*The Cartwrights of
San Augustine*

The Cartwrights
— of —
San Augustine

—

THREE GENERATIONS OF
AGRARIAN ENTREPRENEURS IN
NINETEENTH-CENTURY TEXAS

—

By
Margaret Swett Henson
and
Deolece Parmelee

Texas State Historical Association
Austin

Library of Congress Cataloging-in-Publication Data
Henson, Margaret Swett, 1924–
    The Cartwrights of San Augustine : three generations of agrarian entrepreneurs in nineteenth-century Texas / by Margaret Swett Henson and Deolece Parmelee.
    p.   cm.
    Includes bibliographical references and index.
    ISBN 0-87611-129-0 (alk. paper)
    1. Cartwright family. 2. Businessmen—Texas—San Augustine—Biography.
3. San Augustine (Tex.)—Economic conditions. 4. San Augustine (Tex.)—
History—19th century. I. Parmelee, Deolece. II. Title.
HC102.5.C37H46   1993
338.092'2764175—dc20
93-21498

CIP

10   9   8   7   6   5   4   3   2   1   93   94   95   96   97   98   99

Published by the Texas State Historical Association in cooperation with the Center for Studies in Texas History at the University of Texas at Austin.

The paper used in this book meets the minimum requirements of the American National Standard for Permanence of Paper for Printed Library Materials, Z39.48—1984.

Cover: Matthew Cartwright House, San Augustine, Texas, by Sandra K. Calpakis, 1986. Watercolor on paper, 8 x 12 in. *Courtesy the artist.*

Contents

Preface

~

*T*he descendants of Matthew Cartwright (1807–1870), who had preserved portions of his vast correspondence and that of his six children, began holding family reunions and in 1985 decided to compile a family history. A two-volume genealogy had been privately published in 1939 and 1948 by Emily Griffith Roberts, the wife of Matthew Cartwright Roberts of Terrell and Dallas, a grandson of the original Matthew. The volumes included research and many documents concerning the Roberts, Griffiths, Cartwrights, and other interrelated families, but lacked a historical context. Patty Cartwright Tennison, Pauline Gill Sullivan, Patricia Allen McMillan, James I. Cartwright, Jr., Betty Cartwright, and Sandra Kardell Calpakis formed a committee and employed Mrs. Deolece Parmelee of Austin to explore the collections of papers scattered in private hands, along with the few items then on deposit at the Eugene C. Barker Texas History Center, and to prepare a manuscript. The committee provided Mrs. Parmelee access to individuals for interviews and visits to San Augustine and Terrell for research. Members of the committee contacted the Tennessee State Archives and sought other information to research the Tennessee years.

Mrs. Parmelee was the mainstay in compiling documents concerning family events. She made photocopies and typescripts of the brittle, hard-to-read letters and arranged them in usable order. As her work progressed, interested individuals found more documents, sometimes changing the direction of her narrative. The bewildering array of family names was a particular challenge. Help came from "in-law" Collin Kennedy, who assembled known genealogical facts in his computer. These were augmented by discoveries of forgotten children's names and dates revealed in various letters.

Mrs. Parmelee's 450-page typescript detailing family growth is the basis for the present study. Her heroic efforts in sorting, filing, and deciphering documents, plus researching obscure bits of family history, are a major contribution to this volume.

Errors of fact or interpretation about events and motives of the Cartwrights rest with the primary author. Many of the treasured family stories that cannot be substantiated have been omitted in the narrative or referred to in a footnote.

The author wishes to acknowledge the courtesy extended by the staff of the Eugene C. Barker Texas History Center in the Center for American History, the University of Texas at Austin; the Texas State Archives; the Tennessee State Library and Archives; and Geraldine Smith, the county clerk at San Augustine. The generosity of three colleagues helped with the research and writing of the chapters on the Civil War and Reconstruction: Thomas Nall of Stephen F. Austin University and Cecil W. Harper, Jr., of North Harris County Junior College provided copious notes about the Freedmen's Bureau agents in San Augustine, while Randolph B. Campbell of the University of North Texas critiqued those chapters. The bed and board provided more than once by Sandra Kardell Calpakis at the Matthew Cartwright house in San Augustine and by Steve and Kerry Henson in Austin must be acknowledged.

Margaret Swett Henson
1993

Introduction

⸺

The Cartwrights, unlike the subjects of most Texas biographies, were nineteenth-century businessmen who provided necessary services to the nascent towns on the East Texas frontier. All too often these kinds of settlers are overlooked by historians writing about early Texas because military leaders and political figures are more glamorous, charismatic, and well documented. But in certain respects men like John and Matthew Cartwright also made lasting contributions to the history of Texas: they offered goods and services crucial to making life more pleasant and profitable within their communities, and therefore helped those communities to survive and grow.

John Cartwright settled in the Ayish Bayou neighborhood in 1825 and eight years later helped found the new town of San Augustine. The Tennessee native brought a cotton gin, blacksmith tools, and saleable merchandise to Texas; thus, the family aided the development of the local economy even before Texas became a republic. Cartwright's sons defended the community when needed, and three grandsons served in the Confederate army during the Civil War, but in general the Cartwrights devoted their energies to family and business matters.

Like other Texans with capital, the Cartwrights turned to land speculation in the mid-1830s and built substantial fortunes. John died in 1841, but his eldest son, Matthew, amassed the fourth-largest estate in Texas by 1870 according to the U.S. Census of that year. In each generation Cartwright fathers provided sons and daughters with the best education available and an endowment of property to start their marriages. A strong sense of family pervaded all activities, and sons, nephews, and male cousins were taken into the business at an early age to provide practical experience before and after their academic training. More unusual were Matthew's widow, Amanda, and widowed daughter, Anna, who demonstrated unusual business acumen toward the end of the century when storekeeping and land speculation gave way to ranching, real estate, insurance, and banking endeavors.

The history of the Cartwright family is intertwined with the history of San Augustine and the Redlands of East Texas. Using new sources unavailable to earlier writers, a more detailed picture emerges of events between the 1820s and 1860s. After the challenges of the Fredonian Rebellion, the Battle of Nacogdoches in 1832, and the lack of legal titles to their land, the local residents rallied to send men to battle Santa Anna and to settle conflicts with the local Indians. The village reached its zenith in the 1840s when a number of men prominent in Texas history lived there: James Pinckney Henderson, Oran Milo Roberts, Ezekiel W. Cullen, William B. Ochiltree, and occasionally Sam Houston. Residents took great pride in their town, and after a ball honoring President-elect Houston in 1841, the editor of the local newspaper wrote, "The beauty and fashion of this . . . vicinity, can vie with any portion of the United States." One historian noted the concentration of former Tennesseans in San Augustine, such as the Cartwrights, and concluded that even those from other parts of the South were "given to playing Middle Tennessee Aristocracy." While fond of fine horses and hunting dogs like so many from the rural South, the townspeople also evinced civic ideals, as can be seen in their homes and educational efforts.[1] With two universi-

---

1. William Seale, "San Augustine, in the Texas Republic," *Southwestern Historical Quarterly*, LXXII (Jan., 1969), 345 (2nd quotation), 348 (1st quotation from the San Augustine *Red-Lander*, Oct. 14, 1841).

ties, San Augustine identified itself as the Athens of Texas during the republic. A gradual decline began when travelers to Texas abandoned the old Spanish Road from Natchitoches to San Augustine for the more comfortable steamboat passage between New Orleans and the Texas Gulf ports.

Cartwright descendants saved an unusually complete collection of nineteenth-century letters and account books that add to the understanding of economic conditions affecting merchants in the Redlands from the 1820s through the Civil War. Of particular interest is documentation of the hard times following the panic of 1837 and Matthew Cartwright's decade-long struggle to pay off his debts. Also in the collection are numerous letters to and from the Cartwright sons during the Civil War that describe how the community and troops fared. The lives of the Cartwright men appear in more detail than those of the women; there are fewer letters to, from, or about the women until the 1860s, but occasionally the account books indicate the women's activities. The family records even allow a glimpse into the lives of the black slaves and freedmen who served the Cartwrights through 1868. The Cartwrights, their neighbors, and in-laws—the Robertses, Subletts, Holmans, Garretts, Thomases, Broockses, and Ingrams in particular—participated both directly and indirectly in significant historical events occurring in and around San Augustine. Although not comprising a town history, the activities of these interrelated men and women reveal the challenges, concerns, and texture of daily life in the Redlands of nineteenth-century East Texas.

The Cartwrights *of*
San Augustine

O n e

The Westering Cartwrights

1755–1825

The tall robust man with the auburn hair and dark eyes stood for a moment with his sons atop the bluff at Natchez gazing at the mighty, rolling Mississippi River and the distant Louisiana shore. Soon they would be on board the steamboat, loading at the wharf below, that would take them to Alexandria, Louisiana. There a decision had to be made: If sufficient water covered the rapids, John Cartwright and his family would stay on board to Natchitoches, the last village on the way to Texas. If the Red River was too low, the Cartwrights would have to unload at Alexandria and follow the river road to the old French town. Like most emigrants who left after the fall harvest, John wanted to reach his destination in time to plant corn, the staple of frontier families.[1]

1. The physical description of John Cartwright is from family accounts. Louis Raphael Nardini, Sr., *My Historic Natchitoches, Louisiana and Its Environs* (Natchitoches, La.: Nardini Publishing Co., 1963), 155. Lacking Cartwright sources for the journey, see Jane Long's 1819 journey from Natchez to Nacogdoches via Alexandria as told to M. B. Lamar, in Charles Adams Gulick,

Mary "Polly" Crutchfield Cartwright, thirty-seven years old in early 1825—the same age as big John—watched as the wagons with her possessions descended the steep incline toward the seedy and notorious collection of shacks known as "Natchez-under-the-hill." Once on the wharf, Mary, her daughters Mary and Clementine, ages eleven and six, and eighteen-month-old John Clinton boarded the steamboat while the family slaves and the Cartwright boys helped to secure the four wagons and livestock on the deck under the supervision of the elder Cartwright. Matthew and Robert at seventeen and sixteen resembled their father and in many ways were just as competent, while thirteen-year-old George tried to emulate his brothers.[2]

John Cartwright represented the third generation in his family to move to a new frontier. Mary also descended from pioneers: her mother and father, George and Dicey Hoskins Crutchfield, had crossed rivers and mountains from Virginia into Kentucky and later south into Tennessee. Neither the Cartwrights nor the Crutchfields moved to virgin wilderness, but instead followed others who had established nascent communities. Both families brought modest capital with them and bought land and improvements from earlier settlers. Like many others, the Cartwrights and Crutchfields traveled with family and friends or followed— or were followed—by kinsmen so that their patterns of family life remained the same while their environment changed.

Jr., et al. (eds.), *The Papers of Mirabeau Buonaparte Lamar* (6 vols.; Austin: Pemberton Press, 1968), II, 61–62 (cited hereafter as *Lamar Papers*); also, James Whitesides to George D. Foster, March 29, 1822, James Whitesides Papers (Eugene C. Barker Texas History Center at the Center for American History, University of Texas at Austin; cited hereafter as BTHC).

2. Ages from John Cartwright's Bible (1819) in the possession of James I. Cartwright, Jr. Cartwright owned fifteen slaves and four Dearborn wagons in 1824 (see n. 26 below). For date of emigration: John Cartwright took the oath of loyalty to Mexico in San Felipe and applied for land in Austin's colony on May 3, 1830, saying he came from Mississippi in 1825 (Stephen F. Austin's "Register of Families," General Land Office of Texas, Austin); Robert G. Cartwright in Sabine District, Apr. 7, 1835, says he had lived in Ayish district since March 1825 (Character certificates, General Land Office of Texas, Austin); and John, Matthew, and George W. applied for headrights or augmentations to the San Augustine Board of Land Commissioners in 1838, each saying he had come in 1825 (Gifford White, *1830 Citizens of Texas: A Census of 6,500 Pre-Revolutionary Texians* (Austin: Eakin Press, 1983), 26, 48, 145, 206.

Each generation of Cartwrights improved its standard of living and gradually amassed assets in land and material possessions with the changing times. The parents sent their children to school when schools were available, set an industrious example for their sons in securing a living, and gave sons and daughters a comfortable nest-egg to start their own families. Each generation adapted to new crops and technology in order to accumulate wealth, and John surpassed his father's self-sufficient plantation economy by also engaging in commerce and land speculating. John's sons would continue the tradition in Texas, adding ranching and banking to buying and selling land, while grandsons entered the professions and the nascent petroleum industry. In these respects the westward movement of this branch of the Cartwright family coincided with changes in the national economy, technology, and culture. The San Augustine-bound Cartwrights provide a well-documented example of agrarian entrepreneurship moving west in search of new frontiers.

Because several other Cartwright kinsmen also immigrated to Texas, it is necessary to examine family ties and characteristics to understand more fully the Cartwright wanderlust and drive to succeed. Texas-bound John had not known his grandfather John, who had died in 1780 in Edgecombe County, North Carolina. He had, however, heard the family stories about how old John had left Prince George's County, Maryland, sometime in the 1760s for the North Carolina border. Old John and his family were self-sufficient tobacco farmers who used the proceeds of the cash crop to buy the few things they did not harvest or make themselves. After depleting the soil on their farm, John and wife Sarah sought new, cheaper land on the frontier and moved their eight children first to Granville and Halifax counties in North Carolina before settling on five hundred acres along Town Creek in Edgecombe County. The well-watered and timbered land was not only rich, but it allowed easy access by water to the market at the mouth of the Tar River. Tobacco raisers packed the dried leaves into large barrels and during the winter placed them on flatboats headed downstream to be sold. John could not sign his name, but instead of the common "X," he made a flourishing "C." His sons, however, could sign their names, indicating that they had received basic education.[3]

3. J. Thomas Scharf, *History of Western Maryland* (2 vols.; Baltimore:

After John's sons started their own families, he bought one slave, Primus, to help with the farm. John owned several riding horses, a small herd of cattle, fifty hogs, and a dozen or so sheep. Besides the cash crop of tobacco, the family raised corn and flax, a valued fiber before cotton became popular. The women in the family spent long hours processing flax by carding it and wool into straight fibers to be spun into thread and yarn for weaving. Like their neighbors, the Cartwrights lived off the products of their farm and the forest, even making their own shoes. Old John was particularly proud of his carpentry tools and in his will reserved them and his whipsaw and crosscut saw for his sons. With three guns and a pistol, the Cartwrights obviously could hunt for pleasure and for the table, plus defend themselves if need be. The family had few luxuries—no books, a single candlestick, pewter dishes, a few spoons, and a looking glass.[4]

Edgecombe County residents divided over the question of the Declaration of Independence in 1776. A number of Scottish immigrants in the vicinity preferred for their own reasons to remain loyal to the mother country, and during the revolutionary war the British recruited local loyalist troops. Local patriots mustered, and some were sent to Pennsylvania to join George Washington's army. John's oldest sons moved to neighboring counties but seem not to have served long enough to be eligible for a military land grant. Not that they were reluctant to defend their homes, but an aversion to military duty that would take them far from home seems to have been common among the early Cartwrights and many of their pragmatic neighbors. Amid the

---

Regional Publishing Co., 1968), I, 421; Helen W. Brown (comp.), *Prince George's County, Maryland, Indexes of Church Registers, Protestant Episcopal Church* (2 vols.; [Riverdale, Md.]: Prince George's County Historical Society, 1979), II, 169; Emily Griffith Roberts, *Ancestral Study of Four Families: Roberts, Griffith, Cartwright, Simpson . . .* (2 vols.; Terrell, Tex.: privately published, 1939, 1948), I, 352, II, 946; Halifax County, N.C., Deed Records, X, 89, XIII, 703–704 (microfilm; Clayton Genealogical Library of the Houston Public Library, Houston, Tex. [cited hereafter as CL]); Edgecombe County, N.C., Deed Records, C, 527, D, 148, ibid.; Forrest McDonald, *The Formation of the American Republic, 1776–1790* (Baltimore: Penguin Books, 1968), 77.

4. Will of John Cartwright, Nov. 28, 1789, Edgecombe County, N.C., Will Book, B, 179 (microfilm; CL); Inventory of John Cartwright's estate after death of wife, May 1794, Edgecombe County, N.C., Inventories, 1792–1800, 171, ibid.

unrest, John Cartwright became ill and died at age fifty-five in October 1780, leaving a will to be administered by his sons. John's widow continued to live at the old homestead, retaining Primus and her spinning wheels.[5]

On February 3, 1778, during the early years of the American Revolution, Matthew Cartwright, the father of the Texas immigrant, bought 125 acres in Pitt County and soon married Mary "Polly" Grimmer. The Texas-bound John was born in Pitt County on March 10, 1787, the only son among five daughters. On July 25, 1792, Matthew sold his farm to a neighbor and started for the new frontier over the mountains in Tennessee. Around the same time, two of Matthew's brothers went to the Georgia frontier, leaving their youngest brother, Hezekiah, to care for their mother who still lived on the Town Creek farm in Edgecombe County, North Carolina. She died in April 1794, leaving meager belongings: Primus, a featherbed, a chest, one chair and table, two pewter plates, a churn, and minimal cooking utensils. She still had the looking glass, her spinning wheels, a cow, and a pair of oxen. At the sale of the property to satisfy creditors, Hezekiah bought most of the valuables, including Primus and the livestock.[6]

The Texas-bound John barely remembered the journey to Tennessee in the 1790s when he was five or six years old, and no family story was recollected by his children. His father, Matthew, probably followed the popular route west through the Wautauga settlements in northeastern Tennessee perhaps as far as Knoxville, the territorial capital. Some Edgecombe County neighbors traveled that route: Tennessee Gov. William Blount wrote from Knoxville in May 1792 that his brother had just arrived from Tarboro and had seen many wagons and carts en route to the Cumberland. A second caravan would leave the Tar River for Tennessee in September. The Matthew Cartwright family doubtless joined

5. J. Kelly Turner and John L. Bridgers, Jr., *History of Edgecombe County, North Carolina* (Raleigh: Edwards & Broughton Printing Co., 1920), 92–93; Will of John Cartwright, B, 179 (microfilm; CL); Inventory of John Cartwright's estate after death of wife, 171, ibid.

6. Pitt County, N.C., Deed Records, F, 429, G, 384, N, 520 (microfilm; CL); Inventory of John Cartwright's estate after death of wife, 171, 228. The wills of Peter (see n. 11 below) and Thomas N. Cartwright, filed in Wilson County, Tenn., in 1808 and 1822, indicate that both had claims to land in Georgia.

such a caravan after leaving Pitt County for the road bordering the Tar River and the trail to Tennessee.[7]

Matthew bought two hundred acres on Drakes' Lick Creek in Sumner County in February 1796, the year that Tennessee achieved statehood. During the next five years, county officials called upon him to serve on the local patrol, to help maintain the road in his militia precinct, and for jury duty. Young John attended whatever private classes were available, reading a few classics, developing good penmanship, and learning mathematics useful for business. In July 1803, Matthew sold his land and the town lots he had bought in Gallatin, the county seat, intending to move south across the Cumberland River. To give an example of the potential profits that could be made, Matthew had paid the town's developers $23 for a single lot the previous year, which he sold for $100. But the promissory note he accepted for his two hundred acres was no good, and in 1806 he went to court to collect. In lieu of money, always in short supply on any frontier, he received a title to 640 acres located elsewhere as his compensation.[8]

John was about sixteen years old, an adult by local standards, when the family moved across the Cumberland River and settled in northeastern Wilson County in 1803. His father purchased 640 acres near Cedar Creek along the wagon road that ran east from the courthouse in Lebanon toward Carthage, the seat of neighboring Smith County. Already a thrifty businessman, Matthew continued to acquire more land, giving a portion to each of his six children. He located the court-ordered 640-acre compensation for the unpaid note in the same neighborhood and divided it between two married daughters, Elizabeth "Patsy" Edwards and Polly Ragland, the titles being made in the names of their husbands, James Edwards and Pettus Ragland. Another daughter, Sally, the wife of Richard Hankins, received 150 acres on Round Lick Creek near Matthew's Cedar Creek homestead. When his

7. Albert C. Holt, "The Economic and Social Beginnings of Tennessee," *Tennessee Historical Magazine,* VII (1932), 280–282.

8. Sumner County, Tenn., Deed Book, I, 323, III, 410, 378, 411, IV, 132–144 (microfilm; CL); Sumner County, Tenn., Court Minutes, vols. IV & V, 123, 148, 175, 219, 221, 310, 321, 338, 373, ibid.; Thomas E. Partlow (comp.), *Tax Lists of Wilson County Tennessee, 1803–1807* (Baltimore: Genealogical Publishing Co., Inc., 1981), 3, 29, 94; Wilson County, Tenn., Deed Records, D, 29 (microfilm; CL).

youngest daughter, Susannah, married John Hallum, Matthew gave her 120 acres on the headwaters of Hickman Creek near the Smith County line. While no donations of land are recorded for John or Bethany, who married Littleton Fowler, it is likely that similar portions were made at the time of their marriages because 136 acres of Matthew's 640-acre homestead are unaccounted for in deed records. In 1808, when he was twenty-one, John acquired a cotton gin and a store, probably using capital from his father, an assumption bolstered by the fact that later in San Augustine John entered partnership agreements with his sons in a store and gin. A similar pattern continued in the next generation.[9]

John married Mary "Polly" Crutchfield of Smith County on January 21, 1807, when both were nineteen years old. Her father, a veteran of the revolutionary war, had moved to Hogan's Creek in western Smith County in the early 1800s after a few years in Kentucky. Mary had four sisters and three brothers, most of whom remained in Smith County for the rest of their lives.[10]

Around the time of John and Mary's wedding, his uncle, Peter Cartwright, arrived from Georgia with his wife and eight children and settled on Hickman Creek, southeast of his brother Matthew. John became reacquainted with his cousin John, Peter's eldest son, who was a few years older. Peter Cartwright died in November 1807, less than a year after he had arrived, and left a modest estate composed of three slaves, horses, cattle, and the furniture brought in their big road wagons from Georgia. Peter still had certificates for land to be drawn by lottery in Georgia and $900 due from a debtor.[11]

The confusion of two John Cartwrights in Wilson County was further compounded in 1808 when Matthew's youngest

9. "Wilson County Court Minutes, 1803–1807" (bound typescript by W.P.A., Tennessee State Library and Archives, Nashville; cited hereafter as TSLA), I, 7, 174; Wilson County, Tenn., Grant Books, C, 85, 93, D, 29, 459–461 (microfilm; CL); Matthew Cartwright's will, Feb. 11, 1811, proven March 1812, Wilson County, Tenn., Will Book, 1802–1814, I, 300, ibid.; *The Goodspeed Histories of Maury, Williamson, Rutherford, Wilson, Bedford & Marshall Counties of Tennessee* (1886; reprint, Columbia, Tenn.: Woodward & Stinson Printing Co., 1971), 847; Holt, "Economic and Social Beginnings," 227–228.

10. *The History of Smith County, Tennessee* (Dallas: Curtis Media Corp., 1986), 455. There are no marriage records for this period in Smith County, but the date is in John Cartwright's Bible.

11. Wilson County, Tenn., Deed Records, C, 214 (microfilm; CL); Will of

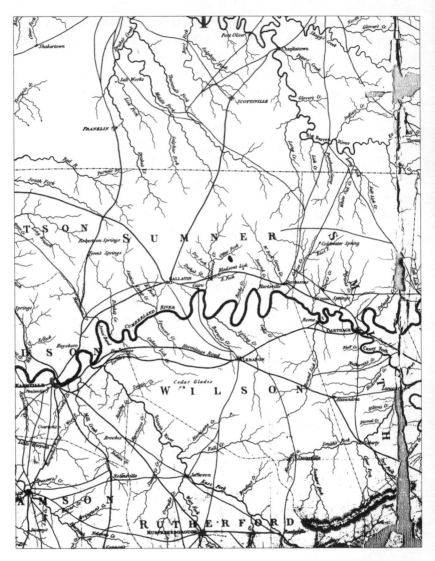

*Portions of Davidson, Wilson, Smith, and Sumner counties, ca.
1832. Matthew Rhea, Map of the State of Tennessee.* Courtesy
Tennessee State Library and Archives.

brother, Hezekiah, arrived from North Carolina with his son John. Hezekiah bought 253 acres on Round Lick Creek just south of Matthew's place, turning eastern Wilson County into a Cartwright settlement similar to Cartwright enclaves in nearby Davidson and Smith counties, where distantly related kinsmen lived. Hezekiah's John married a local girl, Polly Dillard, in 1811, making records even more confusing, with two John Cartwrights with wives named Polly. Moreover, the three cousins named John were about the same age. Which John bought and sold land in eastern Wilson County in the eight recorded transactions between 1810 and 1819 cannot be positively determined. To complete the family circle, Matthew's remaining brother, Thomas Notley Cartwright, also moved to Round Lick Creek from Georgia in 1812 with his sons named Samuel, Thomas, and Hezekiah, but no John.[12] Some of Matthew's sisters may have immigrated to Tennessee, but because North Carolina did not record marriages until 1850 and no family Bible has been found, their married names remain unknown. This clanlike extended family pattern would be repeated in Texas when Thomas's sons, Thomas and Hezekiah, moved to San Augustine.

By the time of Matthew Cartwright's death in 1812, John and Mary had given him three grandchildren in addition to the children of John's sisters and their husbands. John and Mary's first child arrived on November 11, 1807, ten months after their wedding, and was named Matthew for his grandfather. Robert Grimmer Cartwright appeared on March 25, 1809, and Dicey Hoskins, named for Polly's mother, followed on January 21, 1811, around the time that her grandfather Cartwright became ill.[13]

Matthew was fifty-seven years old, two years older than his father had been at his death, when he made his will on February 11, 1811. He did not die, however, until one year later. The will

---

Peter Cartwright, May 23, 1807, Wilson County, Tenn., Will Book, 1802–1814, I, 150–152, 216–217, ibid.

12. Wilson County, Tenn., Deed Records, D, 533, E, 171 (microfilm; CL); Edythe Ruche Whitley (comp.), *Marriages in Wilson County, Tennessee, 1802–1880* (Baltimore: Genealogical Publishing Company, 1981), n.p.

13. John Cartwright Bible.

and inventory of his estate reveal details about the life-style of the Cartwrights in Tennessee. Wealthier than his father, Matthew owned seventeen slaves, but because all are referred to as "boys" and "girls" it is impossible to say how many were adults. There were six female names and the rest were male. The increased ownership of slaves was due in part to the conversion from tobacco culture to cotton and grain, which required more field hands. Matthew willed certain slaves to each of his children, and it is possible that the slaves had already been distributed when each child had married, a common custom and one that continued in the Cartwright family in Texas. In any event, the will legally transferred ownership.[14]

The bequests from Matthew's estate were uneven, perhaps because of previous settlements. Two daughters received a slave and money, one only a slave, others two slaves. John inherited two black men and two stills and their equipment, a bequest that seems to confirm an earlier gift of land and money to buy a cotton gin. The widow, as was customary, received the privilege of the use of two slaves and the homestead for the rest of her life and as much of the furniture and livestock "as she may think proper to keep." Matthew divided his 444-acre homesite between two namesake grandsons (John's Matthew and Sally Cartwright Hankins's Matthew) to be received when they reached twenty-one years of age and after the death of his wife. Giving the homesite to the two grandsons perhaps avoided family arguments.[15]

The widow Cartwright, like her mother-in-law before her, continued to process flax for use on the farm. She had three flax spinning wheels in addition to two cotton wheels. This number suggests that some of the black women must have been trained to use them. Some of the linen cloth woven would have been rough for the sturdy, long-lasting bags and sacks required for picking and storing crops. From the number of sheep in the inventory, it is clear that spinning wool for weaving or knitting woolen garments continued to be important. Polly's house was simple but comfortable. Three folding tables and twelve chairs furnished the

14. Matthew Cartwright's will, I, 300–301.
15. Inventory of Matthew Cartwright's estate, Feb. 28, 1812, ibid., I, 301 (quotation), 302–303 (microfilm; CL).

main room, where tables were set up for meals and taken down afterward. The chest and trunk stored linens and special clothing, as did the two cupboards, although the latter might have been for dining apparatus. The two beds and "furniture" denote massive bedsteads with ticks, feather beds, quilts, and pillows, with drapes for winter and mosquito netting for summer.[16]

Polly's kitchen, doubtless detached from the house, was well equipped with the Dutch ovens, skillets, spider, and pot racks necessary for cooking over an open hearth. She also had such niceties as a tea cannister and kettle, sugar box, and spice mortar. There were two sets of fireplace tools, probably one in the kitchen and the other in the main room. Ironing clothes usually took place in the kitchen, where the smoothing irons could be heated for use on the wooden kitchen table padded with an old quilt. More luxuries adorned Matthew's house than his father's: two looking-glasses, a pair of brass candlesticks, a parcel of books (denoting literate family members), and a gold watch indicate more disposable income than the North Carolina patriarch had possessed.[17] Yet the farm was largely self-sufficient—or could be, if required.

Matthew owned a single rifle in contrast to his father's three guns and pistol. He had a large assortment of farm and handyman equipment, including five plows, four reapers, a shovel and hoe, a number of axes, a foot adze, a froe, iron wedges, two grind stones, and two pairs of steelyards to weigh cotton, wool, and other products. He seemed less interested in carpentry tools than his father, but owned a drawing knife, augers, gimlets, chisels, hammers, and a handsaw. Matthew also owned only one wagon, a yoke of oxen, six horses, one mule, twenty-eight head of cattle, twenty sheep, and sixty hogs. The men recording the inventory listed a number of barrels of whiskey and cider, two hundred barrels of corn, and four hundred pounds of bacon. In addition, they noted a beehive and honey stand, loose boards, a "bunch of wire," and a number of hides that were used for replacement reins and fastenings.[18]

From the debts owed to Matthew Cartwright it appears that he regularly sold commodities to his neighbors such as grain,

16. Ibid.
17. Ibid.
18. Ibid.

bacon, whiskey, and cider. Because there are no imported items such as coffee or tea, he does not seem to have operated a traditional store—perhaps that was John's sphere—but was selling surplus products from his farm.

Polly Grimmer Cartwright remained in her home with the aid of her servants and her children who lived nearby. The census enumerator in 1820 found her widowed son-in-law James Edwards and his children living with her, listed, of course, under his name. The apple orchards provided bountiful crops for sale, and Polly had added turkeys and geese to her barnyard and contined to raise bees, cotton, corn, oats, rye, and flax until her death in 1824.[19]

Matthew had died before the second war with England began in June 1812. Except for wounded national pride, Tennessee residents paid little attention to British seizures of United States vessels in the Atlantic Ocean but worried about possible trouble with the Creek Indians who still held most of the Mississippi and Alabama territory. Florida belonged to Spain, an ally of Great Britain, and Tennessee politicians joined other westerners in demanding military expeditions against British Canada and Spanish Florida in order to add these territories to the United States. All adult men in Tennessee were liable for militia duty but hiring substitutes was permitted. In 1811, one of the three John Cartwrights in Wilson County was chosen ensign by his fellow militiamen, but no evidence or oral tradition exists to verify that Matthew's John took part in the War of 1812.[20]

A brief flurry of high commodity prices due to wartime shortages ended in 1815, and declining agricultural prices prevented farmers from paying creditors for land purchased to increase their production. The economic downward spiral was known as the panic of 1819, when banks called for immediate repayment of loans. When farmers could not pay their debts, the sheriff seized their property and in many states put the unlucky men in jail—for as long as twenty years in Louisiana. John

19. Matthew Cartwright estate inventory upon death of his widow, March 1825, Wilson County, Tenn., Will Book, 1819–1824, 99–105 (microfilm; CL); United States Fourth Census (1820), Wilson County, Tennessee.

20. Mrs. John Trotwood Moore, "Record of Commissions of Officers in the Tennessee Militia, 1811," *Tennessee Historical Quarterly,* VI (Mar., 1947), 62.

Cartwright had difficulty collecting amounts due him and took the defaulters to court in 1818. He employed a newly arrived lawyer, Sam Houston, who had opened an office opposite the brick courthouse in Lebanon, to pursue the case in 1819. Houston won, but the defendant appealed the decision, which postponed payment. Houston remained in Lebanon only ten months before moving to Nashville, but the encounter set the stage for a reunion of the two men in San Augustine in the 1830s.[21]

Thirty-two years old in 1819, John left the county during the summer to take produce to Natchez and was caught up in the excitement of Dr. James Long's expedition. It seems possible that John joined other curious men who visited eastern Texas, although no family story confirms such an adventure. If John visited Texas at this time, it was only for a matter of weeks. More likely, he spoke with men who had seen the Spanish Redlands.

Mississippi Valley residents deplored the actions of Secretary of State John Quincy Adams in giving Texas to Spain in exchange for Florida by the terms of the Transcontinental Treaty made in February 1819. This agreement set the Sabine River as the western boundary of the Louisiana Purchase, although many Mississippi Valley residents believed the boundary should be farther west, at the Neches River. This would have placed Nacogdoches within United States territory. An even more exaggerated claim rested on the French occupation of Texas by La Salle in 1685, which meant that Texas was part of the 1803 Louisiana Purchase. Long and his followers captured Nacogdoches in June 1819, declared Texas independent, and organized a government with Long as president. Some of the party scattered to explore and trade with the Indians while others visited Jean Lafitte on Galveston Island.

The poorly supplied Spanish troops in San Antonio were unable to start east to intercept the invaders until September. By November, however, the Spanish chased the last of Long's men into Louisiana and burned the residences of Anglo-American squatters that were scattered along the principal roads in present-day Sabine, Shelby, and San Augustine counties. Long and others

21. For examples of hard times, see S. F. Austin to James Bryan, Nov. 10, 1821, in Eugene C. Barker (ed.), *The Austin Papers,* in *Annual Report, 1919,* of the American Historical Association (3 vols.; vols. I, II, Washington, D.C.: Government Printing Office, 1924, 1928; vol. III, Austin: University of Texas Press, 1927), I, pt. 1, 426 (cited hereafter as *Austin Papers,* I); *John Cartwright*

returned to Texas in 1820 by way of the Bolivar Peninsula, where they remained until September 1821, when they learned that Mexico had achieved independence.[22]

John had returned to Wilson County by November 1819, when the court fined him for his summer absence. Even though he won a second suit against the debtor, he could not collect what was due to him because of the hard times. Before the end of the year John decided to leave Tennessee and sold his 130 acres of land at $10 per acre, which indicates a highly developed, desirable tract. He used this money or credit to purchase commodities that he could sell in Mississippi and bought passage to the Natchez neighborhood for his family and goods.[23] Pragmatic like his father and grandfather when faced with hard times, John Cartwright ventured to a new frontier in hopes of improving his economic condition.

In 1820 the census enumerator for Wilkinson County, Mississippi, listed John and his family plus five other men and sixteen slaves, all of whom were engaged in agricultural pursuits. At least some of the other young men were probably John's Tennessee cousins because neither Thomas nor the other two Johns were counted in Wilson County in 1820. Moreover, John's sister, Susannah Hallum, and her husband had also left Tennessee and were living in Mississippi. Cousin Thomas Cartwright, a veteran of the Battle of New Orleans in 1815, had settled in Louisiana by December 1820, when he bought an improved homesite on Bayou Chacon (present-day Winn Bayou near Robeline, Louisiana, west of Natchitoches), convenient for Indian trading in Texas. He lived there until 1823, when he sold the property and moved to Texas with his wife and children.[24]

---

v. John Fisher, Suit Pleadings, Court of Pleas and Quarter Session, May term, 1819, "Court Minutes, Wilson County, Tennessee" (bound typescript by W.P.A., TSLA), 123–124, 127–128; Frank Burns, *Wilson County* (Memphis: Memphis State University Press, 1983), 19, 27, 29.

22. F. Trudeau to [Fatio?], June 9, 1819, *Lamar Papers,* I, 32; Report of Col. Ignacio Perez, December 3, 1819, ibid., I, 34–35; Lamar's narrative, ibid., II, 56–60, 64–68. See family records for John in Texas in 1819.

23. Burns, *Wilson County,* 25, 27; Wilson County, Tenn., Deed Records, H, 135, 141, 150; Federal Writers Program of W.P.A., *Tennessee: A Guide to the State* (New York: Viking Press, 1939), 182.

24. U.S. Fourth Census (1820), Wilson County, Tenn.; ibid., Wilkinson and

Mississippi attracted settlers in 1820 because land previously occupied by the Choctaw Indians became available around the town of Jackson. Mississippi had become a state in December 1817. Its only developed area was along the Mississippi River below Vicksburg and the southern tier of counties west of Natchez. Not until 1832 were the Indians removed from the northern half of the state. The United States Land Office at Jackson sold vacant land at $1.25 per acre and offered a new start for those escaping hard times and worn-out land.

Two other Cartwrights, Jesse H. and his older brother Robert M., were living in Wilkinson County when John arrived, and they too would be immigrating to Texas in a few years. They were the younger sons of old Robert Cartwright, one of the founders of Nashville in 1780. Robert had lived in Virginia, but a positive connection with John's Maryland grandfather cannot be made by genealogists, although John and Jesse, born the same year, may have considered themselves cousins. Jesse, a commission merchant at Woodville, had been in Mississippi since 1816.[25]

John and Mary Cartwright remained in Wilkinson County for less than one year and lost nine-year-old Dicey to fever in June 1820. John bought no land there but was taxed for merchandise and slaves worth $5,600. In 1821 he acquired a claim (perhaps

Lawrence counties, Miss.; Bounty Land Claim no. 95728-160-55 for Thomas Cartwright, in Mary Smith Fay, *War of 1812 Veterans in Texas* (New Orleans: Polyanthos, 1979), 63. John Cartwright "of Wilkinson County, Mississippi," deeded two lots in Lebanon to his brothers on November 13, 1820. Wilson County, Tenn., Deed Book I (eye), 217; Index of Conveyances, Vendee, 1800–1880, X, 68 (in Natchitoches Parish, La., clerk's office); "Claims to Land between the Rio Hondo and Sabine Rivers, in Louisiana, 1825," in *American State Papers: Documents of the Congress of the United States in Relation to the Public Lands,* IV (Washington, D.C.: Gales & Seaton, 1859), 97, petition 37. Logic and family stories suggest that John Cartwright had been in Texas before 1825, when he brought his family; one source believes it to have been as early as 1818. The only proof, a letter from S. F. Austin in Arkansas Territory to John Cartwright on Ayish Bayou (date not recalled but possibly 1820), asked about local conditions. This letter was on display in the Texas Memorial Museum in Austin in 1958 but has since disappeared. Patty Cartwright Tennison recalled seeing the letter, and a letter from T. R. Fehrenbach to Tennison (then Mrs. William Y. Harvey) dated Aug. 2, 1983, confirms that he had also seen it.

25. Norman E. Gillis, *Early Inhabitants of the Natchez District* (Baton Rouge: privately published, 1953), 85; "Robert Cartwright," unpublished MS, no. 69-277 (TSLA).

in trade), but not a final title, to 160 acres at Topisaw on the Bogue Chitto River in Pike County near present-day McComb. The booming community, sixty miles northeast of Woodville, was less than ten years old and lay just south of Lawrence County where the Hallums lived. John sent his fourteen-year-old son Matthew and some of the slaves to Topisaw to build a house and plant corn for the family. Pike County levied taxes on John's sixteen slaves and about $3,000 in merchandise in 1822. A daughter was born in September 1822 but lived only two weeks, but the following year Mary bore a healthy son and named him John Clinton. The Cartwrights remained at Topisaw through 1824, when John was assessed a $14 state tax for 328 acres, four Dearborn wagons, and fifteen slaves. John may not have paid this levy because he was preparing to move to Texas, although he had not found a buyer for his land claim.[26]

John finally caught "Texas fever" in 1824, when the new Mexican government seemed to have stabilized. Cheap land and easy profits retailing staple goods attracted many families. James Whitesides, later an innkeeper in Austin's colony, told a friend that he had immediately sold his wagon load of groceries in Nacogdoches at high prices: twenty-five cents a pound for "flower," fifty cents for sugar, and $1 a pound for coffee.[27]

Although Mexican Texas offered economic bonanzas, Anglo-Americans worried about what they considered disturbing negatives, such as swearing allegiance to Mexico and the establishment of the Roman Catholic church as the official religion. One other concern was the security of slave ownership: rumors indicated that Mexico might forbid slavery as practiced in the United States.

26. John Cartwright Bible; Wilkinson County, Miss., Tax records, 1821 (microfilm, Mississippi Department of Archives and History, Jackson; photocopy in Cartwright Research Collection). Pike County, Miss., Tax records, 1822, 1824, show that John Cartwright's claim was still owned by the U.S. government, ibid. John Cartwright, Power of Attorney, June 4, 1825, to sell "any land" in Pike County, in Wilson County, Tenn., Will Book, 1824–1827, 322 (microfilm; CL). Family legend states that fourteen-year-old Matthew and a few slaves traveled from Tennessee to Mexican Texas to develop the land on the Palo Gacho, but it seems more likely that Matthew went to Pike County when he was that age in 1821–1822.

27. James Whitesides to George D. Foster, Mar. 16, 1822, James Whitesides Collection (BTHC).

Thank you for choosing a Texas State Historical Association book. We hope you enjoy it. Please let us hear from you. Complete this postage-paid card and:

☐ Check here if you would like us to send you a complete catalogue of all TSHA publications.

☐ Check here if you would like information about membership in the Texas State Historical Association. Members receive a 15% discount on all TSHA publications.

Name _____

Address _____

City _____ State _____ Zip _____

BUSINESS REPLY MAIL

FIRST-CLASS MAIL   PERMIT NO. 7418   AUSTIN, TX

POSTAGE WILL BE PAID BY ADDRESSEE

TEXAS STATE HISTORICAL ASSOCIATION
2/306 RICHARDSON HALL
AUSTIN TX 78712-9820

Nevertheless, positive attractions outweighed negative. Having won independence from Spain in 1821, the new nation of Mexico chose an emperor who ruled from 1822 to 1823, a development that slowed emigration from the United States.

But in 1824 Mexico became a republic, with a constitution in many ways resembling that of the United States. It provided for three branches of government: an elected president with a four-year term, a bicameral Congress, and a judicial branch. Likewise, the Mexican states each had a governor and a bicameral legislature. Besides the seemingly familiar pattern of republican government, an attractive inducement encouraged immigration to Mexico: a six-year exemption from import duties on necessary goods from the United States. Moreover, Mississippi Valley debtors still suffering from the panic of 1819 learned they would be safe from their creditors because Mexico had no reciprocal treaty with the United States. An immigrant could not be prosecuted in Mexico for debts owed in the United States, nor could he be extradited by creditors.[28]

Equally important was Mexico's generous land policy that gave settlers more acreage than the amount held by rich men in the United States. Each head of a family could claim a league (4,428 acres of pasture land) and a *labór* (177 acres of irrigable farm land) for less than $200 in fees to the state, the surveyor, and a clerk for writing the deed. While vacant land at the United States Land Office cost $100 for 80 acres (the minimum one could purchase), that $100 in Texas gave a man over 2,200 acres! When a Texas settler had little or no cash, arrangements could be made with a capitalist to pay the fees in exchange for one-half of the headright. There was one restriction: the settler had to live on the land for six years and make improvements before the final title would be issued, and if the recipient returned permanently to the United States, the land was forfeited.[29]

The advantages of immigration to Mexican Texas outweighed the disadvantages, especially since most residents of the western states were convinced that the United States would soon acquire the eastern portion of Texas at least to Nacogdoches, and some

---

28. Mexican Constitution of 1824, in David B. Edward, *The History of Texas* (1836; reprint, Austin: Texas State Historical Association, 1990), 322–336.
29. Colonization Laws of 1823, 1824, in ibid., 143, 152, 154, 158.

said to the Brazos River. It therefore became important to get land in Texas immediately, because whenever it became part of the United States, those already in possession of land would have an obvious advantage over latecomers. Another encouraging step was the establishment of Cantonment Jesup in June 1822, about twenty miles west of Natchitoches along the Texas road and eighteen miles east of the Sabine River. Lt. Col. Zachary Taylor had been stationed at Fort Selden six miles north of Natchitoches since 1820, until he moved his four companies of infantry (141 officers and men) to Jesup. Within the year, Col. James B. Many succeeded him.[30] The presence of the United States Army reassured immigrants, and many wrongly assumed that it was a step toward the annexation of Texas.

Anglo-American immigration to Texas increased after 1823 when Stephen F. Austin received permission from the Mexican government to continue his deceased father's 1821 empresario contract to settle 300 families. Only those accepted by Austin could receive titles within the bounds of his grant between the Brazos and Colorado river watersheds. Those who settled elsewhere, such as Ayish Bayou, where John Cartwright was heading, would have no way to receive a title except by petitioning the authorities at San Antonio.

A bad crop year in 1824 and continuing hard times convinced John and others that it was time to try Texas. A number of men in southwestern Mississippi planned to go to Austin's colony in early 1825; one wrote to Austin from Wilkinson County, "The emigrating, or Texas *fever* prevails among all classes." Jesse and Robert Cartwright, deeply in debt in 1824, were among the first to leave for Texas. They left New Orleans by schooner in March 1825 with their slaves and a large assortment of goods, but the vessel went aground in Galveston Bay and they lost some of their cargo. Robert died soon after their arrival, but Jesse settled between the Brazos River and Oyster Creek, where he developed a cotton plantation in what became Fort Bend County.[31]

John Cartwright, however, preferred to travel by steamboat up the Red River and then overland from Natchitoches. He chose

30. Nardini, *Historic Natchitoches,* 137; *American State Papers: Military Affairs,* II (Washington, D.C.: Gales & Seaton, 1861), 456, 558.

31. James A. E. Phelps to S. F. Austin, Jan. 16, 1825, in *Austin Papers,* I, 1020 (quotation); George Huff to S. F. Austin from Woodville, Jan. 29, 1825,

to settle just west of the Sabine, close enough to Jesup and Natchitoches for trade but outside of any colony. It seems likely that sometime between 1820 and 1824 John had visited his cousin Thomas near Natchitoches and made a short trip across the Sabine River to explore and trade with the Texas Indians. The fertile red soil around Ayish Bayou pleased him, and he began planning to move his family.

Frugal, cautious, conservative about money and resources, John was at the same time venturesome, adaptive, and innovative, willing to experiment with new places and changing technology. Like so many other successful men of his day, including his father, John possessed many skills: diversified farming, animal husbandry, carpentry, blacksmithing, distilling, cotton ginning, and storekeeping. Some talents he had learned from his father while others he developed from necessity and experience. Moreover, he was a shrewd agrarian businessman and a patriarch with both white and black dependents. Others might win fame by entering politics or fighting wars, but John Cartwright intended to mind his own business. On the other hand, if anybody challenged his course of action, he could and would defend himself by whatever means were necessary—in or out of law courts.

---

ibid., 1026; Kinchen Holliman to S. F. Austin, Feb. 21, 1825, ibid., 1050–1051; H. Connell to S. F. Austin, Feb. 26, Mar. 1, 1825, ibid., 1051–1053; William Johnson to S. F. Austin, Feb. 28, Mar. 1, 1825, ibid., 1053–1054; Robert Lewis to S. F. Austin, Apr. 11, 1825, ibid., 1074; R. M. Cartwright to S. F. Austin, May 25, 1825, ibid., 1102–1103; Benjamin Carrico to S. F. Austin, June 3, 1825, ibid., 1116; Humphrey Jackson Memorandum, n.d., *Austin Papers*, I, 1116–1117; Woodville *Republican,* May 4, 25, Oct. 5, 1824 (microfilm, University of Texas, Austin; courtesy of Deolece Parmelee).

T w o

Settling in
Mexican Texas

~

1825–1829

O nce John Cartwright and his family reached Natchitoches, they followed the Texas road southwest past Fort Jesup. Two miles beyond the military post lay Shawneetown, the sort of community that grew up around forts to provide entertainment for off-duty soldiers. Besides a race track, there were stores, saloons, gambling halls, and prostitutes, all intent on getting a share of the army payroll. It was not the sort of place John would want to stop for very long, although he may have paused to sell some merchandise.[1]

The Cartwrights continued along the road to James Gaines's ferry and tavern at the main crossing of the Sabine River. Heavily loaded with household and farming equipment plus a cotton gin and blacksmith tools, they chose not to take a smaller ferry on a more direct secondary road that would take them closer to their destination. Gaines, a kinsman of Gen. Edmund P. Gaines, com-

---

1. Nardini, *Historic Natchitoches*, 137. Family lore speculates that John had a store near Jesup.

mander of the eastern division of the United States Army in 1825, had operated the ferry ever since 1813 when he abandoned the ill-fated Gutiérrez-Magee filibustering expedition prior to its defeat by the Spanish army southwest of San Antonio. Instead of joining the Long volunteers in 1819, Gaines sent word to the Spanish authorities; thus, many Anglos viewed him as a traitor. After Mexico won its independence, he moved his domicile to the west bank and later became the alcalde of the Sabine district.[2]

Winding their way out of densely wooded bottoms, the Cartwright wagons reached lightly timbered grasslands along the road to Ayish Bayou and Nacogdoches. They passed scattered dwellings rebuilt since the Spanish army burned the homes of squatters in 1819. Venturesome Anglo-Americans had returned to the area by 1822, and the alcalde at Nacogdoches complained to the authorities in San Antonio that foreigners were again trespassing and did not register their names with him as required. Some immigrants en route to Austin's colony spent a season in the Redlands to plant a crop before continuing to the Brazos River. Others remained in the Ayish neighborhood hoping to secure land by preemption as many had done on the frontier in the United States. John's cousin, Thomas Cartwright, for example, spent a few months in the Ayish Bayou neighborhood in early 1824, but moved to Austin's colony where he received a title to a headright league on December 10, 1824.[3]

2. George L. Crocket, *Two Centuries in East Texas: A History of San Augustine County and Surrounding Territory from 1685 to the Present Time* (Dallas: Southwest Press, 1932), 70, 135; Walter Prescott Webb, H. Bailey Carroll, and Eldon Stephen Branda (eds.), *The Handbook of Texas* (3 vols.; Austin: Texas State Historical Association, 1952, 1976), I, 658; Ramon Quirk and James Gaines to Governor, Sept. 20, 1820, Robert Bruce Blake Research Collection Transcripts (93 vols., ca. 1958; BTHC), X, 208 (cited hereafter as Blake Transcripts); J. Gaines to Juan Seguin, June 9, 1824, ibid., 359.

3. "Journal of Stephen F. Austin on his First Trip to Texas, 1821." *The Quarterly of the Texas State Historical Association*, VII (Apr., 1904), 288–289 (cited hereafter as *QTSHA*); Dill to Governor, Jan. 31, 1822, Blake Transcripts, X, 257; J. E. B. Austin to S. F. Austin, May 15, 1824, *Austin Papers*, I, 792–793; Deed of sale, Thomas Cartwright to Daniel McLean, Sept. 24, 1823, Natchitoches Parish, La., Index of Conveyances, X, 22, 68; Election returns, San Felipe, Dec. 22, 1823, *Austin Papers*, I, 995–996; one league and *labór* granted Aug. 10, 1824 in Austin's colony (General Land Office of Texas).

John chose a site about five miles east of Ayish Bayou near the springs on Palo Gacho Creek. This location was north of the main road from the Sabine crossing and was vacant in 1825, although the house of a previous occupant remained in the vicinity. Nobody challenged his right to the place, called Passons Springs, which had been used by travelers since prehistoric times. In 1767 the Marqués de Rubí camped at "El Palo Gacho" springs during his official inspection tour of the eastern Texas missions and presidios.[4]

Seventeen years later, in 1780, early resident Cristóbal Chonca received permission from the military commander at Nacogdoches to locate his headright league along the stream. He named his ranch Santa Gertrudis de Palo Gacho, but getting a title was slow and difficult on the remote Spanish frontier and it was 1810 before a survey was made and the deed recorded in San Antonio as was the custom. His only neighbor was Juan Pifermo who had received a four-league grant for a ranch in 1794 on the eastern corner of Chonca's league. The Pifermo ranch stretched eastward between the Lobanilla and Boregas creeks. When the invading Gutiérrez-Magee expedition crossed the Sabine heading for Nacogdoches in 1812, the sixty-five-year-old Chonca fled to Natchitoches where he sold his improvements and his rights to the ranch to a Louisiana resident who in turn sold the tract to Lewis Holloway on January 28, 1819.[5]

Holloway was a trader who lived near the mouth of Ironosa Creek in northwestern San Augustine County even before 1819. When Spanish troops chased the remnants of the James Long expedition out of eastern Texas, squatters like Holloway also fled to Louisiana. He settled temporarily in the old Neutral Ground just east of the Sabine River, a haven for the dispossessed and also for renegades. In 1822 Holloway moved his family to the Palo

4. For the conclusion that the springs were vacant, see paragraph about Lewis Holloway and n. 6 below; "Diary of Nicolás de Lafora," in *The Frontiers of New Spain: Nicolás de Lafora's Description, 1766–1768,* ed. and trans. Lawrence Kinnaird (Berkeley: Quivira Society, 1958), 167. *Palo gacho* means "downward curving wood," and is not spelled *gaucho,* as often seen.

5. Crocket, *Two Centuries,* 64; Declaration of Chonca, 1810, in Carolyn Reeves Ericson, *Citizens and Foreigners of the Nacogdoches District, 1809–1836* (2 vols.; Nacogdoches: Carolyn Ericson, 1985), II, 36–37; copy of Chonca's petitions in Blake Transcripts, XV, 279–283; Christopher Chonca to Joshua Blair, Aug. 3, 1818, ibid., XXXV, 274; Blair to Holloway, Jan. 28, 1819, ibid.

Gacho and two years later petitioned San Antonio authorities to confirm his title to the Chonca land. Chonca's 1810 deed was found in the archives and a new survey ordered; one of the 1810 witnesses called to the scene could not identify any landmarks but insisted that they were on the Chonca tract. Beginning at a stream north of Holloway's house, the surveyors marked trees to denote the boundaries of the league, and on October 21, 1824, Holloway received a deed. Almost immediately, he sold two portions of the tract; the southeastern portion was bought by Elisha Roberts, who would become John Cartwright's neighbor, while the other part was occupied only briefly by a transient. Holloway moved his family to the Colorado River in Austin's colony but, ever restless, returned to the Palo Gacho at the end of 1825 and found the Cartwrights on land he still considered his.[6]

Resolution of such controversies began with the sub-alcalde of Ayish Bayou, who was an Anglo; he lacked any instructions from the alcalde in Nacogdoches who, in turn, had no laws to follow as yet from state or national officials. The new Mexican nation was struggling to create a republic in 1824. State government, which would administer the distribution of land, was slow to organize. Because of sparse population, the national congress joined Texas to neighboring Coahuila and named Saltillo, over eight hundred miles from Nacogdoches, the state capital. The eleven legislators, one from Texas and ten from Coahuila, did not complete the state constitution until 1827.

Soon after arriving in the Ayish Bayou community, John Cartwright learned that acquiring a land title would be difficult. The national congress wanted Anglo-American immigrants, but it did not want them to settle close to the Sabine border or along the Gulf coast except with special executive permission. By forbidding Anglo settlement close to the international border, Mexican leaders hoped to prevent the creation of sympathetic communities that might aid an invasion from the United States. The law proscribing settlement in the fifty-two-mile border reserve be-

6. Crocket, *Two Centuries*, 65–66; U.S. Fourth Census (1820), Natchitoches Parish, La.; Chonca title, Blake Transcripts, XV, 282–283; Bill of sale, Oct. 22, 1824, Blake Transcripts II, 13; John P. Coles to S. F. Austin, Jan. 11, 1825, *Austin Papers*, I, 1015; Census of the Colorado District for 1825, ibid., 1244; Petition of Lewis Holloway by attorney at Nacogdoches, Jan. 20, 1826, Blake Transcripts, XI, 223.

tween the Attoyac (west of Nacogdoches) and the Sabine River was passed in 1824 but was not enforced until it had been posted in Nacogdoches in mid-1825. Anglo-Americans, including John Cartwright, who were already living in the border reserve assumed that the authorities would allow them to remain.[7]

The state colonization law passed on March 24, 1825, permitted foreigners already residing in Texas and outside of Austin's empresario grant to appear before the nearest *ayuntamiento* to petition for a headright. The *ayuntamiento* was similar to a city council but had jurisdiction over the surrounding area. Nacogdoches did not qualify for an *ayuntamiento* until 1827, however, so Ayish Bayou newcomers had to send their petitions for land to the *jéfe politico,* a sort of governor, in San Antonio.[8]

Thus, when the Cartwrights arrived in eastern Texas, there was a semblance of order, but in reality the Redlands seethed with unrest because of its mixed population. The newcomers from the United States clustered around Ayish Bayou (present-day San Augustine) and what are now Shelby and Sabine counties; the settlers included poor, honest, hard-working farmers and a number of small businessmen of modest means such as John Cartwright. At the other end of the social spectrum was a large number of unscrupulous and dangerous opportunists, including criminals who had fled the United States to avoid arrest. All segments, however, vociferously espoused traditional Anglo-American rights such as free speech and the right to assemble to voice their opinions. The law-abiding element naively expected to find land laws and criminal justice in Mexico similar to those in the United States because both were republics. One semi-literate immigrant expressed the feelings of many: "Love of change and an Idia that Land could be obtained for a mear Trifle . . . Done caused a considerable Imigration To that country Expecting or thinking It a Republick similar to the one they had left."[9]

In contrast to the Anglo-American character of Ayish Bayou, Nacogdoches remained predominately Spanish in language and custom. It was a poorly educated, cosmopolitan blend of native-born Tejanos with family ties in both Mexican San Antonio and

7. National Colonization Law in *Documents of Texas History,* ed. Ernest Wallace (Austin: Steck Co., 1960), 48.

8. State Colonization Law, ibid., 48–50.

9. Burrell J. Thompson to S. F. Austin, Feb. 17, 1827, *Austin Papers,* I, 1602 (quotation).

French Natchitoches, former residents of the United States and Europe who had become naturalized Spanish citizens in the 1780s, and a large number of itinerant Indian traders of mixed cultural backgrounds. These people were used to Spanish-style authoritarian rule with little participatory democracy and no guarantees of personal freedoms like those in the U.S. Bill of Rights. Unlike the Anglo-American newcomers, these longtime residents understood that civil and military authorities commanded the respect of the populace and that rank brought privileges.

From the beginning the two communities were mutually suspicious, and the Anglos had no interest in understanding Mexican law or even remembering that they were in a foreign country. An Anglo who had broken Mexican law complained that he had been denied the right to take the oath of "Eligence . . . and when I Purchesed land denyed the Right to hold land and could not heave a Deed acnoledged [sic]."[10]

Scattered on the perimeter of the two settlements were small bands of Indians who understood neither system. Cherokees, Delawares, and Shawnees, forced from their homelands in the United States, had settled in the vicinity beginning in 1820 hoping to receive land grants from the Mexican government. Even the Coushattas and Alabamas to the south were immigrants, although they had arrived from Louisiana by the early 1800s. Native East Texas tribes had almost disappeared.

By the time the Cartwrights reached the Palo Gacho, residents of the Ayish neighborhood had already produced and ginned a sizeable cotton crop. At the end of November 1824, Alcalde John Sprowl had a new gin in operation near his home on the hill east of Ayish Bayou. Sprowl had been under pressure from neighbors to complete the gin, which indicates that this was the first one erected in the area. John rushed to put up his gin in time for the 1825 crop, as did John A. Williams, who lived on the west side of Ayish Bayou, because New Orleans prices had been very high—thirty-five cents a pound early that year. A year later, cotton processed at the Williams gin brought only twenty cents a pound.[11]

10. Ibid., 1603 (quotation).
11. John Sprowl to P. de Torres, Nov. 24, 1824, Blake Transcripts, XXVI, 186; Nathaniel Cox to to S. F. Austin, May 27, 1825, *Austin Papers,* I, 1104;

These gins were small, about the size of a modern desk, and the toothed rollers, called saws, that separated the fluff from the seeds were cranked by hand; a slightly larger model could be turned by horsepower. Homemade horsehair brushes pulled the lint away, while the seeds dropped to the floor below. A shed-like gin house sheltered the machine, and a primitive screw press powered by oxen, mules, or worn-out horses stood nearby to compress the cotton into bales weighing 350 pounds or more. Except for having to buy the saws, bagging, and rope, a carpenter and blacksmith could easily maintain these simple gins.

Ginners took a portion of the processed cotton as their fee, and for an additional charge (1¾ cents a pound in 1826) would transport the cotton to market in Natchitoches by wagon.[12] Because there was no commercial treaty between the United States and Mexico until the 1830s, Texas cotton was usually passed off as Louisiana cotton when it was sold in Natchitoches. Merchants there knew ways to overcome unpopular restrictions on imports and had dealt in contraband goods for a long time. John kept a store in connection with his gin and blacksmith shop at the Palo Gacho, and like all merchants of the day, he carried accounts for his customers who would pay when they marketed their crop.

A merchant on the Texas frontier had to resupply his stock at Natchitoches, and in June 1825 John, accompanied by Matthew, returned to the old town. They also visited a well-known lawyer to obtain a power of attorney so that Matthew could conduct business for his father in Mississippi and Tennessee. The document permitted Matthew to "dispose" of the property and allowed him to "apply . . . [the proceeds] . . . to his benefit or my own as he may think proper." Matthew would be eighteen in November 1825, but perhaps his size and adult behavior compensated for his youth. While eager to sell his land east of the Mississippi River, John obviously felt that he could not take the time to go himself and trusted his son to manage well in the adult world.[13]

Arbitration settlement, Oct. 16, 1826, Blake Transcripts, XI, 261.

12. Statement of arbitration, Nov. 2, 1826, Blake Transcripts, XI, 271.

13. Power of Attorney, Natchitoches, La., June 4, 1825, recorded Oct. 4, 1825, Wilson County, Tenn., Commissioners' Court Minutes, I, 301 (quotation) (typescript; TSLA).

Young Matthew had already made one long journey by himself. His grandmother, Polly Grimmer Cartwright, had died in Tennessee in April 1824, and when word reached the family at Topisaw, John sent his son north to see about Matthew's inheritance of one-half of his grandfather's homestead. Matthew also carried a power of attorney from his aunt, Susannah Hallum, and her husband to obtain her share from her mother's estate. Matthew recorded that power of attorney at the courthouse in Lebanon but the records do not show subsequent transactions for the Hallums. His uncle, Richard Hankins, had been named administrator of the old woman's estate and would serve as guardian of the homestead property inherited jointly by his son, Matthew Hankins, and his Texas nephew until both reached twenty-one. Except for the farm, there was little property to divide. The entire estate was valued at only $4,000, and family and friends had bought the most valuable items at the liquidation sale before Matthew arrived from Mississippi.[14]

In January 1826 John Cartwright learned that Lewis Holloway was trying to recover his Palo Gacho property. Holloway evidently believed that his claim would be upheld by the newly elected alcalde of the Nacogdoches district, Chichester Chaplin, a newcomer who had been a justice of the peace in Louisiana. The Nacogdoches alcalde's court, previously controlled by longtime residents accustomed to Spanish/Mexican law, was a court of appeal from the local alcalde courts at Ayish Bayou and Sabine where Holloway seemingly had no influence. Holloway initiated two suits in Chaplin's court: one against Cartwright for forcible possession of Holloway's former residence, and the second against Elisha Roberts, who had bought the southeastern portion of the Chonca tract and who had not paid in full. Roberts had arrived in mid-1824 from Washington Parish, Louisiana, which bordered

---

14. Wilson County, Tenn., Will Book 1824–1827, 322 (microfilm; CL); Wilson County Court Minutes, 1814–1829, 354, in Thomas P. Partlow (comp.), *Wilson County, Tennessee, Miscellaneous Records, 1800–1875* (Easley, S.C.: Southern History Press, 1982), 103; Thomas E. Partlow (comp.), *Wilson County, Tennessee, Will Books, 1802–1850* (Easley, S.C.: Southern History Press, 1981), 49; Wilson County, Tenn., Will Book and Inventories, 1819–1824, 99–105 (microfilm; CL); Report of Richard Hankins, guardian for Matthew Cartwright and Matthew C. Hankins, 1825, Wilson County, Tenn., Will Book, 1825–1827, 274, 277, ibid.; Wilson County, Tenn., Will Book, 1824–1827, 322, ibid.

Pike County, Mississippi, the home of Cartwrights. A native of Tennessee, Roberts settled his large family near a spring close to the old Spanish road crossing on the Palo Gacho. It seems possible that Roberts and Cartwright were acquainted before coming to Texas, and perhaps Roberts urged John to occupy the site near Passons Springs in 1825.[15]

Roberts and Cartwright appeared before Chaplin on March 6, 1826, but Holloway's hopes for a favorable decision were in vain. John A. Williams, former alcalde of Ayish Bayou and attorney for Roberts, denied the validity of Holloway's title. Using typically Anglo-American arguments, Williams asserted that the land was public domain and that substantiating the title was a subject for a higher court in San Antonio. Thus Roberts owed nothing to Holloway. Chaplin declared the case nonsuited, meaning that Holloway had no case. After that decision, the charge against Cartwright was withdrawn. Holloway remained in the neighborhood, displaying no animosity and even occasionally charging items at the Cartwright store.[16]

Chichester Chaplin was the son-in-law of Haden Edwards, a former resident of Mississippi, who had secured an empresario grant from state authorities at Saltillo in 1825 that allowed him to settle eight hundred families in the Nacogdoches neighborhood west of the border reserve at the Attoyac (the boundary between present-day Nacogdoches and San Augustine counties), south to Galveston Bay, and west to the Navasota River. Although the state admonished him to respect the property rights of residents already in place, Edwards announced in October 1825 that he would remove those who could not produce titles or pay him a fee. The announcement caused consternation among longtime residents because almost nobody had a legal title due in part to the Spanish practice of recording deeds in San Antonio, and the invasions of 1812 and 1819 had put those records in jeopardy. By this action it was obvious that Edwards did not understand his

15. Summons for Elisha Roberts and John Cartwright, ca. Feb. 1826, Blake Transcripts, XI, 95, 104. Felix G. Roberts erred in saying he moved in 1823, in John Henry Brown, *Indian Wars and Pioneers of Texas* (Austin: L. E. Daniell, [1896]), 437–438; E. Ross Williams, Jr. (abstractor and comp.), *Legal Records of Washington Parish, Louisiana: Duplicates of Washington Parish Deeds 1819–1840* (2 vols.: [n.p.]: privately published, 1965), II, 93.

16. Blake Transcripts, XI, 95, 104, 112, 118–119.

limited power as empresario under the state colonization law that rewarded empresarios with land for the settlement of every one hundred families and prevented them from collecting fees. Moreover, a state-appointed land commissioner, not the empresario, issued titles, and none would be named until Edwards had settled at least one hundred families.[17]

Insensitive toward Hispanic culture and the history of the community, Edwards was interested only in profits. The order, of course, did not apply to John Cartwright or the others living in the Ayish community, but they were soon drawn into quarrels between longtime residents and newcomers when Edwards successfully manipulated the election of his son-in-law, Chichester Chaplin, as alcalde at Nacogdoches. Old-timers supported their friend and longtime resident Samuel Norris, the brother-in-law of James Gaines. When complaints from Mexican residents reached San Antonio concerning illegal voting and the arrogant attitude of Edwards, the authorities removed Chaplin and installed Norris. However, the Anglo residents of Ayish Bayou and other Redland communities viewed the removal of Chaplin and the installation of the "Mexican party's" candidate as a violation of the democratic process and the sort of thing their grandfathers had opposed during the American Revolution.[18]

Accusations and countercharges from both sides of the Edwards issue increased Anglo contempt for Mexican authority. Anglo agitators demanded redress for alleged grievances, which caused Alcalde Norris to ask Gaines to raise militia companies from among loyal Anglos in the Ayish and Sabine communities to

17. Hayden [sic] Edwards's Contract, in Henderson Yoakum, *History of Texas from Its First Settlement in 1685 to Its Annexation to the United States in 1846* (New York: Redfield, 1855), 462–464. For detailed accounts of the trouble stemming from the Edwards contract, see Eugene C. Barker, *The Life of Stephen F. Austin: Founder of Texas, 1793–1836* (Austin: University of Texas Press, 1969), 148–177, and Edmund Morris Parsons, "The Fredonian Rebellion," *Texana*, VII (Spring, 1967), 11–52. A less balanced account based in part on the colorful but unreliable reminiscences of Alexander Horton appears in Crocket, *Two Centuries,* 133–148, and also in Alexander Horton, "Life of A. Horton and Early Settlement of San Augustine County, [1891]," *QTSHA*, XIV (Apr., 1911), 306–308.

18. Barker, *Life of Austin,* 157–159; see Benjamin W. Edwards to S. F. Austin, July 21, 1826, *Austin Papers,* I, 1380–1386, for rhetoric of the American Revolution.

protect his office. Considering the lack of published laws and the uninformed inflammatory rumors flowing from the drinkers at the "doggeries," it is no wonder that tension mounted.[19]

In keeping with the efficient Hispanic political bureaucratic tradition, reports of the troubles at Nacogdoches passed through the *jéfe politico* in San Antonio to the governor at Saltillo who consulted with national authorities. Although Stephen F. Austin advised Edwards and Edwards's brother Benjamin to be circumspect, their letters to the authorities were not conciliatory and resulted in an executive order on October 2, 1826, that annulled Edwards's contract and banished him from Texas.[20]

When the order arrived in Nacogdoches, even those not counted among Haden Edwards's followers pondered the meaning of an executive order that nullified a contract. Anglo-Americans believed strongly in the sanctity of contract, a concept that had been upheld in the U.S. Supreme Court since the early 1800s. If the Mexican executive could abrogate an empresario contract made under a state law, what might happen to titles or to the pending bill to permit lifetime black slavery in Texas currently under consideration by lawmakers at Saltillo?

Trouble erupted on November 22 when thirty-six armed vigilantes from the Ayish neighborhood rode into Nacogdoches to arrest Alcalde Norris and others. Led by Martin Parmer, the group wanted to replace Norris with someone who would see events from the Anglo point of view. Parmer and four others presided over a drumhead court that tried and convicted the Nacogdoches officials for treachery, corruption in office, and a number of other spurious charges. The vigilantes finally released their victims, but before leaving for home on November 27 they named a new alcalde and offered one hundred pesos for James Gaines, dead or alive. At this time, the rebellion was personal and directed against Alcalde Norris but not against the Mexican nation.[21]

Parmer and a handful of supporters returned to Nacogdoches on December 15 and announced a new course: independence for Texas. A rebellion—just what the Mexican authorities had al-

---

19. Ibid. A doggery was a saloon. Crocket, *Two Centuries*, 122.
20. Barker, *Life of Austin*, 162–166.
21. Parsons, "Fredonian Rebellion," 15–19.

ways feared! Sixteen insurgents including Benjamin Edwards inscribed their names on a red-and-white flag that symbolized the tentative union of whites and Indians who had been recruited as allies. Across the top of the flag were the words Independence, Liberty, Justice. Edwards planted the standard in front of the old stone trading house facing the plaza, which they occupied in the name of the Republic of Fredonia. "Fredonia," coined from "free" and "freedom," was a name once suggested as a label for residents of the United States, but it had never become popular. Volunteers, never more than fifty, joined the rebels and they unrealistically talked about marching to the Rio Grande. Their Cherokee allies came to town on December 21 to sign the Fredonian declaration of independence. The Cherokees were angry with the Mexican authorities because the long-promised title to their Texas land was not forthcoming. Benjamin Edwards promised the Indians the northwestern half of Texas above the old Spanish road in return for their support.[22]

In December Elisha Roberts wrote that the Ayish Bayou residents "are very divided." Although initially they intended to help "put down the revolution," word that the Indians had joined the Fredonians caused a change of heart. They "are now busy moving their families and property to the other side of the Sabine." Roberts intended to "remain neutral, not joining any party." The Cartwrights probably decided to remain also; no family stories indicate that they fled. John, Matthew, Robert, and John's cousin Thomas (who had returned to the Redlands from Austin's colony) were enrolled in the seventy-two-member Ayish Bayou militia on April 1, but there is no evidence that they were among the loyalists called to duty to defend the alcalde or to defeat the Fredonians.[23]

The Mexican authorities were well aware of the unrest in eastern Texas and as early as August 1826 planned to send Col. Mateo Ahumada from San Antonio to Nacogdoches to establish a permanent garrison. However, a lack of supplies and fears of an imminent Indian war near San Antonio detained Ahumada until

22. Ibid., 23–25; Dr. C. F. Sheley, "Whence the Name Fredonia?" *The Bicentennial Commemorative History of Nacogdoches* (Nacogdoches: Nacogdoches Jaycees, 1976), 129–131.

23. Elisha Roberts to S. F. Austin, Dec. 21, 1826, Blake Transcripts, XI, 310 (quotations); Ayish Bayou militia roll, Apr. 1, 1826, ibid., XXIX, 97–98.

mid-December. He left for Nacogdoches with the *jéfe politico*, 110 regulars from the Twelfth Permanent Infantry Battalion, plus twenty cavalrymen, and he expected to be reinforced at the Brazos with militiamen from Austin's colony. Blustery cold and heavy rain in San Felipe, however, delayed the march until January 22, 1827.[24]

Meanwhile the "silly, wild, Quicksotic [*sic*] scheme," as Dr. John Sibley of Natchitoches labeled the rebellion, was winding down. Parmer abandoned his command to Benjamin Edwards, the Indian support vanished, and at the end of January, when rumors reached Nacogdoches that the Mexican army was on its way, some Fredonians defected. The narrative of events becomes confused at this point. Alexander Horton, a youth of sixteen in 1827 living at Ayish Bayou with his mother, recalled a romantic adventure featuring himself in a major role. He said that Stephen Prather, an old Indian trader who lived near the mouth of the Attoyac, brought his two sons, five neighbors, and some Indians to the Ayish settlement where he found only Horton and Ed Teal. Everyone else had fled. According to Horton, this small force attacked and defeated a party of one hundred Fredonians barricaded in cabins west of the ford at Carrizo Creek. However, contemporary official letters unavailable to Horton show that Lt. Col. John A. Williams of the Ayish Bayou militia remained in the neighborhood with a portion of his command. They seized three Fredonians on January 26 and rounded up others during the next few days. Williams reported that an advance detachment from Austin's militia reached Ayish Bayou by February 4 and reinforced the local militia along with Alabama Indians brought up from below the Angelina River by Prather.[25]

Upon learning about the approach of Colonel Ahumada at the end of January, the Edwards brothers and the few remaining Fredonians abandoned Nacogdoches, taking various routes to the Sabine. The colonel entered Nacogdoches on February 8 and

24. James E. B. Austin to S. F. Austin, Aug. 22, 1826, *Austin Papers,* I, 1432; Parsons, "Fredonian Rebellion," 22–23, 34.
25. John Sibley to S. F. Austin, Feb. 18, 1827, *Austin Papers,* I, 1604 (quotation); Parsons, "Fredonian Rebellion," 42–43, 44–46; Horton, "Life of A. Horton," 305–308; John A. Williams to Ahumada, Feb. 12, 1827, Blake Transcripts, XI, 343; Lawrence Richard Kenny to Ahumada, Feb. 9, 1827, ibid., 340–341.

secured the old church ruins to house his troops. Four days later Lieutenant Colonel Williams told Ahumada that his force was in control of Ayish Bayou and that he had 187 men ready for duty.[26] If that number was correct, few had fled—or they had returned quickly.

Colonel Ahumada chose to be lenient toward most of the Fredonians because he wanted to correct the notion that the Mexican government was arbitrary and oppressive. He believed that local residents had been duped by the Edwards brothers and Parmer, and he granted amnesty to all except the leaders. The colonel toured the area as far as the Sabine River and decided that the 168 families living east of the Attoyac in the border reserve had settled in good faith before the law announcing the border reserve had been published. He noted their extensive improvements, such as the Cartwright gin and fields, and he urged the political chief to give them titles.

Jéfe José Antonio Saucedo grudgingly agreed, although he continued to believe that the foreigners should move out of the reserve. Saucedo told residents that he would issue titles on two conditions: (1) proper documents had to be completed in Nacogdoches, and (2) the national government must approve granting deeds to those in the reserve. Before his departure on April 6, the *jéfe* reinstalled Norris as alcalde until an election could be held in June, and he authorized the creation of an *ayuntamiento* for Nacogdoches. This would provide eastern Texas with local government that could grant deeds and settle lawsuits subject to review by his office, instead of the old alcalde system that had little authority. Colonel Ahumada also departed, leaving Capt. Mariano Cosio in command of the 129 men and 10 officers at Nacogdoches until the arrival on September 13, 1827 of Lt. Col. José de las Piedras, newly named commander of the Texas frontier.[27]

26. Parsons, "Fredonian Rebellion," 44, 46; Ahumada to Antonio Elosúa, Apr. 1, 1827 (use of church), Blake Transcripts, Supplement vol. IX, 99; Lawrence Richard Kenney to Ahumada, Feb. 9, 1827, Blake Transcripts, XI, 340–341; John A. Williams to Ahumada, Feb. 12, 1827, ibid., XI, 138.

27. Barker, *Life of Austin*, 175–176; Parsons, "Fredonian Rebellion," 46; Mariano Cosio to Antonio Elosúa, Sept. 18, 1827, Blake Transcripts, Supplement vol. IX, 111.

The Ayish Bayou community remained unsettled, and in June 1827 some of the more strident Anglos called for a meeting of residents who wanted titles to their land. If titles were not forthcoming, they threatened to take up arms. Again, Anglos did not understand Mexican law which forbade this sort of unauthorized meeting. Captain Cosio investigated, decided that it was the "talk of idle drunk men," and dropped the matter. Ahumada's favorable report about conditions east of the Attoyac reached President Guadalupe Victoria, and he sent the necessary permission to the state of Coahuila-Texas to issue titles to the residents who had settled within the border reserve before 1827. But the state government moved slowly. In April 1828, the state named Juan Antonio Padilla land commissioner for eastern Texas, but for a variety of reasons he did not reach Nacogdoches until February 1830. In the interim Ayish Bayou residents took "new life and vigor" when, in August 1829, the *jéfe* in San Antonio officially notified them that "peaceful and useful citizens" could retain their land within the reserve bordering the Sabine River.[28]

Land titles were not the only cause for concern among the Cartwrights and their neighbors. The legal status of black slavery in Texas remained in question. In November 1829, word reached Ayish Bayou that the Mexican government had freed the slaves in Texas. Colonel Piedras reported that the news flew "from mouth to mouth" and the residents of Ayish Bayou were in a "state of consternation." He suggested that the alcalde at Nacogdoches not post the decree, a course already taken by the *jéfe politico* in San Antonio, until reinforcements could be sent to Nacogdoches because his present garrison was too weak to enforce the order. One Ayish resident wrote to Stephen F. Austin, "In the name of God what shall we do . . . we are ruined forever should this measure be adopted."[29]

28. Samuel Norris to Saucedo, June 12, 1827, Blake Transcripts, Supplement vol. IX, 105; Encarnación Chirino to Saucedo, July 7, 1827, ibid., 107 (1st quotation); Barker, *Life of Austin,* 325–326; T. F. McKinney to S. F. Austin, Sept. 9, 1829, in Eugene C. Barker (ed.), *The Austin Papers,* in *Annual Report, 1922* of the American Historical Association (3 vols.; vols. I, II, Washington, D.C.: Government Printing Office, 1924, 1928; vol. III, Austin: University of Texas Press, 1927), II, 259 (2nd and 3rd quotations) (cited hereafter as *Austin Papers,* II).

29. Piedras to Elosúa, Nov. 9, 1829, Blake Transcripts, XII, 178 (1st quotation), 179, 180 (2nd quotation); Barker, *Life of Austin,* 215 (3rd quotation), 216.

The decree abolishing slavery had been issued by the president on September 15 to commemorate the Grito de Dolores that began the 1810 Mexican independence movement. Mexicans did not object to the debt peonage that they practiced, but abhorred the word "slavery." Pragmatic politicians, however, recognized that if the Texas frontier was to become productive, it would be by allowing Anglo cotton growers to bring their slaves. Consequently, neither the national nor state constitutions had forbidden slavery; however, subsequent proposals urged that slavery end by gradual mandatory emancipation of slaves at age twenty-five. Austin and other slaveholders did not like gradual emancipation any better than aboliition, and they were working to get a state law passed permitting slavery to continue in Texas when the president's sudden emancipation proclamation appeared. Austin rallied his Hispanic supporters in the state government; they applied pressure to the national government, and within months the order freeing the slaves was rescinded.[30]

John Cartwright owned about fifteen slaves, one-half the number owned by his neighbor Elisha Roberts. Like many slaveowners, John recorded the births and deaths of his servants in his Bible. Eight were members of one family that John may have owned since the time of his marriage. The parents, Harry and Nancy, had six children born between 1811 and 1823; the other adult slaves were acquired later and there seem to be two family units and perhaps a single man. One concern of Texas slaveowners at this time was that, technically, they could not take their blacks back into the United States. Nevertheless, some owners probably did so from time to time.[31]

Forty-year-old Mary Cartwright bore her last child, Richard Hankins, on April 25, 1828, a year of comparative peace between the Fredonian excitement and the emancipation crisis. At this time, John and Mary's oldest child, Matthew, was twenty and the youngest four and one-half. No correspondence exists between the Cartwrights and the Richard Hankins family in Wilson County to explain why John's brother-in-law was honored by a namesake at this time. Most likely it had to do with favors since 1825 and

30. Barker, *Life of Austin*, 55, 58, 64, 122, 207–209, 212–218.
31. List of slaves from the John Cartwright Bible; compare with those listed in the 1835 Census, Sabine District, Blake Transcripts, XIX, 23.

Matthew's pending visit to Tennessee to claim his inheritance.

Tall, handsome Matthew became twenty-one on November 11, 1828, and sometime in the spring or early summer of 1829 he traveled once again to Wilson County to stay with the Hankins family and enroll in a local college. Perhaps his lack of polish bothered him, or maybe cousin Matthew Hankins was attending classes at nearby Brevard College, which had opened in 1824 in a log cabin four miles east of Lebanon. These schools of "higher education" sprouted throughout Tennessee at this time not only to educate youth but to overcome the previous lack of schools available to young adults such as Matthew. Sometimes these schools lacked regular semesters and the subjects taught reflected the learning of the staff. Greek and Latin classic literature involving much memorization was typical, along with ethics, rhetoric, and logic, the sort of training suitable for those entering law or theology. Practical mathematics for surveyors, navigators, and businessmen was also offered.[32]

Whatever his motivation, Matthew spent some time during the summer writing essays to improve his grammar in a school run by William Pemberton, who in 1833 became president of Brevard. Drafts of two essays by Matthew survive in the Cartwright papers: one dated July 11, 1829, and signed like a letter, "Your most Obt [servant]," deplored wasted time and opportunities; the other, dated September 1 and signed "Your humble sevt," outlined the evils of drunkenness. The subjects, typical of nineteenth-century moralism, were probably assigned, yet they reveal something about Matthew and perhaps hint at his real feelings. Both essays are immature for age twenty-one, but his handwriting, the slanted-to-the-right style popularized by H. P. Spencer in the mid-nineteenth century, shows the result of practiced drill.[33]

Perhaps these essays are autobiographical; if so, they are quite revealing. First Matthew described a vain youth who had been

32. *The Goodspeed Histories of Maury, Williamson, Rutherford, Wilson, Bedford & Marshall Counties of Tennessee,* 858; Notes about curriculum from Lucius Salisbury Merriam, *Higher Education in Tennessee,* Bureau of Education Circular no. 5 (Washington, D.C.: Government Printing Office, 1893), 186–189.

33. Matthew Cartwright draft essay to William Pemberton, July 11, 1829, Cartwright Research Collection; Matthew Cartwright draft essay, Sept. 1, 1829, W. G. Sharp Collection (BTHC).

sent to school by his parents and who wasted time in frivolous, sometimes evil, pursuits. This "Idler" soon discovered that his hardworking "opponent far exceeded him in qualities, qualifications, and the estimation" of his community. "If it is not too late[,] give him an opportunity to improve and he will apply himself with double vigor. . . ." The second essay may be a commentary on life in Texas. Matthew wrote, "Drunkenness . . . impairs the health . . . causes a man to neglect his Business" and indulge in "the most disgracing practices" that destroy his estate and leave his family destitute. Instead of being a worthy citizen, he is "a constant burthen and disgrace" to his friends and family. Matthew abruptly ended this essay in a manner characteristic of an immature student by saying that there were many illustrations he could give of this "important subject but I have not time at present as the time is drawn near for me to start to school." Nevertheless, his mentor wrote a certificate on September 5, 1829, stating that Matthew had studied "the English grammar in my school" and had made "extraordinary progress."[34] Maybe the few weeks with Pemberton were preparatory to fall classes at Brevard although no evidence exists showing that Matthew attended classes while he remained in Wilson County until at least mid-October to complete his business transactions.

On September 29, 1829, Matthew Cartwright "of the Province of Texas" sold to Reuben Satterfield the 222 acres willed to him by his grandfather in 1811. He received $400 and on October 14 bought Jim, born and raised in Wilson County and two years younger than Matthew.[35] Before the end of the year Matthew and his new servant traveled to Texas to join Matthew's father and brothers, Robert and George, in operating the family farm and cotton gin.

34. Ibid., July 11, 1829 (1st and 2nd quotations), Cartwright Research Collection; ibid., Sept. 1, 1829 (3rd–6th quotations), W. G. Sharp Collection.
35. Wilson County, Tenn., Deed Book, M, 510 (quotation); Bill of sale, Oct. 14, 1829, Legal Documents, 1829-1869, Cartwright Family Papers (BTHC) (cited hereafter as CFP).

Three

The Founding of
San Augustine

1830–1834

The Anglo-Americanization of the Redlands increased in
the early 1830s in spite of Mexican efforts to reverse the
trend. At the same time, the Cartwrights broadened their
entrepreneurial activities as John's two oldest sons, Matthew and
Robert, matured and took their places in the community. Robert
would be twenty-one years old at the end of March 1830, and
both young men needed to develop their own capital. Unlike their
father, who married before he was twenty years old, Matthew
and Robert postponed marriage until their late twenties.

John Cartwright was a hard taskmaster. A contract John
made with his sons in 1830 and pages in the extant ledgers reveal
a man who expected total commitment and no waste of resources
from family, slaves, or associates. He charged interest on monetary advances, expected lost time to be made up or deducted
from the profits, and demanded a large share of the proceeds
when his equipment was used. His older sons were thus exposed
to mercantile practices of the day, and Matthew appears to have
benefited from this stern treatment.

On March 6, 1830, John Cartwright made a one-year contract with Matthew and Robert holding them responsible for the cotton plantation, for moving the gin to a new location, and for its operation. Matthew wrote the simple one-page document for the partnership, and perhaps it was he who insisted on a written agreement. A family story relates that earlier Matthew had rented a field from his father to grow a crop, for which privilege he paid one-third of the crop. John later decided that his son had cleared too much profit, while Matthew argued that the one-third payment was the standard levy. The son had learned his lessons well![1]

On the other hand, John may have instigated the 1830 contract, remembering a similar arrangement between himself and his father. While John had been an only son, he was the father of three adult sons and two younger ones; such arrangements needed to be businesslike so that everyone understood his obligations. It is also possible that John wanted to be relieved of the plantation and gin in order to have more time for land speculating, and therefore ordered the formal contract.

By the terms of the agreement, there were seven shares. Matthew and Robert contributed their labor and that of Matthew's slave, Jim, for three shares. John would furnish four shares with the labor of his son George, now eighteen and a blacksmith, and a work force of three slaves: Jack, age thirty-four, Peter, age eighteen, and Jordan, age seventeen (the latter two were sons of old Harry and Nancy). John had trained Jordan, and perhaps Peter, as apprentice blacksmiths. Matthew and Robert were to move the gin to a new location north of the homesite, and the "prophets" (Matthew was a creative speller) from the cotton crop and also from ginning for the public would be split on the three/four share arrangement. John also provided plows and horses to plant the crop and provisions for his four hands. John Cartwright's wagon and team would be available for hauling whenever required, but he would receive two-thirds of the "prophets" for its use. The hours worked by the seven men were to be carefully recorded and deductions made for absenteeism.[2]

1. "An Agreement . . . the 6th day of March 1830," at end of Account Book no. 1, 1832–1834, CFP; Robert L. Cartwright, "The History of John Cartwright Settlement," Cartwright Research Collection.

2. "Agreement, 1830," Account Book no. 1, CFP; Crocket, *Two Centuries,* 87, but Jordan was not sold before inventory of John Cartwright possessions in 1841.

Matthew employed his uncle, Thomas Cartwright, to work at the gin in 1830. The restless older man had lived in Austin's colony during 1824, but upon learning that his cousin John was moving his family to the Palo Gacho in early 1825, Thomas sold his league on the Colorado River and his 177-acre *labór* on the Brazos River near San Felipe in March 1825 and returned to the Redlands with his wife and three sons, James, Jesse, and Thomas. John Sprowl, the alcalde of Ayish Bayou who had known Thomas since 1823, assured the authorities in Nacogdoches that Thomas was an honest peaceable citizen. Thomas returned briefly to Wilson County, Tennessee, to sell his patrimony of 130 acres on Round Lick Creek to his brother Hezekiah. The older praised Texas so much that within a few years Hezekiah moved his family to San Augustine.[3]

Matthew and Robert had to market their cotton in Natchitoches in August and December 1830, taking Peter along as their driver. Matthew also traveled to Nacogdoches to buy cotton and to attend a wedding. Even though the brothers worked hard, their profits were meager after their first year. The accounts showed less than one hundred dollars for each when they settled with their father in March 1831.[4]

In 1830 John Cartwright also concentrated on getting his land on the Palo Gacho surveyed. For more than a year, East Texas residents had expected the arrival of the state land commissioner from Saltillo. In anticipation, Cartwright and others tried to establish boundaries for their headrights. The Cartwright homesite on the Palo Gacho when finally surveyed totaled only five *labores,* or about 885.5 acres. A headright league contained twenty-five *labores,* so John wanted the remaining twenty *labores* to be located along what is now the Shelby County border on the headwaters of Buckley's Creek, where he intended to build a gristmill and sawmill. A headright league was supposed to be a single parcel, and John optimistically expected that the surveyors

3. Election returns, San Felipe, Dec. 24, 1824, *Austin Papers,* I, 995–996; Austin County Colonial Records, II, 83–85, 95–97, 135–137; Sprowl to Nacogdoches Court, Jan. 10, 1826, Blake Transcripts, X1, 171; Wilson County, Tenn., Deed Record, M, 415; Carolyn R. Ericson and Frances T. Ingmire, *First Settlers of the Republic of Texas* (2 vols.; Nacogdoches: Ericson and Ingmire, 1982), II, 161.

4. Account Book no. 1 (near end), CFP.

could join the mill site to his homestead. But when the lines were run, the area totaled more than the 4,428 acres allowed. In order to keep the two favored sites, there would be a 1½-mile gap between the parcels. The surveyor, perhaps cowed by strong arguments from John Cartwright, acquiesced in this irregular arrangement.[5]

Land Commissioner Juan Antonio Padilla and his entourage of two clerks, military escort, and the state-appointed chief surveyor, Thomas Jefferson Chambers, finally reached Nacogdoches in February 1830. Chambers was a contriving, ambitious, Kentucky lawyer who had immigrated to Mexico City in 1826, where he ingratiated himself with powerful men in order to advance his career. His appointment as chief surveyor was a step forward to becoming a licensed attorney and eventually supreme judge for Texas under the Mexican government.

Chambers had a number of Anglo surveyors already at work in the various neighborhoods, and he issued strict written instructions forbidding gaps between the leagues. Surveyors should try to get neighbors to agree peaceably about boundaries, and disputes would be decided by Commissioner Padilla. The surveyors chose where to begin, but they had to proceed in an orderly fashion along the watercourses and roads; in other words, they were not to leave one place and move to another to please an eager settler. Chambers assigned Frank W. Johnson and William Moore to survey Ayish Bayou; both were trained in mathematics, though Moore lacked field experience. Johnson had been in Texas since 1826, when he platted the town of Harrisburg on Buffalo Bayou. He and Moore headquartered at the home of Elisha Roberts and surveyed John Cartwright's homesite first; neighboring tracts are described: "Beginning at John Cartwright's corner. . . ."[6]

5. The first two maps of San Augustine County (dated 1839 and 1841) in the General Land Office of Texas show the Cartwright portions (one by name: the homestead by "C"), while subsequent maps do not.

6. Thomas Jefferson Chambers to George W. Smyth, Feb. 1, 1830, George W. Smyth Papers (BTHC); Webb, Carroll, and Branda (eds.), *Handbook of Texas,* I, 778; Frank W. Johnson, *A History of Texas and Texans,* ed. Eugene C. Barker (5 vols.; Chicago: American Historical Society, 1914), I, 148, 160–161; Elisha Roberts's survey in possession of Sandra Kardell Calpakis; Phillip Sublett's survey, ibid. (quotation).

Mexican politics, however, interrupted the long-awaited surveying in eastern Texas. The arrival of Commissioner Padilla, representing the republican-oriented state government, momentarily eased the rising tensions between the local population and Colonel Piedras, the military commandant for the area, who reflected the centralist, authoritarian views of the national administration and of the powerful military commandant of northeastern Mexico, who had authority over many civilian affairs.[7]

Piedras had been a source of friction since his arrival in 1827, when he tried to follow his instructions to impose Mexican-style law and order in the area. The Anglo population did not understand that the military commander had the authority to supervise the alcaldes, the merchants, and even the manner in which streets were laid off and buildings erected. While this seemed outrageous to immigrants, it was traditional Spanish governing style. Colonel Piedras visited Ayish Bayou in 1828 and told the residents to align their houses with the roads according to Mexican regulations. The colonel noted the home of Elisha Roberts was one of the worst offenders, but Piedras's orders were ignored in Ayish Bayou. Nacogdoches residents complained that Piedras and his troops treated civilians in an arrogant manner and that neither the colonel nor his officers paid their debts to local merchants. Moreover, storekeepers complained that Piedras took away their profits when he ordered supplies direct from New Orleans and sold them to his troops. In fairness to the colonel, the government failed to supply frontier outposts, and payroll and expense money was often late. Piedras constantly worried that his poorly equipped garrison of 150 infantrymen and 60 cavalrymen was outnumbered by hostile Anglo settlers, and he became paranoid about the United States troops at Fort Jesup who seemed poised for an attack.[8]

7. Thomas F. McKinney to S. F. Austin, Feb. 13, 1830, *Austin Papers,* II, 331–332.

8. Thomas F. McKinney to S. F. Austin, Mar. 14, 1828, ibid., II, 24–26; Thomas F. McKinney to S. F. Austin, Nov. 5, 1828, ibid., II, 138–139; Piedras to Antonio Elosúa, July 16, 1828, Blake Transcripts, Supplement vol. IX, 136; T. F. McKinney to Political Chief, Sept. 28, 1828, ibid., XII, 57–58; Merchants to Ayuntamiento, Mar. 28, 1829, ibid., XII, 105–106; Piedras to A. Elosúa, June 26, 1829, ibid., XII, 120–122. Crocket, *Two Centuries* , 153, erroneously says that Piedras was courteous and prudent and cites the seminal study of Edna Rowe, "Disturbances at Anahuac," *QTSHA,* VI (Apr., 1903), 279. Her source

The uneasy situation worsened at the end of April when an order from San Antonio arrived in Nacogdoches for Colonel Piedras to arrest Land Commissioner Padilla. The cause was political, but the immediate charge was the murder of a soldier, the husband of Padilla's mistress, both of whom had come with him from the Rio Grande. His enemies had used the compromising situation to frame Padilla and remove him from office. The commissioner and his two clerks were placed under guard in the army barracks, and Piedras seized Padilla's papers. "The eubullition of public feeling . . . is fearful," Chambers warned, and unrest increased when the residents learned that the land commissioner had also been suspended from office. Although some surveys had been made, nobody had titles yet and the future appeared bleak.[9]

Thomas Jefferson Chambers feared he might lose his position, and he rushed to San Antonio to see what could be done. Unfortunately his appointment as chief surveyor was also abolished. Conservative politicians in Saltillo who disliked the Anglos in Texas had triumphed, and henceforth the state planned to name a commissioner and surveyor for each colony or settlement with fewer powers for better control. Chambers endeavored to legitimize the already-completed surveys, but found that his influence had diminished because of political events at the national and state level. Back on Ayish Bayou, Johnson and Moore collected fees from the surveys they had completed and left the neighborhood in July. Cartwright still owed $25 to Moore for the twenty *labóres*; he finally paid in 1833.[10]

The Mexican republic faced a crisis in 1830 when the conservative centralist faction staged a coup, deposed President Vicente Guerrero (a hero of the 1821 independence movement and an ardent republican federalist) and elevated Vice-president Anastacio Bustamante, a centralist general. The two political factions had

---

was an 1889 reminiscence of Austin's nephew, who was age eleven in 1832, and she later arbitrarily added Piedras to the list of friendly officers. The above cited documents from the Bexar Archives, unavailable to Rowe, prove otherwise.

9. Padilla to S. F. Austin, Apr. 27, 1830, *Austin Papers*, II, 271; T. J. Chambers to S. F. Austin, May 12, 1830, ibid., 373 (quotation).

10. T. J. Chambers to S. F. Austin, May 12, 1830, *Austin Papers*, II, 373; T. F. McKinney to G. W. Smyth, June 28, 1830, G. W. Smyth Papers (BTHC); T. J. Chambers to G. W. Smyth, July 1, 1830, ibid.; Johnson, *History of Texas and the Texans*, I, 160–161; Receipt from Moore to John Cartwright, Sept. 6, 1833, CFP.

struggled for power since adopting the 1824 constitution. The federalists wanted a limited central government and strong states, and many of the residents of Coahuila-Texas belonged to this party composed of ranchers and idealistic republicans. Their opponents, the centralists, preferred a strong central government more in keeping with Hispanic tradition, in which the states were mere dependencies. The centralists included the rich and the powerful: wealthy landowners, army officers, and high churchmen. The first president had been a federalist while the vice-president (always the runner-up in the election) a centralist and a military man, a combination that encouraged discontent. Unfortunately for the new republic, coup followed coup for more than fifty years.[11] At the state level, the republican federalists were friendly toward Anglo Texas, and it was they who had appointed Padillo and Chambers. With the coup in national politics, all was confusion at Saltillo.

John Cartwright, like most Redlanders, cared little for national and state politics. Soon after making the contract with his sons, he traveled to the Brazos settlements to explore the area and buy a certain league of land he had learned was for sale. On April 9, 1830, in San Felipe, the court town for Austin's colony, John paid the equivalent of twelve hundred pesos by deeding a black slave woman named Octavia and her three children to David Bright for his headright on Oyster Creek in present-day Fort Bend County. Bright was a distant kinsman of Elisha Roberts by marriage. The Bright league was just south of present-day Stafford and about six or seven miles from Jesse Cartwright's plantation. John was aware of the agricultural potential of the Bright league for cotton and sugar because two years earlier, young Robert, not quite twenty years old, had bought Bright's *labór* and still owed money for it.[12]

11. Hubert Herring, *A History of Latin America from the Beginnings to the Present* (2nd ed., rev.; New York: Alfred A Knopf, 1965), 307–313. Crocket, *Two Centuries,* 149, relying on erroneous facts in the 1859 *Texas Almanac* (written by the editor of the Galveston *News,* a newcomer to Texas), repeated the myth of Piedras's considerate behavior and other factual errors (pp. 150–151): Victoria was not succeeded by Pedraza but by Vicente Guerrero, and Bustamante did not "seize the reins" (p. 150).

12. Austin County Colonial Records, I, 177–179, 316–319; Fort Bend County Deed Records, B, 77. Noel F. Roberts, a native of Louisiana and resident of Austin's colony, married David Bright's daughter on May 10, 1824. *Austin Papers,* I, 790.

Either Bright or Jesse Cartwright may have urged John to apply for a headright in Austin's colony while he was visiting the Brazos. John Cartwright filed an application in San Felipe on May 3, 1830, perhaps reacting to the bad news from Nacogdoches about the recent arrest of Land Commissioner Padilla and the gloomy prospect of getting a title in eastern Texas. For less than $100 in fees, the current charges, John could be sure of a title in the Austin colony. On his application, John said that he was a farmer in the Ayish district, had come from Mississippi in 1825, and had a wife, five sons, two daughters, and eleven slaves. But like Cousin Thomas, John finally concluded that the Palo Gacho's location close to Natchitoches outweighed the security of a title on the Brazos, because he failed to pay the fees and no title was issued. Encouraging information reached the Redlands in September that a new land commissioner had been named to replace Padilla, which created optimism among the residents.[13]

A new problem for the Anglo-Texans arose with the passage of the anti-Anglo-American "Law of April 6, 1830," banning further emigration from the United States. The order resulted from the report of Gen. Manuel Mier y Terán, who had visited Texas in 1828 at the request of the centralist leaders. Officially he was there to supervise surveying the land along the 94th parallel above the westward turn of the Sabine River to mark the boundary between Mexican Texas and Louisiana under the terms of the 1819 treaty. His report was not unfavorable except in remarking that Anglos outnumbered native Mexicans, and because they continued to speak English and practice the laws of the United States instead of conforming to Mexican statutes, he predicted that they would take over Texas if not checked. Mier y Terán recommended limiting immigration from the United States and at the same time encouraging native Mexicans to move to the northeastern frontier in order to preserve the national heritage and hegemony.[14]

A copy of the law arrived in San Felipe on May 16, and immediately Austin and his associates poured over the wording

13. Austin's "Register of Families," also in Gifford White, *1830 Citizens of Texas*, 26, 48. A copying error for John's application (May 3, 1828, instead of April 9, 1830) appeared in Gifford White (ed.), *Character Certificates in the General Land Office of Texas* (Austin: privately published, 1985), 31.

14. Barker, *Life of Austin*, 261–265.

and discovered an ambiguous phrase that seemed to allow immigrants to continue entering previously established colonies such as his and that of Green DeWitt on the Guadalupe River. Fortunately for the empresario, Mier y Terán, now commandant general of northeastern Mexico and in charge of colonization in Texas, agreed. Anglos with passports to Austin's or DeWitt's colonies could be admitted; at Nacogdoches, Colonel Piedras received orders to enforce the law, and he scrutinized all immigrants carefully and demanded passports showing that newcomers were destined for Austin's colony. The Law of April 6, 1830, did, however, prevent new settlers in the Redlands.[15]

The anti-immigration law coincided with the end of a six-year exemption from national tariffs granted to Austin's colony during its pioneer stage, a privilege subsequently claimed by all Anglo immigrants. True to form, Anglos heard only what they chose to hear, and they were surprised to learn that beginning in May 1830 regular Mexican duties on goods coming from the United States would be collected at all Texas ports of entry. Troops would be sent to major ports to assist the customs collectors with enforcing the tariff regulations. In November, Col. Juan Davis Bradburn and forty men arrived on upper Galveston Bay to establish the town of Anahuac and build a fort at the mouth of the Trinity River to prevent smuggling into eastern Texas. Colonel Piedras, of course, guarded the land route at Nacogdoches, and deputy collectors and a squad of guards would be placed at the mouths of the Sabine and Brazos rivers. A small garrison was placed under the command of Col. Peter Ellis Bean at Fort Terán on the Angelina River south of Ayish Bayou, in the vicinity of an old cattle-smuggling road. West of Nacogdoches along the old Spanish road another garrison, Tenoxtitlán, was installed at the Brazos River crossing. Other troops were assigned to guard the coast below La Bahia and San Antonio.[16]

Meanwhile John Cartwright and his neighbors continued to wait for the arrival of the newly named land commissioner. But

15. Austin to Mier y Terán, May 18, 1830, *Austin Papers,* II, 380–381; Barker, *Life of Austin,* 266–271.

16. Margaret Swett Henson, *Juan Davis Bradburn: A Reappraisal of the Mexican Commander at Anahuac* (College Station: Texas A&M University Press, 1982), 47–54; "Fort Tenoxtitlan" and "Fort Teran," Webb, Carroll, and Branda (eds.), *Handbook of Texas,* I, 633. Again, Crocket, *Two Centuries,* 152–153, is inaccurate.

instead of going directly to Nacogdoches, José Francisco Madero began issuing titles along the lower Trinity River in March 1831. Colonel Bradburn arrested Commissioner Madero and held him for a short time in a quarrel over whether national or state law took precedence in settling families. In May, just after establishing the new town of Liberty twenty-five miles north of Anahuac, the state recalled Madero.[17] Ayish Bayou and Sabine residents were again abandoned without titles to their land.

The Cartwright family had a new neighbor on the southwest corner, Phillip Allen Sublett, whose youngest son would marry John's granddaughter in 1869. Sublett paid $400 to John W. Frith in 1830 for his house and property, which lay along the road from Gaines's Ferry just west of Elisha Roberts, Sublett's father-in-law. Frith had lived there since at least 1826 and had taken an active roll in the Fredonian Rebellion. In early 1828 he was again in trouble with the authorities for supporting some Red River men in a scheme to seize San Antonio and had to leave Texas. Sublett had married Easter Jane Roberts on March 6, 1828, soon after he had taken the oath of citizenship before the Nacogdoches *ayuntamiento* and asked for a headright. He was not a newcomer to Ayish Bayou, having visited the area in 1824 in company with his cousin, Thomas F. McKinney, on a return trip from Chihuahua and Durango. The pair had left Missouri for Santa Fe the previous year and had traded goods along their way, winding up in East Texas to visit McKinney's uncle, Stephen Prather. Both returned to Missouri briefly before deciding to settle in the Redlands.[18]

When John Cartwright's contract with his sons ended in March 1831 it was not renewed. Instead, Matthew clerked at the store on the Palo Gacho and kept the books for his father, while Robert ventured on his own, perhaps on the Oyster Creek land.

17. Henson, *Bradburn*, 58–66.

18. Handwritten deed from John W. Frith to Phillip Sublett, Mar. 15, 1830, signed by alcalde Jacob Garrett, W. G. Sharp Collection (BTHC); List of Free Males Ayish Bayou District, Jn [sic] 9, 1826, Blake Transcripts, XI, 83; Peter Ellis Bean to S. F. Austin, Mar. 5, 1828, *Austin Papers*, II, 23–24; Phillip A. Sublett Bible, in possession of Sandra Kardell Calpakis; Oath of citizenship, May 31, 1828, attached to petition for land, June 9, 1828, Blake Transcripts, XXI, 90; Margaret Swett Henson, "Thomas F. McKinney" (unpublished MS in progress). Crocket, *Two Centuries*, 122, repeats a Sublett family story that Phillip came in 1824 and paid a squatter $50 for the site.

Robert's name does not appear in extant account books between 1831 and February 1833, and a family story maintains that he had a ranch on Oyster Creek.[19]

The year 1832 brought the political crisis in Mexico to a head nationally and in Texas. Colonel Piedras in Nacogdoches received a desperate plea for military assistance from Colonel Bradburn at Anahuac on June 19. About 150 armed Anglo-Americans had appeared at Anahuac on June 9, 1832, demanding the release of a number of Anglo prisoners held by Bradburn. Skirmishes took place, and on June 13 the Anglo insurgents retreated five miles to Turtle Bayou to await the arrival of cannon from Brazoria. With less than 160 troops available for duty, and expecting the Anglo reinforcements to tip the balance against him, Bradburn took advantage of the lull to send messages to Nacogdoches, Tenoxtitlán, and San Antonio asking for help.[20]

Colonel Piedras was aware of the growing quarrel between Bradburn and the residents of Anahuac that had resulted in the arrest of William B. Travis, Patrick Jack, and others in May. He was reluctant, however, to leave his post because of rumors that Ayish Bayou men planned to join the insurgents at Anahuac or perhaps attack Nacogdoches. Moreover, Piedras believed that the entire affair was part of a plan to liberate Texas from Mexico and that he needed to defend his position.[21]

A number of Texans had known Colonel Bradburn in Kentucky and Louisiana before he joined the Mexican republican revolutionaries in 1817. When he first arrived at Anahuac, his former associates thought that he would be sympathetic to their views, but as a career officer, Bradburn intended to enforce the immigration and tariff laws of his adopted country even though it angered his old friends. Bradburn arrested Travis for sedition and expected to send him to Matamoros for trial before the commandant general. Anglos could not understand that under

19. For family lore that Robert owned a ranch, see Matthew Cartwright to Holman Cartwright, Nov. 16, 1909, CFP; Fort Bend County Deed Records, B, 77.

20. Piedras to Elosúa, June 19, 1832, Blake Transcripts, XII, 93; Rowe, "The Disturbances at Anahuac," 285–286. Also see Henson, *Bradburn*, 75–114, for details of the events at Anahuac.

21. Piedras to Elosúa, June 19, 1832, Blake Transcripts, XII, 93; Piedras to Elosúa, June 22, 1832, ibid., 99–102.

Mexican law the military could arrest a civilian, keep him without bail, and hold the trial elsewhere, procedures that would have violated the Bill of Rights of the United States.[22]

Piedras finally left Nacogdoches for Anahuac on June 19 with sixty infantrymen, all of his small cavalry, and nineteen mounted Hispanic civilian militiamen. At Fort Terán he added more cavalry, bringing the total to twenty, plus twenty Indians as militia. He also learned that the Anglo rebels at Turtle Bayou had endorsed the Plan de Vera Cruz, the republican reform promulgated in January 1832 by Gen. Antonio López de Santa Anna, who was leading the victorious federalist forces against the centralist administration. The Mexican civil war, begun in 1829, had finally reached Texas. The Anglo insurgents at Turtle Bayou announced they were aiding Santa Anna and the federalists, and were not revolutionaries trying to sever Texas from Mexico. When Colonel Piedras and his reinforcements reached the town of Liberty, he learned that the residents of the lower Brazos had also joined the *santanista* movement and were marching against Velasco, the small fort at the mouth of the river, before heading for Anahuac. Believing himself outnumbered and in personal danger, Piedras panicked, and on June 28, 1832, assented to the demands of the Anglo insurgents led by Frank W. Johnson, the former surveyor in Ayish Bayou. Piedras agreed to remove Colonel Bradburn from command at Anahuac and to release Travis and the other prisoners.[23]

After a quick visit to Anahuac, Piedras and his troops started back to Nacogdoches on July 8. Three days later the garrison at Anahuac mutinied and declared themselves in favor of Santa Anna. The colonel, however, did not learn about the treason until later. He reached Nacogdoches on July 11 to discover growing unrest over his use of the civilian militia and his allowing armed Indians to accompany him.[24]

Ayish Bayou was restless, but contrary to rumor, no men had started for Anahuac or Nacogdoches. Alcalde Benjamin Lindsay

22. Henson, *Bradburn*, 20–30, 99–100.
23. Rowe, "The Disturbances at Anahuac," 292–295; Piedras to Elosúa, n.d., copied and forwarded by Lieutenant Medina, June 23, 1832, Blake Transcripts, XII, 346–347.
24. Henson, *Bradburn*, 110; Piedras to Elosúa, July 12, 1832, Blake Transcripts, XIII, 37–49.

called a meeting at his home on June 28 during which the majority decided to remain neutral in the matter of Anahuac but named a committee to draft resolutions. A second meeting took place one week later and those in attendance approved the work of the committee and sent copies to Nacogdoches, Tenaha (present-day Shelby County), and San Felipe. Addressed "To the Citizens of Coahuila and Texas," the document endorsed peace and pledged loyalty to the constitution and laws, although the framers expressed concern over the complaints of "brother Colonists." Isolated on the remote frontier and fearing Indian uprisings, the Redlanders strongly objected to Piedras's use of Indian auxiliaries. Then the resolution issued a somber warning: in case of confrontation between civil and military leaders, Ayish Bayou would support the civilian government, which they considered superior in authority to the military.[25] All in all, the resolution made a polite, respectful statement, but a direct challenge to Colonel Piedras.

Whether John Cartwright attended the meetings is unknown. Matthew, still seeking self-improvement, had returned to Tennessee for more education. From August to October 1832 he attended Portershill Academy in western Smith County near the home of the Hankinses. He took part in a debating society and avidly defended President Andrew Jackson's recent veto of the bill to recharter the Bank of the United States. Robert probably was on Oyster Creek. George, almost twenty-one, doubtless attended the meeting along with neighbor Phil Sublett; they both took part in the confrontation on August 2, 1832, in Nacogdoches.[26]

The Ayish Bayou manifesto angered and frightened Colonel Piedras, who began preparing for an attack by ordering the Nacogdoches militia, *ayuntamiento,* and residents to support the garrison. This order caused many Nacogdoches families to leave the village temporarily. Piedras sent a delegation to Ayish Bayou to demand the names of traitors. Leaders denied there were

25. Benjamin Lindsay to Alcalde at Nacogdoches, June, Blake Transcripts, XXIX, 378; Ayish Resolution, July 5, 1832, ibid., XIII, 16–18 (quotations).

26. Drafts of four speeches, Aug. 11–Oct. 6, 1832, Portershill Academy; George's service in Robert Lane Cartwright, "The History of John Cartwright Settlement," Cartwright research files; Geo. W. Cartwright, Pension claim no. 926, Republic of Texas, Pension Applications (Archives Division, Texas State Library, Austin; cited hereafter as TSL).

traitors; everyone supported the Constitution of 1824 and the reforms proposed by Santa Anna to restructure the present cabinet. Thus, Ayish Bayou joined the federalist cause and the residents repeated their promise to support the Nacogdoches *ayuntamiento* against any orders from the military.[27]

The beleaguered *ayuntamiento,* composed of three native Mexicans and two Anglo-Texans, was aware that Stephen F. Austin and the Brazos settlements had embraced Santa Anna's cause in mid-July, and it prepared to do the same. The members accepted the Ayish Bayou support on July 28, admitting that they had previously been "overawed" by Colonel Piedras. Now they wanted to expose his unconstitutional acts: (1) his usurpation of the civilian militia, which had been forced to march to Anahuac, and (2) his use of Indian auxiliaries, so dangerous to the lives and property of the residents. Moreover, they deplored his arrogant and insulting comments equating Anglos and Indians. Then they pronounced, as the Mexicans called rallying to a cause, and called all citizens to rally to the "standard of Santa Anna as the champion of freedom" in support of the constitution and laws of Mexico. Nacogdoches was the third town in Texas to join Santa Anna, following Brazoria and San Felipe; San Antonio would soon follow.[28]

Meanwhile, volunteers from Ayish Bayou, including George Cartwright and Sublett, plus volunteers from Tenaha, Sabine, and Bevil, assembled on Carrizo Creek and were joined by likeminded men from Nacogdoches. Calling themselves the "National Militia," the men agreed—after prayer—to exercise their "natural rights" to oppose a "despot" who had trampled the rights of peaceable citizens and violated the constitution. This rhetoric aimed against Colonel Piedras was similar to that used by their grandfathers in 1776, and had also been used by those who drafted the Turtle Bayou Resolutions on June 13 to explain the attack against Anahuac. The Redland volunteers elected James W. Bullock, a veteran of the War of 1812, to lead them. He and others composed their *pronunciamiento* and resolutions in favor of Santa Anna, and on August 2, 1832, Sublett, Isaac W. Burton,

27. Ayuntamiento of Nacogdoches to Political Chief, Aug. 14, 1832, Blake Transcripts, XIII, 72–73.
28. Ayuntamiento of Nacogdoches to Inhabitants of Ayish Bayou, July 28, 1832, ibid., XIII, 55–56; Barker, *Life of Austin,* 344–345.

and H. W. Augustine took a copy to Colonel Piedras, along with a request that he join the movement within four hours or prepare for an attack.[29]

Piedras remained a loyal officer of the administration and refused to join the *santanistas,* although his superior at San Antonio, Col. Antonio Elosúa, did so before the end of the month. Shortly after noon, Bullock led the volunteers toward the plaza, where Piedras's men fired upon them. The Redlanders took shelter in nearby buildings and returned fire. The Battle of Nacogdoches lasted until dark, during which time George Cartwright, engaged in combat on his twenty-first birthday, was wounded. During the night, Colonel Piedras ordered his troops to withdraw silently west along the road to San Antonio. Their retreat was discovered at dawn. Bullock sent eighteen mounted riflemen in pursuit, and they caught up with the troops near the Angelina River. Piedras immediately relinquished his command to Lt. Francisco Medina and sought refuge at John Durst's house nearby. Without delay Lieutenant Medina surrendered the entire force and they all joined the *santanista* cause. On August 5, the officers delivered Colonel Piedras to Bullock, signaling the end of hostilities. The colonel had lost forty-seven men in the battle, with many more wounded. Of the Texan volunteers, three were killed, including Nacogdoches alcalde Encarnación Chireno, and five were wounded, including George Cartwright.[30]

The volunteers took Colonel Piedras back to Nacogdoches and on August 8, 1832, James Bowie, who was en route to his home in San Antonio, took command of the Mexican troops at their request and made plans to march south. Bowie had been in Texas since 1828 and was a son-in-law of the lieutenant governor of Coahuila-Texas, Juan Martín de Vcremendi of San Antonio. Piedras and the troops reached San Felipe on August 20; the soldiers continued to San Antonio to join the *santanista* move-

29. Ayuntamiento of Nacogdoches to Political Chief, Aug. 14, 1832, Blake Transcripts, XIII, 73 (1st quotation), 74 (2nd and 3rd quotations); Johnson, *History of Texas and Texans,* I, 84.
30. Elosúa to S. F. Austin, Aug. 30, 1832, *Austin Papers,* II, 853–854; Ayuntamiento of Nacogdoches to Political Chief, Aug. 14, 1832, Blake Transcripts, XIII, 75–77; James W. Bullock to Alcalde at San Felipe, Aug. 9, 1832, in Johnson, *History of Texas and Texans,* I, 84–85; Robert Lane Cartwright, "History of the Cartwright Settlement," Cartwright research files.

ment while Piedras, the only prisoner, was escorted to Velasco to embark for Tampico.[31]

Taking advantage of the recent acts of loyalty to the federalist cause, the Nacogdoches *ayuntamiento* asked the state to appoint land commissioners for the East Texas settlements and also to name a political *jéfe* for the District of Nacogdoches. On January 31, 1831, 1½ years earlier, the state legislature had authorized separating Nacogdoches district from San Antonio, but no *jéfe* had been named. Unfortunately for eastern Texas, neither request was honored until 1834 because of the unstable political situation. The council also implored the state to use its influence with the national government to prevent the future placement of troops within any established town and not to allow a military officer authority over civilians. Moreover, in a diplomatic maneuver designed to overcome Mexican prejudice against them, local Anglos asked that officials cease calling them "Anglos" or "foreigners" because they were Mexican citizens.[32]

The recent changes caused Anglo-Texans to call for a meeting to discuss developments. Phil Sublett, Jacob Garrett, Wyatt Hanks, William McFarland, and Donald McDonald represented Ayish Bayou at a convention held in San Felipe on October 1–6, 1832. The San Felipe *ayuntamiento* issued the invitation in August, and sixteen communities sent fifty-eight delegates; unfortunately, no native Mexicans came from San Antonio, which proved harmful to the undertaking. Committees drafted resolutions urging the repeal of the ban on emigration from the United States, reduction in the tariff, and better administration of the customs houses. Resolutions were also drafted requesting land commissioners for eastern Texas, the use of English, and the possibility of severing Texas from its unpopular union with Coahuila. At the same time, the convention created local committees of vigilance and correspondence, similar to those active during the American Revolution, to exchange information. A central committee at San Felipe would be a clearinghouse and was also empowered to call another convention. Not even Stephen F. Austin, who presided, realized that this gathering would arouse such a negative response

31. Bowie to S. F. Austin, Aug. 8, 1832, *Austin Papers*, II, 833; Johnson, *History of Texas and Texans*, I, 85.

32. Ayuntamiento of Nacogdoches to Political Chief, Aug. 14, 1832, Blake Transcripts, XIII, 77–78.

in San Antonio. By Mexican law, such meetings could only be called by the *jéfe politico*, not *ayuntamientos*, and in spite of abject explanations from Austin and others, the *jéfe* believed that it was a first step toward severing Texas from Mexico.[33]

The Cartwrights heartily endorsed the requests for a land commissioner and revision of the tariff. The duties on manufactured goods from the United States collected during 1832 were high and many necessities prohibited entirely to protect Mexican monopolies. The 1832 convention asked for a three-year exemption from the tariff on provisions, iron, steel, machinery, tools, nails, wagons, carts, bagging and rope, coarse cotton goods and clothing for slaves, shoes, hats, tobacco, powder, lead, medicine, books, and paper. Matthew kept a list of the prohibited items in his ledger, but his ledger sheets show he sold such items, which suggests that smuggling goods from Louisiana could not be controlled. There was a collector at Nacogdoches, but no records exist giving details.[34]

The federalist and centralist armies arranged an armistice in December 1832 and agreed to a neutral adminstration until elections could take place in 1833. The federalists won and Santa Anna became president in April 1833, which seemed an encouraging development to the Texans.

The San Felipe central committee, disregarding the advice from San Antonio to avoid calling unauthorized public meetings, called for a second convention to meet in April 1833 with delegates selected on March 1. The Nacogdoches *ayuntamiento*, trying to obey the laws, condemned the call and tore down the posters advertising the election. It also ordered the militia to meet on election day but the summons was ignored—some said because of inclement weather. Nevertheless, elections took place.[35]

Ayish Bayou voters chose Sublett, Elisha Roberts, and Achilles E. C. Johnson as delegates. Nacogdoches selected newcomer Sam Houston and two others. Houston had arrived in Texas from

33. Johnson, *History of Texas and Texans,* I, 91–100.

34. Ibid., I, 93–94; tariff rates, Account Book no. 1, CFP; Musquis to Governor, Jan. 11, 1832 [*sic;* 1833], Blake Transcripts, XII, 293.

35. Ayuntamiento of Nacogdoches to Political Chief, Jan. 29, 1833, Blake Transcripts, XIII, 151; José Ignacio Ybarvo to Political Chief, Mar. 12, 1833, ibid., 173.

Nashville the previous December, crossing the Red River at Fort
Towson and going directly to Austin's colony to apply for a
headright before finishing his official journey in San Antonio. The
U.S. secretary of war sent him to gather information concerning
the numbers and condition of Indian tribes from the United States
residing in Texas, and he returned to Natchitoches in February to
file his report. While there, he wrote his mentor, President Andrew Jackson, that he liked Texas and would perhaps settle there.
He gave Jackson a brief overview about politics in Mexico and
Texas and added that he intended to attend the convention called
for April 1, 1833.[36]

At the meeting, Houston served on the committee to draft a
constitution for a separate state of Texas. The convention re-
adopted the 1832 resolutions and chose Stephen F. Austin to
carry the documents to Mexico City. He departed immediately
for the distant capital, but a cholera epidemic in Mexico City
delayed presenting the petitions. Except for separate statehood,
all were approved by the end of 1833. But Austin, depressed by
the inactivity in October, sent a damaging letter to San Antonio
urging its *ayuntamiento* to take the lead in creating a de facto
separate state. The council had no choice but to forward the
seditious letter to the governor, which resulted in Austin's arrest
in January 1834 and his detention in Mexico City until mid-
1835.[37]

The year 1833 brought changes to Ayish Bayou when residents chose a site for a town and named it "St. Augustine." While
villages like Harrisburg and Lynchburg grew up around the
proprietor's home and business, this was not the way Mexican
towns were created. The land commissioner or the *ayuntamiento*
had authority to designate townsites and the state required a
standard plan regulating the size of blocks, the width of the
streets, and where the government, church, market, military, and

36. Johnson, *History of Texas and Texans*, I, 102; Sam Houston to James
Prentiss, Sept. 15, 1832, in Amelia W. Williams and Eugene C. Barker (eds.),
The Writings of Sam Houston, 1813–1863 (8 vols.; Austin: Pemberton Press,
1970), I, 266; Houston to Ellsworth, Dec. 1, 1832, ibid., 267; Application in
Austin's Grant, Dec. 24, 1832, ibid., 271–272; Houston to Ellsworth and
others, Feb. 13, 1833, ibid. 272; Houston to Jackson, Feb. 13, 1833, ibid., 274–
276.

37. Barker, *Life of Austin*, 359–362, 372–75.

cemetery plazas would be located. Under Mexican law, the city owned the townsite and gave lots to deserving merchants and artisans, selling the rest to raise revenue. San Felipe, Anahuac, and Liberty had been laid off in proper Mexican style.

Facts about the founding of San Augustine (as it came to be called) are few. Sometime in late 1832, local residents held a mass meeting to discuss where the town should be situated and chose fifteen men to make the selection. Alexander Horton, then around age twenty-two, was chosen, and it is he who recalled the fuzzy details later in life. Among the fifteen, he said, were Phil Sublett, Elisha Roberts, William Garrett, and Matthew Cartwright, although John would seem a more likely choice, as would Jacob Garrett, William's father. These men were the investors in a joint stock company to buy the land and plat the town; each would receive seventeen lots drawn at random. John Cartwright, for example, paid surveyor Thomas S. McFarland $10 for his seventeen lots, eight of which were to be on corners. The chosen site was at the northern crossing of Ayish Bayou on land owned by Edmund Quirk, part of a four-league grant he had bought in 1801 from early Spanish settlers. The authorities in San Antonio had approved Quirk's purchase in 1828.[38]

In January 1833, Chichester Chaplin, who lived on the west bank, persuaded Quirk to sell him two square miles (one square mile was equal to the familiar Anglo-American 640-acre section) on either side of the bayou near the crossing for $90. Chaplin, a typical businessman of the day, sold the section on the east bank to Thomas S. McFarland in July for $200, making a nice profit. McFarland and his father, William, had emigrated from Louisiana in 1830, and the father served as alcalde of Ayish Bayou in 1833. The elder McFarland had platted a number of towns in Ohio and Indiana, a skill he evidently was passing on to his

38. Crocket, *Two Centuries,* 61–62, 102–104; T. S. McFarland to John Cartwright, May 8, 1830 [*sic;* 1833], San Augustine Deed Records, B, 202. All other McFarland deeds for city lots are dated 1833; moreover, John Cartwright was in San Felipe in May 1830, and Thomas S. McFarland had barely unpacked. For practice of selling lots to shareholders, see *Journal of the Coincidences and Acts of Thomas S. McFarland Beginning with the First Day of January A.D 1837* (Burnet, Tex.: Nortex Press, 1981), 33 (cited hereafter as McFarland, *Journal*). William Seale, "San Augustine, in the Republic of Texas," *Southwestern Historical Quarterly,* LXXII (Jan., 1969), 347 (cited hereafter as *SHQ*).

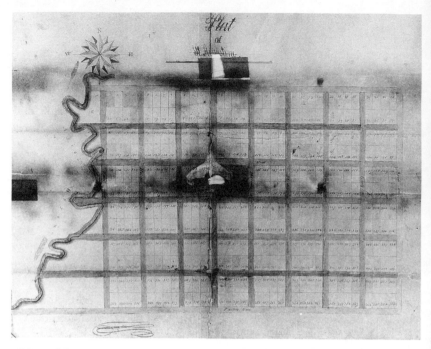

Plat of St. Augustine, ca. 1834, probably by Thomas S. McFarland,
the original surveyor. Courtesy Cartwright Family Descendants.

twenty-three-year-old son. In platting San Augustine young
McFarland laid off a typical American town with a 48-block grid
having 356 lots, each 80 feet wide and 160 feet deep, with 40-
foot-wide streets. He reserved one block in the center for a public
square. Front Street, as in so many American towns, paralleled
Ayish Bayou, and Main Street extended east from the crossing to
the ford at Carrizo Creek.[39]

Historians continue to speculate about why the town was
named San Augustine. The most recent statement perpetuating
confusion is found in *The Lure of the Land,* published in 1988
by the General Land Office: San Augustine County was named
for "a nearby Mexican town of the same name." Historian
George L. Crocket was probably correct when he surmised in his
1939 history that it was named for St. Augustine, the fourth-

39. Crocket, *Two Centuries,* 102–105; Elizabeth LeNoir Jennett (comp.),
Biographical Directory of the Texan Conventions and Congresses, 1832–1845
(n.p., 1941), 130; Webb, Carroll, and Branda (eds.), *Handbook of Texas,* II, 111.

century Bishop of Hippo. He erred, however, in asserting that the state legislature, following a suggestion by the Roman Catholic Church, named it that in March 1834 when it authorized an *ayuntamiento* of San Augustine. McFarland's 1834 plat is labeled "St. Augustine," but the name was in use the year before. Matthew Cartwright headed a letter with "St. Augustine Ayish District" on October 8, 1833, while Isaac W. Burton used the same Anglicized spelling on a document dated February 21, 1834.[40] Probably the founders bestowed the name thinking it would be diplomatic to give the town a Mexican-style name like San Antonio or San Felipe, and one of them recalled St. Augustine from his boyhood studies of the classics.

Besides participating in founding the town, John and Matthew built a second cotton gin and gristmill on the Buckley Creek site to serve a neighborhood without a gin. It was in operation in mid-October 1833, and with the high prices for cotton, Matthew expected "Business to be verry [*sic*] lively" because both cotton and corn crops were "verry good." An incomplete tally sheet for 1833 shows that the Cartwrights ginned 82,000 pounds of cotton by December, which would be 182 450-pound bales, the now-favored size. The other Cartwright gin, located on Patroon Creek, did not do as well. In a new experiment, Matthew planned to ship cotton down the Sabine River instead of "halling" it seventy-five miles to Natchitoches, and he estimated that he would save one-half the expense.[41]

In a letter to Uncle Richard Hankins in Tennessee, Matthew reported that his father had been to Fayetteville, Arkansas Territory, in 1833, where he bought two "warranted" mules that he wanted to sell. Matthew thought Hankins might want them and should send some of his young horses to Texas, where prices were high. Like many residents of the San Augustine neighborhood,

40. Joe B. Frantz and Mike Cox, *Lure of the Land: Texas County Maps and the History of Settlement* (College Station: Texas A&M University Press, 1988), 67; Crocket, *Two Centuries,* 98–99; Matthew Cartwright to Dear Uncle and Aunt [Richard Hankins and Sally Cartwright], Oct. 8, 1833, CFP; Isaac W. Burton, I.O.U., Feb. 21, 1834, Blake Transcripts, XIII, 210; Hand-drawn plat of "St. Augustine, 1834," in possession of Sandra Kardell Calpakis.

41. Matthew Cartwright to Dear Uncle and Aunt, Oct. 8, 1833, CFP (quotation); Amount of Cotton Received in Gin 1833, Account Book no. 1 (near end), CFP.

Matthew appreciated good horses, especially those that raced well, and he offered to buy Hankins's Ulysses for $150 whenever his uncle would send the horse to the Palo Gacho. The nephew urged his uncle and cousins, John and James Hankins, to come for a visit, along with cousin William Edwards, the son of his long-deceased aunt Elizabeth Cartwright Edwards. Edwards was a school teacher and Matthew tempted his cousin to come to Texas by noting that the San Augustine school paid "$30 clear of board" and had been without a teacher since David Brown left to become a surveyor, a higher-paying job. Matthew bragged about local progress: the new town five miles east of the Palo Gacho was "improving rapidly," and interest in religion was increasing. A number of ministers had preached at two camp meetings, which had stimulated the organization of a Methodist society. While Matthew did not give the names of the preachers or the location, the meetings took place in Sabine County with Methodists James Stephenson and Enoch Talley from Mississippi and Cumberland Presbyterian Sumner Bacon. In 1833, visiting Protestant missionaries could be arrested for preaching, but the following year virtual freedom of religion was allowed, except for building a church.[42]

Although Matthew and his brothers remained bachelors, he told his uncle about the impending marriage of his sister Mary "Polly," now nineteen, to "a Respectable citizen" on October 20. Although Matthew thought it unnecessary to give his name, the intended groom was William Garrett, age twenty-five, who had come to Texas in 1827 from Arkansas Territory but was originally from Tennessee. His father, Jacob, served as alcalde of Ayish Bayou in 1830 and was a delegate to the 1832 convention. John Cartwright gave his daughter two slaves as a wedding present, just as his father had done for John's sisters.[43]

42. Matthew Cartwright to Dear Uncle and Aunt, Oct. 8, 1833, CFP (quotations); Yoakum, History of Texas, 538; Homer S. Thrall, A Pictorial History of Texas from the Earliest Visits of European Adventurers to A. D. 1879 (St. Louis: N. D. Thompson & Co., 1879), 743. For surveyor David Brown, see his account for Aug. 18, 1833, Account Book no. 1, p. 54, CFP.

43. Matthew Cartwright to Uncle and Aunt, Oct. 8, 1833, CFP (quotation); Crocket, Two Centuries, 94; Willie Jones to John Cartwright, bill of sale of two slaves, Jan. 11, 1834, Sharp collection (BTHC); John Cartwright to Mary C. Garrett, Jan. 12, 1834, ibid.

Matthew entered land speculating in 1833, a type of venture that would consume his interest for the rest of his life. On May 17 he bought two five-league grants (each 22,240 acres) that had been issued to Coahuila natives Carlos Gil and Ramón de la Serda two years earlier. Neither tract had been located, and Matthew had the privilege of placing them on any vacant lands outside of the settled areas. He paid $500, a little more than two cents per acre, for one, which was not a bargain; Stephen F. Austin, for example, bought thirty-three leagues in this manner for a total of $1,000. The state sold these large unlocated grants at low cost to Hispanics expecting to encourage emigration from Coahuila to Texas, but the native-Mexican purchasers usually sold their documents to Anglos for whatever they could get. Matthew bought one (and probably both) through Nacogdoches speculator Charles S. Taylor and immediately arranged the financing of the purchase and ensuing fees with newcomer Robert A. Irion by giving him one-half of the acreage, a common arrangement. The land was surveyed near the Red River, perhaps in Bowie County, by February 1834 and the paperwork leading to the final title was completed in Nacogdoches in April. But the titles were never officially registered, and it is unknown whether the pair lost their investment or whether they sold it to somebody else.[44]

Matthew and his father continued in business for the next two years as Matthew Cartwright & Company with Matthew managing the store and keeping the records. They each contributed $2,000. John's portion included the stock of goods on hand and the store building on the Palo Gacho; he also would feed and clothe his son, pay for his laundry, and provide a horse to make collections. Each had the privilege of buying goods for personal use at a 25 percent discount. Matthew projected the image of success and indulged his taste for cigars and fashionable clothing,

---

44. Charles Taylor to Matthew Cartwright, May 17, 1833, CFP; Agreement between Matthew Cartwright and Robert A. Irion, May 17, 1833, ibid.; Statement from José M. J. Carbajal, Apr. 18, 1834, ibid.; Virginia H. Taylor, *The Spanish Archives of the General Land Office of Texas* (Austin: Lone Star Press, 1955), 190, 239. For eleven league grants, see Margaret Swett Henson, *Samuel May Williams: Early Texas Entrepreneur* (College Station: Texas A&M University Press, 1976), 45–47; S. F. Austin to S. M. Williams, May 8, 1832, *Austin Papers*, II, 771.

including a beaver felt hat, a silk velvet vest, seasonal dress coats (linen or wool), and silk socks and dancing pumps, in addition to the usual sensible shoes, wool hat, and work pants of jean material. The father bought few luxury items for his family while Robert, back on the Palo Gacho hauling freight and running the gin, charged walking shoes, jeans, and wool socks besides fancier items such as a silk handkerchief, a "Phail [of] Cologn [sic]," plus lots of tobacco, whiskey, and rum. Matthew, unlike most of the community, seems to have avoided alcohol at this time, perhaps due to transitory Methodist influence.[45]

John contracted with Robert W. Russell and W. S. Scott in May 1834 to build a store in San Augustine along Columbia Street, which, because it lay along a ridge, was the choice of other storekeepers. Iredell D. Thomas and Augustus Hotchkiss erected store buildings on the north side overlooking the public square, but before long the plaza was also divided into lots. John owned the southeast corner of Harrison and Columbia and built his store on the corner facing Columbia. He agreed to pay the two men $628 for labor and material, but in the end, like tenant farmers, they both owed over $300 to John Cartwright's store for shingles, planks, hauling, boarding the hands, and personal items.[46]

The spring of 1834 brought several governmental reforms. Because of the increased population, the state created a separate *ayuntamiento* for San Augustine on March 6 with jurisdiction over the present-day counties of San Augustine, Sabine, and Shelby plus portions of Panola, Newton, and Jasper. The council consisted of an elected alcalde, two *regidores* (aldermen), and a *síndico procurador* (treasurer). The *ayuntamiento* appointed a secretary and chose an *alguacil* (constable/sheriff) who served court summons and kept order. Another new law provided for a primary judge for each *ayuntamiento* to relieve the alcalde of judicial duties; local residents would nominate four capable men versed in the law, one of whom the governor would name judge. This same law extended the jury system to both civil and criminal

---

45. Contract between Matthew and John Cartwright, Mar. 4, 1834, Legal Documents, CFP; Account Book no. 3, 58, 60, 66–67, 121, 145, 241, ibid.

46. John Cartwright account with Russell and Scott, 1834, Sharp Collection (BTHC); R. W. Russell and W. L. Scott individual accounts with Matthew Cartwright & Co., Account Book no. 3, 35, 63, CFP; Crocket, *Two Centuries,* 106.

cases, a reform long-sought by Anglo-Texans. Also, the state finally named a political chief for East Texas: Swiss-born Nacogdoches merchant Henry Rueg.[47]

In November 1834, the San Augustine *ayuntamiento* chose the four nominees for primary judge for 1835: Augustus Hotchkiss, Philip Sublett, William McFarland, and John Cartwright. The authorities selected Hotchkiss, who received his notice of appointment on December 28 and immediately secured the judicial records from the alcalde. He must have known that his appointment would be challenged; on December 30, local dissidents named John G. Love primary judge, and even claimed that he had been named by the governor. The matter was resolved quietly and Hotchkiss served his term earning the respect of the community.[48]

Hotchkiss and his kinsman, Capt. Archibald Hotchkiss, probably brothers, had come to Texas in 1834 in connection with the Galveston Bay and Texas Land Company. The company, composed of New York and Boston investors, bought the state-issued empresario contracts from David G. Burnet, Joseph Vehlein, and Lorenzo de Zavala in October 1830 as the basis for their speculation. Selling an empresario grant was of questionable legality, and none of the original empresarios sent colonists or visited their grants before or after the sale. The three contiguous grants covered the annulled Haden Edwards grant: Burnet, a New Jersey native and adventurer to Texas in the early 1820s, received the land north and west of Nacogdoches; Vehlein, a Mexico City businessman, the area south of Burnet along the Trinity River; and Zavala, a Yucatecan and federalist politician, claimed the border reserve along the Sabine River. After many delays because of the prohibitive law of 1830 and the chaos in 1832, the state named George A. Nixon land commissioner for the three contracts held by the Galveston Bay company in June 1834. Nixon arranged for Archibald Hotchkiss to be the "agent" for the

47. Johnson, *History of Texas and Texans,* I, 52–54. Crocket, *Two Centuries,* 99–102, has many factual errors. "Henry Rueg," Webb, Carroll, and Branda (eds.), *Handbook of Texas,* II, 513.

48. San Augustine ayuntamiento to Henry Rueg, Nov. 1, 1834, Blake Transcripts, XIII, 227; Alcalde of San Augustine to Political Chief, Jan. 1, 1835, ibid., 244; Augustus Hotchkiss to Henry Rueg, Jan. 2, 1835, ibid., 246.

empresarios, a ploy intended to imply that the three were somehow still active in the speculation.[49]

Some Ayish Bayou residents, eager to secure titles, went immediately to Nacogdoches to meet with Nixon to start their paperwork. One of the first was Chichester Chaplin, who filed his petition on September 23, 1834. The survey for one league surrounding his homesite on the west side of the bayou was completed on May 13, 1835, and Nixon issued the final title, giving Chaplin a certified copy five days later.[50]

John Cartwright and many others refused to apply, however, when they learned that agent Hotchkiss demanded fees as the representative of the empresario. The outraged Redlanders complained to Henry Rueg, the *jéfe politico,* who demanded that Hotchkiss produce his nonexistent power of attorney. At the end of the year, the state ruled that Hotchkiss could not collect fees because the settlers had moved to Texas at their own expense, and the legislature named special commissioners in 1835 to issue titles to those who had settled in eastern Texas before 1828.[51]

The most significant event in eastern Texas in 1834 was the two-month visit of Col. Juan Nepomuceno Almonte, the special representative of Santa Anna's administration, who arrived from Natchitoches in May 1834. Fearful that the Texans might secede from Mexico, the government dispatched English-speaking Almonte to visit eastern Texas and the Brazos River communities. The son of Father José María Morelos, a martyr to the independence movement, young Juan sought sanctuary in 1815 in New Orleans, where Mexican merchants took him in as an apprentice. There he learned English, French, international law, and bookkeeping.[52]

No doubt Almonte visited the Cartwright store and perhaps the gin as he made his leisurely examination of economic and cultural institutions in San Augustine before continuing his journey to Nacogdoches and eventually San Felipe. He talked with

49. Webb, Carroll, and Branda (eds.), *Handbook of Texas,* II, 663, 841.

50. Chichester Chaplin application and grant, May 18, 1835, Spanish Archives (General Land Office of Texas).

51. Henry Rueg to Archibald Hotchkiss, Jan. 12 [?], 1835, Blake Transcripts, XIII, 254.

52. Juan N. Almonte, "Statisitcal Report on Texas," trans. C. E. Castañeda, *SHQ,* XXVIII (Jan., 1925), 206–207, 209, 212, 213.

merchants, cotton planters, ranchers, and farmers and made detailed reports about their present conditions and expectations for the future and also their perceived problems with the Indians. Like Mier y Terán five years earlier, Almonte deplored the fact that the residents spoke only English, but noted that San Augustine had established a private school better then the one in Nacogdoches. Almonte estimated the population of the entire Nacogdoches district from the Gulf to the Red River at 9,000 and the municipality of "San Agustín de los Aises" at 2,500, while the town itself had 350 inhabitants.[53]

Almonte also reported that San Augustine had "considerable traffic for so small a place," due in part, he thought, to the cotton plantations east of town and the two to three cotton gins. Local planters and those at Pecan Point on the Red River expected to export 2,000 bales that year, each weighing 450 pounds, with a net value of 10 cents per pound, a total of 90,000 pesos. Other exports included hides worth 90,000 pesos and 5,000 head of cattle at 5 pesos each, all exported to Natchitoches. The shortage of specie throughout Texas forced Texans to barter, said the colonel. The only circulating money was old pesos and paper bills from the United States, both of which were often counterfeited; once, even Almonte was cheated. Lacking a law against counterfeiting, the Nacogdoches alcalde could only summon the townspeople with his drum and then escort the note-passer out of town, warning that he would be beaten should he return.[54]

The colonel had no sympathy for the Galveston Bay and Texas Land Company and assured residents that the company's contract was about to expire. He noted that many settlers who had come at their own expense resented its monopoly and complained that they still lacked titles; he urged the government to issue titles "to free them from the cruel uncertainty."[55] All in all, Almonte's report was favorable, and he reported no unrest except over land matters.

No doubt Almonte's recommendations to issue titles to long-time residents at both the state and national capitals paved the way for the appointment of special commissioners Charles S.

53. Ibid., 206, 210.
54. Ibid., 209 (quotation), 212–213.
55. Ibid., 207.

Taylor at Nacogdoches and George W. Smyth at Bevil (present-day Jasper). Almonte reached Monclova, temporarily the seat of government, in September on his return to Mexico City in company with the two lawyers from the Brazos on their way to try to extricate Stephen F. Austin from prison.[56]

Texas seemed quiet in the fall of 1834, and besides hoping that the state would clear up the land matters to his satisfaction, John Cartwright, now forty-eight, looked forward to the birth of his first grandchild. Grandmother Cartwright doubtless attended her daughter when she gave birth to a boy sometime in the fall. Polly and William Garrett named their firstborn John. He was six months old when the census taker made his tally of San Augustine early in 1835. At that time Garrett had fourteen slaves, seven adults and seven children, and was living west of Ayish Bayou. For some reason, the Cartwright homestead on the Palo Gacho, with John, Polly, their three adult sons, three younger children, and fifteen slaves, was enumerated in the Sabine District that year.[57]

On New Year's Day, 1835, nobody imagined the trouble that was lurking around the corner.

56. Henson, *Samuel May Williams*, 58; P. W. Grayson to J. F. Perry, Sept. 16, 1834, *Austin Papers*, II, 1089–1090.

57. 1835 Census, San Augustine and Sabine, Blake Transcripts, XIX, 222, 330.

F o u r

Business and
Texas Independence

1835–1836

*M*atthew and his father again signed their annual contract in March 1835 for the continuation of Matthew Cartwright & Company. This time each invested $3,500. John included $2,500 in debts already on the books, the lot and store on Columbia Street plus another lot on the same block together worth $250, and the rest in cash. John also stipulated that anytime Matthew was absent and John had to take care of the business, John would deduct compensation at the end of the year from the $500 allocated as Matthew's annual salary. Matthew's contribution was $3,100 in goods that he had purchased in New Orleans and his half of the merchandise on hand, amounting to $300. The following March, amid mounting tension over the war against Santa Anna, father and son agreed to continue for one more year.[1]

The Cartwrights had outgrown buying goods at Natchitoches, although they continued to ship cotton to G. A. Constanzi in the

1. "An Agreement . . . March 15, 1835," and at end of p. 2, "Continued until March 15, 1837. . . ," Legal Documents, 1829–1869, CFP.

old village. Beginning in 1833, Matthew began making spring and fall trips to New Orleans to stock the store and to indulge his taste for a good time and the latest fashions. For example, on his fall trip to New Orleans in 1834, he won $1 playing billiards on board the steamboat *Chesapeake,* went to the theatre in New Orleans—first buying a cloak and silk hat—and treated himself to an excursion on the railroad that ran out to Lake Ponchartrain. Moreover, it was evident that Matthew's dedication to the temperance cause had disappeared because he drank "spirits" along with his daily cigar.[2]

The country store near the cotton gin drew its stock from the San Augustine store, especially items designed more for the Indian trade, which still brought in pelts for exchange. John evidently employed others in addition to his sons to work at the gins, the mill, and the country store. In town, Matthew needed a full-time clerk because of his out-of-town trips to make collections and his land business. So he invited a young cousin, William Ragland, to come from Wilson County as an apprentice. William arrived in October 1834 and began keeping the daybooks while Matthew posted the ledgers. William was a poor speller and failed to improve during his fourteen months with Matthew; he also never outgrew his first impression that San Augustine was a "Wild and Wicked place."[3]

Some optimists decided that the East Texas economy was improving in 1835. Wealthy men were immigrating to Texas, and there was "more floating capital" than in all the previous years combined, according to surveyor and land speculator George W. Smyth of Bevil, who continued to believe that the United States would soon acquire eastern Texas.[4]

2. Memoranda Books, 1834–1836, CFP.

3. Account Book no. 2, 1833–1838, CFP, contains memoranda of goods bought in New Orleans from each merchant on different dates and provides an overview of goods sold in San Augustine; Account Book no. 3, 1834–1835, 12, 55, 67, 80, 105, 160, 177, 186, 273, 276, 278, 312, ibid., shows debits and credits for buildings and store stock, venison, and pelts taken in on credit; Ledger sheets for John English in Account Book no. 1, p. 19, and for John Buckley, p. 4, ibid., suggest that they worked for John Cartwright; Day Book no. 3, p. 2, ibid., has a note in William Ragland's hand detailing his journey to San Augustine; Day Book no. 4, ibid., is in Ragland's hand; Matthew Cartwright to Robert Cartwright, Mar. 22, 1836 (quotation), ibid.

4. G. W. Smyth to John Gallagher, May 23, 1835 (quotation), Smyth Collection (BTHC).

While land speculating was booming, all was not well with the merchants. The reason for the influx of immigrants was the return of hard economic times in the United States following President Andrew Jackson's disastrous fiscal policies, intended to close the Bank of the United States and move government funds to favored state banks. The result was a tightening of credit and calling in of loans that affected planters, farmers, and merchants. There was also a worldwide shortage of gold and silver, forcing the use of paper notes issued by local merchants, state banks, and individuals. The United States government did not issue paper money at this time, nor did it regulate the paper that was in circulation. Almonte had noted the lack of money in Texas in 1834, but the problem was widespread and would lead to the devastating panic of 1837.

The specie shortage affected Matthew both locally and in dealings with merchants in Natchitoches and New Orleans. Customer debts amounted to $2,501 in 1835, but Matthew had to continue extending credit to patrons in order to conduct business. Barter increased in order to clear old debts and buy needed commodities. Matthew's ledgers show credits for labor, hauling freight, or for produce such as hides, butter, or pork. John Cartwright, for example, ran an account with ferryman James Gaines in which no money was involved; in exchange for ferriage at $1 per wagon, John freighted a plow and other items for Gaines from Natchitoches at no charge. Lacking gold or silver to pay for goods to stock the store, Matthew shipped bales of hides and cotton to pay suppliers.[5]

Amid the gradually increasing hard times in 1835, the problem of securing land titles for long-time residents in the Redlands was finally resolved. The state named George W. Smyth of Bevil and Charles S. Taylor of Nacogdoches special land commissioners in May 1835 to issue titles to those residents who had arrived before 1828.[6] Both men kept offices in Nacogdoches, as did George A. Nixon, who continued as commissioner for newcomers settling in the Burnet, Vehlein, and Zavala grants that belonged to the Galveston Bay and Texas Land Company.

5. "Agreement . . . March 15, 1835"; Statement from James Gaines, 1832–1833, Sharp collection (BTHC); Various ledger pages in all of the Account Books, CFP.

6. George W. Smyth to his father, May 23, 1835, Smyth Collection (BTHC).

Beginning in May 1835, many Redlanders journeyed to Nacogdoches to take the necessary oaths regarding the date of their immigration, their marital status, and the size of their families that were preliminary to applying for their titles. For some reason John Cartwright did not take this first step, although he was in the old town on May 20 when he witnessed character certificates for two newcomers. For reasons unknown, John delayed applying for his title for six months. The patriarch found traveling difficult because he weighed well over three hundred pounds; he even had a specially reinforced, wide-seated buggy built. The other Cartwrights, however, attended to their headrights: Matthew applied for a certificate early in May and received his 1,107 acres, the amount allotted for single men, which he had surveyed along the Attoyac below the road from Ayish Bayou to Nacogdoches. Matthew's brother Robert filed his status document but procrastinated in applying for his one-quarter league headright. Even cousin Thomas Cartwright applied for and received a headright that he located in present Polk County, although legally he was ineligible, having received a headright in Austin's colony in 1824.[7] No central land office existed at this time, and records remained in the possession of the various land commissioners until after 1836.

John Cartwright had no way of knowing that his delay in applying for his headright would result in the loss of his title, but it seems strange that this keen businessman did not take care of the matter immediately. Perhaps poor health during the summer prevented him from making his preliminary statement, although he could have taken the oath before Judge Hotchkiss in San Augustine. The local *ayuntamiento* was in disarray, however, because Alcalde James Hanks died in the spring and his replacement was not named until July 1835 and by then the community was in turmoil.[8]

7. Robert Lane Cartwright, "History of John Cartwright Settlement," Cartwright research files; John's physical size from oral tradition among descendants; Certificates no. 238 for Michael Chaires and no. 239 for Jesse [Jehu] Peoples, Certificates relative to admission to settle in Texas . . . , no. 662, Texas State Library Genealogy Collection; White (ed.), *Character Certificates,* 31–32.

8. R. C. McDaniel to Political Chief, May 25, 1835, Blake Transcripts, XIV, 120; same to same, June 4, 1835, ibid., 129; A. Hotchkiss to Henry Rueg, July 30, 1835, ibid., 217.

At this same time, the political chief of the Department of Nacogdoches, Henry Rueg, came under fire because of his toryish support for the status quo. The first signs of discontent appeared in May 1835 when leading residents of San Augustine, including Matthew Cartwright, protested that taxes levied by the Nacogdoches court to support the new jury system were burdensome.[9] While Mexico levied no property or income taxes, Anglo-Americans strongly objected to *any* taxes, even the modest sums that supported the jury system they had demanded. They seem to have ignored the fact that in the United States county property taxes paid for such services.

The real crisis erupted in June and July 1836 and was caused by changes in the political course of President Santa Anna. When first elected, Santa Anna took a leave of absence in order to test the political climate. He allowed his federalist vice-president to inaugurate reforms against the special privileges of the church and the army, which eventually proved unpopular. When Santa Anna resumed the reins of government in 1835, it was as a centralist, and he reversed the federalist reforms. He began limiting the powers of states where federalists were strongest by reducing their militias. Early in 1835 the president personally led the army north to punish Zacatecas, Coahuila's southern neighbor, for rebelling against the reduction of its civilian militia. Santa Anna dismissed Zacatecas's legislature and allowed his troops to rape and pillage citizens to demonstrate what happened to rebels. Coahuila-Texas legislators meeting in Monclova included John Durst, the first to represent the Nacogdoches department; the lawmakers quickly moved to raise and arm a force to oppose the president should he continue his northward course. Before the session ended, Gen. Martín Perfecto de Cós, Santa Anna's brother-in-law and commandant general for northeastern Mexico headquartered at Saltillo, sent troops to Monclova to arrest the governor and the legislature. While a few members escaped, the state was without an elected state government in June 1835.[10]

9. San Augustine residents to Political Chief, May 6, 1835, Blake Transcripts, XIV, 76–78; A. Hotchkiss and others to Henry Rueg, July 29, 1835, ibid., 214–216.

10. For details of events at Monclova see Henson, *Samuel May Williams*, 63–73; General Cós to Political Chief in Bexar, June 12, 1835, Blake Transcripts, XIV, 133–134.

Before the governor was captured, he had asked Texas alcaldes to call up the civilian militia to help him, but because of a critical lack of time, only San Antonio responded. The national military commander there tried to stop the civilian militia, thus stirring up the old acrimonious debate over who held superior authority: civilian or military officials, state or national officials. While residents of the Redlands tried to sift the contradictory rumors, Chief Rueg decided to support the national administration.[11]

Meanwhile, there was a reprise of the 1832 attack against Anahuac. Santa Anna needed revenue to maintain his army and so he ordered customs officials back to Texas in January 1835, when the brief two-year exemption expired. Forty troops accompanied the collector to Anahuac, where they found the fort in ruins. Trouble occurred again between merchants and the customs collector, resulting in the arrest of a merchant. On June 28, 1835, William B. Travis, the prisoner of 1832, led a successful attack against Anahuac to free the hostages and also to capture the garrison to prevent a rumored build-up of troops. Travis's rash action upset friends of Austin, who was still in Mexico City on parole; they feared the incident might endanger his pending release. Those who wanted no confrontation with Santa Anna were labeled "tories" or the "peace party," while Travis and his associates were the "war party." Neither faction advocated independence from Mexico at this time, although a few individuals believed it to be the only solution.[12]

Residents in the Nacogdoches district, however, were more concerned about rumors of an impending Indian attack along the northern frontier presumed to be masterminded by Santa Anna's agents. As they had during past crises, San Augustine residents met on July 28, 1835, with Jacob Garrett as chair and adopted resolutions demanding that *Jéfe* Rueg send the militia to thwart the Indians. Rueg asked Jim Bowie, who had just arrived in East

11. Angel Navarro to Secretary of Coahuila, May 16, 1835; Navarro to Ugartechea, May 16, 1835, in John H. Jenkins (ed.), *The Papers of the Texas Revolution, 1835–1836* (10 vols.; Austin: Presidial Press, 1973), I, 110–111 (cited hereafter as Jenkins, *Papers*).

12. Barker, *Life of Austin*, 406–408; Ayuntamiento of Austin to Fellow Citizens, June 25, 1835, Blake Transcripts, XIV, 168; Margaret Swett Henson, "Tory Sentiment in Anglo Texan Public Opinion, 1832–1836," *SHQ*, XC (July, 1986), 14–17.

Texas after barely escaping arrest by General Cós's troops along the Rio Grande, to investigate the situation. Bowie reported that the Cherokees would join an expedition led by himself against the Plains Indians if Rueg would send the civilian militia. Before the plans were complete, men from the Brazos had taken action against the Indians and the issue in the Redlands temporarily faded.[13]

Rueg, however, was more interested in preserving harmony with his superiors than with his constituents. Upon receiving the news about the trouble at Anahuac and the arrest of the governor, *Jéfe* Rueg called on East Texans to support General Cós and denounce the governor and legislators who had participated in what some called the "Mammouth [*sic*] Speculation." A number of Anglo-Texan land speculators at the recent session at Monclova had expected to buy unlocated eleven-league land grants intended to be used to raise and equip volunteers to oppose Santa Anna. But the legislators awarded the grants to insiders, which caused the disappointed speculators to return home labeling the distribution a fraud and contemplating vengeance. Rueg maintained his tory stance, assuring General Cós that the Department of Nacogdoches would observe the orders of President Santa Anna.[14]

Rueg's support of the increasingly unpopular administration caused him to lose more friends in August 1835 when General Cós ordered alcaldes to arrest a number of men considered subversive, a list that included Travis, Frank W. Johnson, and Lorenzo de Zavala. Johnson, who had participated in the events at Monclova, was well known in East Texas since his days as a surveyor, while Travis still aroused sympathy for his incarceration in 1832. Zavala, a native of Yucatán and a noted federalist politician, had recently resigned as Santa Anna's minister to the

13. John Bodine to Henry Rueg, Apr. 16, 1835, in Jenkins, *Papers*, I, 75; Citizens of San Augustine to Political Chief, July 28, 1835, ibid., I, 282; Jim Bowie to James H. Miller, June 22, 1835, ibid., I, 159; Manuel Sabariego to Ugartechea, June 23, 1835, ibid., I, 163; Jim Bowie to Rueg, Aug. 3, 1835, ibid., I, 301–302.
14. Henry Rueg to Citizens, July 8, 1835, in Jenkins, *Papers*, I, 220–221; J. G. McNeel to J. F. Perry, [ca. June 22, 1835], ibid., I, 160 (quotation); Rueg to Political Chief of the Brazos, ibid., I, 281; see Henson, *Samuel May Williams*, 64–75.

French court because of the president's destruction of the 1824 constitution. The idealistic federalist arrived on the Brazos in July 1835 and began advocating the overthrow of Santa Anna. The Texas alcaldes refused to carry out the arrest orders from General Cós, saying they could not find those named. Johnson, in fact, had fled San Felipe and was in Nacogdoches, where he stayed with John Durst and enlightened residents about what was taking place.[15]

As political unrest increased, the old committees of safety and vigilance revived. The Anglo residents of Nacogdoches assembled in the old stone house on August 15, 1835, with Sam Houston and Thomas J. Rusk in attendance. Discussions centered on John Locke's compact theory of government as expressed by Thomas Jefferson in the United States Declaration of Independence. Governments were made, they said, to preserve human rights, and when violations occurred the compact was dissolved, leaving citizens to act in a manner "best calculated to secure the sacred and unalienable rights of life, liberty, and enjoyment of property." Therefore, the oaths taken to become citizens of Mexico were invalidated by the arrest of the governor and members of the legislature and the "invasion of Texas by an army" whose intent was unknown. The crowd unanimously endorsed calling a consultation of representatives from the various settlements, as had been proposed by residents along the Brazos.[16]

Phil Sublett, William Inglish, A. G. Kellogg, and William Garrett, a Cartwright in-law, were named the committee of vigilance at San Augustine on September 7, 1835. After hearing from the San Felipe committee, the leader of the movement, the members of the committee of vigilance endorsed calling the consultation but preferred holding the meeting in Washington-on-the-Brazos rather than San Felipe. The four assured San Felipe that San Augustine's delegates would have plenary powers, relying on them "to do what is right." The residents chose Jacob Garrett, A.

15. Wyly Martin to Ugartechea, Aug. 16, 1835, in Jenkins, *Papers*, I, 347–348; Kerr to S. F. Austin, Sept. 30, 1835, ibid., I, 508; Baker and Johnson, Oct. 23, 1835, ibid., II, 199–200.

16. Nacogdoches Meeting, [Aug. 15, 1835], in Jenkins, *Papers*, I, 343 (quotations), 344–345; Brazoria Meeting, Aug. 9, 1835, ibid., I, 323; Columbia Meeting, Aug. 15, 1835, ibid., I, 342–343.

E. C. Johnson, William N. Sigler, and Almazon Huston to represent them.[17]

At this juncture, on September 8, Stephen F. Austin returned to the Brazos River, no longer a conciliator as in the past, but now in favor of war against Santa Anna because of his destruction of the constitution. This stance, of course, was that of the federalist party and was popular in northern Mexico. Austin's endorsement of the war party against the leader, but not against the nation, ended most tory objections, and events at Gonzales at the end of the month convinced most men that war was the only recourse. In keeping with the reduction of local militias, General Cós had ordered the commandant in San Antonio to recover a small cannon loaned to the residents of Gonzales in 1831 for defense against the Indians. But in view of rapidly changing events, the men at Gonzales refused to give it up and on October 2, 1835, defeated the company sent to get it.

Word traveled swiftly to San Augustine, where Sam Houston was visiting Sublett. Although Houston usually resided in Nacogdoches, he, like many others, preferred Ayish Bayou as a more healthful community during the fever season. Houston and Sublett had become good friends; both loved horse racing, hunting, drinking, telling stories, and playing cards. Houston wrote to a friend on October 5, using capital letters for emphasis: "WAR IN DEFENCE OF OUR RIGHTS, OUR OATHS, AND OUR CONSTITUTIONS IS INEVITABLE, IN TEXAS!"[18]

Events progressed quickly. Political chief Rueg received a letter from Lorenzo de Zavala begging him to come to the consultation, and while the indecisive *jéfe* still had scruples about attending, he replied that he might—just to please Zavala. Phil Sublett suggested to the committee of safety in Nacogdoches that his good friend, Sam Houston, would be suitable for commander-in-chief of departmental troops to "sustain the Constitution of 1824." The committee agreed and gave Houston full power to raise and organize a local force until such time as the consultation made further arrangements. Houston called for volunteers "in defense of our rights" on October 8, 1835; each man was to bring

17. Sublett et al. to Committee of Safety in San Felipe, Sept. 22, 1835, in Jenkins, *Papers*, I, 480 (quotation).

18. Sam Houston to Isaac Potter, Oct. 5, 1835, in Jenkins, *Papers*, II, 46 (quotation), 47.

a rifle and one hundred rounds of ammunition, and without any authorization, Houston promised liberal land bounties for service. Volunteers in the Department of Nacogdoches would be organized into two companies of fifty men each and would elect their own officers.[19]

How could young men resist this charismatic leader and his call to arms? San Augustine quickly assembled a number of armed, mounted volunteers under the command of thirty-three-year-old Col. Phil Sublett. By October 12, a portion of the men joined others from Nacogdoches and started for the Brazos River, perhaps accompanying the delegates to the Consultation. A second group was to follow five days later. In preparation for departure, Sublett visited the Cartwright store on October 16 and bought brass spurs. Capt. William Kimbro was with him and charged one-half gallon of whiskey. Latter-day Cartwrights assumed that Robert and maybe George followed these two men to participate in the siege at San Antonio, but it seems unlikely. Neither brother applied for the 640-acre donation of land awarded to all who fought there in November and December 1835, or for the bounty land of 320 acres for three months' service.[20]

The East Texas delegates to the consultation headed for San Felipe, and by opening day, October 16, 1835, old Jacob Garrett and his three colleagues, five from Bevil, and five from Nacogdoches (including Sam Houston) had arrived. Still lacking a quorum two days later, the meeting adjourned because so many members had gone to join Gen. S. F. Austin and the volunteers en route to attack San Antonio. Those unable to join the army were invited to sit with the General Council, sometimes called the Permanent Council, a de facto governing body that evolved from the San Felipe committee of safety after Austin left for the army on October 8. The council named fifty-nine-year-old Garrett, a trader well-known to the Indians, and two others to visit the northeastern Texas tribes to seek their cooperation or at least their neutrality.[21]

19. Rueg to Zavala, Oct. 6, 1835, in Jenkins, *Papers,* II, 61; San Augustine Committee, Oct. 6, 1835, ibid., II, 61, 62 (quotation); Houston orders, Oct. 8, 1835, ibid., II, 68 (quotation), 69.

20. A. Hotchkiss to John Sibley, Oct. 13, 1835, in Jenkins, *Papers,* II, 113–114.

21. Journals of the Consultation, in Jenkins, *Papers,* IX, 246–327; R. R. Royal to S. F. Austin, Oct. 18, 1985, ibid., II, 156.

Before leaving, Garrett introduced a resolution authored by Sam Houston to restrict the activities of the land speculators: "Whereas certain extensive grants of land have been made by the Congress of Coahuila and Texas since 1833, and the same has been purchased by certain individuals under the most suspicious circumstances, . . . we recommend . . . that they declare all the said grants null and void."[22]

The members approved the resolution, and though the records do not show that they also ordered the land offices to close, such a message was delivered to Nacogdoches on October 31, 1835. Frost Thorn, chair of the local committee of safety, acknowledged the order and reported that the three commissioners, Nixon, Smyth, and Taylor, had suspended surveying. Evidently all action did not cease immediately because two weeks later, John Forbes, the secretary of the Nacogdoches committee of safety, urged a member of the consultation to close the three East Texas land offices and create a single institution such as in the United States. He also accused Smyth and Taylor of issuing between eight hundred and nine hundred orders for surveys "when it is well known that not 2 or 300 families (if that) . . . could be found in their boundaries" that were entitled to the land.[23] This well-meaning order had a disastrous implication for John Cartwright because the land office closed prior to the completion of his belated application for his league.

Meanwhile, Colonel Sublett and his two companies totalling seventy men camped twelve miles east of the Colorado River on October 30, 1835. The Ayish Bayou troops reached the tiny, poor village of Gonzales on November 2, one month after the date of the battle and almost three weeks since leaving home. Most of the male residents of the town had joined Austin's army, leaving a dozen old or infirm men with only three or four weapons to guard the women and children. Unable to cross the river because the flatboat was being repaired, the Redland volunteers had to spend the night in town. Some began drinking and became rowdy,

22. Circular from Council to the People, Oct. 18, 1835, in Jenkins, *Papers,* II, 157–159, 160 (quotation), 161.

23. William Campbell Binkley (ed.), *Official Correspondence of the Texan Revolution, 1835–1836* (2 vols.; New York: Appleton-Century, 1936), I, 3; Thorn to Council, Nov. 1, 1835, Jenkins, *Papers,* II, 293; Forbes to Robinson, Nov. 13, 1835, ibid., II, 393 (quotation).

breaking into homes seeking anything of value and terrorizing the inhabitants until stopped by the officers. The chairman of the Gonzales committee of safety reported a "scene such as in all probability never was exhibited in any civilized country" and asked Austin for twenty guards to prevent a repetition. He added that Colonel Sublett knew who the ringleaders were.[24] There are no details about what happened to the miscreants; perhaps they were sent home.

The Consultation finally had its quorum on November 3, 1835, and heard a report from the Permanent Council including its resolution of October 27 suspending the operations of all the land offices in Texas. For the next ten days the members discussed whether or not to declare independence, what to do about the land offices, and how to supply the army in the field. On November 11, Sam Houston amended the section detailing procedures for the land office to include the appointment of special commissioners to take charge of all public documents immediately, "particularly those in the hands of the political chief of the department of Nacogdoches; and that the said . . . chief cease his functions immediately." Thus, Henry Rueg was to be removed from office. After rejecting a declaration of independence, the delegates agreed to remain part of the Mexican republic but unilaterally severed Texas from Coahuila. They approved twenty-two articles for governing the new separate state of Texas on November 13, 1835. Article fourteen ordered all land commissioners, empresarios, surveyors, and any others concerned with locating lands to cease operations. All records were to be surrendered immediately to "fit and suitable" persons named by the Consultation. The members adjourned on November 14 and headed home or to the army. San Augustine delegates affixing their signatures to the resolution were A. Huston, W. N. Sigler, A. E. C. Johnson, Alexander Horton, and A. G. Kellogg.[25]

John and Matthew Cartwright struggled to stay abreast of events and keep the store open to supply the needs of both the community and the volunteers who were beginning to enter

24. Sublett to Convention, Oct. 30, 1835, in Jenkins, *Papers*, II, 270; John Fisher to S. F. Austin, Nov. 3, 1835, ibid., II, 304 (quotation), 305; Launcelot Smither to Council, Nov. 23, 1835, ibid., II, 493.

25. Journal of the Consultation, Jenkins, *Papers*, IX, 251, 269 (1st quotation), 279–280 (2nd quotation), 283.

Texas from Natchitoches. Although he did not realize it during his lifetime, John Cartwright had lost his headright. He had sent his nephew, William Ragland, to Nacogdoches on October 30, 1835, only days before the opening of the Consultation, with the application for his headright. David Brown, the teacher turned surveyor, had resurveyed the five *labores* (885 acres) homesite on the Palo Gacho and the remaining twenty *labores* on Buckley's Creek. Commissioner George W. Smyth signed the completed petition on November 16, three days after the Consultation ordered the closing of all of the land offices.[26]

During this time San Augustine became the gateway for volunteers from the United States. On November 3, the committee of safety expected sixty such individuals and arranged for them to get horses in Nacogdoches. Moreover, some forty men from San Augustine, Tenaha, and Bevil planned to leave for the army on the 6th. Patriotism was greater in San Augustine than in the Sabine neighborhood, said the committee, and by November 3 residents had supplied thirteen horses and subscribed $400, all duly receipted for future repayment. One month later the town welcomed a group of volunteers from Kentucky with a cannon salute. The former Whig congressman from Tennessee, David Crockett, and his associates found the same welcome when they arrived in January 1836. The recently defeated Whig candidate for Congress wanted to represent the Redlands in the upcoming convention to be held in March and regaled San Augustine with one of his characteristic street-corner campaign speeches on January 8, the anniversary of the victory over the British at New Orleans. James Gaines, an admirer of President Jackson and therefore suspicious of Whigs, did not think much of the speech.[27]

General Austin, chosen by the consultation along with two others to go the the United States to raise men and money for the Texas cause, relinquished command of the army besieging San Antonio on November 24, 1835. He paraded the troops and asked them to remain, and 405 signed up. Austin named Lieutenant Colonel Sublett one of three to appraise the horses and

26. John Cartwright petition, General Land Office of Texas.

27. San Augustine Committee to Council, Nov. 3, 1835, in Jenkins, *Papers*, II, 306; Charles B. Shain to the Louisville *Journal*, June 25, 1836, ibid., VII, 258–265; Davy Crockett to children, Jan. 9, 1836, ibid., III, 453; James Gaines to Robinson, Jan. 9, 1836, ibid., III, 454.

equipment of those who were not going home. Three days earlier, on November 22, Austin had asked his officers to poll their troops about storming the city, and Sublett reported that he opposed the idea as did the majority in his command.[28]

Nevertheless, a number of Redlanders were among the three hundred who entered San Antonio on December 5, 1835, under the leadership of Ben Milam and Frank W. Johnson. They fought from house to house for five days, during which time Milam was killed. General Cós capitulated and signed an agreement on December 11, 1835, to withdraw beyond the Rio Grande and not take up arms against those fighting to restore the Constitution of 1824. Some of the victors remained to join a planned expedition against Matamoros while others returned home thinking that the struggle was over.

Back in San Augustine, Robert Cartwright prepared to leave the country for Tennessee. For the past two years, Robert had his own company; he bought and sold cotton, hauled it, and perhaps kept a small store along with some blacksmith work. Upon at least one occasion, his father hired Robert's slaves, but the ledgers fail to spell out details. Judging by the time that lapsed between visits to the San Augustine store, Robert lived and worked at the mill and gin on Buckley's Creek. But on January 23, 1836, he bought a trunk from Matthew because he was going to visit the Hankins family in Wilson County, Tennessee, and at age twenty-seven he planned to attend nearby Clinton College. Perhaps Matthew had convinced him that the experience was worthwhile, and Robert left around February 1 with cousin William Ragland, who was returning home.[29]

Clinton College was the successor to Porter Hill (sometimes Portershill) Academy, the school that Matthew had attended. Both Porter Hill and Clinton College were founded by Dr. Francis H. Gordon and his son-in-law, James B. Moores, a lawyer. The college opened in October 1833 in a one-story house on a five-hundred-acre farm located along the Trousdale Ferry Pike from Lebanon, the seat of Wilson County, midway between the Jennings Fork Post Office (later Grant) and New Middleton in western

28. Austin's order, Nov. 24, 1835, in Jenkins, *Papers,* II, 495; P. A. Sublett to Austin, Nov. 21, 1835, ibid., II, 486.

29. Account Book no. 3, pp. 60, 121, 126, 131, 197, CFP; [for Ragland] Account Book no. 3, p. 299, ibid.

Smith County. The students lived in small cottages near the main building. Dr. Gordon became famous locally because he introduced Kentucky bluegrass and Durham cattle to the farm in 1835. Robert, however, returned to San Augustine by the end of May, perhaps as early as April 4. Higher education did not fascinate him as it did Matthew, and the news from Texas concerning the fall of the Alamo drew him home.[30]

Matthew, living in town, perhaps at his store as did many merchants, had noted the arrival of a new family from Tennessee who bought the old Lindsey residence about three miles northwest of San Augustine. So many from the Volunteer State lived in the area that it became known as the "Tennessee Colony." Best of all, the Holmans had three attractive and cultured daughters; Matthew wrote to Robert at Clinton College, "I have been to See the Miss Holmans Since you left and found them verry Interesting." He supposed, however, that Robert had found some "Pretty Misses there equally or more Interesting to you." He added that Robert should tell any girls who inquired about Matthew that he would probably see them before he got around to marrying.[31] Matthew was wrong; within a few months he married Amanda Holman.

Amanda's father, Col. Isaac Holman, was a lawyer who, though born in North Carolina, had grown up in Kentucky and married Anne Wigglesworth in Harrison County in 1800. He earned his title as a militia officer in the War of 1812 and served in the Kentucky legislature in 1810 and again in 1816. In 1818 he moved his large family to Lincoln County, Tennessee, where a number of his kinsmen lived. Colonel Holman campaigned for a seat in the Tennessee assembly in 1823, and served Lincoln and Giles counties in the state senate from 1829 to 1831. Like many of his neighbors, he encountered financial embarassment in 1834 with the contraction of credit and decided to immigrate to Texas. His oldest sons, James Saunders and William W., both around thirty years old, were in the San Augustine area in October 1834,

30. *The Goodspeed Histories of Sumner, Smith, Macon, Trousdale Counties of Tennessee* (1887; reprint, Columbia, Tenn.: Woodward and Stinson Printing Co., 1972), 823, 833; *The History of Smith County, Tennessee,* 262; Account Book no. 4, p. 61, CFP.

31. Crocket, *Two Centuries,* 123–124; Matthew Cartwright to Robert G. Cartwright, Mar. 22, 1836 (quotations), CFP.

when William charged a few items at Matthew Cartwright's store. James later became an agent for John K. and Augustus C. Allen in the brothers' Houston venture, so it seems likely that the Holman bothers also spent some time in Nacogdoches. William probably bought the old Lindsey house north of San Augustine in anticipation of the family's move.[32]

The Holman patriarch, his other two sons, John W. and Sanford, and twenty slaves arrived in Texas early in 1835. The senior Holman registered for citizenship in Nacogdoches on February 10, 1835. Holman assured his friends in Tennessee that he "was perfectly satisfied" with San Augustine, which was more refined than he had expected. There was a church within 1½ miles of his house and a good female academy in town only 3½ miles away for his daughters. He also was excited about the bountiful game close to his house.[33]

Holman told his friends that his wife and daughters, Amanda, America, and Elvira, had made the journey from Lincoln County via Nashville, Natchez, and Natchitoches in only fifteen days, a remarkably short time, having connected with steamboats at all three places by mere minutes. In Natchitoches a drove of horses from Arkansas had just arrived and they bought three for only $180. The colonel had sent Sanford, his youngest son, to Tennessee to escort his mother and sisters, but he had unknowingly passed them on the river.[34] From this brief account, it is clear that Anne Wigglesworth Holman was an unusually self-reliant woman, unafraid to travel alone over unfamiliar territory. She and her three teenage daughters were relatively safe on board the steam-

---

32. A page from the Holman family Bible and other genealogical and historical material in *Four Families*, 980–995; U.S. Third Census (1810), Harrison, County, Ky., p. 308 (microfilm; CL); U.S. Fourth Census (1820), Lincoln County, Tenn., p. 11, ibid.; U.S. Fifth Census (1830), Lincoln County, Tenn., p. 216, ibid.; Robert M. McBride (ed.), *Biographical Directory of the Tennessee General Assembly, 1796–1861* (2 vols.; Nashville: State Library and Archives and the Tennessee Historical Commission, 1975), I, 372, 373; Account Book no. 3, p. 98, CFP.

33. White (ed.), *Character Certificates*, 90. Crocket, *Two Centuries*, 123, says William bought it after 1836, but Isaac Holman's letter of Apr. 1835 clearly puts them there in 1834. Isaac Holman to William Moore, Apr. 7, 1835 (quotation), Colgate Dye Van Pradelles Donaldson Moore Collection (BTHC); 1835 census, San Augustine, Blake Transcripts, XIX, 144–145.

34. Isaac Holman to William Moore, Apr. 7, 1835, Moore Collection (BTHC).

boats, but the journey from Natchitoches seems unusual. The ladies must have been accompanied by loyal servants who could hitch the horses to their vehicles and act as an escort past Fort Jesup and through the Sabine bottoms.

In May 1835, the colonel opened an account at Matthew's store, and his wife bought one roll of wallpaper to improve the appearance of her new quarters. Holman bought a map of Texas and went exploring for a site for his headright; Isaac and his son John, age twenty-three and single, had secured headrights from the agent of the Galveston Bay Company and wanted to find a suitable location. The Texas summer proved too much for Isaac Holman and he died on August 10, 1835, six weeks short of his sixtieth birthday. Perhaps he became ill in June when his son William bought calomel, camphor, opium, paregoric, brandy and one-half pound of tea from Matthew. The only purchases in July and August were castor oil, a barrel of whiskey, and more brandy. Alcohol was often used as the vehicle for unpalatable drugs. The family interred the patriarch on his property in what became known as the Holman cemetery. In November 1835, William and James S. Holman answered the call for volunteers to lay siege to San Antonio, taking with them eleven pounds of powder and a bar of lead from the Cartwright store.[35]

After the fall of San Antonio, William Holman returned to San Augustine in time to vote in the February 1 election for three delegates to the convention at Washington-on-the-Brazos. Stephen W. Blount, Edward O. Legrand, and Martin Parmer won the honor.[36] Matthew, believing the trouble with Santa Anna was over, continued business as usual through February and planned to go to New Orleans on business in March 1836.

Meanwhile, Gen. Sam Houston, named commander of the almost nonexistent regular army by the General Council in November 1835, sent James Bowie to San Antonio in January 1836 to destroy the Alamo in order to prevent its use by the enemy if and when they returned in the spring. Bowie lacked enthusiasm for the task, and after the arrival of Col. William B. Travis, who held a commission from the new state government, Bowie joined

---

35. Account Book no. 4, p. 196, CFP; White (ed.), *Character Certificates,* 90; Thomas Lloyd Miller, *Bounty and Donation Land Grants of Texas, 1835–1888* (Austin: University of Texas Press, 1967), 352, 389.

36. Wyatt Hanks to Gov. J. S. Robinson, Feb. 6, 1836, Jenkins, *Papers,* IV, 274.

the effort to ready the Alamo for action to keep any fighting west of the Anglo settlements. Word soon reached Travis that Santa Anna was personally leading the army north far earlier than anyone had expected.

Travis sent letters east on February 12, 1836, designed to bring volunteers: "The Thunder of the Enemys Cannon and the pollution of their wives and daughters. . ." ought to rouse men to rush to the army. Many Texans, still exhausted from the fall campaign, brushed aside the plea, believing there was time to plant a crop before heading west again. Two weeks later Travis wrote again, but it was too late: "I am besieged by a thousand or more . . . [but] . . . I shall never surrender or retreat." After a siege of almost two weeks, Santa Anna attacked the compound on March 6, 1836, and within a few hours most of its defenders were dead. On March 5, the day before the Alamo fell, Nacogdoches and San Augustine received orders from General Houston to send more men and supplies to the front.[37] No San Augustine residents were at the Alamo, but later they remembered how Crockett and his Tennessee friends had passed through their town.

The militia law adopted by the consultation in November 1835 ordered each community to register all able-bodied men over the age of sixteen and under fifty. Each unit of fifty-six men would elect a captain and two lieutenants and were subject to call by the governor. So when Houston called for militiamen, local officers called their men to duty. Relying on old militia tradition, each name was written on a piece of paper and placed in a hat, and a child drew slips to fill the ranks. The militia was divided into three classes: the first would go to the front immediately for ninety days, the second would be prepared for a call at any time, and the third would be a reserve and home guard. In all cases, a man could hire a substitute provided the replacement was not subject to the militia call, which meant boys under age sixteen or newcomers who had arrived within ten days of the call-up. Volunteers were also accepted to fill the first class. Some of those

37. Travis to Gov. Smith, Feb. 12, 1836, Jenkins, *Papers*, IV, 317, 318 (1st quotation); Travis to People, Feb. 24, 1836, ibid., IV, 423 (2nd quotation); Houston to John Forbes, Mar. 5, 1836, ibid., IV, 516; A. Huston to Sam Houston, Mar. 5, 1836, ibid., IV, 517; A. M. Clopper to father, Mar. 10, 1836, in E. N. Clopper, *An American Family* (Cincinnati: privately printed, 1950), 263–264.

who had participated in the fall campaign did not want to serve again and a number of civil officers claimed exemptions, issues that would be clarified in the new militia law adopted at the March convention.[38]

The San Augustine neighborhood was divided geographically into militia and justice-of-the-peace beats, and John and George Cartwright were enrolled in the northeastern sector with Capt. David Brown, surveyor and former schoolmaster. In the northwestern beat were the Garrett brothers and the Holmans under Capt. William Kimbro, a veteran of the siege at San Antonio, as were the Holmans and Milton Garrett. Matthew was enrolled in Capt. William D. Ratliff's company; Ratliff was a brother-in-law of the Garretts and therefore a distant in-law-by-marriage of the Cartwrights. Matthew wrote to his brother, Robert, on March 22, 1836, from New Orleans that their father, age forty-nine and overweight, had been drafted for the second class but said nothing about himself or George. Ratliff's command was not called up until mid-April.[39]

The San Augustine militia rosters lack dates, but both David Brown and William Kimbro served from March 15 to June 15, 1836, so it would seem that both units mustered as quickly as possible upon receiving the orders from General Houston. The Cartwright ledger books show that John hired a substitute and drew $60 on March 8, 1836, to pay for his substitute's three-month service. David Brown issued a certificate on March 15 for "Matthew's" substitute (actually John's), who was leaving that day in Brown's company. George Cartwright, still suffering from his 1832 wound, drew $35 in cash from the store and also a pair of brogans for his substitute on March 14.[40]

Kimbro's company, "The San Augustine Volunteers," received a banner made by the Misses Amanda and America Holman,

38. Powers of the Provisional Government, Nov. 13, 1835, Journals of the Consultation, in Jenkins, *Papers*, IX, 281–282; An Ordinance to organize the Militia, Mar. 7, 1836, Journals of the Convention, in ibid., IX, 315–318; A. M. Clopper to father, Mar. 10, 1836, in Clopper, *An American Family*, 262–263.

39. *Muster Rolls of the Texas Revolution* (Austin: Daughters of the Republic of Texas, 1986), 43, 248–249, 251; Matthew Cartwright to Robert G. Cartwright, Mar. 22, 1836, CFP.

40. Miller, *Bounty and Donation Land Grants*, 131, 395; Day Book no. 5, p. 188, CFP; Account Book no. 4, pp. 10, 25, ibid.; David Brown Certificate, Mar. 15, 1836, ibid.

Mrs. Augustus Hotchkiss, and Mrs. Parks. Evidently the flag was not quite finished when Kimbro marched west, because he asked a friend to thank the ladies and tell them that the company had received the banner while crossing the Angelina River. Sanford Holman probably left with Kimbro, but William did not enroll until April 19, probably delayed by family business—perhaps escorting his mother and sisters to Louisiana. Kimbro's company reached Houston's army on the Brazos River on April 3 and was assigned duty opposite San Felipe, where the company remained for a week until Mexican cannons reached the west bank. Kimbro's men moved north to the main body of the army near Leonard Groce's plantation close to present-day Hempstead. On April 13 Kimbro and his Redlanders joined Sam Houston's army on the march eastward to Buffalo Bayou and the San Jacinto Battleground.[41]

Matthew left San Augustine on March 12, 1836, and reached New Orleans a week later. The latest word from Texas was that the Mexican army had invaded San Antonio on February 23 and that five days later an attack had been repulsed. Other San Augustine merchants were also in the Crescent City: I. D. Thomas had just bought $15,000 worth of goods and A. C. Kellogg, $17,000. Worried about events at home, Matthew limited his buying trip to essentials needed to supply the army: guns, holsters, knives, yard goods, hats, shoes, and saddles. He left for home on March 23 on board the river steamer *Caspian*, which reached Alexandria, Louisiana, on March 26. There Matthew and the other passengers learned that the Alamo had fallen. The next day Matthew and four others took a room in a hotel at Natchitoches. George C. Childress had just arrived from Texas on his way to Washington, D.C., with a copy of the Texas

41. William Kimbro to R. B. Irvine, n.d., reproduced in *Four Families,* 443; Sanford Holman is listed as a private in Kimbro's company under Sidney Sherman at the Battle of San Jacinto, *Muster Rolls,* 59; Family had the Bowie knife Sanford used at San Jacinto, R. L. Cartwright to Mant C. Taylor, Oct. 14, 1826, Cartwright research files; W. W. Holman service dates Apr. 19–July 23, 1836, in Miller, *Bounty and Donation Land Grants,* 352; Holman is listed on Capt. John M. Bradley's roster, Apr. 30, 1836, *Muster Rolls,* 71; Holman missed San Jacinto because on cattle roundup to feed army, *Biographical Directory of the Texan Conventions and Congresses,* 104; Sam Houston Orders, Apr. 3, 1836, in Jenkins, *Papers,* V, 310–311; Baker, Kimbro et al. to Houston, Apr. 10, 1836, ibid., V, 415; Houston Orders, Apr. 13, 1836, ibid., V, 450.

Declaration of Independence adopted on March 2, 1836, which he read to the assembled crowd. Matthew immediately made a gift of a saddle to roommate John F. Moseley; the traveler had intended to speculate in Texas land but now would join the army.[42]

By April 1, Matthew was home and provided army agents in San Augustine with needed items. Previously in February he had sold four pairs of French (Canadian) blankets, receiving a warrant for $40, and now agent Martin Parmer bought $63.37 worth of unspecified items and eleven bridles for $15. Matthew also made a $5 loan to the Republic of Texas to help defray the daily costs of volunteers marching west. Later in the month Matthew sold the army seven rifles at $40 each, two braces of pistols and holsters at $50 each, and one bushel of cornmeal.[43]

Nacogdoches and San Augustine residents became uneasy after March 20, when word arrived about the fall of the Alamo. Had they known that Fannin had surrendered near Goliad on that very day, the situation would have seemed even more dangerous. What was of most immediate interest to the Redlanders, however, was a report that the Cherokees were planning to attack the settlements at the instigation of Mexican agents. Augustus Hotchkiss, the chair of San Augustine's committee of safety, called a meeting on March 21, 1836, at which it was decided that Phil Sublett and Dr. Joseph Rowe should hasten to Fort Jesup to confer with Major Nelson, the commandant. The Redlanders wanted Nelson to restrain the Caddoes in the United States and also to establish regular communication between themselves and the fort. The good news was that Gen. Edmund P. Gaines, recently named commander of the western division of the U.S. Army, was expected to arrive at Jesup within the week.[44]

John T. Mason, an investor in the Galveston Bay Company

42. Matthew Cartwright to Robert G. Cartwright, Mar. 22, 1836, CFP; Account Book no. 2, heading Mar. 23, 1836, purchases in New Orleans, ibid.; John F. Moseley to daughter, Mar. 26, 1836, in Jenkins, *Papers,* V, 202–205. Moseley did not serve in the army until June; see Miller, *Bounty and Donation Land Grants,* 490.

43. John Cartwright and Matthew Cartwright, Audited Military accounts (TSL).

44. John T. Mason to Major Nelson, Mar. 20, 1836, in Jenkins, *Papers,* V, 149; Hotchkiss Report, Mar. 21, 1836, ibid, V, 153–154; E. P. Gaines to Cass, Mar. 29, 1836, ibid., V, 231–232.

and former governor of Michigan Territory, happened to be in Nacogdoches and addressed a private letter to General Gaines on April 1 asking a favor: Because the residents were totally without protection, could he in some way send a detachment of troops to Nacogdoches? Gaines sent word that he could not send troops into Mexican Texas without positive proof that Mexico was fomenting the trouble with the Indians, but he would try to prevent U.S. tribes from crossing into Texas. The thirty-third article of the Mexican treaty with the United States required each nation to prevent Indian attacks against the other, by force if necessary. Because the danger seemed imminent, and having no cavalry at Jesup, Gaines on April 8, 1836, asked the governors of Louisiana, Mississippi, and Tennessee to send mounted militia.[45]

It was at this point in early April 1836 that many Redlanders started packing trunks and loading wagons for Natchitoches. If the Holman women were not already in Louisiana, John W. Holman, who did not enter the army, could have escorted them at this time, along with other refugees. No family stories detail the flight of Holman women, which seems unusual. Cartwright tradition says John left the store, rushed home, and, though dinner was on the table, loaded everybody into wagons and started east. Matthew remained at the store with two pistols and his horse saddled and tied to the porch until word came of the victory at San Jacinto. That welcome information reached San Augustine early in May.

The store ledger adds a few details that corroborate family lore about the Runaway Scrape: John Cartwright made no purchases at the store after April 3; five days later Matthew charged his own account with a holster and pistol for George and another set for himself plus a wallet (a saddlebag), a violin bow, and cigars. At the same time he took four extra holsters and also paid John L. Evans as his three-month substitute in Captain Ratliff's company. No store daybook (journal of daily transactions) exists for the period between March 8 and June 30 to show whether or not the store was open regularly during April. But the ledger for that period shows only George Cartwright among family mem-

45. John T. Mason to General Gaines, Apr. 1, 1836, in Jenkins, *Papers,* V, 288; Gaines to Arbuckle and Vose, Apr. 5, 1836, ibid., V, 327; Gaines to Sec. of War Lewis Cass, Apr. 8, 1836, ibid., V, 373–374; Gaines to Governors, Apr. 8, 1836, ibid., V, 375–376.

bers visiting the store between April 8 and 24, the span of time between Matthew's own charges. George bought items on April 14, 18, and 20.[46] It would seem that the brothers remained in town to guard the store, breaking the tedium by playing the violin and smoking cigars.

Pandemonium erupted at Nacogdoches on April 12, 1836, when residents learned that Indians had camped about sixty miles north of town two nights earlier. Robert A. Irion, the acting commandant, immediately warned John T. Mason, who was en route to confer with Gen. Gaines: "Many women and children must fall victims to the merciless enemy. . . . We all will leave here today . . . concentrating at the Attoyac or at San Augustine." Mason received Irion's frantic, exaggerated message late the same night and forwarded it to Fort Jesup by an express rider. He reached the fort the next day and wrote to the general again, adding his own embellishments: Every inhabitant had abandoned Nacogdoches, which was now probably occupied by Indians. Because the spring rain had caused the Sabine River to overflow its banks, Mason predicted families trapped there would be killed: "The road from Nacogdoches to the Sabine is one unbroken line of women and children, on foot. . . ." In reality Nacogdoches was not abandoned. Irion had not left, and he ordered militia captains Ratliff, Smith, and James Chesser, who were there on their way west to join Houston, to stay in Nacogdoches and protect remaining citizens.[47]

General Gaines reacted quickly to Mason's hyperbole and immediately ordered thirteen companies to march to the Sabine with two field pieces and provisions for twelve days. The six hundred troops would camp on the east bank and begin making rafts to aid the refugees. No Indians appeared at Nacogdoches or San Augustine, and on April 20, 1836, the day before the Battle of San Jacinto, Capt. J. Bonnell, whom Gaines had sent to the Caddo village, returned with good news. Although Manuel Flores,

46. Cartwright, "The History of John Cartwright Settlement," CFP; Ledger Account Book no. 4, p. 25, no. 5, pp. 188, 202, 205, ibid.; Receipt from Ratliff for substitute Evans, Apr. 8, 1836, ibid.

47. R. A. Irion to J. T. Mason, Apr. 12, 1836, in Jenkins, *Papers,* V, 448 (1st quotation); J. T. Mason to General Gaines, Apr. 12, 1836, ibid., V, 449–450; J. T. Mason to General Gaines, Apr. 13, 1836, ibid., V, 459–460 (2nd quotation); R. A. Irion to Captains Ratliff, Smith, and Chesser, Apr. 14, 1836, ibid., V, 473.

a former trader among the Caddo who now claimed to be a Mexican officer, had told the tribes that the Americans planned to kill them and urged them to attack the white settlements, they had refused. The Indians professed great admiration for General Gaines, and said that even if they saw the Americans fighting the Mexicans, they would take no part. Gaines wrote to the governors cancelling his call for militia and tried to place his precipitous actions in a better light in a letter to the secretary of war. While all was quiet for the moment, Gaines begged for cavalry at Jesup and also engineers to map the country. The lack of both, he said, placed the U.S. Army at great disadvantage.[48]

Word of the defeat of Santa Anna at San Jacinto on April 21 reached Nacogdoches on May 11, 1836, but the aftermath of the Indian scare aroused animosity among some of the rowdy element along the Sabine River. They threatened to burn and plunder Nacogdoches because of the tory (Mexican) spirit there. Many women, including the wife of Gen. Thomas Jefferson Rusk, remained in San Augustine for safety. Other families from west of the Trinity River sought sanctuary in San Augustine from the Plains Indians. In May, Samuel T. Allen brought his wife, the former Matilda Roberts, and children 250 miles from the Brazos River frontier to stay with her father, Elisha Roberts. They would remain there while Allen served his three-month militia tour with the army from July 20 to October 20, 1836.[49]

East Texans resumed normal activities in May confident that the war was over. General Rusk, who suceeded Houston when the Hero of San Jacinto had to leave Texas for medical treatment of his wound received in the battle, followed the remnants of the retreating Mexican army from the Brazos River to Victoria. He called for more volunteers because reports from Mexico indicated that a new campaign against Texas was forthcoming. Sterling C. Robertson, ordered to recruit volunteers in the Redlands, wrote to Rusk on May 27 that people in San Augustine and

48. Samuel P. Carson to D. G. Burnet, Apr. 14, 1836, in Jenkins, *Papers,* V, 468–469; Mason to [?], Apr. 16, 1836, ibid., V, 489; J. Bonnell to Gaines, Apr. 20, 1836, ibid., V, 507–508; Gaines to Secretary of War, Apr. 20, 1836, ibid., V, 510–512.

49. H. H. Edwards to T. J. Rusk, May 11, 1836, in Jenkins, *Papers,* VI, 222; Sam T. Allen to brother, May 18, 1836, ibid., VI, 317–318; Miller, *Bounty and Donations,* 71.

Rusk's hometown of Nacogdoches were "luke warm and have but little notion of turning out." San Augustine officals ordered a draft on May 30, but Robertson feared they might not "go if drafted." The reason for the local apathy, he said, was that many believed General Gaines would defend them because the United States considered the Neches River the real boundary with Mexico. Robertson recommended enforcing the law confiscating the property of those who refused to serve in the army. He also noted that East Texas officials changed the word "draftee" to "volunteer" to make the men eligible for more benefits. The forty-five to fifty draftees Robertson recruited in the Redlands reached Nashville in Milam County by June 18, where they were detained for use as frontier rangers to protect those living in Robertson's colony. The attack by Comanches and other Indians at the Parker enclave on the Navasota River on May 19, 1836, was still fresh in the minds of Robertson colonists.[50]

Matthew probably missed the large San Augustine meeting on June 15 protesting the planned release of Santa Anna and the replacement of Houston as commander in chief. Matthew was again in New Orleans at the end of May to restock the store. He bought over $8,500 in clothing, hats, shoes, sewing materials, ribbons, scissors, combs, Queensware dishes, saddles, guns, knives, whiskey, champagne, wine, sugar, red pepper, almonds, and coffee. He also bought a new black coat, shirts, vests, pants, and a silk umbrella for himself, intended to impress Amanda Holman. Paying cash at many stores, Matthew received an immediate 5 percent discount; elsewhere he gave drafts payable in thirty days. Meticulous bookkeeper that he was, Matthew also noted the $13.50 he won while gambling.[51]

Robert Cartwright was called to service in Capt. William Scurlock's company, destined to join General Rusk in Victoria. Robert enrolled on July 4, 1836, along with a number of others, although they did not depart until later in the month. Scurlock was much admired in San Augustine, where he had lived since

50. S. C. Robertson to T. J. Rusk, May 27, 1836, in Jenkins, *Papers,* VI, 392–393 (1st and 2nd quotations); S. C. Robertson to T. J. Rusk, June 18, 1836, ibid., VII, 196, 197 (3rd quotation), 198–199.
51. San Augustine resolutions, June 15, 1836, in Jenkins, *Papers,* VII, 157–158; Account Book no. 2, May 30–June 10, 1836, CFP; Ledger Account Book no. 5, p. 265, ibid.

1834. He had served during the siege of San Antonio and then joined the aborted Matamoros expedition early in 1836. On March 2 his foraging party was attacked by Mexican cavalry, and Scurlock was one of two men to survive by escaping to Goliad. He was spared the execution there on March 27, 1836, to nurse wounded Mexican soldiers, and again managed to escape, returning to the Redlands to raise troops. Robert sold his captain a mule worth $80 on July 4, while Matthew received a receipt for $112.50 for six kegs of powder and loaned the quartermaster $25 to assist in forwarding the troops.[52]

Sam Houston returned to San Augustine from New Orleans in July 1836 and stayed with the Subletts to finish recuperating from his injury. He had hoped to return to the army, but his wound became worse. Houston complained to the authorities that a local recruiter was signing up unarmed substitutes and those who were incapable of performing as soldiers, which was against the law. Houston recommended severe punishment for the infringement.[53]

At the end of July 1836, the Cartwrights and their neighbors were surprised to find columns of U.S. troops marching to Nacogdoches. Convinced that Indians from Louisiana and Arkansas had participated in the attack at Parker's fort in May, General Gaines ordered four hundred men to Texas on July 10, 1836. Four companies of cavalry reached Jesup from Fort Towson on the upper Red River, and they started for the Sabine on July 23; the next day six companies of Jesup's infantry followed. They were to build a breastwork and blockhouse near Nacogdoches and use force if attacked by hostile Indians. One month later, the blockhouse was not built and the infantry remained in town, while the cavalry camped on a hill west of Nacogdoches. Some of these troops, attracted by the generous land grants, deserted to the Texan army, but Gaines ordered them to return or face charges.[54]

52. Miller, *Bounty and Donations*, 160; List of Captain Scurlock's Company of San Augustine Volunteers, enrolled by John G. Love, July 4, 1836 (original in San Augustine County Court House; copy at TSL); Webb, Carroll, and Branda (eds.), *Handbook of Texas*, II, 583; Robert G. Cartwright and Matthew Cartwright, Audited Military Accounts (TSL).

53. Sam Houston to Henry Rueg, July 4, 1836, in Jenkins, *Papers*, VII, 367; Sam Houston to W. E. Harris, July 9, 1836, ibid., VII, 404–405; Sam Houston to T. J. Rusk, July 10, 1836, ibid., VII, 413.

54. Joseph Rowe to Major Anthony, Aug. 6, 1836, in Jenkins, *Papers*, VIII,

The presence of the troops pleased the Anglo-Texans, but many Hispanics departed for their ranches. One traveler noticed that the U.S. commissaries paid cash for supplies in Nacogdoches and that everybody was getting rich; other visitors complained about the inflated prices. Another false alarm about an Indian attack at the end of August caused Houston, temporarily in Nacogdoches, to ask for volunteers from San Augustine for a few days to bolster the U.S. troops until reinforcements could arrive from Fort Jesup. But by early September, all was quiet in the Redlands except for politics. President ad interim David G. Burnet called for the election of permanent officials to take place September 5, 1836.[55]

142–143; Bonnell to General Gaines, Aug. 9, 1836, ibid., VIII, 168–170; William Parker to —, Aug. 4, 1836, ibid., VIII, 122–124; E. P. Gaines to Sam Houston, Aug. 3, 1836, ibid., VIII, 105–107.

55. Traveler to editor of Columbia *Telegraph,* ca. Aug. 20, 1836, in Jenkins, *Papers,* VIII, 279; Sam Houston to Citizens, Aug. 29, 1836, ibid., VIII, 345–346.

Five

The New Republic
and Hard Times

1836–1841

S am Houston's friends entered his name as a candidate for
the presidency of the Republic of Texas exactly three
weeks before the election took place on September 5,
1836. Phil Sublett made the first nomination on August 15 at the
Mansion House in San Augustine. Those attending, probably
including the Cartwrights, unanimously chose Houston along
with Thomas J. Rusk of Nacogdoches as vice-president. The San
Augustine committee sent copies of its resolutions to Nacogdoches,
Sabine, Shelbyville, Jasper, and Liberty. About the same time,
Thomas F. McKinney also nominated Houston at Columbia. In
a letter published in the *Telegraph and Texas Register* on August
30, 1836, the Hero of San Jacinto yielded to the wishes of his
friends and accepted the call to public office because "the crisis
requires it. . . ."[1]

1. Stanley Siegel, *A Political History of the Texas Republic, 1836–1845*
(Austin: University of Texas Press, 1956), 51, 52 (quotation).

When the votes were finally counted, Houston polled 5,119 votes, a crushing defeat for the other two candidates, former Governor Henry Smith with 743 votes and Stephen F. Austin with only 587. In San Augustine, 327 men voted, including John, Matthew, and Thomas Cartwright; Robert was with the army and George evidently was absent. San Augustine voters gave Sam Houston 322 votes and Austin only 5. Shelby Corzine won a seat in the Senate with 199 votes, while William W. Holman and Joseph Rowe, with 192 and 142 votes respectively, defeated four rivals to represent San Augustine in the lower chamber of Congress. Ayish Bayou men approved the constitution 318 to 4, and a straw vote for annexation to the United States revealed 325 San Augustine residents in favor and 4 opposed. Although the neighborhood had given 317 votes to Rusk for vice-president, nationwide Mirabeau Buonaparte Lamar secured the office with a comfortable majority.[2]

Congress met on October 3 in Columbia, the temporary capital, and Sam Houston's inauguration took place on October 22. Texas faced dreadful problems: an empty treasury, hard times, high prices, Indians on the northern and western frontiers, and a possible return of the Mexican army. Between October and December 22 1836, Congress struggled to meet those needs in addition to organizing counties and selecting a site for the capital.[3]

Far from the seat of government, San Augustine was more concerned with commerce than with coping with the republic's problems, except for the fear of Indian attacks. Most residents, however, expected that Texas would soon be annexed by the United States, and that the more powerful nation would overcome all difficulties. The Cartwright correspondence fails to record what the family members thought about these matters.

Matthew, however, had matrimony on his mind in 1836. Almost twenty-nine years old, he began courting Amanda Holman as soon as widow Anne Wigglesworth Holman and her daughters returned to San Augustine. Sometime in the summer, perhaps June or July, Matthew wrote a note to Amanda in stilted, formal nineteenth-century style, indicating his serious purpose:

2. Ibid., 55; San Augustine tally sheet, Sept. 5, 1836, Election returns, Secretary of State records (TSL).
3. Siegel, *Political History,* 56–57.

Miss Amanda Holman:

Please allow me to address you for the first time with the most profound respect. I admire your person, your address and appearance. . . . I have come to the conclusion that of all other objects met with in this life . . . you are the one. Therefore, I now address you for the purpose of requesting permission to pay my suit on that of which is of the most importance to me and I hope not indifferent to you. Please reply as soon as convenient and relieve the suspense of one who is desirous to unite his fate and happiness in life with yours.

Your obedient servant,
Matthew Cartwright

Barely nineteen years old, Amanda replied in the correct manner of the day:

Dear Sir:

In compliance with your request I drop you a few lines to inform you that I was not aware of your regard . . . the subject being entirely new to me leaves me wholly unprepared to give you a satisfactory answer . . . I therefore deem it my interest to reflect seriously upon the matter before I address you further.

Yours with respect,
Amanda Holman

A third undated note from Matthew begged Amanda to relieve him of the painful suspense because she was his "choice and favorite."[4]

Amanda soon accepted Matthew's proposal and scheduled the ceremony for Tuesday, October 18, 1836, little more than one year after the death of her father. On August 2, she bought seven yards of French muslin and two bonnets at Matthew's store, and later pink silk and gauze ribbon, all suitable for a wedding. Early in October, Matthew went to Natchitoches, where he bought merchandise for his store and also purchased rings and other jewelry. Five days before the wedding, John Cartwright bought fancy tableware, a set of silver spoons, and a dress coat, while

---

4. The two notes from Matthew Cartwright to Amanda Holman and the note from Amanda to Matthew are in CFP.

Robert, just returned from the army and once a beau of the Holman sisters, purchased a new stock, the fashionable neckwear of the times. Other kinsmen and friends charged boots, coats, and pants at this time, apparently readying themselves for the wedding. The day before the ceremony, Mary Cartwright sent young Clinton to the store for a dozen candles and one pound of tea, the latter unusual except during illness or entertainment. Matthew closed the store in honor of the occasion, but on the days before and after, he diligently entered transactions into his daybook and recorded the proceedings in a ledger.[5]

The ceremony doubtless took place before San Augustine's primary judge because Congress had not yet authorized county governments. Thus, there was no means of recording a marriage, and, unlike some couples married by bond prior to 1836, Matthew and Amanda saw no need to record their marriage at the county courthouse at a later date.

With his store closed on his wedding day, the methodical Matthew made an inventory of his assets. He owned nine parcels of land scattered in nearby counties totaling 12,177 acres, and two twelve-acre lots in Mina (Bastrop), but he failed to mention any town lots in San Augustine. He also held a number of notes from debtors, and added them to his valuation of the land, the grand total reaching $10,616.37. This tally also omitted his interest in the store, which remained in partnership with his father.[6]

Where the newlyweds resided at first is unknown. Matthew may have lived in the store while a bachelor and taken meals at the hotel or a boardinghouse. By April 1838, he owned three of the four lots where he was living in 1849, and because they had belonged to his father earlier, maybe that is where he and Amanda lived after their marriage. Two were corner lots on the south side of Livingston Street but were divided by Broadway.[7]

5. Ledger Book no. 4, 1835–1837, pp. 74, 226, 259, CFP; Day Book no. 6, 1836–1837, ibid.

6. "Inventory of the property & effects of M. Cartwright on the 18th day of Oct. 1836," loose sheet in Ledger Book no. 3, 1834–1835, CFP.

7. On Dec. 27, 1849, Matthew sold lots 75, 76, 77, and 116, "where I now live"; he had bought lots 75, 76 (corner lots John Cartwright had secured from Thomas S. McFarland in 1833) and 77 on Apr. 7, 1837, and acquired lot 116 on Apr. 15, 1839. San Augustine County, Deed Records, H, 200 (quotation), 201, E, 30–31, 228.

Matthew Cartwright (1807–1870), ca. 1840s.
Courtesy Cartwright Family Descendants.

From pictures later in life, Amanda must have been a pretty and curvaceous bride, and her doting husband indulged her wishes. Items charged to his account soon after their wedding included clothing, earrings, silver spoons, a music box, a toothbrush, six Windsor chairs, and artificial flowers. A bottle of cordial might have been medicinal, but the two bottles of champagne just before Christmas must have been for social drinking. In January, Matthew took garden seeds from the store, but also a looking glass, hat pins, a set of table china, and more champagne.[8] He had gotten over his earlier aversion to alcohol, and subsequent events suggest that he, like most of his contemporaries, indulged himself with liquor.

Almost immediately Amanda became pregnant, and the first child, Clinton Columbus (always called Columbus or Cumby), arrived on August 23, 1837. Amanda may have gone to her mother's larger house for the event; this birth was special for Anne Holman because her two older married daughters were childless and her other grandchildren, offspring of James S. Holman, lived in Tennessee. Columbus was Mary and John Cartwright's first grandchild to carry the Cartwright name, and though Matthew and Amanda broke the old tradition of naming first sons for grandfathers, little Cumby was adored by all. The names suggest that the parents each chose part of his name, a precedent also used in naming the second son. "Columbus" was the name of Amanda's uncle and his son, while "Clinton" was for Matthew's younger brother.[9]

Two family weddings took place during the summer and another during the winter months. On June 27, Amanda's sister America, called "Meck," married Robert Lane, a Tennessean, before Judge William McFarland; they became the first couple to have their union recorded by the county clerk in San Augustine. Perhaps Amanda, then seven months pregnant, gave a party for her sister because during June she bought a folding-leaf table, table covers, draperies, new earrings, and two breast pins. Her purchase of eight dozen eggs on one day suggests she was making cakes or custard, or even eggnog. Two weeks before Amanda gave birth to Columbus, Matthew's brother Robert married Mary

8. Ledger Book no. 5, pp. 259, 289, Oct. 5–Jan. 29, 1836–1837, CFP.
9. Cartwright and Holman family genealogical records, Cartwright research files.

Lanier in San Augustine. Her father, A. H. Lanier, a refugee from hard times in Tennessee, charged a few items at Matthew's store; the debt remained for two years until Robert finally paid his father-in-law's bill. On January 14, 1838, Amanda's brother Sanford Holman wed Matthew's sister Clementine. She was not quite nineteen and he was twenty-one, and their union was destined for tragedy with both dead within a decade.[10]

In March 1837, John Cartwright, now fifty years old, finally agreed to sell his half of the store to Matthew. As part of their arrangement, Matthew spent the next two years collecting accounts due his father and tried at the same time to settle the partnership's debts due to merchants in Natchitoches and New Orleans. In marked contrast to their previous businesslike contracts, John gave Matthew the following receipt, which failed to mention a sum: "Recd of M. Cartwright in full for my Interest to all goods, Invoices, belonging formily [*sic*] to M Cartwright & Co this 29th March 1837."[11]

John did not retire to his country home but, instead, continued speculating in land and took an active role in the gin, mill, blacksmith shop, and country store on Buckley's Creek with Robert and George. Moreover, during the summer of 1837, John built a commodious two-story building on the southeast corner of the public square, the block having been divided into regular lots. Upstairs the structure was probably a rooming house or hotel because there are receipts for monthly rent of numbered rooms, while downstairs was a store operated by John and, later, Clinton Cartwright. Fourteen years old in 1837, young Clinton was errand boy and perhaps clerk for both his father and Matthew. John acquired his stock in staples, iron, and tools for the country store from Matthew, and Clinton often transported bulk orders of coffee, sugar, and rice to Buckley's Creek. As in the case of Matthew's store, country customers paid their accounts in produce, services, and land. Credits for cotton, pork, butter, eggs, pelts, and hauling goods locally and to Natchitoches appear on ledger sheets. James Gaines, for example, paid Matthew with one $100 "shear" in the town of Pendleton in July 1838.[12]

10. Ibid.; Ledger Book, 1837–1839, 1, 49, CFP.
11. John Cartwright Receipt, Mar. 29, 1837, Legal Documents, 1829–1869, CFP (quotation); Ledger Book, 1837–1839, 23, 46, 171, 225, ibid.
12. Ledger Book, 1837–1839, 23, 46, 50, 51, 171, 180 (Gaines), 182, 202, CFP; Crocket, *Two Centuries*, 219.

Economic hard times increased in March 1837 when the price of cotton fell almost 50 percent at New Orleans, reflecting a worldwide glut. This decline began a downward spiral of the agrarian-based economy and was known as the panic of 1837. In May, banks in New York, Philadelphia, Boston, and Baltimore suspended gold payments and New Orleans money lenders soon followed, affecting the Cartwrights and other merchants in the Republic of Texas. Although banks eventually resumed exchanging paper money for coins, the next seven years saw repeated suspensions and a reluctance to accept paper money except at a substantial discount. The causes for this severe depression, which lasted until the late 1840s, included the acute shortage of gold and silver worldwide, land speculating at inflated prices, and the proliferation of often worthless paper money issued by state banks, private merchants, states, and the Republic of Texas.[13]

The new republic had to solve its own economic woes when annexation to the United States failed to take place in 1837. The republic owed huge sums to merchants, particularly McKinney and Williams (over $90,000), commission merchants at the mouth of the Brazos and in Galveston who had used their credit in the United States to supply the Texas army and navy. Sam Houston's administration was besieged by creditors, not only large firms but individuals who lost horses during battles and merchants like the Cartwrights who had supplied small amounts of provisions and arms for soldiers. John and Matthew sent powers of attorney and their receipts from army quartermasters with Representative W. W. Holman and Senator Joseph Rowe to the first session of Congress and successfully collected about $800 in Texas treasury notes for items they had furnished to the Texas army.[14]

Already committed to paying its soldiers with land, the new nation hoped to use its vast unpopulated resource to borrow money in the United States. But Texas agents trying to arrange loans backed by public land in Texas at fifty cents per acre found no investors in the United States because of the banking panic. Efforts to secure loans in Europe fared no better. The new republic was forced to levy taxes, and the Texas Congress reluctantly

13. "Money of the Republic of Texas," Webb, Carroll, and Branda (eds.), *Handbook of Texas,* II, 221–222.

14. John and Matthew Cartwright, Audited Military Claims, Treasury Department of the Republic of Texas (TSL).

passed legislation to raise revenue knowing how unpopular taxes were among its constituents.

As members of an agrarian society with no manufacturing, Texans disliked import duties, as witnessed by the acts of 1832 and 1835 under Mexico. Nevertheless, in order to raise money on which to operate, Congress ordered a 12½-cent ad valorem levy on imported goods and a number of direct taxes, including a poll tax (not for voting, merely a head tax) of 50 cents and later $1 on each white male over twenty-one years of age. Real and personal property were taxed as well: levies on land began at 25 cents per hundred acres and 25 cents per town lot; 50 cents on each slave over ten years of age; 12½ cents (one bit) on each horse over two; the same amount on cattle beyond an exemption of twenty-five animals; 25 cents per wheel on wagons and buggies, but 50 cents for pleasure carriages.[15] Many could not pay, while others would not, a situation that within a few years resulted in many sheriff's sales. Subsequent congresses fiddled with the tax rates, but the republic never succeeded in becoming solvent nor in making the taxpayers happy.

As a partial solution to the lack of circulating money in the fall of 1837, the Republic of Texas began issuing promissory notes in amounts from $1 to $500 bearing 10 percent interest payable in twelve months. At the same time, the Congress forbade the circulation of private IOUs as money and also further use of state bank notes from the U.S. to pay duties or taxes. At first paper money circulated at par with specie but declined to forty cents on the dollar within one year. Subsequent issues of paper money dropped even lower, to two cents on the dollar in 1841. From 1843 to 1845, rumors about annexation to the United States gradually restored the value of Texas money as the economy began to recover.[16]

The Cartwrights, like others, failed to comprehend immediately the seriousness of the hard times. At first they conducted business as usual in land speculating and at the store, resorting to barter when necessary. It was not until 1840, when the price of cotton fell dramatically, that everyone realized the depressed economic conditions would be with them for awhile.

15. H. P. N. Gammel (comp.), *The Laws of Texas, 1822–1897* ... (10 vols.; Austin: Gammel Book Co., 1898), I, 1514.

16. Webb, Carroll, and Branda (eds.), *Handbook of Texas*, II, 222.

Matthew's experience was typical. In 1838, he shipped very little cotton to his New Orleans agent because an infestation of worms destroyed much of the crop in eastern Texas. Peyroux, Arcueil & Company, a commission house located near the foot of Toulouse Street and the levee, did not buy the cotton themselves, but sought purchasers, always endeavoring to sell when the market was to their customer's advantage. To pay for the merchandise ordered for his store through Peyroux, and unable to pay with cotton, Matthew sent a $1,000 certificate of deposit on the City Bank of New Orleans in September 1838 as partial payment. Peyroux did not accept Texas Treasury notes, and in December the agent advised Matthew that the notes had declined to a 50 to 61 percent discount in the Crescent City. He suggested that Matthew dispose of any he might hold even at a loss. Cotton was then selling at from 11 to 14 cents a pound in New Orleans and was not expected to decline.[17]

When Matthew sent four bales of cotton to New Orleans early in 1839, he told his factors that more bales would arrive soon because the crop then being ginned and baled was very good in contrast to the previous year's. He received 15¼ cents a pound for the first four bales, weighing a total of 1,800 pounds, which netted $257.64 after Peyroux, Arcueil & Co. deducted freight, storage, marine and fire insurance, weighing, and their 2½ percent commission. But later that year the agents advised that though the demand for cotton was high, the price had fallen and Philadelphia and New Orleans banks had again suspended specie payments.[18]

The price of cotton continued to decline as the economic depression worsened. In January 1840, Matthew received only 8½ cents per pound for fifteen bales, giving him a total credit of only $528.42. The next month the price dropped to 7¾ cents and in April to 5 cents per pound. The markets were glutted, said the agent, and transportation costs were rising: "We hope that this sale tho' not so satisfactory as either you or we could wish it to

17. M. Cartwright to Peyroux, Arcueil & Co., [Mar./Apr., 1839], CFP; Peyroux, Arcueil & Co. to M. Cartwright, Dec. 10, 1838, ibid.
18. M. Cartwright to Peyroux, Arcueil & Co., [Mar./Apr., 1839], CFP; Statement to account of M. Cartwright, Apr. 27, 1839, enclosed in Peyroux, Arcueil & Co. to M. Cartwright, Apr. 30, 1839, ibid.; same to same, Oct. 25, 1839, ibid.

be in regard to price, will yet be considered as having been effected to the best of our judgment in the present situation."[19]

How could Matthew survive? The declining prices for cotton in New Orleans were hard to explain to store patrons in San Augustine who had bought merchandise on credit in the expectation of earnings based on the previous year's prices. Nevertheless, Matthew did not lose faith in his New Orleans factors and named his second son, born March 27, 1840, Americus Peyroux. Amanda, of course, had chosen the baby's first name, the masculine version of her sister America's name. The continuing hard times forced Peyroux to close briefly in 1841 and Matthew's inability to pay his debt to the New Orleans firm resulted in a rupture of their relationship.[20]

Matthew was not alone in suffering from the depressed economy. Thomas S. McFarland, who had platted San Augustine, became convinced in 1838 that his town speculation was unprofitable and moved to Belgrade on the Sabine River in present-day Newton County. He returned to San Augustine to collect debts in 1839 and noted "money as scarce in the red lands" as it was in Belgrade. At Crockett, ninety miles west of San Augustine, a resident reported, "Times here are perfectly ruinous. Our most solvent men are unable to meet their lightest obligations and property of every description is unsaleable." About the same time, Adolphus Sterne in Nacogdoches observed, "Grog Shops all Shutt up *no Cash*. Credit very Sick. . . . times have never been so hard in Texas."[21]

During these difficult days, the Cartwrights forged various partnerships in order to remain in business. John and Matthew Cartwright became partners with in-law William Garrett in a cotton warehouse in Sabinetown at the mouth of the Palo Gacho in anticipation of a boom in steamboat traffic that failed to develop. Matthew joined Amanda's brother William in buying

19. Peyroux, Arcueil & Co. to M. Cartwright, Sales statement, Jan. 25, 1840, CFP; statement, Feb. 3, 1840, ibid.; letter and statement, Feb. 8, 1840, ibid.; statement, Apr. 6, 1840, ibid.; letter, Apr. 11, 1840 (quotation), ibid.

20. Peyroux, Arcueil & Co. to M. Cartwright, Apr. 30, 1844, CFP.

21. McFarland, *Journal,* 68 (1st quotation); J. H. Kirchoffer to James H. Starr, Jan. 5, 1841, quoted in William Ransom Hogan, *The Texas Republic: A Social and Economic History* (Austin: University of Texas Press, 1946), 94 (2nd quotation); Archie P. McDonald (ed.), *Hurrah for Texas: The Diary of Adolphus Sterne, 1838–1851* (Austin: Eakin Press, 1986), 78, 86 (3rd quotation).

land and also acquired various partners to operate the store. On the inside cover of Matthew's 1837–1839 ledger, somebody wrote that in 1842 Matthew Cartwright, Samuel T. Burrus, David Brown, and John C. Brooke "were the store" during "the hard times." Surveyor Brown remained busy in his profession and in land speculation, while Brooke was a newcomer who served as clerk for the Board of Land Commissioners in 1838 and as San Augustine County judge for a portion of 1839. Sam Burrus had come in 1835, and though lacking the polish of the others in handwriting and spelling, he remained Matthew's partner for a decade. How much interest these men took in the store before 1842 is not clear; while Matthew continued to keep the ledgers, the daybooks show different handwriting. One hand was Burrus's, who at an early date may have been the person who wrote "Cartright," without a "w." Matthew's younger brothers Clinton and Richard perhaps served as bookkeeper-clerks as part of their education, but they would not have misspelled the family name.[22]

Land matters absorbed much of the Cartwrights' time. President Houston kept the republic's land office closed as long as possible in order to secure the scattered records from former commissioners and alcaldes and to determine legitimate titles from the fraudulent documents issued in 1835. Meanwhile, even with the land office closed, Congress offered generous grants to encourage immigration: heads of families who had arrived prior to March 2, 1836, were eligible for one league and *labór,* and augmentations were allowed single men like Matthew who married after receiving a bachelor's portion. Those who came between March 3, 1836, and October 1, 1837, qualified for 1,280 acres if head of a family or 640 acres if single. After October

22. "George W. Cartwright" Day Book, 1839–1845, CFP, p. 1 on M. Cartwright account, says "yr part Corporate Tax for Sabine Warehouse"; Ibid., p. 6, Cartwright and Garrett billed for installing French lock on warehouse [ca. Mar. 1839]; Inventory of property belonging to estate of John Cartwright, Nov. 9, 1841, one-third lot and warehouse in Sabinetown, ibid.; Samuel Davis of Shelby County to Wm. W. Holman and Matthew Cartwright of San Augustine County, deed, Mar. 1, 1837, for one-half league of land issued to Wm. [John] Vaughan in 1835 on Neches River three miles below the saline works, filed Dec. 16, 1846, in San Augustine County, ibid.; Matthew Cartwright ledger, 1837–1839, Day Books nos. 6–12, ibid. The Sabine County courthouse burned in 1875, making searches for early deed records impossible.

1837, a family received only 640 acres and a bachelor one-half of that amount.[23]

Beginning in 1838, when the Boards of Land Commissioners began holding hearings in each county, each applicant presented his claim and needed two witnesses to confirm the date of arrival. Those with a certificate as evidence of their right to land, such as discharged soldiers, could sell their documents to an "assignee," which sometimes led to fraud, along with those who lied before the county boards. An 1839 investigation of the records discovered between three hundred and four hundred questionable claims issued to assignees in Sabine County, and in San Augustine a special examiner reported that "more than 1300 Certificates have been issued . . . many of which . . . are believed to be spurious."[24]

Unfortunately, on January 5 and February 7, 1839, Matthew bought three of those fraudulent certificates issued by the Sabine Board. On February 7, 1839, in San Augustine, one man sold Matthew his certificate for one unlocated league and *labór* (4,604 acres) for $600, which in devalued Texas treasury bills was $240, or five cents per acre. They went to the county judge's office that same day to acknowledge the transaction. The scoundrel must have told of his good fortune to cronies, because the sale was repeated exactly on February 20 and 21 with two other men. All three swindlers told the Sabine board they had come to Texas in 1834, but their names appear on no records before or after that date. Matthew kept the three certificates, perhaps in hopes of finding the trio. George Cartwright had better luck with his purchase of a certificate for one-third of an unlocated league issued on January 8, 1838. The seller also claimed that he had arrived in 1834, but George located the 1,476 acres in Sabine County.[25]

The San Augustine Board of Land Commissioners began hearing petitions on January 8, 1838, and Robert was the first in the family to appear. On January 29 he asked for a league and

23. Carolyn Reeves Ericson, "Introduction," in Ericson and Ingmire, *First Settlers of the Republic of Texas,* I, i–iii.

24. Gifford White, *The First Settlers of Sabine County, Texas* (St. Louis: Ingmire Publications, 1983), 5 (quotation).

25. Certificates nos. 1059 (Hiram Godell), 1060 (Charles G. Small, Jr.), and 1065 (Elbert Lauden), CFP; Certificate no. 95 (James Connally), assignee G. W. Cartwright, in White, *First Settlers of Sabine County,* 14.

labór, while George, still unmarried, applied for and received his headright of one-third of a league on February 7, 1838, although he did not locate it until 1840 in Bell County. Matthew submitted the required statement signed by two witnesses on February 14, saying that he had come in 1825 and that he did not leave Texas during the campaign in 1836 nor refuse to participate in the war. Then he asked for his augmentation of two-thirds of a league because he was now married. John, not suspecting that he did not have title to his league (see Chapter 4), petitioned on March 8, 1838, for the *labór* to which he was entitled and located it in Sabine County. Robert ultimately located his headright in what is now Kaufman County ten miles northeast of Kaufman, then the Kingsborough fort. Robert sold his 1837 military certificate for 320 acres earned by three months' service during the summer of 1836, as did many others who also had headright tracts.[26]

Many of the land certificates acquired by Matthew and John were in payment for debts incurred at the store. Some debt settlements occurred only after adjudication. Between 1838 and 1839, Matthew, represented by different attorneys, often appeared as either defendant or plaintiff in debtor suits before San Augustine county judges E. O. Legrand and John C. Brooke, the latter his business partner. Matthew had served on a coroner's jury at an inquest in 1837, but never sat in judgment in the county court in those early years, although his brothers and brothers-in-law did. Robert, for example, was on the jury in January 1839 when the San Augustine customs collector, John G. Love, sued a number of prominent men including William W. Holman for failure to pay duties. It was convenient for the customs collector to attend court because the rectangular building on Montgomery Street just below Columbia housed both. The Holmans, W. W. Lanier (Robert's brother-in-law), and Phil and Henry W. Sublett occasionally sat in the jury box when Matthew's suits were

26. Oaths to Board of Land Commissioners (Robert and Matthew), in Linda Cheves Nicklas (comp.), "San Augustine County, Texas, Courthouse Records and Loose Papers, 1831–1906," Inventory and Index (typescript; Special Collections, Ralph W. Steen Library, Stephen F. Austin University, Nacgodoches, 1984), 26; San Augustine County, County Court Minutes, W.P.A. transcripts (BTHC). Robert G. Cartwright's headright appears on the Kaufman County Original Land Grant Map, General Land Office of Texas: John Cartwright form and survey in Sharp Collection (BTHC); Miller, *Bounty and Donation Land Grants,* 160.

argued. In one instance on April 16, 1838, Phil Sublett was a member of the jury that ruled in favor of Matthew in one case and, minutes later, decided against him in another.[27] In the small close-knit community, a totally impartial jury was impossible.

Moreover, friends sued friends and fathers sued sons, perhaps as a means to record the settlement of disagreements rather than personal vendettas. Settlement of these suits usually was for the amount of the debt, plus interest, often 15 percent or 25 percent from the date that the note was given, plus court costs. Sometimes the amount was substantial, and in view of the lack of cash and the reluctance to accept an IOU from a debtor, real estate or personal property such as slaves had to be forfeited. The court became more professional in 1840, when Congress established district courts served by visiting district judges for civil and criminal cases. County courts thereafter concentrated on probate cases and administrative duties such as road building.[28]

Besides widespread hard times, troubles with the local Indians and Mexicans kept residents of eastern Texas uneasy between 1837 and 1839. The Cartwrights and the Holmans worried over Amanda's brother William, who belonged to Alexander Horton's company at the time of the Cordova Rebellion in 1838, and later over James Cartwright, the teenage son of cousin Thomas Cartwright, who served in 1839 against the Cherokees.[29] Doubtless the rumors of impending attacks against the settlements disturbed the family, but actual fighting took place north of Nacogdoches. Besides, San Augustine residents took comfort in the presence of Fort Jesup just across the Sabine River.

The first trouble came in March 1837 when rumors indicated that Mexican agents from the Rio Grande intended to unite the northeastern tribes with discontented Nacogdoches-area Mexicans to attack the Anglo settlements. Ownership of land was at the center of the controversy. Ever since the arrival of the agents of the Galveston Bay Land Company in 1834, both the Chero-

27. Nicklas (comp.), "San Augustine County Courthouse Records," 30, 32–34, 69–71. For George on jury, Jan. 28, 1838, see ibid., 22. John Cartwright appeared in court as late as January 1840; see ibid., 125, 130, 133, 137. For details about the courthouse see Crocket, *Two Centuries,* 109.

28. For example, Jacob Garrett sued Milton. Nicklas (comp.), "San Augustine County Courthouse Records," 49, 56.

29. Republic of Texas militia rosters (TSL).

kees and native Mexicans had found Anglo intruders on land they considered theirs but for which they lacked titles. In order to secure the neutrality of the sedentary and civilized Cherokees, Shawnees, Delawares, and Kickapoos in February 1836, Gen. Sam Houston promised titles to land north of the old Spanish Road. The Texas Senate, however, influenced in part by speculators who coveted the Indian lands, refused to ratify the treaty, which caused widespread resentment among the tribes. Moreover, by 1837, the wide-ranging Caddoes from Louisiana occupied an area of northeastern Texas and threatened to unite with the more fearsome Plains Indians.[30]

In response to rumors of a concerted attack, the San Augustine militia mustered to plan a defense for the neighborhood in March and April 1837. But action taken by President Sam Houston through General Rusk, commander of the Nacogdoches district, temporarily defused the feelings of the discontented Mexicans and Indians. Seventeen months later, on August 10, 1838, the threat resumed when Vicente Cordova, a former alcalde of Nacogdoches, and other Mexicans gathered on the Angelina River northwest of the old town with a force of perhaps three hundred. The Hispanics sent a letter renouncing citizenship in the Republic of Texas to President Houston, who was visiting in Nacogdoches. Cordova resented the ever-increasing Anglo rule in his hometown and had recently visited Matamoros seeking support. Houston immediately sent word to his Cherokee friends asking that they and their associates not join Cordova, a request that was honored by most. The president ordered the militia to rout Cordova but to respect the lives and property of Mexican and Indian women and children. General Rusk ignored the latter stipulation and sent Henry W. Augustine, San Augustine's former senator, with half of the militia, perhaps including Amanda's brother William, to destroy the Mexican camp. Cordova escaped while many of the local Mexicans returned home. Houston granted them amnesty although this generosity was not popular in Nacogdoches or among the military.[31]

30. See Anna Muckleroy, "The Indian Policy of the Republic of Texas," *SHQ*, XXV (Apr., 1922), 229–260, XXVI (July, 1922), 1–29, XXVI (Oct., 1922), 128–148.
31. McFarland, *Journal*, 18–19, 22–23; Sam Houston to T. J. Rusk, Mar. 25, 1837, in Williams and Barker (eds.), *Writings of Sam Houston*, II, 74–75;

Houston's policy was soon reversed. President Houston could not succeed himself in office, and in the election of September 1838, Mirabeau B. Lamar and David G. Burnet became president and vice-president. In contrast with Houston, neither man was sensitive to the needs of the Indians or the Mexican inhabitants of Texas, and during their term they actively worked to eliminate both groups. During the regular session of Congress in November 1838, San Augustine Senator John A. Greer and his Redlands colleagues in the lower house, Isaac Campbell and Ezekiel W. Cullen, helped pass an act calling for a special session of the district court at San Augustine to try the Mexican rebels for high treason. An indictment was returned against one hundred men, and at least one was sentenced to death. The misconduct of the jury and doubt over the man's guilt led to his pardon by President Lamar, however, and soon all the cases were dismissed. Greer and his colleagues next proposed a three-man commission to confiscate the property of the rebels and post it for sale in 640-acre tracts.[32] This blatant racism caused uneasiness among the Mexican families and many abandoned their homes.

Lamar's administration could now concentrate on removing the Cherokees, Shawnees, and Delawares from northeastern Texas. Lamar argued that the Mexican government had never promised land or civil rights to the Indians, and that they remained in Texas "against the public wish, and at the sacrifice of the public tranquility." Rumors, perhaps manufactured, again surfaced in early 1839 that the Indians would attack the white settlements in collaboration with Mexican agents. Amid popular outcry, Lamar sent agents to negotiate the immediate removal of the Cherokees, offering to pay for their improvements and the cost of moving into the U.S. Indian Territory north of the the Red River. Tribal leaders reluctantly agreed but wanted to wait until they could harvest their crops, a request that was denied. Some Texans interpreted the request as a ploy to seek allies in order to resist. In June, Capt. William Kimbro, the sheriff of San Augustine

---

President Houston's message to the Texas Congress, May 5, 1837, ibid., 84–85; Houston's general orders, Aug. 18, 1838, ibid., 278; John M. Henrie to M. B. Lamar, Aug. 17, 1838, *Lamar Papers,* II, 205.

32. Gammel (comp.), *Laws of Texas,* II, 6, 33, 146; "Cordova Rebellion," Webb, Carroll, and Branda (eds.), *Handbook of Texas,* I, 412–413.

County, led his volunteer company to the Shawnee village and forced them to surrender their gun locks as a pledge of peace. His company continued north to the upper Neches River in present-day Van Zandt County to meet Col. Edward Burleson and Gen. Kelsey H. Douglas, who intended to destroy the Cherokee emigrant train en route north. Chief Bowles and perhaps one hundred Cherokee men were killed in mid-July 1839, while the remnant of the tribe fled toward the Red River. Soon after, the Shawnees agreed to leave Texas if the government would pay them for their improvements and moving expenses. Most other bands departed in 1839, thus ending tribal occupation in eastern Texas.[33]

Through this period of racial conflict and economic hardship the Cartwrights continued to mind their enterprises and acquire land. The 1840 tax assessments make it possible to compare the land holdings and material possessions of the Cartwrights with others in Texas. John owned over 20,000 acres located in six counties and 9,735 acres in certificates as yet without titles. The tax assessor listed Matthew as liable for taxes on 19,545 located acres in six counties. John still had twenty town lots in San Augustine, six in Sabinetown, and nineteen others in speculative towns, while Matthew owned twelve lots in San Augustine and twenty-eight in other villages. John owned fifteen slaves, while Matthew held only six; both had clocks and watches that were taxable items, and John also had forty-one head of cattle over the untaxed twenty-five animals and a four-wheeled carriage. Robert owned 3,238 acres in San Augustine County, no slaves, three saddle horses, and a watch while George was assessed for three horses, thirty-five cattle, a watch, and sixteen lots divided between San Augustine and Shelbyville, but no acreage.[34]

33. H. Allen Anderson, "The Delaware and Shawnee Indians and the Republic of Texas, 1820–1845," SHQ, XCIV (Oct., 1990), 238–245; Lamar's Message to Both Houses, Dec. 21, 1838, Lamar Papers, II, 353 (quotation); Crocket, Two Centuries, 191–193.

34. Gifford White (ed.), The 1840 Census of the Republic of Texas (Austin: Pemberton Press, 1966), is an edited, published version of the 1840 tax rolls that often serves as a substitute for a decennial census because the first U.S. census for Texas was in 1850. The original tax rolls have been microfilmed, and examination of San Augustine and Sabine counties reveal discrepancies with White's published account. In the 1840 San Augustine roll, for example, John, Matthew, and Robert show totals of land owned in various counties as assessed

At this time John Cartwright was San Augustine's largest landholder of tracts both in and out of the county, followed by Matthew and Elisha Roberts. But in the matter of slave ownership as an indicator of wealth, John ranked only eighth with fifteen chattels, behind Roberts, who with forty-five was the largest slaveowner, and son-in-law William Garrett, the fourth-largest slaveholder in San Augustine County, with twenty-three. John was among the fifteen who owned carriages in San Augustine County, the largest concentration of vehicles in Texas. Carriages remained scarce because of poor roads; second after San Augustine County was Galveston with twelve, Harris with ten, Brazoria with eight, and Nacogdoches with only six.

John Cartwright's land holdings compared with others in Texas found him behind Nacogdoches residents Frost Thorn, who owned over 191,000 acres, and partners Raguet and Logan, with over 50,000. William Hardin's estate in Liberty County claimed similar acreage. A number of Texans held over 40,000. This comparison places the Cartwrights among the moderately wealthy in real and personal property in 1840. With taxes high and times so hard, many men would try to reduce their holdings over the next few years.

Perhaps it was a desire to lessen his tax burden or to settle inheritance matters that prompted John to deed Robert the 2,655-acre-Buckley's Creek tract "where Robert G. Cartwright now lives" on January 1, 1839. The record says title was given "for the natural love and affection which I have for my son . . . and diverse other good causes," common legal phraseology for deeds of gift that avoided putting a monetary value on exchanges between relatives. The deed also noted that John's other heirs had agreed to the transfer, which suggests it was a matter of inheritance. This acreage was part of John's headright that had never been legally recorded, but that was not yet known.[35]

John, overweight and in declining health, made his will 1½ years later on August 21, 1840, assisted by lawyer W. W. Frizzell

---

and collected by the San Augustine assessor (to be sent to the other counties per law) that differ from what appears on the various county lists prepared by White. Assuming that the San Augustine assessor was correct, those figures (in most cases) have been used in the above statements.

35. San Augustine County, Deed Records, E, 113–114.

of San Augustine. Although the document seems uneven at first glance, he most likely felt that it represented a fair division of his property. Documents do not exist detailing property given at the time of his children's marriages, nor is there oral history to illuminate the matter. The 885-acre homesite on the Palo Gacho was left to minor sons Clinton, almost seventeen, and Richard, twelve, along with all of the household goods and livestock, plus the fifteen slaves including four infants. Mary Grimmer Cartwright retained a life interest in the homestead, which could not be sold until after her death and after Richard, the youngest child, reached age twenty-one in 1849. Moreover, the widow was entitled to all money owed to John. Robert was not mentioned with a specific endowment, evidence that the Buckley's Creek acreage was his inheritance, nor was Clementine. Matthew was given one-half league in Jefferson County, Mary Garrett one-half league in Travis County, and George 1,060 acres in Sabine County plus the cancellation of money owed to his father. The rest of John's real estate at the time of his death was to be divided equally between Mary Garrett, Clementine Holman, Robert, and George. Whether or not John was seriously ill at the time he made his will in August is unknown.[36]

In December 1840, John's peace of mind was disturbed when neighbor Burrell J. Thompson filed suit against Cartwright, Elisha Roberts, and others who were living on the old Cristóbal Chonca grant. Thompson had bought whatever claim Lewis Holloway had in the Palo Gacho tract, a claim that had been rejected in 1826. The county court advised John and the others that a resurveying would take place on January 20, 1841. The suit lingered in the court until 1844, three years after John's death, when a judge again declared there was insufficient evidence to support a claim against the current owners.[37]

John died on July 18, 1841, at age fifty-four, and Mary buried her husband of thirty-four years on the bluff overlooking the Palo

36. Will of John Cartwright, Aug. 21, 1840, recorded Aug. 16, 1841, San Augustine County, Probate Records, pp. 187–190, certified typescript copy dated Mar. 2, 1965 (the original has disappeared from the courthouse since 1965; photocopy provided by Patty Cartwright Tennison), CFP.
37. San Augustine County Clerk to Sheriff, n.d., to notify John Cartwright of survey, Sharp Collection (BTHC); *B. J. Thompson v. Elisha Roberts et al.*, San Augustine County, District Court Minutes, A, 2, 37, 38, 55, 57.

Gacho. The summer was exceedingly hot with noontime temperatures above the mid-90s for days at a time. Adolphus Sterne in Nacogdoches noted that a number of people suffered from fever and several died during the month. Four days after John died and on the same day that the San Augustine *Red-Lander* carried his obituary, Amanda's mother passed away at her home northwest of San Augustine. Anne Wigglesworth Holman, age fifty-eight, was buried next to her husband in the Holman family plot on her farm. While no local people identified the sickness that summer, it may have been yellow fever. Two men who left Nacogdoches in September died of the dread disease as soon as they reached Vicksburg.[38]

The two bereaved families, so intertwined by marriage, solaced each other. The adventuresome, immigrant parents were disappearing, but their offspring, also from the eastern states, would spend their lives improving San Augustine and its environs and enjoying the bounty of Texas. During the sixteen years that John Cartwright lived in Texas, he laid the foundation for a comfortable estate for his family through diversified business interests and investments in land. Having weathered the political and military upheavals between 1826 and 1836 and subsequent rumors of Indian attacks, John and his sons faced the economic challenges following the panic of 1837 in the same resolute manner, paying close attention to business. Focusing on commerce, agrarian services, and land trading instead of investing in slaves and growing cotton, the Cartwrights survived the hard times better than some of their neighbors.

38. San Augustine *Red-Lander,* July 22, 29, 1841 (obituaries); McDonald (ed.), *Diary of Adolphus Sterne,* 48, 52, 64.

Six

The Years of Adversity

1841–1846

*W*hen John Cartwright's will was offered for probate on August 16, 1841, Matthew and Robert challenged it. Most likely Matthew consulted one of the lawyers in San Augustine who confirmed what he doubtless suspected: the document was not in keeping with the community property laws adopted by the Republic of Texas in January 1840, whereby the wife was entitled to one-half of the estate amassed during the marriage. Moreover, John had exceeded his testamentary powers in the distribution of his property to his children.[1]

Texans had discovered two advantages in Mexican law to protect property from creditors, and the new Republic adopted both, establishing precedents later extended to other states in the United States. The first was the homestead exemption excluding a man's home and "tools of his trade" from seizure by his creditors and the other was the wife's right to one-half of the fruit of the couple's labors since marriage. In contrast, the laws of the

1. San Augustine County, Probate Minute Book, A, 173, 178.

United States based on English common law generally left widows with less property. Although a Texas wife was unable to manage her one-half of the property during her marriage, as a widow she had full control over one-half of the estate after the payment of debts, as well as the management of the share of the minor children if she was named executor.[2]

John may have composed his own will, but because only a typescript copy remains, there is no way to determine by handwriting. It might well be the work of newcomer William W. Frizzell, who signed the instrument as a witness. Frizzell, a brother-in-law of respected jurist George W. Terrell, had settled north of town in December 1839, but in 1843 moved to Cherokee County where he devoted himself to farming and keeping a hotel, not practicing law. Apparently Frizzell was unaware of the community property provisions under Mexican law or the new law passed in February 1840 defining marital rights in the republic.[3]

Mary Cartwright immediately renounced her executorship in order to contest John's will so as to "receive in common with my children such portions of said estate as we are by law entitled to." The court nevertheless named her interim executor when it set aside the will. Son-in-law William Garrett applied to be coadministrator in October, probably at the widow's request, and when no objection was made, he was confirmed the following month.[4] Few women felt competent to act alone, and because her eldest sons were involved with their own business affairs, they agreed their brother-in-law should assume the task.

In January, the court named three commissioners to divide the estate. They had two inventories to work from. The first was a September listing of assets made by Phil Sublett and two others that failed to include all of the property John owned outside of San Augustine, particularly land jointly owned with others. Values attached to the various items totaled just under $50,000.00,

2. Gammel (comp.), *Laws of Texas,* II, 177–179, 180 (quotation).

3. John Cartwright's will, Aug. 21, 1840 (typescript copy in CFP); Ericson and Ingmire (eds.), *First Settlers of the Republic of Texas,* II, 169; McDonald (ed.), *Diary of Adolphus Sterne,* 138; *Cherokee County History* (Jacksonville: Cherokee County Historical Commission, 1986), 8; U.S. Seventh Census (1850), Cherokee County, Texas (microfilm).

4. San Augustine County, Probate Minutes, A, 180 (quotation), 181, 185, 188.

including $22,233.00 in real estate. A more detailed listing dated November 9, perhaps assembled by Garrett with Matthew's aid, appears in family papers. The real estate alone, excluding the 885-acre homestead, was worth $43,628.00; the value of slaves, tools, livestock, and the home place with its furnishings added $29,180.00, for a grand total of $72,808.38. No list of outstanding debts survives, so what the heirs actually divided is not clear.[5]

The family reached a settlement in January 1842. Because a listing of what each heir received appears in the back of an old Cartwright account book and seems to reflect each one's particular interest, Matthew and his brothers evidently worked closely with the commissioners to apportion the property. Matthew received much of the land that he had held jointly with his father resulting from titles acquired while collecting debts. Mary Cartwright retained the homesite on the Palo Gacho and the most valuable slave, Jordan the blacksmith, along with Jincey, perhaps the wife of Jordan, and her five children. As guardian of Clinton and Richard, Mary also kept a second man and woman. The widow received one wagon and team of oxen, three horses, sixty hogs, and ten head of cattle. In addition to the homestead, valued at $11,505, she received the titles to all of the San Augustine town property, some with buildings, worth almost the same amount. She also kept the New Orleans carriage, bought in 1837 for $350, but she may have given it to her daughter, Mary Garrett. A $500 carriage was assessed to William Garrett in 1843 as administrator of John's estate. For some unexplained reason, in 1842 the widow deeded the same inventory (plus one more slave infant) to her sons, one not yet twenty years old and the other only fourteen.[6]

5. San Augustine County, Probate Minutes, A, 205; "A List of Property belonging to the Estate of John Cartwright, dec., as taken on the 22 day of Sept. 1841," CFP; "An Inventory of property belonging to the Estate of John Cartwright, decd, taken and valued on 9th Nov. 1841," MS, ibid.

6. San Augustine County, Probate Minutes, A, 211; "George W. Cartwright Daybook, 1839–1845," 14-19, CFP; Ledger, 1837–1839, 271, ibid.; San Augustine County, Tax Roll, 1843 (microfilm; CL); San Augustine County, Deed Records, F, 244–245. Subsequent tax records show Garrett with two carriages. Crocket, *Two Centuries*, 87, mistakenly says that John sold Jordan to George Teal and Jacob Garrett, but a deed discarded from the courthouse in 1929 and salvaged by W. G. Sharp reveals that his son, Richard H. Cartwright, sold Jordan to George Teal in 1853 after the death of his mother. Sharp Collection (BTHC).

The household items in the inventory reveal a comfortable life-style but with only a few luxuries, such as John's gold watch and chain valued at $150. A dining table and four small pine tables along with four Windsor chairs and twenty-four ordinary chairs suggest commodious living and dining rooms; the writing desk, the "fine Bureau," and one of the two clocks were probably in the main rooms too, along with the silver spoons, tinware, crockery, five candlesticks, and United States map, which were listed together. Perhaps the spinning wheel and books found farther down the list were also located there. Mary seldom, if ever, used the wheel since factory-loomed fabric and ready-made hosiery were readily available and of better quality than the old-fashioned homespun. Perhaps she kept it for its symbolism of former industriousness or in case of emergency. The sleeping areas were amply furnished with three "fine bedsteads," two common beds, and two cots. Four feather beds, six mattresses, ten pillows with three dozen cases, four dozen sheets, one dozen blankets, ten quilts, four good coverlets, and eighteen calico and checked spreads indicate that Mary Cartwright could provide accommodations for a large number of family and guests, although some of these items may have belonged with the roominghouse. The family's clothes and bedding were stored in a clothes press, two trunks, and two walnut chests. But instead of listing each kitchen item separately, the commissioners lumped them together along with andirons, tongs, water vessels, and three sad irons.[7]

The three adult sons and two daughters received two slaves each along with their bedding and a table plus a few head of cattle. The horses, mules, oxen, plows, and wagons were insufficient for equal distribution, and some chose mules over horses, or a wagon and a mule, or whatever each could best utilize. The land was more difficult to distribute. The remaining 3,611 acres of rich Brazos River land in the David Bright league in Fort Bend County was split into five 722-acre portions, each valued at $2,888, while the other tracts were divided as evenly as possible. Each adult heir received an estate amounting to about $10,000, which included previous donations such as Robert's 2,655 acres

7. "Inventory Household & Kitchen furniture," Jan. 20, 1842, "George W. Cartwright Account Book," CFP.

on Buckley's Creek or the forgiveness of debts. The first figure on each individual's list was labeled "To Property Recd Formerly" or "Amt Inventory Rendered," and another tally listed those same sums as "Recd formerly." The two daughters' shares, of course, were administered by their respective husbands, and in the old account book only the husbands' names appeared.[8]

Matthew, as the eldest son, took his place as the family patriarch and also assumed his father's mantle in town matters. He took his seat as one of the trustees of the University of San Augustine alongside Amanda's brother William W. Holman, Phil Sublett, and other neighbors. The ambitious institution was chartered in June 1837, at the same time as the Independence Academy in Washington County; these were the first institutions of higher learning in Texas. Congress awarded both schools certificates for four unlocated leagues of land to be used as an endowment. Getting the school underway, however, took nearly five years. A suitable building had already been erected in 1839 by developer-builder Sidney A. Sweet, who wanted to sell it to the county for a courthouse, but instead the school trustees bought it in 1842 by giving Sweet one of the leagues. The impressive forty-foot square, two-story frame building crowned with an "observation" cupola dominated a wooded slope on one of the large outlots just east of town along the south side of Main Street.[9]

Finding a suitable faculty was next. The trustees interviewed the Scottish-born Rev. Marcus A. Montrose, a Presbyterian minister, in the summer of 1842. According to local lore, merchant Iredell D. Thomas asked Montrose if he could "figure," while Matthew Cartwright inquired about his ability to calculate interest. These practical questions were answered affirmatively, and he was hired. Classes opened in the fall with Montrose teaching the senior division, which may have included Clinton Cartwright, age nineteen; Richard Cartwright, at age fourteen, would have been among the junior division. The impressive curriculum outlined in the prospectus, but not necessarily implemented in full, included logic, rhetoric, philosophy, mathematics, Greek and Roman writers, and the constitutions of the United States and

8. Ibid.
9. Crocket, *Two Centuries,* 111, 301.

Texas. These were the same kinds of subjects offered at the Tennessee schools attended by Matthew and Robert, courses that exposed students to both classical and practical knowledge.[10]

The University lost Reverend Montrose in mid-1845 when he moved to Nacogdoches to take over its university, but the school continued for two more years under the direction of Rev. James Russell. The university lost some students, however, when a second school, Wesleyan College, a Methodist institution, opened in San Augustine in late 1843. The Methodists, the predominant sect in San Augustine, built an even larger building, forty-by-eighty feet and three stories tall, on the north side of Main Street one block east of the University of San Augustine. Its "female" department opened in the former Isaac Campbell house fronting on Main Street opposite the university, a handsome home that Matthew Cartwright would acquire within a few years. But civic pride and even a desire to make San Augustine the "Athens of Texas" could not support two schools with similar advanced classes, a grammar school for those under age twelve, and a separate girls' school. The university closed in 1847, as did its Methodist rival; the latter had graduated two men, one being Franklin B. Sexton who became a lawyer and also represented Texas in the Confederate Congress. After such an ambitious beginning, San Augustine residents were chagrined when the town went without an institution of higher learning for the next three years.[11]

Besides its interest in education, the community was active in politics. In 1841 citzens including Sam Houston deplored the Lamar administration's "useless extravagance and . . . most unprincipled profligacy." A group of Redlanders met on April 5, 1841, at the request of Stephen W. Blount and Kenneth L. Anderson, lately the customs collector and now candidate for Congress, to nominate the Old Hero for president. Houston spoke at a rally in town on April 19, and two days later, on the anniversary of the Battle of San Jacinto, he addressed a crowd at the old stone fort in Nacogdoches. Houston was not as popular in Nacogdoches as he once had been because of his attacks against land speculators in former Cherokee lands when he was San Augustine's represen-

10. Ibid., 301–303.
11. Ibid., 305–308.

tative in Congress during 1839–1840. On election day, September 6, Nacogdoches residents voted 212 to 105 for Harris County's David G. Burnet, but San Augustine and the rest of Texas preferred the Hero of San Jacinto and gave Houston a landslide of 7,508 votes to Burnet's 2,574. The president-elect and his bride of one year remained in San Augustine through September, visiting at the town house of Iredell D. Thomas and also the country home of Phil Sublett.[12]

How Matthew and Robert Cartwright voted in the election is unknown, but given the circumstances, they probably favored Houston. Robert, who now lived about three or four miles northeast of town on the former J. B. Dillard place, had been elected justice of the peace for his neighborhood on February 1, 1841, a position he held for one year. In September 1842, doubtless as a reward for Holman and Cartwright support, President Houston named Amanda's brother, twenty-five-year-old Sanford Holman, customs collector at San Augustine to replace John G. Berry, who had resigned. The position paid $800 per year plus 15 percent commission, a comfortable income for a young man.[13]

Collecting tariff duties on goods coming from the United States was as unpopular in East Texas during the republic as it had been under Mexican Texas. Desperate for income, the first Congress of the Republic of Texas levied ad valorem duties on both necessities and luxuries except for food, tools, and building materials. When Lamar became president at the end of 1838, the economic crisis was deepening, and he ignored calls from eastern Texas to allow free trade. On December 17, 1840, sixty-three San Augustine citizens petitioned the Texas Congress to abolish the "onerous & Burthensome" tariff in favor of a direct tax to support the government. Although none of the Cartwrights signed

12. Llerena B. Friend, *Sam Houston: The Great Designer* (Austin: University of Texas Press, 1969), 100–101 (quotation); McDonald (ed.), *Diary of Adolphus Sterne*, 57–58, 62.

13. *Compiled Index to Elected and Apppointed Officials of the Republic of Texas, 1835–1846* (Austin: Texas State Archives, 1981), 21, 59; San Augustine County, Deed Records, G, 221; Case no. 986, *Sam Houston et al. v. Wm Holman et al.*, Exhibit A, accounts of Sanford Holman (copy provided by clerk of district court to Clementine Holman), Sharp Collection (BTHC); McDonald (ed.), *Diary of Adolphus Sterne*, 78.

the document, many of their friends did, including John W. Holman, Phil Sublett, Elisha Roberts's sons, and fellow merchant I. D. Thomas.[14]

The Congress, however, agreed that the tariff must remain to produce revenue until a loan was secured from a foreign country, a hope that bore little success during the worldwide economic depression. In fact duties increased in 1841 when the Texas Congress doubled many specific tariffs and raised the ad valorem rate to 45 percent. While some San Augustine and Nacogdoches importers registered their manifest lists and paid their customs duties with deputies at Sabinetown, San Augustine, and Nacogdoches, others tried to evade the tax, and the collector at San Augustine took them to court.[15]

Sanford was in trouble within ten months of his appointment and was removed from office by July 30, 1843. No details exist explaining the difficulties in either personal or official records, but the republic believed his accounts were short over $2,500. Copies of his quarterly reports beginning in October 1842 reveal that he had deducted and paid his commission and that of his deputies out of his collections, but that was not a crime. Perhaps serious miscalculations occurred in the collection of exchequer bills for tax purposes; they were valued at their ever-changing market rate, which was twenty-five cents on the dollar in mid-1842. At the time of Sanford's dismissal, the republic's treasurer figured Holman's salary for nine months and twenty-nine days at $664.44, but then deducted $312.34, the amount of former commission claims. Altogether, Sanford owed the republic $2,679.34.[16]

President Houston named a replacement, William M. Hurt, on July 11, 1843, several weeks before Sanford Holman's removal from office. Because of the lack of details, one can only assume that the blow to Sanford's pride was devastating, and the fact that he died on December 23, 1843, added to the family tragedy. While no mention of suicide is recorded, it was a strong possibility given family events during this time. Sanford's brother-in-law Isaac Campbell had died in September 1843 of unspecified

14. Webb, Carroll, and Branda (eds.), *Handbook of Texas*, II, 706; Petition, Dec. 17, 1840 (quotation), Memorials and Petitions (TSL).

15. San Augustine Court Records, "Loose Papers" (Special Collections, Ralph W. Steen Library, Stephen F. Austin University).

16. *Sam Houston et al. v. Wm Holman et al.*

causes after suffering severe economic losses. Sanford Holman left his widow, Clementine Cartwright, age twenty-four, with two small children, Anna, four, and William, barely one year old. The probate court named the widow and Sanford's brother, William W. Holman, administrators on January 16, 1844. The Treasury Department pursued the Holman debt in the spring and summer of 1845 by forwarding evidence to Oran M. Roberts, the district attorney of the Fifth Judicial District that served San Augustine. The republic won its suit and Sanford Holman's heirs became liable for the debt.[17]

At the time of his death, Sanford was living in the old Holman house northwest of town, not far from the popular Stedham race track, where he was usually in attendance. Afterward, Clementine and her children returned to her mother's home on the Palo Gacho because she had little means of support. During the first years of their marriage, before the deaths of John Cartwright and Anna Holman in 1841, tax rolls reveal that Sanford owned two adult slaves, three horses, and a watch but no land. Both Sanford and Clementine inherited land from their parents that totaled about 15,000 acres in 1842. The year after Sanford's death, Clementine owed taxes on four slaves and one silver watch as reported by her brother, the administrator of the estate, plus acreage. The continuing hard times slowed land sales, but Clementine managed to pay some debts by transferring some acreage, while other tracts were sold at sheriff sales for back taxes and other debts. By 1846, the struggling widow owned only 1,476 acres valued at a mere $369, an average of twenty-five cents per acre.[18]

While the Holman tragedies absorbed the Cartwrights and their extended family, a rash of violence known as the Regulator-Moderator War erupted in Shelby County, some of which spilled over into San Augustine and caused concern among residents. The trouble began in 1838 over fradulent land claims issued by

17. *Compiled Index,* 62; *San Augustine County, Texas, 1828–1940, Probate Cases* (Friends of the San Augustine Library, n.d.), 68; James B. Shaw to Wm. M. Hurt, Mar. 8, 1845, O.M. Roberts Papers (BTHC); James B. Shaw to Oran M. Roberts, July 16, 1845, ibid.

18. Adolphus Sterne spent the night at Holman's on Nov. 24, 1842, after a day at the track. McDonald (ed.), *Diary of Adolphus Sterne,* 128; San Augustine County, Tax Rolls, 1837, 1839, 1840, 1843, 1844, 1845, 1846 (microfilm; CL).

Shelby County officials that were purchased by trusting persons who found later that they had been swindled. In an area populated in part by unsavory men accustomed to defying the law and seeking revenge, a series of vendetta-like murders took place between 1838 and 1840. Judges who endeavored to enforce the law in Shelby County were intimidated and mob rule was the result. Some men grew angry over the inability or disinclination of public officials to end the corruption and violence; these men became vigilantes, calling themselves "Regulators."[19] The name had been used by a somewhat similar group in the back country of North Carolina between 1768 and 1771 protesting the arrogant disregard of their needs by the tidewater gentry who governed the colony. Indeed, some of the Shelby County Regulators may have had grandfathers who had been Regulators at the earlier date.

The opponents of the Regulators first called themselves "Reformers," and later "Moderators." Some Moderators, such as their leader, Col. J. J. Cravens, were less inclined toward revenge, wanting instead to restore legitimate law and order. One contemporary believed that Moderators tended to be family men with property, at least more so than were the Regulators.[20]

In 1841 Charles W. "Watt" Moorman assumed leadership of the Regulators after the murder of Charles W. Jackson, the founder of the movement. The six-foot-tall, reckless son of a respectable Mississippi planter fled to Shelby County to avoid arrest for forgery, a hanging offense at this time. The muscular, charismatic leader with shoulder-length hair and piercing black eyes always wore a military coat, pistols, and a Bowie knife. It was Moorman who ambushed John M. Bradley, veteran of 1832 and 1835, outside an evening Baptist meeting at the Masonic Hall in San Augustine in 1844. Each man had sworn to kill the other "on sight" after Bradley abandoned the Moderators and moved to San Augustine. Bradley, not without faults, died almost instantly of the gunshot wound while Moorman escaped to Shelby County.[21]

19. Dr. Levi Ashcroft, "History of the Moderators and Regulators," unpublished MS, [ca. 1850s] (typescript; BTHC); Yoakum, *History of Texas,* II, 439.

20. Ashcroft, "Moderators and Regulators," 37.

21. Ibid., 20, 38 (1st quotation), 40 (2nd quotation).

Riding high on his popularity in 1844 and against the proposed annexation of Texas to the United States, Moorman wanted to form an independent country. The Regulator movement had changed from personal vengeance to civil rebellion. In the surrounding counties the charismatic Regulator chief recruited supporters who had also fled from the United States and who might face prosecution if annexation occurred. In July 1844, the rebellious Regulator governing body in Shelby County proscribed twenty-five residents, charging them with disturbing the peace and resisting Regulator law. The indicted group included the sheriff and a number of Moderators who were ordered to leave Shelby County within two weeks or face death. The Regulators built a fort three miles southwest of Shelbyville in August and sent to Harrison County for reinforcements. Likewise, the more law-abiding Moderators recruited men from San Augustine, bringing the total on each side to perhaps 150 men. The Moderators attacked the log fort, forcing the Regulators to retreat to their campgrounds near Hilliard's Spring northwest of Shelbyville.[22]

When word about the insurrection reached President Houston at Washington-on-the-Brazos, then the capital of the republic, he started for the Redlands. He reached San Augustine on August 15, 1844, and issued a proclamation ordering the combatants in Shelby County to "lay down their arms, and retire to their respective homes." The following morning he sent an open letter "to My Countrymen," warning the Regulators that he would "suppress all insurrectionary movements" by ordering the militia to arms. He also advised the Moderators against vigilante activities: "If persons . . . have rendered themselves obnoxious to the laws, it remains with the laws to punish them—but not for individuals . . . [to] . . . assume to themselves powers which belong to the constituted authorities." He added that as yet he did not have all of the facts of the controversy at hand and would "therefore abstain from making any decision as to the merits or demerits of the parties." Nevertheless, if they did not disperse immediately, return home, and abstain from further violence, the president would have to take measures "unpleasant to myself." Four days later he ordered the San Augustine militia commanded by Col. Travis G. Broocks to march immediately to Shelby County

22. Ibid., 42–55; Crocket, *Two Centuries*, 199.

to restore order and also called out the militia in Sabine, Rusk, and Nacogdoches counties.[23]

The San Augustine men had mixed emotions as they hurried north. This was a civil war, and they might have to fire at friends and neighbors. When Broocks reached the Moderator camp, he ordered them to lay down their arms, which they did immediately. Following orders, Broocks arrested ten leaders and sent them under guard to Shelbyville. The San Augustine men then marched toward Moorman's Regulator camp but found it deserted. Gen. James Smith, commander of eastern Texas, and the three other militia units arrived, making a force of several hundred. Nine Regulator leaders voluntarily surrendered and joined the ten captive Moderators, all of whom were sent to San Augustine. The San Augustine militia finally captured Moorman, and he joined the others in San Augustine to appear before President Houston. After a stern reprimand, the twenty leaders were released on bail and on August 26, 1844, Houston returned to the Brazos. As soon as Moorman was released, he was arrested by the San Augustine sheriff for killing John Bradley and was taken to jail to await trial. A jury eventually acquitted Moorman on the grounds of self-defense when he convinced his listeners that Bradley had previously threatened him.[24]

While peace generally prevailed in Shelby County because of the continued presence of mounted militia through December 1844, bad feeling remained. Finally District Judge William B. Ochiltree and other eminent East Texans met with leaders of the two factions and drew up a document designed to ease the tension. Two prominent men from each side signed the paper denouncing the recent anarchy. They promised to aid civil authorities in maintaining law and order and to end animosity. The four swore never to use the terms "Regulator" and "Moderator" and to forgive and forget past activities. The pledge was copied and circulated throughout the area and was endorsed subse-

23. Sam Houston to "The Moderators and Regulators" of Shelby County, Aug. 15, 1844; Sam Houston to My Countrymen, Aug. 16, 1844, in Williams and Barker (eds.), *Writings of Sam Houston,* IV, 361 (1st and 2nd quotations), 361–362 (3rd quotation), 362 (5th and 6th quotations).

24. Ashcroft, "Moderators and Regulators," 58–61; Sam Houston to Gen. James Smith, Aug. 26, 1844, in Williams and Barker (eds.), *Writings of Sam Houston,* IV, 367; Sam Houston to Washington D. Miller, Aug. 26, 1844, ibid.

quently by a large number of citizens. Nevertheless, cautious visitors to Shelbyville always carried their guns.[25]

Robert Cartwright, convinced that the trouble was over, moved to Shelbyville, where his wife's family lived, in 1845. Besides farming and raising livestock, he entered into a partnership in a saloon and store in town. Three years earlier Robert had sold his sawmill and gristmills and the 2,655 acres on Buckley's Creek for $5,000. Not long afterward, he sold his 250-acre homesite northeast of San Augustine to Eliza P. Lovell. In 1845 Robert owed $19.64 in taxes to the Shelby County assessor-collector for nine slaves, two work horses, a herd of cattle, and 10,940 acres of land in various counties, about two-thirds the amount of land Matthew owned. Doubtless there was rivalry between the pair, which might explain Robert's departure from San Augustine. Over the next few years, as times improved, Robert gained in wealth and changed mercantile partners several times. When he and Mary had first moved to Shelbyville, they had only one daughter, Amanda, born in 1843, but two sons, Matthew and Robert, Jr., arrived in 1847 and 1849 respectively.[26]

Robert took a small interest in the Kingsborough project sponsored by Dr. William P. King and his Southern Land Company located in present-day Kaufman County. King headed a group of Mississippi speculators who had acquired certificates for 115 leagues of land (509,220 acres) that they intended to locate between the three branches of the Trinity River in what was then upper Nacogdoches County. In 1840, after the Indians had been expelled from northeastern Texas, a surveying party built a fortified building, King's fort, near the site of present-day Kaufman, soon known as Kingsborough. Robert located his 1838 headright league northeast of the settlement as a speculation. Dr. King left his family in San Augustine while he traveled between Mississippi and Kingsborough endeavoring to attract more settlers. Unfortunately for the project, King became ill with yellow fever after a visit to Nacogdoches and died in September 1841 in Vicksburg, Mississippi. Dr. King's second wife and the four children of his first marriage remained in San Augustine, and

---

25. Ashcroft, "Moderators and Regulators," 62–64.

26. San Augustine County, Deed Records, E, 113, F, 374, G, 221; Shelby County, Tax Rolls, 1845, 1846, 1848 (microfilm; CL).

in February 1842 Robert petitioned the probate court for letters of administration on King's estate in order to collect debts owed to him, and also to become guardian of Samuel and John Randolph King. Although Robert resigned three months later, he maintained an interest in helping the orphaned King boys.[27]

Matthew's business affairs absorbed all of his energy during the continuing hard times. Around the time of his father's death in June 1841, Matthew had received a form letter from his New Orleans agent, Peyroux, Arcueil & Company, announcing that they had reopened for business after having had to close due to bankruptcy. Matthew had sent them forty-seven bales of cotton in May 1841, some of which they had sold and credited his account with by July, when they reopened. Matthew still owed them a large sum for merchandise sent to San Augustine, however, and Peyroux, writing in the common business style of the day, assured Matthew that "feeling every confidence in your integrity, we are satisfied that you will do all in your power to liquidate it at as early a day as possible."[28]

Matthew, however, was unable to send either money or cotton because of a bad crop year and also family matters. Merchants, including Matthew, usually totaled their books in March and November and sent their customers statements or reminders of their indebtedness. In November 1841 Peyroux noted that "it is some time since we had the pleasure of hearing from you. . . . We regret that our late difficulties . . . compels [sic] us to press somewhat urgently for balances due from our friends." Matthew could do nothing, and at the end of February 1842, Peyroux wrote again: "Annexed we beg to duplicate our respects of

27. Webb, Carroll, and Branda (eds.), *Handbook of Texas*, I, 960 (the *Handbook* lists three W. P. Kings and has several errors); Kate Efnor, "Historical Sketch of Kaufman County," *The American Sketch Book, An Historical and Home Monthly* (Austin: American Sketch Book Publishing House, 1880), V, 36, 37; "George W. Cartwright" account book, 1837–1839, 218, 301, CFP; Undated hand-drawn map of the "King Surveys, Kaufman Co. Texas," ibid.; Wm B. Martin to M. Henderson Moore Mar. 11, 1841, given to R. G. Cartwright, May 3, 1842, ibid.; Petition of R. G. Cartwright to Probate Court, San Augustine County, Sept. 1843, ibid.; McDonald (ed.), *Diary of Adolphus Sterne*, 54, 64; San Augustine County, Probate Records, A, 139, in W.P.A. file (BTHC).

28. Peyroux, Arcueil & Co. to Matthew Cartwright, July 6, 1841, CFP.

November 6. . . . We ask your consideration . . . this debt being a heavy and old one."[29]

Matthew went to New Orleans in March 1842 determined to make arrangements with his creditors by mortgaging several large tracts totalling almost 12,000 acres of land to secure his indebtedness of $9,590. He signed notes promising to pay installments beginning in one year at 10 percent interest and to be cleared in April 1845. While this was reasonable and generous on the part of the New Orleans creditor who did not want Texas land, Matthew failed to make his first payment of $1,640 on April 1, 1843. Peyroux wrote a week later, "Disappointed, we shall beg of you to endeavor to put us in funds for at least a part of this amount being very much oppressed at this moment on account of the present low rate of Cotton and the want of Collections." The agent reminded Matthew that the mortgage "was merely a formality because we have . . . more confidence in the morality of our Correspondents then [*sic*] in the property they mortgage."[30] It is clear that Matthew was not the only one in debt to Peyroux and that even New Orleans merchants did not fully comprehend the long-term impact of the depressed times.

The hard-pressed agent sent Matthew a reminder in June 1843, tactfully adding that his April 10 letter must have miscarried and therefore he was sending a duplicate. Matthew, of course, had received it but could make no reply in either April or June, being unable to send money or cotton. Finally, after waiting one year, Peyroux, Arcueil & Company sent an agent, Leon Chabert, to San Augustine. "All what Mr. Chabert shall do for the settling of our business," Peyroux warned sternly, "shall be duly approved by us before hand." The tone of the letter was cold, and the writer reminded Matthew that the partial payment that he had made prior to the mortgage in 1842 was in personal drafts on which the firm made no profit. At that time, Matthew had offered to pay in Texas treasury notes which he was willing to discount as much as 50 percent. Peyroux, however, thought such a gesture unwarranted and suggested that Matthew use the Texas money to buy cotton to ship to them. Now, Peyroux said,

29. Peyroux, Arcueil & Co. to Matthew Cartwright, Nov. 6, 1841, CFP; same to same, Feb. 28, 1842, ibid.

30. San Augustine County, Deed Records, F, 116–120; Peyroux, Arcueil & Co. to Matthew Cartwright, Nov. 10, 1843, CFP.

they had lost faith in Matthew but they "still expect more from you than from many others." As of April 20, 1844, Matthew owed them $11,550.46 including interest.[31]

When Matthew received this unpleasant letter from the hand of Leon Chabert, negotiations were in progress for the United States to annex Texas. For Matthew and other debtors, however, the blessings of annexation were mixed: Peyroux would find it easier to collect the debt.

The proposed annexaton of Texas to the United States dominated politics in Texas in 1844. Ever since the Mexican raids on San Antonio in the spring and fall of 1842, Texans felt vulnerable and wanted the security implied by being a part of the United States. President Houston, without funds and opposed to confronting Mexico, reluctantly ordered a force to the Rio Grande to appease public opinion. But his worst fears were confirmed when an unauthorized contingent of Texans crossed the river and was captured. The survivors of what was known as the Mier Expedition were marched to prison near Mexico City. Many Texans felt that the republic was so weak and vulnerable that annexation to the United States was the only recourse.

In early 1844, when certain politicians in the United States suggested that the time was auspicious for annexation, President Houston dispatched San Augustine resident James Pinckney Henderson to Washington, D.C., to aid chargé d'affaires Isaac Van Zandt of Harrison County in the negotiations. Old Sam was cautious: having once been the abandoned bride at the altar of annexation in 1837, as he described the ill-fated earlier effort to join the United States, he began a series of conferences with the agents from France and Great Britain as a means to explore all options and keep the United States guessing as to his motives. Houston even sent agents to Mexico to discuss its recent offer to allow Texas autonomy if the recalcitrant province would return to the Mexican republic.[32]

31. Peyroux, Arcueil & Co. to Matthew Cartwright, June 15, 1843, CFP; same to same, Apr. 20, 1844, ibid.

32. For the best discussion of annexation, see Friend, *Sam Houston: The Great Designer,* 115–160; for the analogy of Texas as a bride, see Sam Houston to Andrew Jackson, Feb. 16, 1844, in Williams and Barker (eds.), *Writings of Sam Houston,* IV, 265.

Houston's masterful subterfuge was successful. When the U.S. Senate voted against the proposed treaty of annexation in 1844 because of pressure from northern states opposed to the addition of such a large slave state, canny politicians found an alternate method. Annexation supporters, fearing that Texas might become a satellite of France or Great Britain, proposed acquiring the Lone Star republic by a joint resolution of Congress, which required a simple majority in both houses instead of the impossible-to-achieve two-thirds majority needed to approve a treaty in the U.S. Senate. The joint resolution passed at the end of February 1845, just before the inauguration of President James K. Polk of Tennessee, who had campaigned in favor of annexation. Mexico had never recognized the independence of Texas and, viewing the annexation of its province by the United States as an act of aggression, immediately broke diplomatic relations. In June 1845, just before the Texas convention met to accept the offer of annexation, President Polk ordered Gen. Zachary Taylor to move his troops from Fort Jesup to Corpus Christi to protect Texas residents. Doubtless the Cartwrights gathered to watch the U.S. Army march through San Augustine on its way south.[33]

San Augustine sent James Pinckney Henderson and Nicholas Henry Darnell to the Texas convention called for July 4, 1845, to approve annexation and to write a state constitution suitable for joining the Union. On October 13, 1845, Texas voters approved annexation 4,254 to 257 and ratified the proposed state constitution 4,174 to 312. In San Augustine 227 men voted for annexation and 13 against; the constitution was approved by a similar margin, 221 to 5. The United States Congress accepted the constitution and on December 29, 1845, Texas joined the union as the twenty-eighth state.

Texans chose Henderson as the first governor of the Lone Star State, and on February 21, 1846, Sam Houston and Thomas Jefferson Rusk became Texas's first two United States senators, while David S. Kaufman, who practiced law in Nacogdoches and later Sabinetown, represented the Eastern District of Texas in the United States House of Representatives. The Redlands were well represented in the seats of government.

33. Friend, *Sam Houston: The Great Designer*, 158.

Meanwhile, last-minute efforts by the United States to buy Texas from Mexico and set the Rio Grande as the boundary failed. While the Nueces River at Corpus Christi was the traditional boundary between the province of Texas and Tamaulipas and Coahuila under Spain and Mexico, the Texans had unilaterally claimed the Rio Grande as its border since 1836. In 1846 Mexico, not recognizing the independence of Texas, regarded the Sabine River as its boundary with the United States; thus, when President Polk ordered Taylor to move from Corpus Christi to the Rio Grande, war was inevitable. Skirmishes between the two forces took place in April, and in May 1846 President Polk asked Congress to declare war. General Taylor requested that Texas supply two regiments of infantry and two of cavalry, and the Texas legislature granted Governor Henderson a leave of absence in order to take command of state troops.

In San Augustine some seventy to eighty men, including Amanda's brother William Holman, who always seemed ready for military action, joined a company of mounted volunteers. Other Cartwright neighbors going to war were Samuel and John R. King, the latter a clerk at the store of Travis G. Broocks, whose oldest son John also joined; John G. Berry; a son of Callaway Dean; and Richard F. Slaughter, who would later marry Clementine Cartwright Holman's daughter. The legislature provided that the volunteers elect their own officers, and they chose Otis M. Wheeler, the thirty-three-year-old brother of District Judge Royal T. Wheeler, as their captain. Otis Wheeler would become a Cartwright in-law within three years. The San Augustine contingent finally rode into Taylor's camp at Point Isabel in June 1846 in company with groups from other communities.

The San Augustine recruits became Company A of the Second Regiment of Texas Mounted Volunteers commanded by Col. George T. Wood and were sworn into the United States Army for three months' service on June 24, 1846. Before they mustered out on October 2, they had marched up the Rio Grande to Mier and then southwest to Monterrey, a distance of almost four hundred miles, where they forced the Mexicans to surrender on September 24. Fighting continued elsewhere, but because the ninety-day enlistments were up and the Texans were starting for home, General Taylor lost most of the volunteers, which postponed the end of the war for more than a year.[34] Most Texans, however, felt that the war was over after the victory at Monterrey and settled down to enjoy their new status as citizens of the United States.

34. Charles D. Spurlin (comp.), *Texas Veterans in the Mexican War: Muster Rolls of Texas Military Units* (Corpus Christi: privately published by author, 1984), 35. Charles P. Roland, *Albert Sidney Johnston: Soldier of Three Republics* (Austin: University of Texas Press, 1964), 125–139, gives good details about the Texas troops.

Seven

Surviving the Trials
of Job

1846-1849

*T*he year 1846 was not good for Matthew. In the waning days of the republic, the district attorney of the Fifth Judicial District called on Matthew to pay $1,000 in customs duties stemming from an incident in 1844. Matthew had weathered similar charges in 1843, as had other local merchants when the local court was reluctant to prosecute. Surviving court records fail to explain details, but local antipathy toward the collection of customs duties might have intimidated both prosecutors and witnesses. Bending to pressure on January 10, 1846, Matthew promised to pay, but failed to do so, perhaps hoping that the pending annexation of Texas to the United States would somehow make the payment moot. The prosecutor finally petitioned the court to bring Matthew to trial at the spring term meeting at San Augustine. Incomplete records fail to show whether or not the case was heard or if Matthew paid the duties.[1]

1. Incomplete petition to Judge Royal T. Wheeler of the Fifth District Court, Spring term 1846, *Republic of Texas v. Matthew Cartwright,* 4 pp., San Augustine District Court Records (Special Collections, Ralph W. Steen Library,

The inventory of goods Matthew allegedly imported on March 1, 1844, provides a glimpse of the life and needs of San Augustine residents. Among the items were: $250 worth of ready-made clothing; $500 in hats, bonnets, boots, and shoes; $1,500 in "callico" [sic], cotton, woolen, and silk yard goods; $250 in "saddels" [sic]; $500 in hemp bagging and "roap" [sic]; $250 in manufactured tobacco; 5,000 cigars, both Spanish and American made; 1,500 pounds of brown sugar; 400 pounds of coffee; 50 pounds of spices; 200 pounds of bar soap; 250 pounds of sperm candles; 20 barrels of flour; 100 bushels of salt; 130 gallons of whiskey; and 250 gallons of brandy. This inventory reveals that, despite the economic hardship that was prevalent in 1844, some Redlanders were living in style and comfort, providing a demand for the luxury items that Matthew could supply.

In addition to the annoyance of the January dispute over the old customs charge, Matthew also had to settle a debt owed to brother Robert in April. Matthew had paid his indebtedness to Robert by endorsing three IOUs made by others: one for $1,787, another for $280, and a third for $396, totaling $2,463. This sort of exchange was common where money was in short supply, but when Robert could not collect the sums from the original makers, Matthew became legally liable. For some reason, the older brother was unwilling or unable to pay and in the litigious atmosphere of the times, Robert took him to court. The judge ordered Matthew to pay the notes, and by April 15 Robert received the money and surrendered the notes to Matthew. Because the documents remained in his papers, it appears that Matthew was also unable to collect from those who had made the original notes.[2]

Since his difficulty with Peyroux, Arcueil & Company, Matthew no longer visited New Orleans—where he might be arrested—to buy goods for the store. Instead, his partner, Samuel T. Burrus, went to the Crescent City to purchase merchandise and arranged for the disposition of cotton. Five or six years younger than Matthew, with a wife and several children, Burrus was buying an interest in the store. Burrus journeyed to New Orleans early in 1846 where he arranged business with commission mer-

Stephen F. Austin University). Numerous similar charges can be found against merchants between 1842 and 1845.

2. Robert G. Cartwright receipts to Matthew, Apr. 1 and 15, 1846, CFP.

chants Bonner & Smith. But whereas in the 1830s Matthew had purchased several thousand dollars' worth of goods for the store, Burrus carried only $323 in cash plus thirty-two bales of cotton that had been warehoused at Grand Ecore. The new steamboat landing west of Natchitoches had become popular with Texas merchants since the main channel of the Red River had changed course, leaving the old French town without navigable water. At the current price of six cents per pound for cotton at New Orleans, the bales brought only $871, which, when added to his cash, totaled not quite $1,200. With that sum, Burrus paid what he owed for goods previously purchased and used the rest as partial payment for new stock to take back to San Augustine. Burrus returned to New Orleans in July with $700 in notes and coins, a sum that Matthew loaned Burrus at 4 percent interest per month to be repaid as soon as possible. That meager sum included $180.50 in gold, $59.50 in silver, $235.00 in bank notes issued by banks in the United States, plus two notes made by prominent individuals. In October 1846 Burrus paid Matthew $50 against his debt, all that he could manage because business was slow, and he was unable to clear his account until the next year.[3]

Amid the depressed economy and the stifling summer heat, and approaching his fortieth birthday, Matthew began keeping a journal on July 22, 1846, noting business transactions, listing things to be done, and also recording his thoughts. He continued the diary, begun at a time when his oldest sons were ill, for only ten days, but it is a revealing document that illustrates both his business practices and loving devotion to his family. One fact is clear: Matthew reveled in the intricacies of sharp trading, whether for land, livestock, or produce, always maneuvering for profit. At the same time, he was a tender caregiver towards his children and toward an ill slave woman, although he worried about the cost of the slave's treatment and feared losing her productivity. Matthew's journal pictures life in San Augustine and also offers insight into Matthew's personal philosophy as shaped by his brief education and ongoing reading. While he had not yet joined the

3. Fragment of a contract between Matthew Cartwright and Samuel T. Burrus, Jan. 1, 1845, loose sheet in back of Ledger no. 10, CFP; U.S. Seventh Census (1850), San Augustine County, Texas (microfilm); Receipt of Burrus for cash and cotton, Jan. 22, 1846, CFP.

order of Freemasons, some of his phrases echo its ritual. What follows is an edited version of excerpts from the ten loose sheets, the only evidence that he ever kept a diary. Matthew's nineteenth-century grammar and spelling have been preserved.[4]

"July 22nd [1846]: Rose at 7 oclock. Made a slight promise in my mind that I would rise sooner. Americus and Columbus [ages six and almost nine] on the mend Though doubtful whether they will recover without more Medicine. [Dr. J. T.] Patterson has been their phisician; though he is in debt to me, more than he can possibly charge . . . Yet he has called on me . . . for a little coffee, making a poor mouth. . . ."

Matthew noted arrangements he had made with two local men regarding land and letters to be written to three others in distant counties. He worried that annexation to the United States and its implied promise of protection against the Plains Indians would make men restless for cheaper land on the frontier, which would injure San Augustine's economy. "Today I have seen or heard of ten or twelve persons going up on Trinity, Looking [for] Land to move to, indicating a decline in population of this County this fall." This observation in 1846 was prophetic and helps explain San Augustine's decline in importance.

"I consider the day rather an idle one though my Mind has been engaged or employed with my sick boys, reading, Writing, and Reflecting on Matters of interest Generally. It is now after Nine oclock and my usual bed time. My humble thanks for the many blessings I enjoy and my prayers to do more and better in time to come. So may it be."

The next morning, July 23, he arose at six A.M., read from the works of Roman poet Marcus A. Lucan (39–65 A.D.), and went into his garden to sharpen his pocket knife. "Now 7 oclock, ready for Brakefast." The San Augustine *Red-Lander* arrived, which Matthew read before writing a deed for a portion of one of the large outlots that ringed the village. He completed an arrangement with James Perkins, who "Rented . . . the Lovell property [brother Robert's old home] for one Year for One Hundred . . . [dollars, and] improvements he makes to be valued at a fair . . .

4. Journal, July 22–29, Sept. 1–2, 1846, CFP. Editorial identifications are from Crocket, *Two Centuries;* census tracts; or information derived from Cartwright letters.

price . . . out of the Rent." If Perkins preferred buying instead of renting, he could pay $350 before November and would not have to pay any rent. After noting several other pending transactions, Matthew continued: "Boys mending. Fine shower this evening . . . wife out of sugar. The day has not resulted in much of profit or interest." Then he made a list of tasks to be performed: beginning lawsuits against three men; posting his account books; consulting the tax assessor; buying some calico and sugar; and several other reminders about trading land, slaves, and livestock. Matthew, like many men of this period, bought the groceries and dry goods for his family.

"July 24th 1846: Rose . . . before 6. Walked in the Garden to the union peach Tree and ate 1 doz or more . . . Wife and children came in and joined in the Sport. Found that the apple Tree Rob^d of all . . . except two. Returned from Garden at 7 oclock. To day wife's Birthday." Amanda was twenty-eight, married for almost ten years, and the mother of five children. Matthew went to town and "Procured 16 lbs Sugar, . . . 5 [cents] worth calico . . . [and played] . . . 1 Game Billiards. Sold . . . 3520 ft. plank for 95$." He also heard the latest gossip, which he recorded: that A. J. Fowler, who taught mathematics at Wesleyan College, "and old Parson [Francis] Wilson is at Loggerheads, and that Fowler will sue the Westleyan [*sic*] College for six hundred Dollars." Matthew was relieved that he did not sit on the board of that school.

"I have ate more peaches to day than any day for 5 years past, apple dumplings from apples of our raising for Dinner. Verry fine indeed." The sugar had been put to use and more apples must have been found.

"I was under the impression that Columbus and Americus were getting well, but find that Americus quite unwell in evening. So that I have given one dose medicine and expect to give him another." Matthew's younger brother Clinton and his wife, Elvira "Ella" Holman, visited after supper, and when they left Matthew resumed his journal. "Now 40 minutes after nine O.C. at Night and the second dose of calomel [mercurous chloride, a purgative] and dover powders [ipecac and opium for pain or to cause sweat] given Americus for fever and worms."

Matthew was a little gloomy after a rain that threatened both hay and cotton. "I consider the Notes taken to day verry indifferent and the day rather Barren of anything important . . . [and]

being warm and a dull season of the year . . . does not fully account for it. . . . I now close my remarks for the day, Surrendering myself to the Stream of time. . . . If I Live I shall have in Course of five Years some interest and to me important things to note. May our father guide and direct for the welfare and Glory of all his Creators. Closed.

"25th July 1846: Awake at 1/2 after 4, to Sleep till 5, then in bed and awake till 6 O.C. then Rose. . . . Found both Jane's [a new slave, age sixteen] eyes badly affected, so much that I fear that she will go blind.[5] Preparing Irish potatoe patch for Turnips. Give Americus Oil & Spt[s] Turpentine, Shaved and put on a clean shirt, went to the Store . . . [and after reading newspaper] . . . Swept the store and then came to Brakefast."

The concerned father believed Meck was better "from the operation of Medicine Given Last Night. . . ." Matthew completed details for some mule trading and delivered twenty-one barrels of corn to a customer, payment due January 1. Another man borrowed eighteen barrels of "old" corn and promised to pay with twenty barrels of "New Corn" at harvest time. Matthew went home at noon to find Meck better, "his Medicine having operated twice. . . . He is now asleep and appears to Rest well. Old Pres[t] Russell [Rev. James Russell, president of San Augustine University] Came about one hour since to see Columbus and Americus. Appears [to] think much of the boys, particularly Columbus."

While awaiting dinner, the master of the house went to the garden and "got some verry Ripe Peaches from the union Tree" but "Found some Hogs in Garden that came in by the Carriage Door left open by Dan [servant]. I find that ripe peaches agree verry well with me. Keeping my Bowels in proper order." Mrs. Watson, an elderly seamstress working for Amanda for the day, joined the family for dinner at one o'clock and ate "verry hearty."

Returning to the store, Matthew measured and delivered "upwards two thousand feet of plank" and sold "considerable Salt, Tobacco, &c." He bought some venison, eggs, and melons to take home to Amanda and "found my sick boys much better, Clear of fever and Resting finely. Eat Supper, went to Store with my wife and remained a Short time and returned. Found all quiet

5. Matthew Cartwright's Bible lists the birthdates of Nancy and her children and Jane and her children (in possession of Patty Cartwright Tennison).

at home." While Matthew congratulated himself on good health because his bowels were "in fine order," he worried about a growth near his eye. "The Idea of a cancer on my eye and probability or Posibility of it Brakeing in an eating Cancer ultimately annoys me Verry much. Yet I try to quiet my fears and reconcile myself to my fate as much as possible." Pictures in mid-life show him with no blemishes or disfigurement, suggesting that the growth was not serious, perhaps only a sty. By the next year, however, Matthew had bought a pair of spectacles that may or may not have cured his problem.[6]

"Sunday 26th July A.D. 1846: The morning clear and pleasant. Rose at 6 oclock. Jane complains that She cannot see. We gave her some soot from the impression that it would cool her Blood and Lower the excitement and also placed on the back of her neck a Blister for the purpose of Drawing the excitement from her eye." Matthew ordered her to remain inside without exercise or eating and at noon Jane said she had little pain unless the light shone in her eyes. "The idea that she will become intirely blind forces itself upon my mind . . . verry unpleasant," wrote Matthew. It is possible that Jane was playing sick in order to avoid chores.

Happily, all was not business and worry. "At about 10, my wife went with me into the Garden and Gathered some fine peaches, some from the union tree and some Verry Large Plum peaches from the N.W. Corner of the Garden. Then we had our Horses caught for a ride, the Grey Eagle for the Madame and W. W. Holman's work horse Charley for me." Amanda's brother, a bachelor at this time, was with the Texas Mounted Volunteers en route up the Rio Grande on their way to Monterrey, so Matthew was keeping his horse. But on this day Leonidas and Anna, ages not quite four and just over two, demanded to go be taken along on a ride, "and to please them and avoid the cries and importunities, we agreed . . . Anna in my lap and Leonidas behind his Ma. So up we got, Mant on the Grey . . . and . . . I on old . . . Charley." The gray "in full Glee" dashed ahead while Charley was "not so Lively." They rode over to Ayish Bayou, where some "Little Boys were in swimming, that scampered off" at their approach; they

6. Matthew bought spectacles on July 17, 1847. Account Book, 1847–1849, 156, CFP.

crossed the stream and circled a field before starting home to see about Cumby and Meck. It appears that Amanda, even after bearing five children, remained an avid horsewoman.

While Matthew mentions the four oldest children in his diary, nine-month-old Mary seems not to have attracted much attention, evidently remaining at home in the care of one of the slaves. Matthew and Amanda owned seven servants besides Jane in 1846: Nancy, who was thirty-six, and her four children, Dick, Emeline, Virtue, and Walker, ranging in age from ten to an infant, plus Dan, Mary, and one other. Mary was soon to be traded to James Perkins, as noted in the list of tasks. Subsequent tax rolls and family documents show that Nancy and Jane and their offspring remained part of the Cartwright family until slavery ended.[7]

In the evening, Matthew recorded his thoughts in his journal, and the dispassionate businessman confronted the caring patriarch. "The past week has been one Rather trying to the spirits. 1st Two fine boys sick. 2 the trouble and expense to giving them aid, the idea of weakening and destroying their constitutions, the fear of being sick ourselves. . . . The idea of all expenses and no profit." He estimated that he had spent $100, which coupled with nothing coming "in for one week is enough to alarm any person that has a Young family." Matthew felt sorry for himself: he was "becoming old, not used to work, and . . . weaker in body and mind" while demands on him increased. Furthermore, "the Idea of a verry Likely and Valuable Girl worth 500$ becoming blind, and . . . an expense and trouble—makes the week more trying. May our Father Guide and direct all things . . . is my present prayer."

Morosely contemplating the "Dark View of the Past Week," the consummate bookkeeper totaled his losses, including the $400 he had paid for Jane. They came "to $479, which in ten weeks would be $4,790, and in two years, $47,900! More than

7. San Augustine County, Tax Rolls, 1837–1864; Matthew Cartwright's Bible. Dan is mentioned in the 1846 journal, and documents among legal papers reveal his purchase along with Mary's. Other transactions regarding slaves appear to involve blacks Matthew acquired as payment for debt and whom he must have been traded immediately. The 1867 voter registration for San Augustine County, Texas State Archives, and the U.S. Ninth Census (1870) for San Augustine County list "Dick Holman" and Walker "Cartwright."

I am worth or expect to be." Matthew promised himself that beginning Monday, "I must Rise earlier, do more when up . . . be more agreeable and profitable." Hopefully next week would be better: "But Cautiousness and past experiences say sir do not flatter Yourself. The troubles are many in store. Prepare to meet them for the happiness and joy wished for by man is not things of the earth . . ." but of Heaven. "What a subject for man who has been taught to Strive for things of earth. . . ." The pleasures most valued by mankind astonished Matthew; despite the gloom of the past week, he went to breakfast, where he "enjoyed [himself] finely": "Our fare was sumptuous, and a good variety."

In a revealing outburst Matthew wrote, "What should a person do when he finds his expenses to overrun his income? Curtail them, but that is verry unpleasant after Living well and free from economy. . . ." Only the "firm and Noble" could discipline himself in frugality. "I fear our case is sealed. The fact is We have not even learned the value of things, much Less the want. How can we then, who has been floating along on a smooth stream for the Last ten Years with[out] pulling an oar, or putting forth any . . . exertion. Can we, who have no real experience, Stand the storm of adversity?" No, and the only hope was to find "some good harbor and there ride in security till the storm subsides." It seems clear that Matthew and Amanda had been enjoying a luxurious life-style, and he feared he might have to economize, and that neither one was prepared for self-denial. Matthew continued to worry about the upcoming court session in which Leon Chabert, the agent of Peyroux, Arcueil & Company, would demand payment of the old debt.

Matthew did not write anything on Monday, but on Tuesday, July 28, he regretted arising later than he had planned. He had been up "Frequently Last Night to Watch Jane under the operation of Medicine." Jane's case, he wrote, "is one of some importance and Interest" and he needed to "manage it well."

"8 O.C., Concluded to go to Garretts." When he arrived an hour later he found his ill sister, Polly, with company. Nancy Curl, the remarried widow of Matthew's cousin Hezekiah Cartwright, was there, and soon two other friends arrived. Matthew visited for an hour or so "Quite Lively and merry, considering that sickness caused the meeting."

Matthew went home and then to the store where he left his "trunk of papers." If similar to others of the period this trunk was probably small enough to carry under one arm. Then he went to various stores, buying three yards of calico for the slave Mary's dress and a bottle of aloes, a bitter purgative made from the century plant, to be given to Jane. He returned home and read Lucan until dinner. Afterward, he continued reading until he "had become tired" and decided to go to the store. But someone brought him "a Lot of fine peaches, of which I eat verry hearty . . . [then] . . . Columbus Brought a Mellon, which eat of also finely. I then felt better, and in order for reading until the children brought a Lot of Candy. I then eat of that occasionally while Reading till about 4 O.C." Then he walked to the gin where he found his slave Dan "lazying about." From his eating habits, it is easy to see why Matthew was growing stout like his father.

At home again, Matthew found the pigs "helping themselves to Mellons" until Columbus came into the garden and the two found some watermelons "of which I ate." The master was disturbed that two doses of medicine failed to "operate" on Jane, but she finally recovered. "To day is spent and Nothing in the [way] of business done," wrote Matthew, adding "Very warm." He ended his journal entry with a homily: "He that will not Reason is a bigot. He that Cannot Reason is a fool, he that dare not reason is a slave."

The month of August passed without Matthew recording a single word, and events fail to explain this long hiatus. On September 1 he noted that the Reverend Russell "cowhided J. M. Ardrey," an unembellished statement concerning two upstanding citizens. Ardrey was Matthew's current lawyer, around thirty years old, while the Methodist minister was considerably older. Russell died the following year, shot by the brother of a woman he had defamed in print.

Matthew continued his journal for two days in September. The sale of some mules demonstrated the continuing shortage of cash and the dependence on bartering: in exchange for Matthew's mules, prospective buyers offered a 4,605-acre certificate for land, a gristmill, or an unstated amount of tobacco. It was also time to think about providing meat for the family; Matthew was "inclined to put some small pigs up for Roasting," but a neighbor wanted to buy his "two sows and their 15 pigs." It appeared that the fall ginning season would be unfavorable because worms had destroyed most of the cotton in the San Augustine area, a fact that perhaps contributed to Matthew's overall gloom and Sam Burrus's inattention to business. Matthew commented that his partner, who had a "soar leg," had "begun to muck about."

Moreover, illness plagued the community. Clinton and Ella's son William, about one year old, was "verry low this morning [September 2], Not expected to live." Dr. Patterson visited Clinton's home every few days beinning in mid-August to treat William and Ella who was pregnant. Contrary to Matthew's notation, William recovered, and on September 8 the doctor delivered Ella's second child, who seems to have died soon afterward. Matthew's sister, Mary "Polly" Garrett, did not survive her illness; she died on September 30 at age thirty-two, leaving two daughters, Mintie, ten, and Mary, eight.[8]

When District Court Judge Oran M. Roberts, a Cartwright neighbor, convened court in San Augustine in October, law partners Ardrey and Charlton Payne represented Matthew in the case brought by Leon Chabert for Peyroux, Arcueil & Company. The New Orleans firm had ceased to exist by 1846 and old Silvain Peyroux had retired from business, but his agent was still trying to collect on the notes given by Matthew in 1842 and secured by mortgaged Texas land. By this time, Matthew preferred to close the matter by surrendering the mortgages.[9]

Matthew's attorneys seized every opportunity to postpone the decision. Two technical errors, misspelling Chabert with an "o" instead of an "a" and the omission of a proper seal on the documents by the district clerk, caused a motion to quash the writ. But the clerk filed for permission to add the seal, and Judge Roberts ruled that the case might continue. Chabert's attorney asked that the name be corrected while Ardrey and Payne demanded Chabert post security for the court costs. That maneuver forced a continuance until the spring term, at which time the

8. Journal (quotation); Dr. J. T. Patterson statement to J. C. Cartwright, San Augustine County, Probate Records, J. C. Cartwright file; Genealogy of William Garrett, Cartwright research files.

9. *Matthew Cartwright, Plaintiff in Error v. Leon Chabert, Defendant in Error,* MS transcript of record from San Augustine County, Nov. 24, 1848, Texas Supreme Court, 1849, MSS. M-296, pp. 1–24 (TSL); *New Orleans City Directory,* 1842, 1843, 1846, 1849 (microfiche; CL).

lawyers moved and countermoved, resulting in more delay until the fall of 1847, when Matthew added former Gov. J. Pinckney Henderson to his legal advisors. Nevertheless, the San Augustine jury decided in favor of Chabert on October 18, 1847. Judge Roberts ordered Matthew to pay $15,812.17, which represented the $9,559.00 principal plus $6,253.17 in interest. Court costs were an additional $37.35. Lawyer Ardrey advised Matthew to enter an appeal to the Texas Supreme Court on writ of error because of the lack of the seal and the misspelled name, thus again postponing a final decision until early 1849.[10]

The legal problems were not Matthew's only concerns between 1846 and 1848, when both of his sisters, a brother, and his mother became ill and died. Mary Garrett died and was buried on her husband's plantation just before the district court convened in 1846. Old Mary Cartwright, now fifty-nine years old, grieved not only for the loss of her eldest daughter but for her two granddaughters, who probably went to live on the Palo Gacho with their grandmother and widowed aunt, Clementine Holman. William Garrett observed mourning for one year, and in November 1847 married Lucette Teal, who eventually bore him seven more children. His daughters then returned to their father's home west of Ayish Bayou.[11]

The old widow would suffer more bereavements in Job-like succession. Six months after the death of Mary Garrett, her surviving daughter, Clementine "Mintie" Holman, became seriously ill at age twenty-eight. Since Sanford's death in 1843, Mintie had raised cotton on her mother's farm; how successful she was is unknown, but she ran an account at brother George's store. On her deathbed she made her will on March 6, 1847, and died three or four days later. Following the custom of the day, the family ordered printed notices to be distributed around town on March 10, 1847: "The friends and acquaintences [sic] of Mrs. C. C. Holman, deceased, are respectfully invited to attend her funeral tomorrow at ten o'clock, at the residence of her mother, Mrs. Cartwright, four miles east of San Augustine." Clementine was not buried in the Cartwright cemetery; her body was taken by wagon to be interred next to her husband in the Holman

10. *Matthew Cartwright v. Leon Chabert*, 3 *Texas* 261 (1849).
11. Genealogical material, Cartwright research files; San Augustine County, Marriage Records, William Garrett, Nov. 15, 1847.

family plot northwest of town. The bereaved grandmother, in poor health herself, surrendered Clementine's two children, Anna and William, to Holman kin. William Garrett, executor of Clementine's will, finally took Clementine's two children into his home soon after his marriage.[12]

The widow Cartwright still had her youngest son, Richard, living at home in 1847, while Matthew and Clinton lived in town and the other two sons, Robert and George, were within a day's ride. Matthew and Robert had been married for a decade, but George had remained a bachelor until age thirty-two, when he wed fourteen-year-old Ann Oliver in San Augustine on February 14, 1844. A native of Ireland, she may have been a foster daughter of the native-born Olivers who moved into Sabine County in the early 1840s. By 1846 George owned a farm along Bayou Tebo in Sabine County where he was modestly comfortable with four slaves, seven horses, a number of hogs and cattle, and a pair of oxen. One month after George's wedding, John Clinton Cartwright, not quite twenty-one, married Amanda's youngest sister Elvira, the "Ella" of Matthew's 1846 diary. The newlyweds occupied the building on the northwest corner of Main and Harrison, the boardinghouse and store that Clinton inherited from his father's estate. Clinton also entered into a partnership in a blacksmith shop in town with William T. White, where he kept his slave Jordan, the valuable blacksmith given to him by his mother, employed.[13]

12. Single ledger page, Clementine C. Holman, debtor, to George W. Cartwright, n.d., reproduced in Roberts, *Four Families*, I, in section labeled "Old Family Papers"; Funeral notice (quotation), in possession of Sandra Kardell Calpakis; *San Augustine, Texas, 1828–1940, Probate Cases*, 69, and also in W.P.A. files, San Augustine County, folder 1 (BTHC); U.S. Seventh Census (1850), San Augustine County, Texas (microfilm) [Anna and William with Garrett].

13. San Augustine County, Marriage Records, G. W. Cartwright, Feb. 14, 1844; Ibid., J. C. Cartwright, Mar. 19, 1844; Sabine County, Tax Roll, 1846 (microfilm; CL); Petition of J. C. Cartwright, San Augustine County, Probate Minute Book, B, 59; Blacksmith shop with White mentioned in Oct. 29, 1849, addenda to Inventory of J. C. Cartwright's property, San Augustine, Probate Records; U.S. Seventh Census (1850), San Augustine County, Texas (microfilm) [Wm. T. White, blacksmith]; Sheriff's sale, J. C. Cartwright's town lots, Nov. 3, 1850, clipping, Sharp Collection (BTHC); Crocket, *Two Centuries*, 219; Clinton's "homestead" on Lot 177, Inventory and List and Appraisement of the Real and Personal Property of the Estate of John Clinton Cartwright, San Augustine County, Probate Records, J. C. Cartwright file.

Clinton's family was sick a great deal in 1847, and Dr. Patterson visited at least once a month to treat Ella, little William, Jordan, or one of the other slaves. In November, Clinton became quite ill with malaria, and after two weeks of treatment with quinine and cough syrup, he was still convalescing when Ella gave birth to a third child on November 15. Perhaps this was a still birth because there are no subsequent references to a child. This infant and the one that died several weeks after its birth in 1846 were buried in the John Cartwright cemetery on the hill overlooking the Palo Gacho. There was no church or city cemetery in San Augustine at this time. Ella recovered slowly, but Clinton suffered a relapse and received the usual treatment for malaria, often called ague or intermittent fever. Patients shivered with chills accompanied by severe pain in the back, arms, and legs and often within an hour became feverish with excruciating headaches. Usually the seizures lasted three or more days, and the painful symptoms were relieved by taking gradually decreasing doses of quinine every few hours. Some patients did not have seizures again for months, but the cycle could continue for years.[14]

On December 17 and 18, 1847, Clinton's pain was so severe that Dr. Patterson brought his Galvanic battery to the house. This device was a popular medical treatment, and the shock it provided was supposed to relieve rheumatoidal pain. Clinton took more quinine every few days through the end of December and once a dose of cayenne pepper and Blue Mass, a soft pill made of mercury thought to be good for biliousness. He temporarily improved and Dr. Patterson called only once during January, but in late February 1848 Clinton needed morphine, and the following month quinine and Blue Mass pills were again administered. The doctor came every day in April, repeatedly giving Clinton morphine and quinine and by April 20 was making two and three calls each day. Clinton, not quite twenty-five years old, was dying, and by May 8 was perhaps in a coma because Patterson called but made no more charges. Somebody, perhaps Matthew, clipped a lock of Clinton's hair and tied it with thread, a common practice at that time, and Matthew placed it in his ledger. Matthew recorded Clinton's death (as he had those of his sisters) in

14. Dr. J. T. Patterson statement to J. C. Cartwright, San Augustine County, Probate Records; Prof. Henry Hartshorne, *The Practical Household Physician: A Cyclopaedia* (rev. ed.; [n.p.]: W. E. Scull, 1901), 405–407.

the old John Cartwright Bible as taking place on May 10, 1848. The family bought the necessary black cloth to line the casket and 275 "coffin tacks," along with the required crape and black clothing mourners wore, from J. B. Johnson's store. Clinton's account in Matthew's ledger also shows funeral items and an infant's coffin.[15]

Ella Holman Cartwright agreed that Clinton should be buried in the Cartwright graveyard near the small graves of his two infants and beside his father. In July she asked the probate court for letters of administration; Clinton had died without a will, and besides the town property, six slaves, furniture, and a gold watch, he still owned acreage in common with Richard, who was a minor. The young widow, barely twenty-three, soon shocked San Augustine residents. On January 18, 1849, only eight months after the death of Clinton, she married Otis Marshall Wheeler, veteran of the recent war and a merchant and land trader. Matthew was taken completely by surprise and wrote in his daybook:

> Mrs. John Clinton Cartwright married O. M. Wheeler in 8 mos & 8 days from Death of her Husband. Myself & wife recd invitation from the Madam late in the evening to take supper at candle lighting. She intended moving to the country and making her home at Col. Wheelers. We went in the dark and Rain through the mud and saw the last of John C. Cartwright's fond and ever adoring wife.[16]

Old Mary Cartwright was also dying in the spring of 1848. She too had suffered from recurring malaria since at least 1847. Dr. Patterson rode out to the Palo Gacho to visit her on April 20 and stayed three days. While he had charged Clinton only $2.50 for house calls in town, his fee was double when he rode five miles out of town and spent the night. During some of these visits Dr. Patterson also cared for the slaves and for Richard, who also suffered with malaria. On May 20, ten days after Clinton's

15. Ibid., 311; Statement to John C. Cartwright from J. B. Johnson & Co., San Augustine County, Probate Records, J. C. Cartwright file; Clinton Cartwright ledger sheet, Account Book, 1847–1849, 198, 210, CFP.

16. San Augustine County, Marriage Records, O. M. Wheeler, Jan. 18, 1849; Matthew's remarks, Jan. 18, 1849 (quotation), Day Book no. 18, 1847–1849, CFP.

demise, the doctor brought his Galvanic battery to ease Mary's pain, but the treatment seems not to have helped her and was not repeated. On June 7 she worsened and the doctor stayed at her house around the clock on some days. Mary died on June 16, 1848, or early the following morning. At the time Richard was severely ill, and Matthew was in Jefferson on business, having left home soon after Clinton's funeral in May. Amanda apparently did not know her mother-in-law lay on her deathbed when she wrote her husband on June 14 saying that they were all well. Just who notified Robert and George is unknown, but surely they came to bury their mother next to her husband in the family plot overlooking the old homestead. In twenty-two months, the three Cartwright brothers had lost two sisters, a brother, and their mother.[17]

Clinton's long illness had kept Matthew from his regular spring tour through northeastern Texas to collect debts and check on his various properties. He had expected to return by the last week of May 1848, when the probate court met in San Augustine, but unexpected business delayed him. He complained from Jefferson on May 18 that "times are very much changed since I was here Last, for the worse." He had collected "only about 70$, made no trades and think it is doubtful whether I will be able to affect any for cash." One purpose of the trip was to accumulate cash for the Peyroux debt, and he needed gold. In the peculiar romanticism of the day and somewhat morbid after his recent bereavement, he signed his letter "Your affectionate companion even in death," while Amanda replied, "Your affectionate and devoted wife untill [sic] Death."[18]

Amanda asked her brother William, who was leaving for Marshall, to take a letter to Matthew. Little Mary had developed severe diarrhea a few days after Matthew left home, and Amanda, like her husband, seemed to have little faith in local doctors. The letter, the first that was saved after their courtship notes, reveals a very competent woman used to dosing sick children and slaves: "I disliked to send for Dr. [Charles J.] Smith so much that I could not bare the idea." So she gave the 2½-year-old toddler "brandy

17. Dr. J. T. Patterson statement to Mrs. Mary Cartwright, deceased, for $261.25, notarized Oct. 21, 1848, CFP.

18. Matthew Cartwright to Dear Amanda, May 18, 1848 (1st–3rd quotations), CFP; Amanda to Dear husband, June 14, 1848 (4th quotation), ibid.

and pepper for two days without any effect." Finally she bought a vial of laudanum (tincture of opium, ten drops of which would stop diarrhea) and gave "it to her 3 or 4 times without any relief whatever. What more to do I did not know . . . I felt about as bad as I could. I knew something more must be done verry soon or we would . . . loose [*sic*] her. . . . I gave her 1/2 teaspoonful which seemed to do her good in a few hours. . . . She then commenced mending and is now as harty [*sic*] as ever." Writing after her child was better, Amanda seemed almost frivolous when she added: "Your new books has been quite a treat to me since you left . . . time has passed off faster than usual." The titles show that Matthew liked popular reading as well as Roman poets: Amanda liked *The Bride's Keepsake* best and was halfway through *The Ladies Wealth*. Amanda also reported that the new "sopha" and chair had arrived safely by wagon from Natchitoches.[19]

One year earlier, in April 1847, Matthew started closing his interest in the store in order to devote more time to his land business. He continued to keep the ledgers but Sam Burrus assumed all other mercantile duties. Storekeeping was not as profitable as it had been; cotton prices remained low while the costs of merchandise, transportation, and operating increased. Although import duties had ceased with annexation to the United States, the state and the county levied substantial annual fees for retail licences and for selling liquor in bulk (meaning a quart or more). Matthew inventoried the goods on hand prior to turning the business over to Burrus. The store no longer carried groceries, only tools, hardware, ready-made clothing, shoes, sewing materials and notions, plus a few pieces of jewelry and silverware coming to a total value of $1,329. The charge accounts due Matthew came to $646, bringing his entire interest to $1,975, a sum to be credited to Matthew's account. Interesting items on hand were artificial flowers, three pairs of common spectacles, eight dozen wooden pocket combs, forty-five pounds of sad irons, and seventy-nine assorted violin strings. The Cartwrights and the Holmans had been steady customers for "bunches" of violin strings since the 1830s. Matthew, Robert, and Clinton played the instrument, as did William Holman. Robert had paid

19. Amanda to Dear husband, June 14, 1848, ibid. It is interesting to note that Amanda's son Americus married Dr. Smith's daughter in 1869, and the pair lived with Amanda after Matthew's death.

$4 for a violin in 1837, and Clinton purchased a bass violin in 1843. Afternoon and evening musicales by the Cartwrights were common occurrences. Matthew taught young Columbus to play as soon as he was able to manage the bow and finger the strings, lessons that were repeated with the other children.[20]

Matthew, as the eldest son, continued to oversee many time-consuming tasks associated with his father's estate and had assumed the responsibility for training Clinton and Richard in business practices. Both had worked at his store and the gin at different times and learned to keep the daybooks and ledgers. John Cartwright's estate would finally close in April 1849 when Richard became twenty-one years old. When Mary Cartwright died, Richard, still a minor, chose Matthew to oversee his affairs for the next few months. A major task was separating real estate, slaves, and furniture that Richard had held in common with the now-deceased Clinton; in September 1849 Matthew applied to the probate court for a division, which was concluded in November. In January 1850 Matthew held a sale of his mother's household goods, which, as usual, were bought by family and friends. While Robert and Matthew bought many items, so did O. M. Wheeler, Elvira's new husband, in spite of Matthew's sarcastic remarks the previous year. The old spinning wheel that had come from Tennessee was not valued as an antique or for future emergency use and was sold for only ninety cents.[21]

In April 1849 Matthew traveled to Austin to attend to land business and also to be present when the Texas Supreme Court heard arguments regarding his appeal in *Cartwright v. Chabert*. Attorney Ardrey had filed the documents in December 1847 after the decision of the district court. The Mississippi native was one of the best lawyers in San Augustine and a good friend of District

20. Licences issued to Matthew Cartwright from May 1846 through Dec. 1847, CFP; "Inventory Mdze [*sic*] Furnished Store, 26 April 1847," on sheet pasted into Account Book, 1847–1849, ibid.; Violin items in Ledger no. 5, 1836–1837, 201, 265; Ledger, 1837–1839, 46, 202, 227; Account Book no. 7, p. 145; Account Book, 1847–1849, 120, 160, ibid.

21. Matthew Cartwright's ledger sheets, 1847–1849, are written in different hands, perhaps those of his younger brothers. Account Book, 1847–1849, 172, 184–185, 187–188, 193, CFP; Partial list of items sold, no date but a cross-lined inscription "purchased by M. Cartwright Jany 1849," a loose sheet in ibid.; San Augustine County, Probate Minute Book, B, 137, 143, 140, 150, 159, 160, 189.

Judge Roberts. Ardrey was impressed with the newly organized Texas Supreme Court, which, since statehood, was composed of three appointed justices instead of the district judges sitting *en banc* as had been the case during the republic. Ardrey worried that Judge Roberts's decision in *Chabert v. Cartwright* might not be reversed and urged his client to be present in Austin.[22]

Matthew left home riding a new horse that was "a good traveller," but heavy rains slowed his progress because the rivers were hard to cross. He had to stop nine miles east of Nacogdoches the first night and, after reaching town the next day, had to spend two more days waiting for word that the Angelina and "Naches" rivers had receded. He assured Amanda on April 7, 1849, that he would return from Austin "as soon as possible, say 3 weeks."[23]

He worried that Amanda was uneasy about their financial difficulties and told her again that the Peyroux-Chabert debt "was still under the old Law" and could be paid with property, which would be no problem, since Matthew had "Lands sufficient to pay the am^t 5 times over." She should "have no fears as to our means or independence." He bolstered her confidence, and perhaps his own, by writing "I feel Buoyant and in good sp^{ts} amd feel myself competent to the task before me. . . . The *Omens* of fortune are favorable for this trip." Annoyed that he had to leave his family, he would resign himself "to circumstances and depend on your discretion . . . to manage home." In quaint language he told her to "enforce the Government of our family and little pledges [the children] strictly and mildly as possible." After all, what they learned at home about "Government & truth . . . is that much Capital." Amanda should "bear up against Care and Gloomy prospects—patience and hope for the Best." Then, in straightforward business style unlike the earlier somewhat morbid closings, Matthew signed the letter to his wife: "Yours truly, M. Cartwright."[24]

When the case was finally heard, the three justices could find no reversible error and let the decision of the district court stand. Royal T. Wheeler, former resident of San Augustine and brother of Otis Wheeler, Amanda's new brother-in-law, wrote the opin-

22. Matthew Cartwright to Amanda, Apr. 7, 1849, CFP; James M. Ardrey to Hon. O. M. Roberts, Feb. 4, 1848, Roberts Papers (BTHC).
23. Matthew Cartwright to Amanda, Apr. 7, 1848, CFP.
24. Ibid.

ion.[25] Matthew's ride home must have been less than pleasant, knowing as he did that Chabert demanded cash, not land.

Matthew, however, was not without resources. For example, in one month's time from December 20, 1849, to January 20, 1850, just three months before the dreaded Supreme Court decision on his appeal, he had acquired sixteen tracts of land totaling 14,294 acres in Upshur, Panola, Shelby, and Cass counties for $1,782, an average of twelve cents per acre. Just how he paid for this speculation is not recorded; perhaps it was by trade, debt collection, or credit instead of specie. When he listed the properties, each with its estimated value, the total came to $3,400—almost double the cost. Such were the "animating pursuits of speculation," a phrase used earlier by Sam Houston to describe the excitement and euphoria of a successful deal so enjoyed by Matthew Cartwright and others.[26]

Matthew's best investment in 1849, however, was a new house. On October 22, 1849, he paid $900 for the ten-year-old Isaac Campbell house on Main Street just east of town and across the road from the university building. The New England-style, two-story frame house had been built by Augustus Phelps, a master carpenter from the northeast, who also constructed other San Augustine homes. Carpenter Sidney A. Sweet contracted to frame and roof the dwelling for $1,800 in Texas money, with Phelps finishing it inside and out for an additional $2,000 and one league of land. The total cost was $3,800 plus perhaps $442.80 for the vacant land if it was valued at a low of ten cents per acre. Texas money was worth 37½ cents for one dollar in specie in 1839, meaning that the house cost $1,425 to build in United States funds plus whatever value Campbell placed on his acreage. Thus, Matthew's purchase of the house in United States money represented about two-thirds of its original cost, and was still quite a bargain.[27]

25. *Matthew Cartwright v. Leon Chabert, 3 Texas* 261 (1849).

26. "Investments for lands, 20th Dec 1848 to 20th Jany '49," loose paper in back of Account Book, 1847–1849, CFP; Sam Houston to John A. Wharton, Apr. 9, 1835, in Williams and Barker (eds.), *Writings of Sam Houston*, I, 293 (quotation).

27. Contract between Isaac Campbell and Sidney A. Sweet to frame and roof the house, May 30, 1839, and another between Campbell and Augustus Phelps to finish the house, June 1839, San Augustine County, Deed Records, E, 275–276, 400–402.

*The Matthew Cartwright (1807–1870) house, San Augustine, Texas.
The house, which remains in the possession of Matthew's descendants, was built in 1839 by Augustus Phelps for Matthew's brother-
in-law, Isaac Campbell. Matthew acquired it in 1849.* Courtesy
Cartwright Family Descendants.

Campbell planned the house in 1839 as a bridal present for
Mrs. Elizabeth "Betty" Holman Dye, Amanda Cartwright's older
sister, a recent widow who had moved to Texas to join her
mother. Campbell had come to Texas in 1836, represented San
Augustine in the Texas Congress during 1838–1839, and was one
of the five commissioners who chose Austin as the new site for the
capital of the republic. When criticism of the frontier site began
in 1842 after the first Mexican raid on San Antonio, Campbell
published a defensive letter in the San Augustine *Red-Lander*
saying that he had not voted for far-off Austin. Instead, he
preferred some more central site on the Brazos River. Soon after
moving into his new home, Campbell was so deeply in debt that
on March 2, 1840, he temporarily deeded it to Sanford Holman.
The ploy was intended to give Campbell a chance to settle his
debts, but the times remained severe. Two years later he borrowed $738.75 at 10 percent interest from Matthew Cartwright,
but his creditors took him to court and the judge ruled that
Campbell's property must be sold. On September 5, 1842, the
sheriff auctioned the house and its four lots to the highest bidder,

William Holman, at the minimum bid of two-thirds the value—$633.33.[28]

Two days later, on September 7, Campbell died at age thirty, and Matthew recorded funeral purchases in his ledger the following day. While nobody said his death was a suicide, it would not be surprising. William Holman soon sold the property to Rev. Francis Wilson and three trustees of the Methodist Wesleyan University for use as a residence for the staff and classrooms for its Female School. Classes met there until 1847; the following year the trustees sold the house to fellow Methodist Dr. Richard Ratliff, brother of a board member, probably as a means of extinguishing a debt to him.[29]

The church rented the house as a manse for Rev. Jesse Witt in 1848, but by August Ratliff was in dire financial trouble. The following details illustrate the continuing hard times and the complexity of financial arrangements. Ratliff mortgaged the property to Elijah Price for a loan of $425 in order to pay a debt owed to merchants S. W. Blount and James B. Johnson. At the same time, Ratliff sold his interest in the house to former Wesleyan trustee John C. Brooke for a series of notes totalling $1,045, to be paid annually beginning in January 1849. In the meantime, merchant Charles Stewart sued Ratliff and his wife for $1,325, and the court ordered payment with half allocated to Brooke. With no money available, Stewart received the deed to the old Campbell house and in turn sold it to Matthew Cartwright.[30] It appears that everybody lost money on the house except Matthew.

The Cartwrights liked the convenient arrangement of the handsome, sturdy house built out of heart of long-leaf yellow pine, even though it had suffered hard usage during the school years. The front door faced south on Main Street and opened into a ten-foot-wide passageway between the parlor on the east and a

28. Holman genealogical material, Cartwright research files; *Biographical Directory of the Texan Conventions and Congresses*, 63; San Augustine County, Marriage Records, June 6, 1839; San Augustine *Red-Lander*, Aug. 12, 1841, Sept. 1, 1842; Promissory note Isaac Campbell to M. Cartwright, Feb. 28, 1842, CFP; San Augustine County, Deed Records, F, 279.

29. San Augustine *Red-Lander*, Sept. 9, 1843; Ledger Book no. 7, p. 78, CFP; San Augustine County, Deed Records, F, 279, 321–325.

30. San Augustine County, Deed Records, G, 308, 310–311, 424–426; O (oh), 9.

bedroom on the west, each about fifteen feet by twenty feet with fireplaces on the east and west walls. A handsome, curving staircase engineered by neighbor Travis G. Broocks rose from the central hall to the second floor, where the floor plan was repeated: two large bedrooms with fireplaces flanked the wide center hall. The ten-foot-high ceilings and the free circulation of air through the many windows and doors with transoms, all protected by louvered shutters, made the hot summers endurable. On the northeast corner was a one-story attached dining-room wing forty-three feet by twenty-eight feet, also having a fireplace on the north wall. A fifteen-foot-square kitchen built similarly to the house stood a few feet away and was later joined to the dining room. The main portion, forty-two by twenty-two feet, and its one-story wing sat on brick piers, and the exterior was covered in beveled, lapped siding. Altogether, the house had 2,268 square feet of living space. Later Matthew built a wide porch, or gallery, on the west side of the dining room that extended at right angles to run north along the downstairs bedroom, creating many more square feet of liveable space during pleasant weather.[31]

Matthew's property stretched 750 feet along Main Street and extended 340 feet north to Columbia Street, covering all but 120 feet of the modern block between Ayish and Milam streets, and totaling almost six acres. Eventually the grounds included three servants quarters, a stable, a carriage house, a smokehouse, and other outbuildings. There were three brick-lined wells—one just outside the kitchen door and the others near the servants' quarters and the garden and orchard. Fences separated the cows, horses, pigs, and hunting dogs on the property. Matthew even built himself a detached office, similar in style to the house and with its own fireplace, just east of the parlor. No inventory exists for furnishings of the house but purchases recorded in the account books through 1866 suggest a comfortable and sometimes elegant life-style.[32]

31. Works Progress Administration, Historic American Buildings Survey (Texas, 238, 1934), copy in Cartwright research files; Elevations and brief discription of Matthew Cartwright house, in Paul Goeldner (comp.), *Texas Catalog: Historic American Buildings Survey* (San Antonio: Trinity University Press, 1974), 211; also in Anne Clark (comp.), *Historic Homes of San Augustine*, ed. Carolyn Allen (Austin: San Augustine Historical Society, 1972), 22–23.

32. Ibid.; Plat W ½ Out Lot no. 24, San Augustine County, Tax Appraisal District.

Moving into the house at the end of 1849 must have been a joyous occasion after the trials of the past decade. Only three years earlier, Matthew had worried about enduring "the storm of adversity," but now the future looked brighter. Although Matthew was encumbered by a large debt to Chabert, land values were rising because of an influx of immigrants seeking homes, which would prove profitable for the Cartwrights during the 1850s.[33]

33. Matthew Cartwright journal, 1846, CFP (quotation).

Eight

"It Was the Best of Times . . ."

THE AFFLUENT 1850S

*M*atthew Cartwright was the wealthiest man in the county in 1850 measured by the value of the land he owned—$165,000. The San Augustine enumerator for the first United States census taken in Texas began his count on September 6 and did not finish until April 16, 1851. He found 2,087 white persons living in 350 dwellings and males outnumbering females 1,146 to 941. A total of 1,561 slaves lived in the county and were almost equally divided according to sex. Therefore, 57 percent of the population was white and 43 percent black. While Matthew had only seven slaves and William Garrett twenty-one, the two largest slaveholders in the county were Amanda's brother-in-law Iredell D. Thomas, who had married widow Betty Holman Campbell in 1845, and Philip Sublett's widow, Easter Jane. Both owned forty-three slaves.[1]

1. U.S. Seventh Census (1850), San Augustine County, Texas, summary of statistics on last page. San Augustine County Slave Schedule (1850) gives number of male and female slaves and their ages but no names. Matthew Cartwright's Bible lists Nancy, b. 1810, and her four children: Dick, b. 1836;

Several residents had just returned from California, where the promise of gold had proved to be a difficult and disillusioning reality. Many Texans returned home after California entered the Union as a free state in September 1850. One of them, Abner G. Roberts, wrote, "It is a fine country . . . but owing to the people . . . I could not be induced to live here . . . among the Yankees particularly one can see no peace." Abner, the son of Isaac Roberts, and his cousin Felix G. Roberts, the son of Elisha, returned in time to be counted in the census. The pair had spent the rainy winter of 1849 at San Jose, south of San Francisco, without making much money. To get to the gold fields, a number of Redlanders rode horseback across Central Texas to Fredericksburg, where they joined organized companies for protection during the long trip to El Paso, Santa Fe, and San Diego before turning north to the gold fields. Abner told his family, "I do not wish to travel the long road but once and then I expect to ride the waves . . . to New Orleans" when he returned home. He had seen "A. D. Alexander and his Mrs." in San Francisco, and other San Augustine neighbors were at Stockton. Word was that other San Augustine residents were on their way to California as well.[2]

Matthew's former partner Sam Burrus also tried his luck in California. He and four or five associates left San Augustine early in 1850, but instead of the arduous overland trip, they went by way of New Orleans and Panama, crossing the isthmus to catch another boat for San Francisco. Sam told Matthew that one of their party was drunk from the time they left Grand Ecore on the Red River, and he lost all but $220 of his money gambling on board the ship. Moreover, the drunkard had "caught the gonerhear [sic] and we had him to weight [sic] on all the way over the pacific." The group separated in San Francisco, and Burrus staked a claim on the Yuba River seventy-five miles northwest of Sacramento, the closest post office. He sent a sample of gold dust in a

---

Emeline, b. 1838; Virtue, b. 1840; and Walker, b. 1846. It also lists Jane, b. 1830, and her daughter Harriet, b. 1849.

2. A. G. Roberts to sister, Jan. 20, 1850 (quotations), typescript from Betty Carver (in possession of Sandra Kardell Calpakis); *Four Families,* 46; U.S. Seventh Census (1850), San Augustine County, Texas. See Mabelle Eppard Martin (ed.), "From Texas to California in 1849: Diary of C. C. Cox," *SHQ,* XXIX (July, 1925), 39, 41–42, for a typical train.

letter to his wife and told Matthew that each letter cost $1.50 to mail. Some days Burrus made about $10 panning for gold, but it was "the hardest work . . . that I have had any hand in." Burrus wrote that if any "of the Boys wishes to Come . . . tell all of those that cant take a spade and grubing [*sic*] hoe and dig up that branch between Genl [James P.] Hendersons and town and wash all of the mud and sand out . . . to stay at home." Everything was expensive. The waterproof boots that Burrus had bought in New Orleans for $6 sold in Sacramento for $20–$30; butter was $4 per pound, and Irish potatoes forty cents per pound. Burrus had sworn off gambling and expected to be home within the year with $5,000 in cash. He must have succeeded, because his personal property increased tenfold in value between 1850 and 1860.[3]

George Cartwright may have taken his wife and small daughter Mary to California. The tax assessor in Sabine County listed him as a nonresident, and his name appears nowhere in Texas in the 1850 or 1860 censuses. His five-year-old son Sanford lived with Richard Cartwright in San Augustine in 1850 and went to school in Shelby County the next two years. George was back in Sabine County on June 5, 1860, however, when his steam mill exploded, damaging the machinery. He told a friend that he was "not dispirited" and thought he could repair it.[4]

Only the deaths of Robert G. Cartwright and his wife Mary marred the early 1850s for the Cartwright family. Robert was a respected citizen of Shelby County, having served as a county commissioner and as trustee of the ambitious Shelby University. By 1850 he had an estate of about $13,000, comfortable by local standards but not as impressive as that of Matthew. His various enterprises included a mill and a store in addition to his farm in the Jonathan Bittick league, and, like Matthew, Robert had several thousand acres in speculative land. He owned nine slaves who helped him raise cotton, corn, cattle, hogs, and sheep.

3. Samuel T. Burrus to Matthew Cartwright, May 12, 1850 (quotations), CFP; U.S. Eighth Census (1860), Panola County, Texas (microfilm).

4. Sabine County, Tax Rolls, 1846–1861; U.S. Seventh Census (1850), San Augustine County, Texas. See Dr. W. Ragland statement to R. G. Cartwright, Sept. 30, 1851, June 26, 1852, CFP, for presence of Sanford with Robert G. Cartwright. Martin (ed.), "Diary of C. C. Cox," 49, mentions a company of families from eastern Texas including a blacksmith. Letter from "MAT," in San Augustine *Red Land Express*, June 16, 1860 (quotation).

Beginning in 1851, Robert's family and slaves were treated for intermittent fever by Dr. William J. Ragland, a Tennessee kinsman. Mary Lanier Cartwright became very ill in 1852 and died by the end of September; Robert survived her by less than seven months, dying on March 1, 1853. He had named Matthew his executor and co-guardian of the three children with W. W. Lanier, his brother-in-law.[5]

Matthew's financial problems with Leon Chabert finally ended in 1852. After the decision of the Texas Supreme Court, Matthew's lawyers, Henderson, Ardrey, and Payne, maneuvered to postpone the settlement, and in May 1851 Chabert sued Matthew's guarantors, Sam Burrus and William Garrett, in an effort to collect his money. The trio of lawyers defeated Chabert, and another delay allowed former Governor Henderson to arrange a private settlement with the New Orleans agent. If Chabert agreed to drop his demand for an additional $5,000 in interest that had accrued since 1848, Matthew would pay $8,000 in cash in May 1852 and include an $8,000 note endorsed by Governor Henderson and payable in May 1854.[6] This concluded the decade-long financial nightmare in which a debt of $9,500, amply covered by mortgaged Texas property, had almost doubled.

Matthew was chastened by the experience. Since 1847 he had traveled for long periods of time in order to sell land to raise the funds for his debt and also to support his family. In an introspective note to Amanda shortly after making the arrangement with Chabert, he "ventured to Look at myself free of Debt and Draw some fancy sketch of the pleasure in Store for us—though I find on a sober view that we have many duties ahead of us as well as pleasures."[7]

Amanda at thirty-five had matured during Matthew's absences and felt sufficiently confident to criticize her husband's behavior, including his indulgence in alcohol. Replying to a recent

5. Shelby County, Texas, Tax Rolls, 1850–1853 (microfilm; CL); Gammel (comp.), *Laws of Texas*, II, 847; Statement, Dr. W. J. Ragland, 1851–1853, Inventory of estate of R. G. Cartwright, May 31, 1853, CFP; Amanda Cartwright (Matthew's wife) to son Americus, Apr. 10, 1856, ibid.

6. J. M. Ardrey to O. M. Roberts, May 9, 1851, Roberts Papers; Leon Chabert to J. P. Henderson, Mar. 22, 1853, CFP.

7. Pencilled scrap, June 8, 1852, on road to Austin with business papers of that date, CFP.

letter from her spouse discoursing on friendship and happiness, she wrote frankly: "I infer that you will entertain the subject *Know Thyself*. . . . Every man has his foibles, and you have yours . . . but knowing you to be a lover of truth, I approach you on the subject without fear." Too often, she said, Matthew dwelled on his virtues and was blind to his faults: "Your great fault . . . is your fondness for excitement. Stimulating drink . . . heats the imagination and paints things in too high colours when compared with realities." As "the keeper of your happiness," she did not wish to "dictate . . . but if he would moderate his desires, be more charitable to mankind, and cultivate goodness and love," she thought that he would be happier.[8]

Amanda also suffered anxiety during his absences. Left alone with the children, she not only had to cope with their illnesses but with their education. A few years earlier, returning from a trip, Matthew discovered that eleven-year-old Columbus, usually a good student, did not know his multiplication tables, and Amanda had not been able to force him to master memorization. The stern father drew a chart and decreed that Cumby would know the tables "in Three Days or explain the Reason."[9]

His children's education was important to Matthew. When the university and college closed in 1847, the trustees of both schools joined to create a nondenominational institution, and in 1848, the state issued a charter for the University of East Texas located at San Augustine. Matthew Cartwright and William Garrett were among the trustees when the new school opened in the former university building under the leadership of James M. Wells, a graduate of West Point. Like its predecessors, it had primary and preparatory classes for both sexes, and in 1850 Matthew sent his three sons and Anna to the struggling school, while William Garrett enrolled his two daughters and the two orphans of Clementine and Sanford Holman, Anna and William.[10]

Monetary problems soon caused the new university to fail, and in late 1850 members of McFarland #3 A.M. & F.M. lodge (soon to be called Redland #3) quickly organized the more realistic Masonic Institute, which was more like a modern high

8. Amanda to husband, Aug. 15, 1852, CFP.

9. Chart, July 25, 1849 (in possession of Sandra Kardell Calpakis).

10. Crocket, *Two Centuries*, 309–310; U.S. Seventh Census (1850), San Augustine County, Texas.

Amanda Holman (1817–1894), ca. 1850s.

Matthew Cartwright (1807–1870), ca. 1850s. Courtesy Cartwright
Family Descendants. *A similar pose appears in John Henry Brown,*
Indian Wars and Pioneers of Texas *(1896).*

school. The members bought the university building across the street from Matthew Cartwright's house and began classes in 1851 with a separate branch for girls. Tuition for the children of Masons and non-Masons was the same, but Matthew, perhaps taking Amanda's advice to seek friendships, finally joined the lodge in 1857.[11]

Educators for the institute generally came from out of state: James T. Thornton headed the Male Institute and Thomas Smith the primary department; Mrs. Mary DeCamp, formerly the head of a New Orleans girls' school, guided the Female Institute; and Miss Willie Bate, the primary classes where Matthew's two daughters, Anna, seven, and Mary, six, were enrolled. Except for Miss Bate, who married in 1852 and was replaced by the wife of the Episcopalian minister, these men and women shaped the education of the Cartwright children and their Garrett and Holman cousins for a number of years.[12]

The Masonic Institute, the longest-lasting school in San Augustine, continued even after Thornton married Mrs. DeCamp and the pair returned to her home in New Orleans where they could make more money. The female department continued under the leadership of J. Thomas Fulton and his wife, a music teacher, as well as an art instructor and another who taught English composition. Most parents expected their daughters to study music, painting, and fancy sewing rather than advanced academic subjects, and Anna and Mary took advantage of Mrs. Fulton's talent. In 1859 Amanda wrote to Matthew that the girls practiced their music, presumably the piano and violin, for hours each evening. The boys' institute was harder to staff, but finally newcomer S. W. Bewley, a lawyer, became principal. The school continued until the end of the decade, but more and more parents began sending their teenage children to schools in the eastern United States, not only for a better education but for family prestige.[13]

11. Crocket, *Two Centuries*, 310–311. Miss Bate married Noel G. Roberts in July 1852; Matthew Cartwright was initiated in San Augustine on March 4, 1857, and was passed and raised two years later. Masonic Grand Lodge Library and Museum of Texas, Waco.

12. Crocket, *Two Centuries*, 311; List of students at Masonic Institute, George L. Crockett Papers, Blake Transcripts, XXXV, 27.

13. Amanda Cartwright to Matthew Cartwright, Feb. 10, 1859, CFP; Crocket, *Two Centuries*, 312–313.

One of the first local boys to go to the Kentucky Military Institute near Frankfort was the Cartwrights' neighbor, Moses A. Broocks, and in 1853 Matthew sent Columbus to join him. In July, sixteen-year-old Columbus and two other boys traveled by steamboat down the Red River and up the Mississippi and Ohio rivers to Louisville, from which they rode the train, the first they had seen, to the Kentucky capital. "We had a fine ride from Louisville to Frankfort on the cars," Columbus wrote. "At first we were surprised to see them go so slow, but . . . [soon] . . . we were going faster than we ever went before." Classes did not begin until September, and Columbus suffered severe homesickness during the interim because he had received no letters: "My Dear ma . . . if you dont wright to me I am coming home and see you." He sent love to each member of the family, especially "to my Pa who has worn himself nearly out so that he might be able to make something out of his Children." Amanda's firstborn remembered her too. He wrote, "Ma you . . . have encouraged me to learn ever since I have been large enough to recollect," and he promised to study hard so that they might be proud of him.[14]

One week after classes began Columbus still missed home, but assured his mother that "I shall not let that bother my mind" because he was determined to do well. He wanted Meck to join him the following year and told his brother to "studdy" hard. Although Cumby was impressed by the splendid buildings and bought notepaper with an engraved illustration, he was surprised to find that the cadets slept on mattresses laid out each night on the floor. He liked the morning routine, when the booming cannon and the fife and drum summoned the boys to roll call. He sent his father a catalog and wrote, "This is the place for a boy that wants to studdy." While others took fencing lessons, Cumby was "studding," which he believed more advantageous. The two debating societies, so dear to his father's heart from his own college days, did not tempt Columbus as much as the Temperance Hall, which he planned to join to continue his commitment to avoid alcohol, as he had pledged four years earlier when he was twelve. Like other poorly prepared students from Texas, Columbus was placed in the freshman preparatory department, where

14. C. C. Cartwright to Dear Pa, Aug. 1, 1853 (1st quotation), CFP; Columbus Cartwright to Dear Ma, Aug. 26, 1853 (2nd–4th quotations), ibid.

he studied arithmetic and grammar and was tutored in Latin. Besides buying textbooks, Columbus spent money for uniforms, boots, shoes, gloves, and an overcoat from the $200 Matthew had deposited with the school. Tuition was $102 each semester and included board, lodging, washing, fuel, lights, and necessary medical attention.[15]

Conscious of his duty, Columbus missed no classes and worked very hard to please his parents. Upperclassman Moses A. Broocks wrote to his father that Columbus was "one of the finest and healthiest looking" cadets and "no boy in the Institute . . . is more studious"; he predicted that "Colum" would head the freshman class. Matthew received a report in January 1854, at the end of the semester, commending Columbus's "Exemplary" behavior in deportment, application, personal habits, and progress and giving him a grade of 10 out of a possible 10 in geometry, arithmetic, English grammar, composition, and declamation, but 9.9 in algebra.[16]

Columbus still missed home and wrote Meck in the spring of 1854 complaining about the difficulty of required studies in geometry, algebra, and composition and his struggle with French. The latter would prevent him from registering in the upper-level classes. He wrote, "I tell you Meck I am getting mighty tired of staying away from home but I will have to bear it one more year." He did not think he would return after that "for I dont like Kentucky very well and I dont like the way that this school is going on." Some of the teachers were partial to certain students, he said, which affected his grades. "Oh! Meck how I want to come home when I get to playing my old fiddle. . . . I have learned some of the prettyest tunes you ever heard."[17]

At this time, fourteen-year-old Meck was traveling with his father because the Male Institute was without a staff. Americus had been ill, and because a change of scene was sometimes

15. Columbus Cartwright to Dear Ma, Sept. 18, 1853 (1st and 2nd quotations), CFP; Columbus Cartwright to Dear Pa, Sept. 19, 1853 (3rd quotation), ibid.; Statement from KMI to C. C. Cartwright, Sept. 8, 1853–Jan. 20, 1854, ibid.

16. Moses A. Broocks to Travis G. Broocks, Dec. 12, 1853 (1st quotation), CFP; U.S. Seventh Census (1850), San Augustine County, Texas; Kentucky Military Institute Report for session ending Jan. 28, 1854 (2nd quotation), CFP.

17. Clinton Columbus Cartwright to Americus, Apr. 21, 1854, CFP.

beneficial, Matthew took him along when he visited Tyler on land business. From there they continued southwest to the General Land Office in Austin. Heavy rains delayed them in the state capital and prevented travel to San Antonio.[18] Matthew intended that the trip would educate Meck in the ways of land trading, practical training that Matthew provided to each of his sons as they matured.

Columbus returned home for the summer and in August 1854 left again for Kentucky with Meck, Thomas William "Billy" Blount, and Lycurgus "Gus" Broocks, all fourteen years old. They had to travel to Alexandria by wagon because the river was too low for steamboats. Gus became ill, which slowed their progress, but he recovered somewhat on the boat to Memphis. They decided to take a stage from Memphis to Nashville and Louisville, which would take about four days, instead of continuing by boat to Louisville, which would take a week. Gus became worse one day out of Memphis, however, and went home. Meck and Billy wanted to go back too, but Columbus made them continue even if they were homesick.[19]

The two younger boys roomed together while Columbus joined a friend next door in order to "keep them from getting demerits" and to help them study. Cumby gloated when Billy Blount was assigned the usual preparatory work instead of entering the sophomore class as he had expected. "The Gentleman was too short in the breach yet," he confided to his mother. Columbus was studying French, trigonometry, and physiology, and expected to begin descriptive geometry soon.[20]

The institute was crowded with new boys, but its founder, the popular Col. R. T. P. Allen, a graduate of West Point, planned to sell his interest and open a military school in Texas. Columbus urged his mother to support the plan when the colonel visited San Augustine to talk with "Pa and Genl Broocks and Col Blount," because the eleven Texas boys would like to attend school closer to home. Columbus was careful with the money his father had

18. Matthew Cartwright to Dear Companion, May 24, 1854, CFP.

19. Columbus Cartwright to Dear Ma, Sept. 9, 25, 1854, CFP; Columbus Cartwright to Sister, Oct. 16, 1854, ibid.

20. Columbus Cartwright to Dear Ma, Sept. 25, 1854 (quotations), CFP.

given him and had paid $150 for Meck's tuition and expenses, but only $102 for himself because he did not need as much.[21]

Columbus managed to earn 9.97 in physiology and trigonometry, though he failed French; Meck's report was not preserved by the family. Near the end of the term Columbus fell ill with scarlet fever, which became epidemic among the cadet population. Several died, which forced the school to close until February 1855. Cumby and Meck moved to a private boardinghouse six miles away in Frankfort; Meck enjoyed the respite. Cumby wrote to his father on New Year's Eve about his illness and disappointing report and also asked for money for the next quarter. Matthew sent $250 and advice: "I sympathize . . . but hope you will have nerve and firmness . . . to soar above Difficulties"; otherwise the world would be a dark place. He urged the boys to "Look ahead . . . Prepare for your Station . . . [because] . . . Education . . . [and] . . . Knowledge" cannot be taken away and only become brighter with time.[22]

Columbus also wrote to his cousin Anna Holman, the daughter of the deceased Clementine and Sanford Holman, explaining their plight. Like their male kinsmen, a few San Augustine girls were sent off to school. Anna and her cousins Mary Garrett and Victoria "Tory" Thomas, the stepdaughter of Elizabeth Holman Campbell Thomas, and therefore a stepniece of Amanda's, had been sent to St. Mary's Hall, an elite Episcopalian finishing school founded in 1837 in Burlington, New Jersey, near Philadelphia. Episcopalian Frances Cox Henderson, wife of the former governor of Texas, escorted the trio to the much-admired school. Like the Texas boys, the girls endured terrible homesickness and culture shock upon their arrival in November 1854. Seventeen-year-old Mary Garrett begged her father to "come for me . . . We have no fire in our room and . . . it is so cold we do not know what to do." Moreover, like Cumby the previous year, she had received no mail from home: "This is a very lonesome place although there is so many girls, but they will not go with us they think that they

21. Ibid. (quotation). Colonel Allen founded the Bastrop Military Institute in January 1858, and Sam Houston, Jr., among others, attended the following year. Webb, Carroll, and Branda (eds.), *Handbook of Texas*, I, 121.

22. Kentucky Military Institute Report, Nov. 23, 1854, CFP; Mary Garrett to Dear Pa, Jan. 13, 1855, Garrett family papers (in possession of Sandra Kardell Calpakis); Matthew Cartwright to Columbus, Jan. 29, 1855, CFP.

are too good." It is not known when the three returned, perhaps in the summer when the Thomases visited New York City.[23] This experience perhaps convinced Matthew that his daughters should be educated closer to home.

Meck resumed classes at KMI in the spring of 1855, but Columbus returned to San Augustine to recuperate at home because his health was so bad. Billy Blount wrote "Friend Cumba" giving almost no news of the institute but instructed Columbus to "Tell my little *Duck*" to write.[24] Apparently San Augustine girls were not dependable correspondents either.

Amanda was four months pregnant when Columbus arrived home. It had been ten years since her last pregnancy, and she found it more burdensome. Matthew had left in January 1855 to ride his circuit in northeastern Texas through Marshall, Jefferson, and Gilmer, but reported gloomy market prices. The best cotton sold for six cents a pound at Jefferson and buyers were few. Unlike so many others, Matthew's land trading provided an alternative source of income and he did not have to depend on the fluctuating cotton market. But money was again scarce and Matthew feared a parallel decline in land prices. Although absent, he was concerned about the children's education and told Amanda to impress upon Leonidas and the two girls "the importance of the improvement of their minds and a proper course in life." She was also to make sure that Leonidas rode Matthew's horse to water three times a day for the exercise. Aware of Amanda's state of mind during his absence, he closed with husbandly advice: "Be cheerful in the station of wife, mother and Governess."[25]

Matthew left again in June 1855 for a horseback tour to Upshur and Wood counties and then south to Athens in Henderson County, where he took time to write. Five years earlier, at the request of the Henderson County commissioners court, Matthew had donated a section (640 acres) out of a large tract that he owned so that the county could relocate the courthouse in its geographic center. Understandably, Matthew took particular in-

23. Ralph K. Turp, *West Jersey Under Four Flags* (Philadelphia: Dorrance & Co., 1975), 243; Mary Garrett to Dear Pa, Dec. 31, 1854 (quotations), Garrett family papers; Elizabeth Thomas to Amanda Cartwright, June 7, 16, 1855, CFP.

24. W. T. Blount to Friend Cumba [Columbus Cartwright], Apr. 12, 1855, CFP.

25. Matthew Cartwright to Dear Companion, Jan. 16, 1855, CFP.

terest in the growth of Athens, growth which, of course, made his land more valuable. He was delighted to find that Henderson County, which unlike San Augustine had been suffering from drought, had received rain and that the crops were growing well, which would stimulate land sales. Matthew, however, could not return home immediately as he had intended because he needed to go to Austin. He hoped to be home by the end of July, close to the expected time of Amanda's confinement. It will be "pretty Late—," he wrote. "I hope . . . the cares of home affairs may be light."[26]

Thirty-eight-year-old Amanda was without sisterly support during the summer of her last pregnancy. Her youngest sister, Elvira Wheeler, had moved to Polk County, and Bettie Thomas left San Augustine with her husband in June for Tennessee and New York on business and pleasure. The Thomases took the steamer to New Orleans, where they remained only one day because "there was so much sickness." Betty could not complete some shopping for a neighbor, and she asked Amanda to relay a message that she would shop instead in New York. The Thomases continued to Mobile by water and then traveled overland for five days to Shelbyville in Bedford County, Tennessee, to visit Polly Ann, the oldest Holman sister, and her husband, Dr. James E. Barksdale. The other sister, America Lane, called "Meck" by her family, had lost her husband in 1849 and had lived with the Barksdales until her recent marriage to merchant J. C. Akin. Betty assured Amanda that Mr. Akin was "very much of a gentleman" and that she liked him and so would Amanda.[27]

Amanda had not visited her native state since her marriage, apparently by choice. Betty tried to describe everything: both Shelbyville sisters had "beautiful homes," but "I should never have known America, she has changed so much . . . she is a beautiful woman . . . her children are very hansome [sic]." The eldest, Sarah, was "nearly grown" and played the piano well. "Polly Ann is geting [sic] very large, but not near as corpulent as

26. Matthew Cartwright to Dear Companion, June 20, 29, 1855, CFP.

27. *Four Families,* 981; Elizabeth Thomas to Amanda Cartwright, June 7, 1855 (quotations), CFP; U.S. Seventh Census (1850), Bedford County, Tennessee (microfilm); Bedford County, Tenn., Marriage Records (microfilm; CL); *The Goodspeed Histories of Maury, Williamson, Rutherford, Wilson, Bedford and Marshall Counties of Tennessee,* 875.

you and I. She will weight [sic] about 140 pounds." Betty added that the Tennessee sisters longed to see Amanda and "Mr. Cartwright."[28] "Meck" Lane Akin, of course, remembered Matthew when he was courting Amanda, but Polly Ann had never met him.

Back in Texas, Matthew reached home in time for Amanda's confinement, and on August 11, 1855, she gave birth to a son whom she named Matthew. The doting father remained at home until November, when he and his brother Richard went to Austin on business. Richard, always in poor health, became very ill, which threatened to delay their return until just before Christmas. Matthew promised that they would come as soon as Richard could travel because he longed to see "our laughing Matt."[29]

Twenty years older than Richard, Matthew felt protective toward his younger brother, and this trip was intended to bolster the younger Cartwright's spirits. Not only was his health bad, but Richard and his wife had separated four years earlier after only two years of marriage and the birth of a daughter. For a Cartwright heir, Richard seems to have been constantly short of funds, which suggests perhaps gambling and drinking too much. (Family letters in 1873 refer obliquely to the tragedy of too much alcohol but do not mention names.) Richard had married Ann Eliza Berry, the daughter of John G. Berry, on September 15, 1849, when she was sixteen years old. No documents exist detailing their marital difficulties except for what is revealed in deed records and tax rolls. Just before his marriage, Richard sold his half of the old John Cartwright homestead (the other half belonged to Cinton's heirs) to Matthew for $3,000. The family was still unaware that they had no title to the Palo Gacho homestead. When Ann took her daughter and five slaves and returned to her father's home in 1851, Matthew returned three hundred acres of the Palo Gacho land to Richard for a pasture for his cattle. Richard still owned Jordan, the blacksmith he had inherited after the death of Clinton, and, needing money, Richard sold him to George Teal in 1852 for his tax value of $1,625. After 1852, Richard's name no longer appeared on the San Augustine tax roll, not even a poll tax, which means he must have been living

28. Elizabeth Thomas to Amanda Cartwright, June 16, 1855, CFP.
29. M. Cartwright to Dear Companion, Dec. 9, 1855, CFP.

elsewhere temporarily. When Matthew and Richard returned to San Augustine in late 1855, the younger brother returned to the house on the Palo Gacho, apparently not in need of nursing.[30]

Although Matthew never took an active role in politics, he was interested in civic betterment. For some time San Augustine officials had wanted to build a new courthouse on the old town square, which was somewhat cluttered with buildings on its perimeter. San Augustine's courthouse was in the old Republic of Texas customs house and it was too small. County offices were scattered all over town, and in the early 1850s the county fathers began soliciting donations for a new building. Progress was slow until 1852, when a windfall from the federal government allowed

30. San Augustine County, Tax Rolls, 1849–1856; Matthew Cartwright [Jr.] to Leonidas Cartwright, Apr. 28, 1890 [Richard's daughter], CFP.

Texas state legislators to return nine-tenths of each county's taxes for six years. This munificence resulted from the ten million dollars appropriated by the United States Congress to settle Texas's old unilateral claim made during the republic to the portion of New Mexico west of the 103rd meridian. In exchange for the money, Texas agreed to the present-day border with New Mexico. One-half of the sum to be paid to Texas had been reserved by the federal government to pay creditors of the defunct republic, while the remaining five million dollars was deposited with the state. After paying some indebtedness, state legislators set aside two million dollars for a public school fund while the remaining money allowed the state to relieve county taxpayers.[31]

San Augustine, like many other counties, used the returned tax funds to build a courthouse. The two-story, forty-five-foot square brick building was completed in 1854 in the center of the old town square even though there were buildings scattered around the square's edges. County officials urged those who owned such property to give it to the county, and in September 1855 Matthew Cartwright deeded lots #143 and #144 facing Columbia Street, where he had a houselike structure that had been used at different times as a store, to the county for $1. Other property owners seem not to have relinquished their claims as readily. Historian George L. Crocket said that the buildings around the courthouse remained until 1901, when the entire block was cleared.[32] The old Cartwright store on the corner across Harrison Street, however, remained in family hands.

Columbus planned to return to KMI in January 1856, but word arrived that a fire had damaged the buildings. By the time he learned that school would open anyway, it was too late to go to Kentucky. In the meantime, Meck had trouble with a recurring infection in his left eye, and asked to come home. Matthew discouraged him, urging him to remain if the eye was improving: "I wish you to soar . . . and move on in pursuit of knowledge which is power and wealth." Amanda sympathized with her son, and thought perhaps a special doctor somewhere might be able

31. Crocket, *Two Centuries*, 109, 256; Rupert N. Richardson et al., *Texas: The Lone Star State* (3rd ed.; Englewood Cliffs, N.J.: Prentice-Hall, 1970), 140, 142.

32. San Augustine County, Deed Records, D, 322–323; Crocket, *Two Centuries*, 110.

to cure the ailment. She had recently become interested in religion and told Meck that "the Scriptures says there is nothing impossible with God."[33] Meck eventually lost his left eye.

Unable to return to school, Columbus left on a business tour with his father. On their way through Harrison, Upshur, and Wood counties in January 1856, they discussed long-range plans. Perhaps if the Male Institute reopened soon, Cumby and thirteen-year-old Leonidas could attend. Meck was expected to graduate the following year, and Matthew presumed that he would come home and farm. At present, however, the father had no farming land in San Augustine County to give his sons. The Joses Hobdy place south of town that Matthew had been cultivating during the past year had been sold to William W. Holman. Hobdy and his wife, the former Lizetta Cartwright, a granddaughter of old Robert Cartwright of Nashville, had come to San Augustine County in 1829, and Matthew had helped them secure a headright along Ayish Bayou. Both had died by 1854 and Matthew was the executor of the estate. In typical fashion, he enrolled two of the orphaned Hobdy children in the institute, paying their fees from the estate.[34]

Amanda again assumed control of the family while Matthew and Cumby were gone. The winter of 1855–1856 was the coldest she could remember. The ground remained frozen from Christmas until the end of January, and she was never "so tired of cold weather in my life." No doubt washing and drying clothes for a five-month-old was a trial. When warmer weather returned, little rain fell, and by April the ground in San Augustine County was so hard and dry that people were unable to plow and plant cotton. Amanda's immediate situation was even more difficult because old Nancy's two sons required attention from the mistress. Twenty-year-old Dick had broken his leg in a fall when he drove the horse too fast over a slick bridge. Dick was unable to walk for two months, while ten-year-old Walker had bilious fever. Also, Amanda's namesake, the twelve-year-old orphaned daughter of Robert Cartwright, had temporarily joined them. Matthew

33. Matthew Cartwright to Americus, Jan. 6, 1856 (1st quotation), CFP; Amanda to Americus, Jan. 22, 1856 (2nd quotation), ibid.

34. Matthew Cartwright to Americus, Jan. 6, 1856, CFP; John H. Cartwright [brother of Lizetta Hobdy] to Matthew Cartwright, June 24, 1854, ibid.; List of students at Masonic Institute.

had brought young "Mandy" from Shelbyville the previous September to attend the Masonic Institute and board with its principal, S. B. Bewley. Mandy arrived a few weeks after the birth of young Matt, and evidently Amanda decided that it was better that her niece live with the Bewleys. Mandy's two young brothers, Robert and Matthew, remained in Shelby County.[35]

In April, Ella Holman Wheeler, evidently forgiven by Matthew Cartwright, arrived for a visit along with her husband and four children. "You never saw such a nest of little fellows in your life," Amanda wrote her son, adding that her sister, Betty Thomas, kept them sometimes. Besides nine-year-old William Cartwright, son of the deceased Clinton, Elvira's three Wheeler children ranged in age from five down to an infant who was "the very image of her Mother." Amanda was unable to write Meck in Kentucky as often as she wished because "I have such a heavy charge on me now . . . I hardly know what to do."[36]

An additional concern was the terminally ill Richard, who had not recovered from his bout the previous fall. He had been confined to his house on the Palo Gacho for some time and died on April 25, 1856. Matthew was again absent and George Cartwright not living in Texas when Amanda and Columbus decided to bury him next to Clinton in the old family cemetery on the Palo Gacho. After Matthew returned and began settling Richard's affairs, he finally discovered that his father had not acquired title to the Palo Gacho land, and in 1859 Matthew ceased paying taxes on the old homestead.[37] Matthew seemed to have had no sentimental attachment to the old place and let it be acquired by strangers.

Cotton prices began to recover from the distressing lows of the 1840s, and with the debt to Chabot cleared in May 1854, Matthew decided to return to the commission business and storekeeping in 1856. At the time of Richard's death Matthew was in New Orleans making arrangements with merchants there for next year's crop. On April 27, he boarded the luxurious steamboat *Niagara* for a trip upriver to Louisville on his way to

35. Amanda Cartwright to Americus, Apr. 10, 1856, CFP.

36. Ibid. (quotations); John Cartwright Family Bible.

37. Amanda Cartwright to Americus, Jan. 22, 1856, CFP; John Cartwright Family Bible and graveyard; San Augustine County, Tax Rolls, 1859. This is the last year for the Palo Gacho property.

visit Meck at KMI. He arrived on May 3 and spent two days with his second son, whom he had not seen for almost two years. Both had changed. Matthew had gained so much weight that Meck "didn't hardly know him." Nevertheless, in true nineteenth-century admiration of girth as an indication of well-being, Meck told his mother that "Pa looked better than I ever saw him" and proudly noted that his father was "not much taller than I am." Matthew approved of his tall, handsome son, and told Meck that he wanted him to finish school soon so that he could help with business matters. Seeing his father caused Americus to be "a little homesick," and Matthew told him if the rivers were high enough in June, Meck could come home for a visit. The son cried when the father offered his "hand in farewell."[38]

Matthew paused at Louisville on the journey downriver and bought $250 worth of merchandise intended for family use. Evidently he failed to find everything he needed, for he returned to New Orleans, where he spent another $400, before going home on May 14. The following year Matthew made a long list of dry goods and groceries to be bought during his April visit to the Crescent City. The 500 pounds of sugar, 200 pounds of coffee, 240 pounds of lard, and 350 pounds of hams were intended for the store, along with the 1,000 yards of domestics, prints, ginghams, and muslins, but Matthew also had a long list of items for his family.[39]

That Matthew's financial affairs had recovered is evident from the personal items he bought in New Orleans in April 1857. Amanda, and perhaps Matthew himself, felt that it was time to refurbish the house. First on his list were wallpaper for all rooms and heavy oilcloth for the dining room floor. Amanda needed twelve new dining room chairs, six damask tablecloths, and twenty-five yards of linen for napkins. Matthew was also to buy a 120-piece set of white-and-gilt china, one dozen "fine" knives and forks, and a set of silver castors (cruets). When he reached New Orleans, Matthew added more china, totaling 173 matching pieces, plus tumblers, vases, a tea set, and two marble washsinks. The most expensive items were the $100 china set, the forty-five

38. Printed menu, steamboat *Niagara*, Apr. 27, 1856, for Mr. Cartwright, table 1; Americus to mother, May 6, 1856 (quotations), CFP.

39. Receipts, May 6, 1856, Louisville, and May 14, 1856, New Orleans, CFP; "Memorandum, March 31, 1857 for New Orleans," Account Papers, ibid.

yards of oil cloth at $63, and the $60 mohair mattress for their bed. Matthew also bought a "Verry fine" carriage for $500 and a carriage robe for $10.[40] Obviously the Cartwrights intended to keep up with or surpass their neighbors by displaying the latest in home decor and carriages.

Likewise new clothing was required. Matthew's list included three pairs of pants, two fine coats, three vests, a cloak, six shirts, cravats, handkerchiefs, a pair of fine boots, and two hats (one black silk and the other white beaver felt), totaling $170. Amanda wanted a braid of hair and a back comb to help create the fashionable hairstyle of the day, along with a suitable lady's "headdress," the fancy cap worn by married women at home. One-half dozen fine Pickett finger gloves, black silk hose, assorted collars and cuffs, two painted jaconet (a thin India cotton) dresses, a plaid silk, a pair of jet bracelets, and a pair of gold earrings to match her breastpin completed her list. Matthew's oldest daughter Anna wanted sheet music, a saddle and bridle, and a white "hair" summer bonnet trimmed with white ribbon. Amanda ordered Matthew to buy similar bonnets for second daughter Mary and niece Mandy, two pairs of shoes for each girl, and thirty yards of English brown merino (cashmere) for three dresses, plus three summer dresses and three dozen pairs of ladies' hose. Matthew deducted the expenses for his niece from the assets of Robert's estate just as he did for keeping his nephews in school in Shelby County.[41]

In the spring of 1858, Columbus and Meck decided to attend Cumberland University in Lebanon, Tennessee, near the old home of the Cartwrights. The university had opened in 1842, evolving from Cumberland College, which had been founded by the Cumberland Presbyterian Church in Kentucky. Lebanon impressed the site selection committee with its growth and importance; in addition, the city promised $10,000 toward a suitable building. Two years later the imposing structure was completed, and Cumberland University soon earned a reputation as one of the finest colleges in the South, with an outstanding faculty and a commodious campus.[42]

40. "Memorandum."
41. Ibid.; Robert G. Cartwright estate settlement papers, CFP.
42. Merrit (ed.), *History of Wilson County,* 114–116.

The brothers left San Augustine in April and stopped to visit their mother's sister, Aunt Polly Ann Barksdale, in Shelbyville, Tennessee, about eighty miles south of Lebanon. Aunt Meck Lane Akin and her husband, however, had moved to McMinnville, perhaps fifty miles to northeast. During an extended visit with the Akins, Columbus fell in love with his sixteen-year-old cousin, Sarah "Sallie" Lane, who had recently completed studies at Mary Sharp College. Cousin marriages were quite common in the nineteenth century and caused no particular notice. Cumby wrote his parents asking their consent because he was two months and a few days shy of twenty-one. Matthew did not approve; after all, he had waited to marry until he was almost twenty-nine and well established with property, but he left the matter to his son's discretion and generously sent $200. Meck attended the June 25, 1858, evening ceremony and told his mother that he was pleased with his smart and pretty sister-in-law.[43]

Matthew finally concluded that marriage and settling down to farming would be more beneficial for Columbus than school because Cumby's "health and constitution requir[ed] an active life." (The scarlet fever in 1854 had left Columbus with a chronic kidney infection.) Should Cumby want some land, his father was ready to assist. The newlyweds left McMinnville in September 1858 in a carryall with a pair of handsome matched horses and accompanied by Sallie's inherited slaves. The blacks drove a wagon pulled by two mules belonging to Sallie's stepfather that would be sold for him in Texas. Columbus told his parents that the "very dark dappled claybank" horses "can knock the shine off of Col Blount's or any other pair of horses that ever made a track in San Augustine." The Cartwright love of fine horses was still much in evidence and Cumby intended the pair as a gift for Amanda, writing that they were "exactly the horses to please Ma." Having softened the parental mood over such extravagance, the bridegroom added, "I did not have enough money to pay for the horses, wagon and carryall besides our expenses . . . and I wish you would let me have about $600 to settle with Mr. Akin when I get home." Cumby explained that it would be a loan because there was inheritance money "due Sarah but we cannot

43. A. P. Cartwright to Mother, June 25, 1858, CFP; Matthew Cartwright to Columbus, July 14, 1858, ibid.

Columbus "Cumby" Cartwright (1837–1901), the eldest son of Matthew and Amanda, and his wife, Sarah "Sallie" Lane (1841–1895), 1870s. Courtesy Cartwright Family Descendants.

get it at present." The newlyweds planned to camp along the way, and took the "dry rout" [sic] north through Kentucky and Illinois, then across the Mississippi River and south through Missouri and Arkansas in order to avoid the marshy, fever-ridden bottomlands on the eastern shore.[44]

Meck had enrolled at Cumberland University in September 1858 and found "an excellent boarding house" and "was studying hard." Meck wrote to his father on September 8, carefully omitting the details of his pleasant summer passed in parties, although he had unwisely described his frivolous activities in a letter to his sister Anna. Instead, Americus assured Matthew that he would work hard to "make myself a man" as his father had urged in a recent letter. Meck wrote, "I know that nothing could please you and Ma more than for me to acquit myself with honor." He added that he had grown an inch and a half and was now six feet tall and weighed 140 pounds.[45]

When Anna shared Meck's letter with her parents, Matthew became furious with the prodigal scholar. The businessman was irritated that eighteen-year-old Americus had spent three weeks at a summer resort "dancing nearly every night" and that he had lost his money. Matthew added, "Your time and money for the last six months I consider to be lost and I hope that you do not wish to continue in the same course." Meck should "determine on a proper . . . course. . . . Will you do it? Speak plain. Say nothing that you will not carry out." Matthew sent $150, wondering how Meck had been sustaining himself since the loss of his money.[46]

Parental discussions about Americus's transgressions filled the ears of sixteen-year-old Leonidas, and he wrote to Meck in October repeating his father's rhetoric, sounding more like a parent than a younger brother: "I am in hopes that you will make use of your time and opportunities . . . to make us proud of you. . . . [T]he time that you spend foolishly passes away never to be recalled." Lon was attending the Masonic Institute and had classes with Mr. Bewley and Mr. Edward Eels, the Presbyterian

44. Matthew Cartwright to Columbus, July 14, 1858 (1st quotation), CFP; Columbus Cartwright to Dear Pa, Sept. 26, 1858 (2nd–6th quotations), ibid.

45. Columbus to Dear Pa, Sept. 26, 1858; A. P. Cartwright to Dear Father, Sept. 8, 1858 (quotations), CFP.

46. Matthew Cartwright to My Dear Son [Americus], Sept. 8, 1858, CFP.

minister, who was "even more strict" and an excellent scholar. There were ninety boys, while Anna, Mary, and cousin Amanda were among only fifty-five girls in the female branch.[47]

When Columbus and Sallie arrived in November 1858, Amanda and Matthew discovered that they were about to become grandparents. The trip had been a grand adventure with nobody sick except one of Akin's mules that died after eating green corn. Columbus bought a replacement mule by giving an IOU drawn on his father in order to finish the journey. The patriarch generously financed the purchase of 415 acres east of town from Felix G. Roberts and Widow Easter Jane Sublett for a farm for the young couple and also helped them buy horses, cattle, hogs, and chickens. Columbus paid taxes in 1859 on five horses, thirty-five head of cattle, and three slaves. Matthew recorded the sums of money provided in a memorandum book so that all of the children would be treated equally in the future.[48]

It was Lon's turn to accompany his father on the spring business trip to Henderson and Upshur counties. Amanda wrote to Matthew on February 10, 1859, that Anna and Mary had started classes and were studying hard. Every evening they practiced their music in the parlor. During the day, Amanda visited Sallie and Columbus and also supervised the plowing and planting of her garden. Responding to rumors that abolitionists were trying to stir slave rebellions, Amanda kept "the gun at the head of my bed" and made one of her slave women sleep in the house, but added, "I presume we will not be pestered with [abolitionists] as none has made their appearance yet." Three-and-a-half-year-old Matthew slept with his mother and promised to "kill every one that comes." She also worried about the scarlet fever that had struck nine members of a nearby family, leaving one dead. Perhaps Matthew returned in time for the birth of his namesake first grandchild on March 17, 1859.[49]

47. Unsigned draft by Leonidas Cartwright to Dear Brother [Meck], Oct. 13, 1858 (quotations), CFP; Crocket, *Two Centuries,* 286–287.

48. Columbus Cartwright to Matthew, Nov. 1, 1858, from Marshall, CFP; Amanda Cartwright to Dear Companion, Feb. 10, 1859, ibid.; San Augustine County, Deed Records, J, 172–173, 182; San Augustine County, Tax Rolls, 1859; Leather memorandum book, CFP.

49. Amanda Cartwright to Dear Companion, Feb. 10, 1859, CFP.

Niece Mandy, now sixteen and finishing school, lived with Matthew and Amanda and needed a white Swiss muslin dress along with appropriate slippers and bonnet for the May fete. Like others who could afford to pay a dressmaker, the Cartwright women did not make their own clothes. Mandy had a beau, A. D. McCutchan, a newcomer who was the printer at the local newspaper and who joined the musical evenings when Anna and Mary played the piano while the others sang. The young couple became engaged, and Anna and Mary helped their cousin assemble her trousseau and hope chest. Besides her wedding dress, Mandy bought material and trimmings for four other dresses, each requiring fifteen yards to cover the hoopskirt petticoats fashionable at this time.[50]

Mandy and A. D. were the first couple to be married in the Cartwright parlor, and the pair said their vows on Wednesday, September 14, 1859, before Rev. A. Kimble. Two weeks later, they had an ambrotype made, as did Anna and Mary, and the cousins exchanged pictures. At the end of October, the newlyweds left for Austin by stagecoach, and Mandy wrote to her cousins about the exhausting five-day trip. The McCutchans returned to San Augustine and took a room at the home of the Widow Anderson adjacent to Columbus and Sallie's farm. Beginning in May 1860, McCutchan edited and published the *Red Land Express,* which advocated Gov. Sam Houston for the presidency of the United States. When his chances faded, McCutchan supported John C. Breckinridge, the candidate of the southern Democrats.[51]

As tensions mounted over state and national politics at the close of the 1850s, Matthew Cartwright recorded nothing on paper about his political views or position. That he was a Democrat seems evident: in 1858 he named Jane's fourth child

50. Amanda, Minor heir R. G. Cartwright, Account Book no. 12, 1859–1868, 12–14, CFP.

51. [Ambrotype], ibid., Marshall *Texas Republican,* Sept. 24, 1859; *Texas State Gazette* (Austin), Oct. 8, 1859; Amanda McCutchan to Dear Cousin Anna, Nov. 2, 1859, CFP; U.S. Eighth Census (1860), San Augustine County, Texas; Marilyn McAdams Sibley, *Lone Stars and State Gazettes: Texas Newspapers before the Civil War* (College Station: Texas A&M University Press, 1983), 364.

"Buchanan," for Pres. James Buchanan, and in 1861 called Emeline's son "Jefferson Davis."[52] As usual, Matthew was more interested in taking care of his land business than in politics, although what was going on in the world of politics would soon affect his family's comfortable life-style in San Augustine.

52. Matthew Cartwright Bible.

Nine

Pride, Confidence, and War

1860–1863

*M*atthew Cartwright was not only the wealthiest man in San Augustine County in 1860, but also the sixth richest in the state. Although he was unaware of his statewide rank during his lifetime, he may have suspected it. His wealth was in land, not slaves or merchandise like the other eight men who had estates valued at over $500,000. Listing his occupation as "Land Trader" on the 1860 census, Matthew estimated his real estate at $500,000 and his personal property near $75,000, but with only thirteen slaves, a total wealth of $575,000. His brothers-in-law trailed him in total wealth on the 1860 census as in the previous decade, but they held more slaves: "Planter" William Garrett had a $171,651 estate including 132 slaves, while "Farmer-Merchant" Iredell D. Thomas had $166,000 in property and 52 slaves. Proud of his accumulated wealth, Matthew Cartwright urged his sons to "prepare yourself for your future station in life."[1]

1. Ralph A. Wooster, "Wealthy Texans, 1860," *SHQ*, LXXI (Oct., 1967),

Since 1850, Matthew had increased his land holdings by 94,000 acres scattered over fifty counties. Most tracts were in northeastern Texas, where farmers liked the good prairie soil. Certain acreage dramatically increased in value during the decade because of nearby economic development, but average tracts brought $1 per acre if conveniently situated, while remote, undeveloped land sold for fifty cents per acre. In this era before railroads, the most desirable land was along navigable streams. Inflation was not a factor, as demonstrated by Matthew's long-held, fertile, twenty-eight hundred acres on Oyster Creek in Fort Bend County: the costliest single tract Matthew owned, it had been roughly appraised at $10,000 and retained the same value of $3.50 per acre through 1870.[2]

Fifty-two years old when the 1860s began, Matthew was a handsome, tall, portly man weighing almost 250 pounds. Wearing spectacles for close work, he was sufficiently vain to dye his graying auburn hair. Even though he was heavy, he still enjoyed riding his big sorrel horse, Red-Buck, as he traveled around the state on business. Everyone except his wife addressed him by the courtesy title of "Colonel," the popular deferential nomenclature awarded to prominent Texans regardless of their actual military service or lack thereof.[3]

At forty-two Amanda was also properly stout, evidence of good living, and a handsome woman. The energetic horsewoman of 1846 now rode sedately in her carriage behind the matched claybanks. She, too, was vain; when her oldest grandson, Bobby, began talking in 1862, he called her "granny," no doubt repeating what he heard from his parents. But Amanda was dismayed and playfully threatened to "whip him for it" unless he called her "mistis," which, of course, was how the servants addressed her.

165–166, 178; Matthew Cartwright to Columbus, Jan. 29, 1855 (quotation), Cartwright Research Collection.

2. San Augustine County, Tax Rolls, 1851, 1859. These tax rolls were used because they were complete and legible, while others were not.

3. Matthew Cartwright to Leonidas, Apr. 7, 1863, CFP; Account Book no. 12, 1859–1868, 20, ibid. The first evidence of the use of "Colonel" is in a letter to Matthew from T. B. Howard, Aug. 7, 1857, CFP. For the Texans' disposition for titles as early as 1839, see the remarks of an English visitor, *Galveston Island; or, A Few Months Off the Coast of Texas: The Journal of Francis C. Sheridan, 1839–1840*, ed. Willis W. Pratt (Austin: University of Texas Press, 1954), 13.

Like most of her contemporaries, she devoted her efforts to home and family. Although her daughters had not attended fashionable schools elsewhere, their letters and those of their friends indicated that local teachers had instilled firm training in grammar and penmanship plus a knowledge of eighteenth-century and modern literature. In their mid-teens in 1860 and finished with their academic education, Anna and Mary enjoyed music and painting and practiced ladylike domestic skills. They could sew, knit, crochet, and do fancy embroidery, but they also learned to cook and tend the garden under the direction of their mother.[4]

Meck finished his studies at Cumberland University in early 1859 and returned home to clerk in the Burrus and Cartwright store now run by Anthony A. Burrus, who still owed Matthew money. Within a year Meck was unhappy in what his mother called "this dull town." She told Lon that "Meck begins to think his cake will be doughy . . . he has a strong notion of going to school again."[5] But before Americus could resume his education, the Civil War began.

It was Leonidas's turn to go to school away from home in 1860. He and two or three others started for Lebanon, Tennessee, by taking a stagecoach from San Augustine to Alexandria, Louisiana, which, Lon explained, was "very rough and unpleasant" because they had to help get the coach "out of the mud." At Alexandria, the boys boarded the steamboat for New Orleans, which Lon found "very pleasant," and spent a day wandering the Crescent City. Impressed by the equestrian statue of Jackson in the square, the first statue he had ever seen, Lon reported that the "monument of General Jackson . . . looked very natural." The young men traveled by steamboat to Memphis, where they transferred to a train to Nashville and a stage to Cumberland University, arriving by the end of January 1860.[6]

---

4. Anna to Brothers, Jan. 22, 1862 (quotations), CFP; also see Jennie Blount to Leonidas Cartwright, Mar. 30, 1863, ibid., in which she (a schoolmate of Anna and Mary) quotes Thomas Gray, "Elegy Written in a Country Churchyard" (1751), and Edgar Allen Poe, "The Raven" (1845).
5. Amanda Cartwright to Leonidas, Sept. 2 [?], 1860 (quotations), CFP; Matthew Cartwright to Americus, July 12, 1861, ibid.; San Augustine *Red Land Express*, Oct. 20, 1860, p. 2 [Burrus-Cartwright store]; also see n. 19 below.
6. Leonidas Cartwright to Dear Ma, Jan. 23, 1860 (quotations), CFP; Leonidas Cartwright to Dear Pa, Jan. 29, 1860, ibid.

For some unexplained reason, Lon left Lebanon and returned home in June 1860, although his friend, John H. Massey from Nacogdoches, remained behind to struggle with classes. In July, however, Lon and the Sublett brothers, Phillip and Henry, started for Bastrop Military Institute, which had opened two years earlier under the direction of Colonel Allen, formerly of the Kentucky Military Institute. En route they spent a week fishing and hunting deer at the Trinity County plantation of Franklin Bolivar Sublett, Phil and Henry's older brother. After a month at school, Leonidas told Columbus that he liked Colonel Allen, who was "a very clever old gentleman." There were about 130 boys at the school and more arriving every day. Lon's only complaints concerned getting up so early in the morning and the drilling, sentiments echoed by the Subletts. Lon proudly reported that he had entered Latin classes at the senior level and mathematics as a sophomore. But like his brothers before him, Matthew's third son suffered from homesickness and chided his family for not writing.[7]

Lon changed his opinion about the colonel in November, he told his father, when he received lower grades than others "who I did not think deserved high marks. . . . I was very much hurt . . . and would have quit school but I did not have permission from you." Lon confronted Colonel Allen about what he considered an unfair grade, explaining to Matthew that if it happened once, it might again unless he stood up for himself. Then "my name would be down with the common stock" instead of at the top of the class where he belonged. Colonel Allen told Lon that he had "the native talent to stand at the head," but that he was poorly prepared due to inferior teaching before coming to BMI. Lon was not convinced and asked Matthew for a letter allowing him to leave in case "my feelings are thus trampled upon again . . . I can quit this school and go to another."[8]

Lon had a double burden to carry. Not only did he have to perform as his father expected, but he had to be as good as or better than his two older brothers. He overcame his hurt pride and worked very hard so that his recitations were better during

7. Leonidas Cartwright to John [H. Massey], July 31, 1860, CFP; Leonidas Cartwright to Joel [V. Massey], Aug. 26, 1860, ibid.; Leonidas Cartwright to Dear Pa, Aug. 31, 1860, ibid.; Leonidas Cartwright to Columbus, Sept. 22, 1860 (quotation), ibid.

8. Lon to M. Cartwright, Nov. 16, 1860 (quotations), CFP.

the next month. He told his sister that his marks "have been very high" and that he intended to maintain his position to "prove to those who have . . . considered me as the shabb of the Cartwright stock that they were mistaken." Bolivar Sublett, the guardian of his younger brothers, was so upset when Lon's grades were better than those of Phillip that he complained to Colonel Allen. The headmaster doubtless had received such complaints before and replied that Phillip would have to prove his "academic excellence." Lon still considered changing schools and thought the one at Independence would be good. By December 1860, however, a number of boys were sick with typhoid fever, including Colonel Allen's son. Although BMI remained open through April 1861, Leonidas and the Sublett brothers returned home at the end of the year and attended classes in San Augustine for a few months.[9]

The ominous political situation at the close of 1860, of course, encouraged parents to call their sons home. National politics became heated that election year when Northerners and Southerners disagreed over the issue of allowing slavery in the territories west of the Mississippi River. The issue was not new, but had supposedly been settled in the 1854 Kansas-Nebraska Act that permitted local voters in the territories to decide whether they wanted a slave state or a free state. The act pleased neither side: most Northerners were not abolitionists, but they did not want slavery to spread into new states, while Southerners demanded that Congress protect the rights of slaveholders to take their property wherever they liked. In 1860, Southern Democrats walked out of the Democratic national convention, which then nominated Stephen A. Douglas of Illinois, who favored popular sovereignty. Those who abandoned the party, including the Texas delegates, called their own convention and named John C. Breckinridge of Kentucky as their candidate. The Republican party, created in 1856 to oppose the extension of slavery into the territories, nominated Lincoln on a platform proclaiming no expansion of slavery but said nothing about abolition. Former Whigs and others in the South who feared disunion formed the Constitutional Union Party with John Bell of Tennessee as their leader. With a four-way split—two Northern and two Southern

9. L. Cartwright to Anna Cartwright, Dec. 3, 1860 (quotations), CFP; William B. Sayers to Lon, Apr. 11, 1861, ibid.; Joel V. Massey to Leonidas, Mar. 17, 1861, ibid.

parties—the Republicans won the election by carrying the populous Northern states. Lincoln received 180 electoral votes compared with a combined total of 123 for his three opponents.[10]

In the month before the November election, Lon had gone to hear "Old Sam Houston" speak at the Bastrop Military Institute. Houston had left the U.S. Senate and was elected governor of Texas in August 1859 as an independent, old-fashioned Democrat, meaning he was a unionist and opposed to the vocal Democrats who were willing to endanger the Union over the issue of slavery. Old Sam was stumping against the Texas extremists and appealing to Texas unionists; he had not, however, joined the national Constitutional Union party. Lon did not say how the audience received Houston's speech, one of a series he made in Central Texas. After the election of Lincoln in November, however, some of the cadets joined local leaders in making speeches at a protest meeting. Lon wrote, "The Disunion flag has been spread out to float in the air here."[11] The Cartwrights did not mention what they thought about secession in their letters.

The results of the November election spread by telegraph to major cities throughout the nation, and within three weeks even the smaller towns in Texas heard the disturbing news. Negative Democratic campaign rhetoric about the dangers the Republican party posed to the South convinced many Texans that they should quit the Union rather than endure Republican rule. While there was no widespread sentiment for secession in Texas before the election, almost immediately leading Democrats began a series of meetings to arouse the movement. On November 24 the Marshall *Texas Republican,* read by the Cartwrights, fed the fire for secession: "From every portion of our State . . . where intelligence has been received on Lincoln's election, there has been manifested but

10. For Texas reaction to this split, see Walter L. Buenger, *Secession and the Union in Texas* (Austin: University of Texas Press, 1984), 48–52, and Randolph B. Campbell, *A Southern Community in Crisis: Harrison County, Texas, 1850–1860* (Austin: Texas State Historical Association, 1983), 193–197.

11. Leonidas Cartwright to John H. Massey, Oct. 13, 1860 (1st quotation), CFP; L. Cartwright to Columbus, Nov. 23, 1860 (2nd quotation), ibid.; Buenger, *Secession,* 54; also see James Alex Baggett, "The Constitutional Union Party in Texas," *SHQ,* LXXXII (Jan., 1979), 233–264; Randolph B. Campbell, *Sam Houston and the American Southwest* (New York: HarperCollins College Publishers, 1993), 142–149.

one feeling . . . the people of Texas will never consent to Black Republican domination."[12]

The perceived danger was twofold: forbidding slavery in new territory suggested a moral condemnation of the system and a step toward its destruction, which threatened the economic well-being and social system of Southerners. Second, the widely believed notion that all Republicans favored immediate abolition and Negro equality stirred irrational fears of both slave insurrection and the dreaded amalgamation of the races. Texas Democrats labeled the series of fires in North Texas during the hot, dry summer of 1860 an abolitionist plot to incite a slave rebellion, and though the rumor proved untrue, many Texans remained uneasy. The *Texas State Gazette* in Austin carried an typical editorial on November 17: "The negros would of course be set free, and . . . would prey . . . upon the industrious white population."[13] Thus the Republican victory and its implied threat to the Southern way of life led to the demand for secession and ultimately to the fight for "states' rights."

Conservative unionists including the Old Hero of San Jacinto opposed separating from the nation they had struggled so hard to join. In an "Address to the People of Texas" published in pro-Houston newspapers, including San Augustine's *Red Land Express,* edited by Matthew's nephew-by-marriage A. D. McCutchan, Governor Houston warned against demagoguery and pleaded for reason. He delayed convening the state legislature, the only body empowered to call for a convention to discuss recent developments; instead, he favored a consultation of all the Southern states.[14]

The call for reason, however, drowned in a sea of inflammatory secession rhetoric. On December 1 the residents of San Augustine held "one of the largest, most united and best conducted public meetings" with old Alexander Horton presiding. Merchant S. W. Blount, former district clerk Calloway Dean, and others formed a committee to adopt resolutions and to write a petition asking

12. Marshall *Texas Republican,* Nov. 24, 1861, quoted in Buenger, *Secession,* 130.

13. Buenger, *Secession,* 55–60, 119; *Texas State Gazette* (Austin), Nov. 17, 1861, quoted in ibid., 20.

14. Houston's Address to the People, in Williams and Barker (eds.), *Writings of Sam Houston,* VIII, 206–212.

Governor Houston to convene the legislature. Men everywhere in East Texas, said San Augustine lawyer Rufus Price, are "against tamely acquiescing in this election." At the same time, Texas Congressman John H. Reagan wrote to Texas Supreme Court Justice Oran M. Roberts that if Sam Houston "still stands in the way of the popular" call for a convention, the people should do it themselves. Reagan hoped his old friend would be a member of such a convention. Following Reagan's advice, a second meeting took place in San Augustine on December 27 at which a resolution was passed asking the county judge to order an election for delegates to such a convention. One hundred and forty-four men unanimously chose Calloway Dean to go to Austin.[15]

While Governor Houston continued to argue that Americans who believed in the democratic process should accept Lincoln's election, the convention delegates met in Austin on January 28, 1861, and chose O. M. Roberts president. On February 1 they voted 166 to 8 to secede from the Union and sent the ordinance to the people for their approval. Texans went to the polls on February 23 and endorsed the secession ordinance 46,129 to 14,697, with a favorable vote in most East Texas counties. In San Augustine County, out of about 490 eligible voters, 265 men went to the polls and cast 243 votes for secession and 22 against. This meant that about 92 percent of those voting in San Augustine favored leaving the Union, but almost one-half of the males over twenty-one did not vote. Texas seceded on March 2, 1861, and joined the Confederate States of America. Governor Houston refused to take the oath of loyalty to the CSA; the convention declared the office of governor vacant and elevated Lt. Gov. Edward Clark of Marshall to the position.[16]

15. Rufus Price to O. M. Roberts, Dec. 2, 1860 (1st and 2nd quotations), Roberts Papers; Crocket, *Two Centuries,* 332; John H. Reagan to O. M. Roberts, Dec. 7, 1860 (3rd quotation), Roberts Papers; San Augustine *Red Land Express,* Dec. 29, 1860, Jan. 12, 1861. For an excellent discussion of the causes for secession in East Texas, see Campbell, *Southern Community in Crisis,* 193–197.

16. Ralph A. Wooster, "Statehood, War, and Reconstruction," in Donald W. Whisenhunt (ed.), *Texas: A Sesquicentennial Celebration* (Austin: Eakin Press, 1985), 110–111; Stephen B. Oates, "Texas Under the Secessionists," in Ralph A. Wooster and Robert A. Calvert (comps.), *Texas Vistas: Selections from the* Southwestern Historical Quarterly (Austin: Texas State Historical Association, 1987), 147; Joe T. Timmons, "The Referendum in Texas on the Ordinance

Even before Texans voted to secede, and acting on the dubious authority of the Secession Convention, Col. Benjamin McCulloch, a celebrated Texas Ranger and veteran of the Mexican War, successfully led 1,000 volunteers against the United States Army post at San Antonio on February 15, 1861. Not a shot was fired by the 250 U.S. cavalrymen who were allowed to evacuate the post, a stunning victory soon celebrated throughout Texas. This action preceded by two months the incident at Fort Sumter in Charleston harbor on April 12 that signaled the start of the war. The arms, ordnance, and equipment captured in San Antonio would help supply Texas Confederate troops.[17]

In February 1861, in response to a call from the Secession Convention, the de facto state government, San Augustine County commissioners appropriated $1,000 for "fitting out a company of volunteer infantry . . . to serve for twelve months" as a home guard. On February 23, the day voters went to the polls to endorse secession, the Red Land Minute Company received a flag from fifteen young ladies representing the fifteen Southern states. The procession formed at the old Wesleyan College at nine in the morning and marched past the Cartwright house to the university, where Miss Martha Anderson gave a "patriotical" oration and presented the banner to Billy Blount. The entire group paraded around town and back to the university, where Bolivar Sublett delivered an address that was followed by a barbecue. Two weeks later the *Red Land Express* announced that the Red Land Cavalry company would drill on Friday mornings while the infantry would meet at the college on Tuesday and Friday nights. Daniel M. Short, a veteran of the Mexican War, and others eager for a military appointment from the governor rushed to Austin.[18]

Although excitement remained high, no units left San Augustine until summer. In the meantime, Lon studied for and passed oral examinations in San Augustine while Matthew ordered car-

---

of Secession, February 23, 1861: The Vote," *East Texas Historical Journal*, XI (Fall, 1973), 18.

17. Oates, "Texas Under the Secessionists," 148–149.

18. Campbell, *Southern Community in Crisis*, 200; Minutes of the County Court, San Augustine County, cited in Crocket, *Two Centuries*, 333 (1st quotation), although pp. 333–336 have incorrect chronology; San Augustine *Red Land Express*, Feb. 23, Mar. 16, 1861; Joel V. Massey to Leonidas, Mar. 17, 1861 (2nd quotation), CFP.

pet, piano sheet music, two Leghorn hats, and two fine silk dresses from New Orleans, as if unconcerned about the coming war. Except for holding a note on the Burrus store, Matthew was again divorced from storekeeping and had leased Clinton's two-story store and roominghouse on the southeast corner of the square to Col. Richard Waterhouse, a veteran of the Mexican War who moved to San Augustine in 1852. Toward the end of April 1861, Lon accompanied his father on a trip to Upshur, Hopkins, Kaufman, and Wood counties. He told his mother that they collected only $750, and that many debtors told them it was entirely "out of the question" to make payments. Rumors that federal troops might invade Texas soon raced through the northern counties, and some of Lon's friends had joined a volunteer company to start towards the Red River. "I am getting anxious to be at home for if I have to go . . . I want to go with the San Augustine company," Lon wrote. He was five months past his eighteenth birthday.[19]

Short received his appointment as captain and announced at the end of April that he would be recruiting cavalrymen from Sabine and San Augustine counties. Lon returned to San Augustine in time, and on May 25, 1861, he and Meck and twenty other volunteers rode to Shelby County, where Captain Short lived, to enlist in his company. Cumby, with a young family and in poor health, remained at home. Short's company left in June to rendezvous near Dallas, where, along with other East Texas units, they were sworn into Col. Elkana Greer's mounted regiment on June 13. Greer was from Marshall and also a veteran of the Mexican War, having served with Jefferson Davis's First Mississippi Rifles. The ten companies from East Texas composing the regiment eventually were designated the Third Texas Cavalry, and Short's company became Company E. The regiment spent several weeks drilling while it waited for mule-drawn wagons coming from the Alamo with captured U.S. Army arms, tents, and other supplies.[20]

19. Joel V. Massey to Lon, Apr. 28, 1861, CFP; M. Cartwright to A. A. Burrus, Apr. 24, 1861, ibid.; Statement of A. A. Burrus & Co. to M. Cartwright, June 17, 1861, ibid.; Matthew Cartwright to Leonidas, Jan. 11, 1862, ibid.; Leonidas Cartwright to Dear Ma, May 1, 1861 (quotations), ibid.

20. San Augustine *Red Land Express*, Apr. 27, May 25, 1861; Judge David D. Jackson and Col. James Q. Erwin, "Rebels from the Redlands," unpublished MS, 1990, pp. 29, 31–34.

Americus P. "Meck" Cartwright (1840–1873) in Dallas, July 1861, as a volunteer in D. M. Short's Company E (San Augustine and Sabine counties), Third Texas Cavalry, CSA. This image is reversed.
Courtesy Cartwright Family Descendants.

Benjamin Thomas Roberts (1837–1887), future husband of Anna W. Cartwright, a member of Americus and Leonidas Cartwright's company. Courtesy Cartwright Family Descendants.

Leonidas "Lon" Cartwright (1842–1922), 1863 or 1864, while serving east of the Mississippi River as a member of Company E, Third Texas Cavalry. Courtesy Cartwright Family Descendants.

Leonidas proved to be the most faithful correspondent of the brothers; he wrote to his father on July 6, 1861, that the mule train had arrived and that the unit expected to leave for Fort Smith, Arkansas, in three days. Lon and his five messmates from San Augustine had their pictures taken and sent them home in a box to be distributed to their parents. Volunteers furnished their own clothes, horses, and equipment, for which they received a government allowance. At Dallas the Texans received horse pistols.[21]

At this point the volunteers considered army service a lark, rather like a prolonged hunting trip with good friends. The war was expected to be short, contrary to Sam Houston's prescient warning that it would be long and bloody. The editor of the Clarksville *Standard* unrealistically wrote on March 23, 1861, that Northern people would accept the legal arguments for secession, because the North feared the combined strength of the Southern states. One month later the editor was still convinced: "We cannot think the contest will last long. . . . Without the authority of Congress—with a Treasury bankrupt—with the heart of great bodies of Northern People all adverse," the effort to subdue the South was the "supreme folly of the age."[22]

The first disaster that awakened the troops to the dangers of their undertaking occurred when the regiment reached the Red River at Colbert's Ferry. The mounted units and some of the wagons had crossed to the north bank before nightfall, but one artillery battery with its guns and baggage wagons camped on the south beach with its animals unhitched, waiting for morning. Suddenly a wall of water roared downstream. The frantic men worked to get the animals and equipment back on the high bank, but some washed away. Men dashed into the water and managed to save some things, but Charley Baker from San Augustine had both arms broken and was left at the ferry to recuperate. The Texas troops passed through the Choctaw Nation (now southeastern Oklahoma), where Lon admired the country. The Choctaws were "hand and hand with us . . . [and] . . . are going to have a

21. Leonidas Cartwright to Dear Pa, July 6, 1861, CFP; Jackson and Erwin, "Rebels from the Redlands," 47.

22. Clarksville (Texas) *Standard*, Mar. 23, 1861, quoted in Buenger, *Secession*, 128; Clarksville *Standard*, Apr. 28, 1861, quoted in Ralph A. and Robert Wooster, "A People at War: East Texas During the Civil War," *East Texas Historical Journal*, XXVIII (Spring, 1990), 5.

war dance tomorrow." One member of the regiment recalled that during the ceremony the Texans learned the "warwhoop, which many of them were soon able to give just as real Indians do."[23]

Lon and Meck arrived at Fort Smith on July 27 after "a long and tiresome march." Lon had been sick for a few days, as had his eighteen-year-old cousin William S. Holman, the orphan son of Sanford and Clementine, but Meck was "getting on finely." The troops received rifles on the 28th, and Lon had "one of the finest in the company." The regiment was moving toward Gen. Ben McCulloch's headquarters about eighty miles from Fort Smith, where there were about 25,000 to 30,000 men. Rumors circulated that McCulloch intended to capture the 11,000 Federals at Springfield, Missouri.[24]

Amanda penned a letter to her sons that echoed the pride and fear of all mothers:

> San Augustine July the 11th 1861
>
> My Dear children
>
> With feelings of deepest solicitude I write these few lines . . . I have been very anxious to go to Dallas since you have been there. . . . If I could have been there the day that you were mustered into the service I should have mustered you homewards in a hurry . . . I think every patriotic Mother ought to be proud to see her boys go forth . . . and acquit themselves like soldiers . . . particularly when we are fighting for our fire sides and independence but I must acknowledge my weakness. . . . I have regretted many times that you had to leave home at such an unfavorable season.
>
> Often have I invoked the blessings of the Allmighty in your behalf. I know that the South is fighting in a just cause and providence will be in their favor. . . .
>
> Your Affectionate and devoted Mother
>
> Amanda Cartwright

23. Leonidas Cartwright to Dear Pa, July 22, 1861 (1st quotation), CFP; S. B. Barron, *The Lone Star Defenders: A Chronicle of the Third Texas Cavalry, Ross's Brigade* (New York: Neale Publishing Co., 1908), 30–31, 33–34 (2nd quotation).

24. Leonidas Cartwright to Dear Mother, July 28, 1861 (1st and 2nd quotations), CFP; Leonidas Cartwright to Dear Pa, July 29, 1861 (3rd quotation), ibid.

That Amanda prayed for her sons and consulted the big thick family Bible is obvious from its worn binding and well-thumbed pages.[25]

San Augustine parents waited anxiously for letters and news about the war. Most letters to and from the soliders were carried by individuals who were constantly coming and going from the encampments. Twenty-year-old Henry Hanks, for example, brought a letter from Leonidas to his sister on July 11 and returned to the army a few days later with packages and letters for the troops. Some letters from east of the Mississippi River came by the weekly mail carrier, who also brought newspapers from New Orleans and other towns. San Augustine residents shared the news from their sons, while newspapers were posted for all to read. On July 12, 1861, Matthew wrote, "Our Town has been verry Dull, since you left except Thursdays when all gather to hear the news. We were disappointed Yesterday as the mail failed."[26]

The homefolks not only worried about their sons, but they began to feel the economic pinch in the summer of 1861. San Augustine residents began hoarding staple goods, buying on credit if possible. "Mr. Burrus is selling goods about as fast as when You left," Matthew wrote Meck, but Burrus had collected only $320 to pay on his note held by Matthew. The senior Cartwright was glad to get even that small sum because it "enables me to pay my Taxes which is $2125, Some more than I expected. . . . Several of our best men are hard pressed to Raise means to pay Taxes." Hard times were returning, and supporting the Confederacy was not going to be easy.[27]

Mosquito-borne fevers also troubled San Augustine. "There . . . has been more sickness within the Last month than at any time before, but generally Billious fever, easily controlled," wrote Matthew. He had suffered for about a week and lost weight, but Columbus was so sick that he spoke of dying to his father before his slow recovery. Sallie, his wife, also had two chills but seemed to be better; Matthew probably did not know that she was

25. Amanda Cartwright to Dear children, July 11, 1861, CFP; Matthew Cartwright Bible (in possession of Patty C. Tennison).
26. Matthew Cartwright to Americus, July 12, 1861, CFP.
27. Ibid.

expecting her third child. Other neighbors were very ill and some were dying.[28]

Almost four weeks later, Matthew received a letter from the Choctaw Nation and wrote a reply to be carried by Charley Baker's mother. She was on her way to visit her son in camp at the Red River with his broken arms, and Mrs. Baker was taking clothing and other things he had requested. Matthew gave all of the news that absent soldiers might want to know: August 5, 1861, was election day and lawyer Richard F. Slaughter, cousin Anna Holman's husband, was running for the state legislature against neighbor Noel G. Roberts. (Slaughter won.) Two companies had been raised recently in San Augustine with one hundred men each, many recruited from other counties. One was a cavalry company under Capt. John H. Broocks that included as lieutenants men well-known to the Cartwrights, such as Carroll R. Ballard and James M. Ingram of Sabine County. Ballard would later cause trouble for young Matthew Cartwright, while Jimmie Ingram would wed Meck and Lon's sister Mary. The other was an infantry company commanded by Benjamin Franklin Benton in which the Massey brothers of Nacogdoches, friends of the Cartwright boys, enlisted. Benton had encountered great difficulty in recruiting infantry since receiving his commission in April; Redlanders, like other horse-oriented Texans, preferred the cavalry. Benton needed thirty-five men from San Augustine to fill his company, along with a like number from Nacogdoches and Sabine counties. Finally he resorted to visiting each militia beat to enroll volunteers. The news about "the Glorious Victory . . . at Manassas Gap" in July 1861 raised spirits in San Augustine, wrote Matthew, and "we now have no fear of our ultimate success and hope for an early peace . . . by 1st Nov. next."[29] Like so many others, Matthew remained confident that the war would be short.

The social life of San Augustine's young people revolved around the war. Almost no couples married between April and September 1861, while the young men readied themselves to go

28. Ibid. (quotation); Mary Cartwright to Dear Brother, July 11, 1861, CFP.
29. Matthew Cartwright to Lon, Aug. 5, 1861 (quotation), CFP; San Augustine *Red Land Express*, May 4, 18, 25, 1861; Wooster and Wooster, "A People at War," 6.

to war, though some may have become engaged. Seventeen-year-old Anna Cartwright turned down a marriage proposal from an unidentified Mr. Broocks at the end of June. It might have been Gus Broocks, brother of John H., who had gone to KMI with Anna's brothers, or John M. Broocks, perhaps a cousin, who boarded with a family near the Subletts in 1860. Anna struggled to draft her reply and finally wrote, "I consider marriage the most important step in life," and too many marriages begun in haste "resulted in the destruction of the happiness of both parties; therefore I defer giving a definite answer at present."[30]

Capt. John H. Broocks's mounted company did not leave for Missouri until October 10, 1861, but Benton's infantry started for Virginia on September 12. Local women including Anna and Mary Cartwright spent six weeks during the hot summer making uniforms and knitting wool socks, gloves, and caps. Anna saved some items to be taken by Captain Broocks to her brothers in Missouri and presented a flag to Benton's men upon their departure. Upon this occasion she also made a brief speech to a crowd of nearly eight hundred in front of Chaffin's Hotel. The *Red Land Express* published her remarks and also those of Thomas Irving, who received the banner, the next day. Gen. Travis G. Broocks, father of the captain, and Bolivar Sublett formally bade the soldiers farewell, while Captain Benton "said, as many appropriate things, in a few minutes, as one could expect or desire." The crowd filed over to the courthouse where Rev. S. A. Williams offered a prayer, and townspeople passed a hat for donations to help the troops on their journey. The foot soldiers marched to Alexandria, where they boarded a vessel to New Orleans and then went by rail to Richmond.[31]

Anna and her family watched Broocks's cavalry company pass by the house in October, and she wrote to her brothers that "they looked to be quite well mounted. When this company leaves there will be but two or three young men about the place."

30. Mrs. Frances Terry Ingmire (comp.), *San Augustine County, Texas, Marriage Records, 1837–1880* (St. Louis: n.p., 1980), 12–13; Anna W. Cartwright to Mr. Broocks, June 30, 1861 (quotation) (in possession of Eugenia Porter); U.S. Eighth Census (1860), San Augustine County, Texas (microfilm).

31. Mary Cartwright to Brothers, Oct. 1, 1861, CFP; typescript copy of San Augustine *Red Land Express* article (quotation), ibid.; Crocket, *Two Centuries,* 334–335 (has incorrect chronology).

One remaining behind was her cousin Lucius Holman, the son of the long-deceased Isaac Holman, Jr., an older brother of Amanda; Lucius lived in Gilmer, Upshur County, and sometimes in San Augustine, where he worked for his Holman and Cartwright uncles to learn about business. Currently he was too ill to leave and "looks wretchedly," Anna wrote. His sister, Mrs. Anna Traylor from Gilmer, was making an extended visit with the Cartwrights while her doctor-husband was with the army. Anna added, "I never knew the town to be so dull."[32]

Columbus was still at home. He not only had suffered from malarial chills and fever, as had Sallie, but he then took bilious fever. He and Sallie had a second son, Robert Lane, born on March 15, 1860, but the following November lost their first born, Matthew, at age twenty months. The parents sent out printed funeral notices that little Matthew would be buried on November 21; the procession would begin at their home and "proceed to the Family Burying Ground of Col. W. W. Holman." Having lost the title to the John Cartwright cemetery, which would have been more convenient, Sallie and Cumby concurred that the Holman plot was the best alternative, though more distant. After all, their mothers were both Holmans. Sallie would name her next child John Matthew after his grandfather, great-grandfather, and deceased infant brother. Sallie's mother America Lane Akin, still living in Tennessee, worried that Columbus would join the volunteers. Writing in April 1861, the least well-educated of the Holman sisters urged, "if he joines the army . . . he must send you hear to stay with me." America was expecting a visit from sister Polly Ann Barksdale, while Sallie's brothers Billy and Bobby Lane, seventeen and fourteen, were still in school though many Tennessee colleges had closed. "There is great excitement among the people at preasant, some are for secession others for the union," but most believed Tennessee would soon secede.[33]

Meanwhile, Greer's regiment had moved from Fort Smith into southwestern Missouri. In Barry County, Leonidas began having chills and fever the first week of August 1861, as did many others, including his lieutenant, Preston B. Word. The officers

32. Anna W. Cartwright to Dear Brother, Oct. 10, 1861, CFP.
33. Columbus Cartwright to Dear Brothers, Sept. 1, 1861, CFP; Funeral Notice (1st quotation) (in possession of Sandra Kardell Calpakis); America Akin to Mrs. S[ally] A. Cartwright, Apr. 25, 1861 (2nd and 3rd quotations), CFP.

allowed the sick to remain behind the moving army and usually left someone to care for them; so Meck had stayed with his brother. He and Lon hoped to catch up with their unit by traveling with the artillery company that was expected to reach their camp soon. Lon missed home more than ever and inquired about Anna Kaufman, the orphaned daughter of the deceased former congressman David Kaufman. She had returned to visit in San Augustine, and Lon had fallen in love. Meck also wrote home and assured the family that Lon was "mending very fast." The regiment was about fifty miles ahead, near Springfield, and was expected to have attacked the Union army there on August 5. Meck had heard that the enemy was retreating toward St. Louis and that CSA general McCulloch "was in hot pursuit." Every skirmish so far, he said proudly, had been won by the Confederate troops.[34]

Americus misjudged the date for the battle at Oak Hills, which actually took place on August 10, 1861. McCulloch had camped fifteen miles south of Springfield on August 9, intending to attack the federal troops the next day, but Union general Nathaniel Lyon learned of McCulloch's approach and surprised the Confederate camp at dawn. Fierce fighting ensued, during which General Lyon was killed; by mid-morning Greer's Texas cavalry had attacked the Union right flank, but Union artillery halted their advance. Nevertheless, the Texans' cavalry charge confused the federal troops, allowing CSA general Sterling Price and his Missouri troops to pound the Union lines, driving the Yankees back to Springfield. Although minor skirmishes continued, the battle was over. The South outnumbered the North two to one, but both suffered heavy casualties. Had McCulloch been able to pursue the retreating Yankees, he might have achieved a total victory. But both armies, exhausted and low on ammunition, were forced to quit the fight.[35]

The Cartwright brothers had missed the first battle. Meck wrote to his parents on August 17 and described secondhand "the great Battle" of the previous Saturday. Only one member of

34. Leonidas to Dear Mother, Aug. 6, 1861, CFP; A. P. Cartwright to Dear Sister, Aug. 6, 1861 (quotations), ibid.
35. Jackson and Erwin, "Rebels from the Redlands," 55–57.

Company E had been killed, although Elisha Berry had had his horse shot out from under him. Lon suffered another bout with fever, and he and Meck had remained behind; he was not as ill as cousin Billy Holman, however, who had been sent to the hospital along with Oliver Anderson (who died shortly thereafter) and Frank H. Tucker.[36] Many of these members of the small, closely knit San Augustine community who fought in the Confederate army were to reappear in the lives of the Cartwrights.

The Redland cavalrymen continued their interest in racing and trading their horses during the boring lulls between battles. Matthew had asked his sons about the value of their horses, perhaps as a guide in his own horse-trading negotiations. Lon currently had a race horse that was valued by the army at $200, seventy-five dollars less than that of cousin-by-marriage Iredell D. Thomas, Jr., an animal that Lon's horse had beaten. "There was no justice in the way they valued our horses," Lon wrote. He had only raced his horse twice, and finally ran him again against I. D.'s horse because I.D. had "bragged so much . . . and bantered me for a race for ten dollars." Lon's horse won, which stopped I. D.'s crowing. Meck added that his horse was valued at $175. He thought he and Lon "have as good horses as there is in the Regiment" and that they had stood the trip well.[37]

September 1, 1861, was a day of relief for Matthew and Amanda when they received Meck's August 6 letter saying their regiment would not reach McCulloch's headquarters for several days. The parents had just learned about the battle near Springfield when the welcome letter arrived. "We had suffered a great deal from suspense previous to the receipt of your letters," Anna wrote her brothers. An extra edition of the Dallas *Herald* reached San Augustine on August 31, reporting that fifteen Texans had died on the battlefield but providing no list of the dead and wounded.[38]

36. A. P. Cartwright to Dear Parents, Aug. 17, 1861 (quotation), CFP; Leonidas Cartwright to Dear Pa, Aug. 17, 1861, ibid.
37. Leonidas Cartwright to Dear Pa, Aug. 17, 1861 (1st and 2nd quotations), CFP; A. P. Cartwright to Dear Parents, Aug. 17, 1861 (3rd quotation), ibid.
38. Anna W. Cartwright to Dear Brothers, Sept. 1, 1861, CFP.

Amanda's letter to her sons was more poignant:

> We were almost certain that you . . . were in the fight
> and probably one or both killed or wounded. My imagi-
> nation was very lively. . . . I never received a letter that
> afforded me so much relief as the one you wrote on the
> 6th. . . . We were truly sorry to hear that you were sick
> . . . [and] . . . If you are not . . . well . . . before this reaches
> you . . . I think you had better return home. . . . may the
> God of heaven let his arms . . . rest over you . . . and
> permit you to return safely home where we can enjoy
> peace and happiness.

Matthew, still expecting to receive Lon's letter, wrote a short note on September 2 to send with Ebb Kellogg, a new recruit from Jasper who was in San Augustine on his way to Missouri.[39]

Greer's regiment remained near Carthage in southwestern Missouri to deter any Union invasion of Arkansas. When John H. Broocks's company left Texas in October 1861, Matthew sent along for his sons the winter clothing made by their sisters. He also sent $50 in gold, "being informed that paper money would not answer. You will learn the difficulty of getting Specie here from the boys, also the worth of money." Confederate notes, wrote Matthew, would be useful for the $3,000 in taxes he owed. Therefore, Columbus and Lon should not "dispose of them without full value." The troops were paid in Confederate money, and Matthew envisioned his sons spending it unwisely among Missouri merchants and farmers when he could use the depreci-ating notes to pay taxes. Matthew had provided five horses, one mule, and $200 for Broocks's company and also $10 to cover the expenses of the team carrying the winter clothing sent to Com-pany E by their families. Matthew told his sons that he was leaving for Jasper to attend court, and from there would go north to Gilmer for another session. Wistfully he added, "Will be compelled to travel by myself which you know does not suit me."[40]

39. Amanda Cartwright to Dear Children, Sept. 1, 1861 (quotations), CFP; Matthew Cartwright to Americus, Sept. 2, 1861, ibid.

40. Jackson and Erwin, "Rebels from the Redlands," 72; Matthew Cartwright to A. P. & L. Cartwright, Oct. 11, 1861 (quotations), CFP.

Lon and Meck boarded in the town of Carthage, Missouri, in October 1861 while recovering their health but soon returned to camp. Many of their company were ill with typhoid fever, including I. D. Thomas, while others had measles. Rumors said that Greer's regiment would go to Kansas to fight the Jayhawkers who terrorized the residents. The regiment, however, was ordered into winter quarters in December south of Van Buren, Arkansas, where a lumber mill provided boards for the troops to use in building shelters. Good horsemen that they were, Lon's group built stables for their horses first and expected to finish their house by Christmas. Horse trading occupied a lot of their time, and Lon traded his race horse for $300: $150 in cash and a horse worth $150. The new animal, "though undersize," had "carried a large man . . . [from Texas] . . . and looks as well as when he left." Moreover, he had just won a race. While Meck remained well, Lon was having chills and fever again.[41]

As 1861 came to a close, civilians were suffering shortages. Matthew collected little money on his semiannual collection tour, but contracted for about one hundred bales of cotton to be delivered to Jefferson for transshipment to New Orleans. But, he said, unless the Union blockade of the Gulf coast was lifted, nobody would buy the cotton. San Augustine merchants had no goods to sell and could not make collections. Like the young people, Matthew agreed that San Augustine was "a verry dull place," but for different reasons: "no billiard Table nor whiskey in town." He hoped that peace would come soon so things could return to normal.[42]

Leonidas's health improved in January 1862, but amid the disagreeable rain and snow, Americus succumbed to chills at the end of the month. He dosed himself with his mother's favorite remedy, cayenne pepper, which seemed to cure him. Meck warned his mother not to believe the stories that might be circulating in San Augustine that he and seven or eight others were "killing ourselves drinking whiskey." It was "as base and black a lie as ever escaped the lips," and he knew none of the family would

41. Jackson and Erwin, "Rebels from the Redlands," 78–79; Leonidas Cartwright to Dear Father, Dec. 11, 1861 (quotation), CFP.
42. Matthew Cartwright to Americus and Leonidas, Nov. 20, 1861, CFP; Matthew Cartwright to Leonidas, Jan. 11, 1862 (1st and 2nd quotations), ibid.

believe such a story.[43] Given the tedium of winter camp, however, and the overindulgence in alcohol by most men that was common at this time, the rumors were probably true.

As early as January, Amanda wrote her sons that she was "looking forward to the 13th of June with great pleasure," that being the day that their twelve-month enlistments would end. She and many others would be disappointed when they learned that in April 1862 the Confederate government extended enlistments to three years for all men ages eighteen to thirty-five, with the privilege of hiring a substitute. But as early as January, officers urged their troops to reenlist. Meck told his mother on February 2 that "they are trying to get this regiment to enlist for two years . . . but few say that they would" even when offered a sixty-day furlough with expenses paid. "It was some time," he told his brother later, "before I gave my consent to reenlist, for I am exempt by military law." He referred, of course, to his closed left eye. The "Conscript Act," Lon wrote, "has produced some confusion . . . and some say they are going home anyhow when their term is out." Lon would stay, and in April 1862 wrote that he believed "our country at this critical moment demands the service of every one . . . to uphold her noble cause."[44]

The Cartwright brothers participated in the Battle of Pea Ridge, or Elkhorn Tavern, in northwestern Arkansas on March 6–8, 1862. During the hard-fought struggle, Gen. Ben McCulloch was killed and Colonel Greer took command of the fallen hero's troops, while Lt. Col. Walter P. Lane filled Greer's place at the head of the Third Texas Cavalry. Despite superior numbers, CSA general Earl Van Dorn ordered a retreat after two days of heavy fighting. Lon described the withdrawal: "We retreated in good order slowly all day Saturday . . . unpursued by the enemy I suppose being glad enough to get off as they did and not knowing really that we were retreating." No San Augustine men were killed, but two badly wounded men were taken prisoner along with San Augustine's Dr. B. M. Watson.[45]

43. Meck to Dear Mother, Feb. 2, 1862, CFP.
44. Amanda Cartwright to My Dear Children, Jan. 22, 1862 (1st–3rd quotations), CFP; A. P. Cartwright to Dear Mother, Feb. 2, 1862, ibid.; Leonidas Cartwright to Dear Mother, Apr. 23, 1862 (4th and 5th quotations), ibid.
45. Jackson and Erwin, "Rebels from the Redlands," 96–102; Leonidas Cartwright to Dear Mother, Mar. 20, 1862 (quotation), CFP.

The Confederacy suffered a blow on April 7, 1862, when the much-admired West Pointer, Gen. Albert Sidney Johnston, was killed at Shiloh in southern Tennessee. His replacement, Gen. P. G. T. Beauregard, called for reinforcements, including the Third Texas Cavalry, to be sent immediately to Corinth, Mississippi. The Cartwrights and their friends were ordered to Little Rock and then to Duvall's Bluff, where their horses were sent home. There was a great need for infantry, and cavalry mounts suffered from lack of forage in Mississippi. The Texans boarded a steamboat for Memphis, from which Leonidas wrote to his mother on April 23. Three days later, after riding the train, they arrived in camp near Corinth. A number of San Augustine friends were nearby, including John H. Broocks's infantry company. Cousin Lucius Holman had recovered from his illness and was in camp doing well. Word reached the troops that New Orleans had fallen to Federal forces on April 25; Leonidas "regretted" the loss but thought it inspired everyone to fight even harder.[46]

Upon the reorganization of the regiment on May 8, Meck Cartwright became 2nd lieutenant of Company E, chosen by the the majority of the forty-seven members voting. He received thirty-two votes while his two rivals together received only fifteen. Word was again chosen lieutenant and Billy Holman and Ben T. Roberts 2nd and 3rd sergeants. Elisha Roberts and I. D. Thomas became corporals. The day after the election, a long-expected skirmish against federal troops occurred. Company E and others marched through twenty miles of tangled thicket to out-flank the enemy in order to force the Union troops to retreat. Although many members of the Third Texas were ill, the Cartwrights remained healthy. Meck told Columbus that "Lon looks better now than I ever saw him," and jokingly added, "The infantry service seems to agree with him much better than cavalry." The unit remained in the fever-ridden camp until the end of May 1862, expecting a major battle any day while more and more troops became ill. Finally General Beauregard ordered a withdrawal on May 29 south toward Tupelo, where the army was placed under Gen. Sterling Price. There the dismounted

46. Leonidas to Dear Mother, Apr. 23, 1862, CFP; Leonidas to Dear Father, May 1, 1862 (quotation), ibid.; Barron, *Lone Star Defenders,* 79–82.

Third Texas Cavalry was assigned to a new brigade commanded by Gen. Louis Hebert.[47]

Company E's horses reached San Augustine, where they were to be cared for until again needed, in May 1862. The Cartwright horses went into the stable on the back of the lot, and Anna and Mary enjoyed riding Meck's dun horse, but Lon's bay war horse scared them. The senior Matthew had been very ill in the spring, but by mid-May he was able to travel his collection route. To his disappointment, he discovered that nearly all of his debtors were away from home with the army. Hot weather and little rain in June and July 1862 threatened the corn crop upon which everyone was depending for food.[48]

The new draft law meant that Columbus might be called for service. Both Meck and Lon advised their brother not to join the army because it would be too hard on his health and his family: "San Augustine has enough men in the field already . . . [and] . . . it is necessary for some to be left at home to keep the negroes in their places. For I haven't the least doubt that Old Lincoln has his emissaries all through our country." By the end of the year, Columbus had a substitute for the Confederate service, but a call for sixty men from San Augustine for service in the state militia along the Gulf coast meant he had to hire a second substitute. Matthew's ledger book for 1863 and early 1864 shows a number of payments of $50 or more to two men to serve in Cumby's place. Larkin G. Gothard served as Columbus's substitute in the Confederate army from late 1862 through January 1864, receiving a total of $371.50 from the Cartwrights. John Matlock of Shelby County, age sixteen, was accepted on September 19, 1863, as Columbus's six-month substitute in Company A of the Texas State Troops under Maj. F. B. Sublett at Camp Simpson in Nacogdoches. Matlock had received $300 in payments by January 31, 1864. Because of criticism that rich planters and their sons were hiring substitutes and avoiding service, the Confederate government forbade substitutes in 1863 and in February 1864

---

47. Leonidas Cartwright to Dear Sister, May 6, 1862, CFP; A. P. Cartwright to Columbus, May 10, 1862 (quotation), ibid.; Leonidas Cartwright to Dear Father, May 10, 1862, ibid.; Jackson and Erwin, "Rebels from the Redlands," 117–123.

48. Matthew Cartwright to Dear Sons, June 26, 1862, and its postscript of July 24, 1862, CFP.

called on all men between seventeen and fifty. Matthew was safe, being fifty-six years old. Only the state continued to permit substitutes.[49]

In May 1862, Lon and Meck asked their father to find clothing and boots for them, and Matthew had the local tailor make the pants and coats, evidently from material wisely put away earlier. At the end of June Matthew tried to send them to Meck and Lon in Mississippi, along with twenty-six-year-old Dick, old Nancy's son, but could find no safe conveyance across the Mississippi River. Lon had asked for a servant to be sent to him during the previous winter when he was ill in Arkansas, but Matthew was unwilling to risk sending a slave to such a cold climate. Another chance to send Dick and the clothing occurred in July 1862, but again Matthew hesitated because rumors indicated that Price's army would be transferred to the west side of the Mississippi River and that the Third Texas would be re-mounted.[50]

Meanwhile, the troops in Itawamba County spent a dull summer drilling and trying to stay healthy. The ever-impatient Meck fretted and suffered problems with his eye and the hearing in his left ear. Finally, on August 13, 1862, he asked for a medical discharge, which was approved by Dr. Dan Shaw, surgeon with the Third Texas Cavalry, and signed by his captain. The doctor certified that Meck suffered from a painful neuralgic "affection [*sic*]" resulting from the loss of his left eye two years earlier, and now his hearing was impaired and thus he was "unfit for duty." Meck sent his resignation to the secretary of war and started for home.[51]

49. A. P. Cartwright to Columbus, May 10, 1862 (quotations), CFP; Leonidas to Mother, June 20, 1862, ibid.; Matthew Cartwright to Lon, Dec. 23, 1862, ibid.; Acceptance of John Matlock as substitute, Sept. 19, 1862 [printed form], W. G. Sharp Scrapbook (BTHC); Account Book no. 12, 1859–1868, Feb. 10, June 3, Aug. 17, Sept. 23, 26, Oct. 3, Nov. 26, 1863, and Jan. 23, 31, 1864, pp. 19–24, CFP; Campbell, *Southern Community in Crisis,* 207.

50. Matthew Cartwright to Sons, June 26, July 24, 1862, CFP; Statement from W. A. McClanahan to M. Cartwright for tailoring, May 12, 1862, ibid.; Matthew Cartwright to Leonidas, Jan. 11, 1862, ibid.

51. Leonidas to Anna Cartwright, June 25, 1862, CFP; A. P. Cartwright to Columbus Cartwright, May 10, 1862, ibid.; Service Record of A. P. Cartwright (quotations) (copy in possession of David D. Jackson).

Meck's resignation coincided with the long-awaited order to remount the Third Texas Cavalry. He left Saltillo, Mississippi, on August 22 in company with those detailed to collect the horses. Lon took this opportunity to ask his father to send Dick to Mississippi with the horses. He worried that if his horse was driven in a herd "he will be in bad condition" when he arrived in camp. Dick, however, would see that his horse and that of Billy Holman were properly fed, watered, curried, and exercised. Confident that Dick would be coming, Lon instructed his father, "I expect that you had better give him a few dollars to buy corn." Forgetting that home was not the same as when he had left over a year earlier, Lon gave more orders: "My saddle needs some repairs . . . and probably my bridle also . . . send me a pair of good saddle blankets."[52]

While the Third Texas Cavalry awaited its mounts, the troops took part in the disastrous battle at Iuka on the night of September 13, 1862, in which the unit suffered twenty-two killed and seventy-four wounded. No letters detail what role Lon and his friends played in the battle. Three weeks later Lon was ill with diarrhea and missed the debacle at Corinth on October 4 and 5, where poor leadership by General Van Dorn caused the loss of 4,638 men while the Yankees lost only half as many. The army retreated west through Ripley to Holly Springs, Mississippi, where Lon wrote to his father on October 12 to tell him he was all right. Bill Holman survived the battle unscathed, and Ben Roberts, who had been taken prisoner at Iuka, had been paroled. Ben, however, had to remain at Iuka to care for wounded Confederate prisoners. The regiment retreated south towards Grenada, where they received their horses at long last.[53]

Americus reached San Augustine on October 27 and by late November was considering joining the state militia for three months. The militia was made up of those who were exempt from the draft and served as a home guard, and Meck wrote Lon that "Pa and Ma are very anxious for me to go." One presumes that public opinion was critical of seemingly able-bodied men remaining at home. Matthew found it difficult to keep Meck busy, and when the father left for Panola County for a week, he sent the

52. Leonidas Cartwright to Father, Aug. 21, 1862 (quotations), CFP.

53. Barron, Lone Star Defenders, 105–108, 120–126; Leonidas Cartwright to Father, Oct. 12, 1862, CFP.

twenty-two-year-old to round up cattle in nearby Shelby County. Within two weeks Meck again wrote to his brother about "this dull county. I am getting very tired of it."[54]

Matthew suffered a personal loss on December 7, 1862, when "old Red-buck . . . died after a few hours illness." The big sorrel horse had carried Matthew many miles, and Mary wrote Lon that "it was quite a trial to Pa to give him up." Meck and young Matthew, age seven, supervised the burial of the "fathiful, old servant" the next day. Meck gave his father the sorrel horse that he had ridden home from Mississippi, and he wrote Lon that "he suits Pa very well." Matthew was grateful and planned to buy a replacement for Meck, who was "very much at a loss" without a horse. Meck, however, was "very choicey" and Matthew knew finding a horse would be difficult. But within two months, Matthew decided that Meck's horse was "rather wild for me." He began looking for another one for himself because he needed to make a long trip. He finally found what he wanted in Jefferson and paid $1,200 in Confederate money for a black horse. By this time, CSA dollars had depreciated 75 percent, meaning that this horse would have cost $300 in 1861.[55]

Lon's sisters kept him informed about what the home front was doing at the end of 1862. Mary, Anna, Anna Kaufman, and one other had joined the Methodist Church at its quarterly meeting in San Augustine. The Cartwright sisters and Jane Blount had visited with Anna Kaufman for two days; she had been to Nacogdoches earlier and everywhere she went "she saw hanks of thread hanging about the house." While many people were forced to wear homespun clothing, and Tempe Price McLaurine, a young married friend, had paid $24 "cash" (gold?) for a homespun dress recently, Mary assured Lon that "we have not had to resort to . . . [it] . . . for ourselves yet, and if we meet no misfortune, I do not think we shall for some time to come." The girls reported that their mother had been carding cotton at home, but her cards

54. A. P. Cartwright to Leonidas, Dec. 1, 1862 (1st quotation), CFP; same to same, Dec. 16, 1862 (2nd quotation), ibid.

55. Mary Cartwright to Lon, Dec. 8, 1862 (1st–3rd quotations), CFP; A. P. Cartwright to Lon, Dec. 10, 1862 (4th quotation), ibid.; Matthew Cartwright to Lon, Dec. 23, 1862 (5th and 6th quotations), ibid.; Matthew Cartwright to Lon, Feb. 28, 1863 (7th quotation), ibid.; Account Book no. 12, p. 20, ibid.; Campbell, *Southern Community in Crisis,* 208.

were worn out and new ones unobtainable. Neighbor Crabb Griffith, a Mexican War veteran, offered to go to Matamoros to buy cards and other necessities for several households, and in one day he collected $600 in gold to buy needed items. The Cartwrights had been hiring neighbor women to weave cloth for slave clothing, but few housewives wanted to weave. Moreover, having common jeans cloth woven cost from $3 to $5 a yard, so Amanda decided to buy a loom and have some of the slave women learn to weave.[56]

Personal matters were also shared in letters to the boys at the front. The Cartwrights' cousin Clementine "Mintie" Garrett, who had married Benjamin F. Price and had three small children, died of typhoid fever on December 18, 1862, after an illness of seven weeks. Mary Garrett, an old maid at twenty-two, also had typhoid, but recovered to help care for her deceased sister's children while their father was with the army. Anna and Mary were unable to visit Mary Garrett, who lived at her father's home about two miles away, "not having any way to go." Evidently the matched carriage horses had been sold.[57]

A minor problem concerned the slave Dick's wife. Matthew wrote Lon, "I hope you find Dick a good boy and of much advantage to you but I feel that you will allow him to [sic] much liberty and I understand that he is sending money to his wife." Matthew thought that was a waste. "I want you to take charge of the money that Dick made and take care of it for him[,] for there is no necessity for him sending it back to his wife to fool away for nothing." Besides, Lon would need the money for Dick's expenses when they returned home.[58] The fact that Dick was earning money and finding a way to send it to San Augustine from Mississippi during the war challenges popular views about slavery.

56. Mary Cartwright to Lon, Dec. 8, 1862 (quotations), CFP.
57. Mary Cartwright to Lon, Dec. 1, 1862, CFP; Anna Cartwright to Lon, Jan. 31, 1863 (quotation), ibid.; U.S. Ninth Census (1870), San Augustine County, Texas (microfilm). The three Price children, John, Mary, and William, lived with William Garrett. Mary Garrett married H. W. Sublett on July 15, 1869. San Augustine County, Marriage Records, also, U.S. Ninth Census (1870), San Augustine County, Texas.
58. Matthew Cartwright to Lon, Dec. 23, 1862 (1st quotation), CFP; A. P. Cartwright to Lon, Dec. 10, 1862 (2nd quotation), ibid.

Overall, people remained optimistic that the war would end soon. In a letter at the end of December 1862, Matthew hailed recent Confederate victories at Fredericksburg, Virginia, and Holly Springs, Mississippi, where General Van Dorn redeemed himself by cutting Gen. U. S. Grant's supply lines. He also heard, erroneously it turned out, that Emperor Napoleon III of France would recognize the independence of the Confederate States. Matthew thought that the mid-term elections in the North showed the peace Democrats defeating the "abolitionists" in some states, but the isolated Redlander failed to understand that the Republican Party controlled Congress.[59]

San Augustine residents were short of manufactured goods and some staples like coffee and flour, but in general they lived comfortably from their gardens. Cornbread replaced wheat biscuits and honey was used instead of refined sugar, but that was not unusual in the region. Prices for everything had quadrupled since the war began, but a man could still hunt the woods for meat if he could not afford beef or pork.

The first twenty months of the war had not hurt the Cartwrights as much as it had many other families. They had not lost a son, and Matthew continued to work his land business, although it was hard to collect money. Their pride and confidence was intact, except perhaps for Cumby and Meck, both of whom found their inactivity caused by health problems to be onerous. Nevertheless, the Cartwrights and their neighbors were growing apprehensive at the close of 1862, and the holiday season from Christmas through New Year's Day brought little cheer. Rumors indicated that the Union planned action in the Red River Valley, a step that might endanger Texas as well.

59. Matthew Cartwright to Lon, Dec. 23, 1862, CFP; Jackson and Erwin, "Rebels from the Redlands," 144–145.

Ten

"... It Was the Worst of Times"

1863–1865

*D*uring the first two years of the war, fighting had taken place far from San Augustine, but by January 1863 the people in the Natchitoches area began to worry about a Yankee invasion fleet ascending the Red River after recent rains made navigation possible. Some San Augustine residents had cotton stored there, and the commission merchants asked them about moving the bales to safety as Louisiana clients had already done. By summer the Confederates took protective measures in Sabine County. Anna wrote her brother in August, "We are expecting [the Yankees] this winter. Sabine Town is being fortified, which I think will only entice them here."[1] In reality, the Union generals were more interested in capturing Vicksburg and Port Hudson, the two major ports on the east side of the Mississippi River, before risking an invasion of the Red River or Texas. The attack against Vicksburg began in late 1862 and lasted until

---

1. Anna Cartwright to Lon, Jan. 31, 1863, CFP; Anna Cartwright to Leonidas, Aug. 24–25, 1863 (quotations), ibid.

July 4, 1863; Port Hudson, below the mouth of the Red River, surrendered a few days later.

While the Union was still struggling with Vicksburg, some federal troops penetrated the bayou country southwest of Baton Rouge in April 1863 and briefly occupied Alexandria before withdrawing to concentrate on the Mississippi River campaign. Many frightened Louisiana slaveholders sought sanctuary in Texas, and their caravans passed the Cartwright house especially after the fall of Vicksburg. "I think Texas will be filled with them," Mary wrote. Matthew received a letter from one Louisiana man looking for a haven in Henderson or Anderson counties at a "reasonable price," payable in Confederate bonds and notes. He preferred a place away from a public road, well-watered, with plenty of timber, and already developed with houses and cabins. The records do not reveal if Matthew was able to find such an Elysium for him or was willing to accept Confederate money.[2]

Leonidas and the Third Texas Cavalry, now remounted, remained east of the Mississippi River for the remainder of the war. He participated in the morale-boosting raid on Holly Springs, Mississippi, on December 20, 1862, when the Confederates forced the federal troops to abandon their comfortable winter quarters and a large depot of supplies. Anna wrote, "I suppose you had rare times the morning you entered that place arousing the vandals from their sweet repose by your yells and shrieks." Despite her seeming devotion to proper behavior for "young ladies," a favorite phrase used by the Cartwright sisters, Anna retained a tomboyish streak: "I imagined I should liked to have been a participant. . . . They must have been greatly surprised and mortified."[3]

Matthew learned firsthand about the successful attack when Col. John Summerfield Griffith, Crabb's brother, visited San Augustine. He told Matthew that Lon's division was ordered to Tennessee to cooperate with Gen. Braxton Bragg in his campaign to oust Union general William C. Rosecrans from Nashville. In

2. Anna Cartwright to Leonidas, Aug. 24, 1863, CFP; Mary Cartwright to Leonidas, Nov. 13, 1863 (1st quotation), ibid.; Robert C. Hynson to Matthew Cartwright, Dec. 26, 1863 (2nd quotation), ibid.

3. Anna Cartwright to Lon, Jan. 31, 1863 (quotations); CFP.

writing to Lon, Matthew spelled the Yankee general's name "Rosencrantz," evidently remembering his reading of *Hamlet*.[4]

Almost two years in the army had hardened Lon and his friends. During the March 4–5, 1863, battle at Thompson's Station south of Nashville, Company E took part in a gory victory over Union forces, and Lon described the details in a letter. He and the others had dismounted and sent their horses to the rear before advancing up a barren hill to meet the enemy. Lon, Drew S. "Bully" Polk, and Hugh Leslie were in the front line during the charge when suddenly a Yankee skirmisher "raised up in about twenty feet of us and aimed at Bully. My gun failed to fire, and in an instant he shot Bully dead, the bullet entering the upper lip and coming out through the top of the head." But Hugh killed the enemy. Twenty-one-year-old Lon had seen enough battlefield deaths by this time that he could suppress the horror and write stoically that he "regretted that my gun did not fire." Like a true Spartan, Lon took pride that Bully fell "in front of his Regt. bravely discharging his duty." Others had performed well under fire. Cousin Bill Holman, now 2nd lieutenant of Company C, "acted nobly and received compliments from Maj. Stone [Absolom B. Stone of Harrison County] for his gallant behavior." Lon added that brothers Ben and Noel G. Roberts "behaved well and stood to their posts."[5]

The Confederates lost only 300 men, while the Federals had 100 killed, 300 wounded, and 1,306 missing. Another San Augustine loss was the death of Capt. James A. Broocks, who had succeeded to command Company C, Twenty-seventh Texas Cavalry (Gen. John W. Whitfield's Legion), the day before the battle, when his brother John was promoted to lieutenant colonel. Their father, Travis G. Broocks, made the long journey to Tennessee, passed through the lines, and brought James's body home to San Augustine. Only five years earlier, he had performed a similar sad duty when his second son Moses, who had attended KMI, drowned after a steamboat accident on the lower Red River.[6]

A few days after the Battle of Thompson's Station, the enemy

4. Matthew Cartwright to Leonidas, Feb. 28, 1863, CFP.

5. Leonidas Cartwright to Father, Mar. 22, 1863 (quotations), CFP; Barron, *Lone Star Defenders*, 150.

6. Jackson and Erwin, "Rebels from the Redlands," 160 note; Crocket, *Two Centuries*, 336.

forced the Texas cavalry to retreat southeast along the Duck River toward Shelbyville, the home of Aunts Polly Barksdale and America Akin. Lon made inquiries and learned that the Yankees had occupied the Barksdale house, destroyed their furniture, and stolen their slaves. Dr. Barksdale "is a strong Southern man," wrote Lon, and talked "straight out to the Feds . . . which I suppose was the cause of their treating them as they did." Neighbors said that the Barksdales had fled to Chattanooga and the Akins had gone to Texas. A later report placed both Holman sisters in Dalton, Georgia, southeast of Chattanooga, which also had to be evacuated.[7] Lon and his associates remained in central Tennessee until May 1863 when they returned to the Vicksburg area in an unsuccessful effort to relieve the siege.

Meanwhile, San Augustine residents continued to receive less than accurate reports about the Tennessee campaign. "The last papers received stated that we were receiving large reenforcements," wrote Anna, "and we are in hopes that it will not be long ere . . . [Tennessee] . . . will be relieved of the galling chains with which the tyrants are attempting to encircle it." Anna had adopted the rhetoric of the newspaper editors who wrote in this style, and six months later used the same phrases: "how many lives have been sacrificed at the altar . . . by the ruthless hand of Disease or by the deadly missiles hurled at them by the ruthless vandals of the North who are striving to encircle our beloved Sunny south with the galling chains of despotism"? Not only did Texas readers have to endure editorial excess, but they were seduced by censored and manipulated accounts emanating from both the Confederate government and the generals. Aware of the value of deceiving Yankee readers, most Confederate generals barred reporters from their armies and allowed only statistics and facts favorable to their campaigns to be published.[8]

Both Anna and Mary had commenced writing letters to "care-worn soldiers" other than their brothers. Benjamin T. Roberts,

7. Leonidas Cartwright to Father, Mar. 22, 1863 (quotations), CFP; Leonidas Cartwright to Mary, Aug. 7, 1863, ibid.

8. Anna W. Cartwright to Ben T. Roberts, Mar. 30, 1863 (1st quotation), CFP; Anna W. Cartwright to Ben T. Roberts, Oct. 6, 1863 (2nd quotation), ibid.; David C. Humphrey, "A 'Very Muddy and Conflicting' View: The Civil War as Seen from Austin, Texas," SHQ, XCIV (Jan., 1991), 385–386.

seven years older than Anna and a neighbor since childhood, asked her to begin a "friendly correspondence." Although she "never corresponded with young gentlemen before the war . . . [and said] I never would," she decided it was a "duty imcumbent on the fair sex" to contribute to the soldiers' happiness. The exchange of letters between Anna and Ben encountered major difficulty before their marriage in 1869, but that between sister Mary and Capt. James M. Ingram of Sabine County blossomed into an engagement and marriage at the end of the war.[9]

The ever-restless Meck was bored at home and Mary reported that he "spends a good deal of time fishing . . . [and has] caught a great many this spring, some weighing three pounds." When Henry H. Sibley's brigade passed through San Augustine on its way to Louisiana early in March 1863, Meck had an opportunity to visit with a distant Cartwright relative who had served in the New Mexico campaign. Several weeks later, the family heard vigorous knocking at the door and assumed it was Lon. But it was Columbus Holman of Austin, the forty-year-old son of Amanda's oldest brother James S., en route to Mississippi for duty with the commissary department. Like the unidentified cousin, he spent the night.[10]

These visits and the inactivity caused Meck to start east in May to rejoin the Third Texas Cavalry. When he reached Natchitoches, he learned about the federal occupation of Alexandria. Being "apprehensive of the yankees capturing him," Anna wrote Lon, "he concluded to remain on this side of the river and join Lane's regt, Edwards Company." Walter P. Lane, once colonel in the Third Texas Cavalry, raised the First Texas Partisan Rangers in northeastern Texas in mid-1862. The regiment fought a major battle in Arkansas, but Lane became ill and returned home to Harrison County to recuperate. His cavalry regiment

9. Anna W. Cartwright to Ben T. Roberts, Mar. 30, 1863 (quotations), CFP; Anna W. Cartwright to Ben T. Roberts, Oct. 6, 1863, ibid. Mary Cartwright to Leonidas, Mar. 30, 1863, ibid., mentions she had just finished another letter to be carried to the army by Colonel Griffith. W. Sanford Holman to Anna W. Cartwright, Mar. 27, 1864, ibid. Leonidas Cartwright to Anna, Mar. 22, 1865, ibid., refers to Mary's letters to Ingram.

10. Mary to Lon, Mar. 30, 1863, CFP.

was ordered to Natchitoches in April 1863 to harass Yankee gunboats operating on the lower Louisiana waterways.[11]

By the time Meck joined the unit, the Texans had been incorporated into Col. John P. Major's Texas Cavalry Brigade, which started toward New Orleans by riding along the high ground between the Atchafalaya and the Mississippi rivers below Port Hudson. On June 15, 1863, three weeks before the fall of Vicksburg, Meck was on the Atchafalaya when over six hundred horses crossed the wide stream on two flatboats. For two days they scouted the west bank of the Mississippi River opposite Port Hudson and found nothing. Another Confederate regiment captured Plaquemine, where "a good supply of . . . stores" provided coffee and other "eatables." They continued south through twelve miles of swamp surrounded by thirty-foot-high canebrakes and finally arrived at "Thibodeauxville" on Bayou Lafourche, where they captured Union troops and a number of negroes. During the battle "a bullet passed very close to my head," Meck told his parents, and "I came very nearly being killed . . . [but] I . . . turned my head just before the ball reached me." It caused his horse to rear and he "soon led the crowd" until a clod of dirt struck Meck in his good eye, removing him briefly from cavalry duty. Instead, he escorted prisoners to Donaldsonville under a white flag on June 24, but did not participate in the doomed assault there on June 28.[12]

The surrender of Vicksburg to the Union army caused consternation among the Confederates in Louisiana. Meck wrote on July 28, 1863, "Some of the men . . . have been rather low-spirited since the fall of Vicksburg and Port Hudson, but the most of them are getting over their scare and have come to the conclusion that there is something else to do before the Yankees can whip us." Unreliable information even reached brigade commanders; Colonel Majors announced that General Lee had captured Washington and was on his way to Baltimore! In fact, Lee was in retreat to Virginia from the disaster at Gettysburg on July

---

11. Anna W. Cartwright to Leonidas, Aug. 24, 1863 (quotation), CFP; Jackson and Erwin, "Rebels from the Redlands," 169; Walter P. Lane, *The Adventures and Recollections of Gen. Walter P. Lane* . . . (Austin: Pemberton Press, 1970), 104–106.

12. A. P. Cartwright to Parents, June 30, 1863, CFP.

3. But the rumor that the Yankees would try to invade Texas in the fall was true, and only luck allowed the handful of young men under Lt. Dick Dowling at Sabine Pass to defeat the plan on September 8.[13]

Around August 1 Meck became forage master for Major's brigade and traveled several times by boat up the Teche above New Iberia to purchase corn. Because his pay was uncertain, Meck asked his father to send him "three or four hundred dollars," explaining that "money is a great friend to the soldier" and commenting on the high prices along the coast. In Franklin Meck met a man from the Third Texas Cavalry who told him that Lon and the San Augustine "boys" had been a part of Gen. Joseph E. Johnston's army that had been trying to relieve Vicksburg. "We were close together last month but I did not know it," Meck wrote his mother. "The Miss. River only separated us. If I had have known it I would have swam the river certain."[14]

By August 1863 Lon was stationed at Pelahatchie Depot near Jackson, Mississippi, and had become obsessed with getting a furlough. The previous spring, still hopeful that the war might end soon, he had not asked for a furlough even though he had been gone twenty months. He told his parents that he could wait and return when "our liberty and peace . . . [are] established." But as more and more friends obtained permits, he became determined to go home. At a time when there were many desertions, commanders could not furlough an entire company as some soldiers desired, and they finally resorted to drawing lots for the few dispensations each month. Some of the lucky recipients sold their furloughs for exorbitant amounts. On August 7 Lon wrote, "We received the gratifying news yesterday that all of the furloughs were approved," but he had not drawn one nor been able to buy one as had I. D. Thomas. Two days later Thomas was also disappointed when he learned that the furloughs were not approved for anyone who intended to cross the Mississippi River.[15]

13. A. P. Cartwright to Father, July 28, 1863, CFP.

14. A. P. Cartwright to Father, Aug. 13, 1863 (1st quotation), CFP; A. P. Cartwright to Mother, Aug. 16, 1863 (2nd and 3rd quotations), ibid.

15. Matthew Cartwright to Leonidas, Feb. 28, 1863 (1st quotation), CFP; Leonidas Cartwright to Father, Apr. 22, 1863, ibid.; same to same, May 9, 1863, ibid.; Leonidas Cartwright to Mary Cartwright, Aug. 7, 1863 (2nd quotation), ibid.; Leonidas Cartwright to little Brother, Aug. 9, 1863, ibid.

The change in plans also upset Lon because he planned to send Dick home with I. D. so that the slave could bring back needed winter clothes and equipment. "I don't know what I will do for clothes," Lon wrote, because they were scarce and very expensive in Mississippi. He added the list of his requirements to his letter saying that Ma should get the things ready in case an opportunity to send them occurred. Somehow the policy about crossing the river changed, and I. D. and Dick reached San Augustine by September 23, 1863. Lon's bookkeeper-father entered Lon's order for an overcoat, pants, coats, shirts, underwear, wool socks, boots, linen towels, blanket, gloves, handkerchiefs, a cap, and a new halter into the account book on October 6 with a total cost of $362 against Lon's account. Matthew also paid I. D. Thomas for Dick's travel expenses and sent Lon $1,000 in cash to buy necessities when I. D. and Dick returned to Mississippi. Confederate paper dollars were worth less than thirty-three cents in gold at this time.[16]

Meanwhile, Lon's sisters wrote long, gossipy letters to him whenever there was a means to send one. Their mother had been "rather delicate . . . this summer" but was improving and had "never been confined to her bed." At age forty-six, Amanda was suffering the symptoms of menopause, as indicated by both language used to describe her condition and $10 paid to a midwife in July. In mid-August Matthew "suffered a good deal . . . with rheumatism in his right knee," Anna confided to Lon, but assured her brother that their father was getting better. Matthew consulted Dr. Smith and bought a hickory cane (and silver to trim it) that allowed him to go "everywhere he wants." Matthew and Amanda went to Marshall on November 17, 1863, so that she could visit a dentist and to do some shopping. They traveled as far north as Jefferson and on their return stopped at Carthage, where they found a pair of wool cards that Amanda desperately needed to clean the wool sheared from the sheep that many Redlanders were raising. Returning home after eight days on the road, Matthew rested for ten days before leaving for a two-week tour to Gilmer, Canton, and Palestine on land business.[17]

16. Leonidas Cartwright to little Brother, Aug. 9, 1863 (quotation), CFP; Account Book no. 12, p. 22, ibid.
17. Anna W. Cartwright to Leonidas, Aug. 24, 1863 (1st and 2nd quotations), CFP; Mary Cartwright to Leonidas, Nov. 13, 1863 (3rd quotation), ibid.; Account Book no. 12, pp. 21, 23–24, ibid.

Anna also sent Lon details about a tableau that she, Jane Blount, and Penelope "Nel" Thomas, I. D.'s sister, had organized to benefit the soldiers' hospital in Galveston. They also sang "The Bonnie Blue Flag" and "Dixie" accompanied by guitar and violin and raised $106, which included a small donation of $2 from Matthew Cartwright. Tableaux were popular among young women who enjoyed posing in costumes for still-life scenes representing historic events or literary characters. Anna's production presented a white-clad "young lady" representing each state in the Confederacy; each wore a coronet "after the fashion of those worn by queens with the initials of the state she represented" at the peak. Anna "represented fair Texas, the land of my birth," and her coronet had the "Lone Star" plus a long, white plume. Mary Blount, dressed in mourning clothes and with "her hands in fetters . . . assumed a kneeling posture" as Maryland.[18] The theatrical scene demonstrated sympathy for Maryland, considered by Southerners to be in bondage to the Union after President Lincoln had acted to quash a rebellion in the state, in such close proximity to the national capital. While the majority of Marylanders opposed secession, a faction of prominent Confederate sympathizers had rioted in Baltimore in April 1861, resulting in casualties when the Sixth Massachusetts Regiment passed through the city on its way to Washington. To prevent any future occurrences so close to the national capital, Lincoln took the unusual step of suspending habeas corpus, resulting in long imprisonment for a number of Maryland Confederates.

Mary and Anna also needed dental work, "plugs" in the parlance of the day, and Columbus escorted them to Shreveport in May 1863. The dentist was not there, so they went sightseeing and shopping instead. "We went on board the 'Missouri,' an ironclad . . . being built there," Anna explained, and "we also saw the 'Webb.'" The latter was the W. H. Webb, a ram that had been built as a New York City harbor tug and moved to the Mississippi River in 1858. The Confederacy seized it in 1861 to carry mail and passengers. The town was "so much crowded we could scarcely procure rooms" because the legislature was in session and "Genl Kirby Smith's troops were encamped but a mile or two from Town." Gen. E. Kirby Smith, commander of the Trans-

18. Anna W. Cartwright to Leonidas, Aug. 24, 1863 (quotations), CFP; Account Book no. 12, p. 20, ibid.

Mississippi Department, had moved his quarter master corps to Shreveport in March 1863, and a month later transferred all other departments to Marshall, Texas. In July, Matthew took his daughters to Marshall, "where we succeeded in getting our teeth plugged." They took rooms in a boardinghouse where Uncle Jimmy Holman was staying; he "is very popular" and was "the particular friend of everyone we met." Anna added, "we, *of course,* received a great deal of attention." The girls found Marshall "a beautiful place," just as Lon had told them they would after his visit there before the war.[19]

Young Matthew, approaching his eighth birthday, entered Mr. Swindle's school in April 1863; the Masonic Insititute had closed when its staff and older pupils went to war. Matthew was reluctant to go the first day since the others had started classes in January, but he immediately went to the head of his class in recitation and the next day was eager to go to school. Amanda had been teaching her youngest to read and do arithmetic at home the previous fall, and apparently had succeeded because "he progressed rapidly . . . through the 2nd reader and . . . six or seven lines of the multiplication tables." At the end-of-school examination ceremony, Matthew made a speech and "was the finest looking little boy you ever saw." Anna warned Lon that "you would scarcely know him he has grown so much." She confided that Matthew and Mary had mastered spinning cotton on the recently purchased spinning wheel, and though Anna could weave, she still could not spin thread or yarn.[20]

While Leonidas continued to struggle for a furlough through the fall, Meck returned home on sick leave at the end of October 1863. Since September, he had recurring chills and fever and in mid-November was "looking very pale." Adding to Amanda's

19. Anna W. Cartwright to Leonidas, Aug. 24, 1863 (quotations), CFP; Account Book no. 12, pp. 20–21, ibid.; Campbell, *Southern Community in Crisis,* 213. The *Missouri* failed to enter service before the end of the war, and after word of the surrender in April 1865, the *Webb* tried to run past Union gunboats and was sunk below New Orleans. Lilla McLure and J. Ed Howe, *History of Shreveport and Shreveport Builders* (Shreveport: J. Ed Howe, 1937), 37.

20. Anna W. Cartwright to Lon, Jan. 31, 1863, CFP; Matthew Cartwright to Leonidas, Apr. 7, 1863, ibid.; Anna W. Cartwright to Leonidas, Aug. 24, 1863 (quotations), ibid.; Mary Cartwright to Leonidas, Dec. 8, 1862, ibid.; Account Book no. 12, p. 19, ibid.

cares, young Matthew had chicken pox. Even Billy Holman received a furlough from Mississippi and visited his aunts and uncles in San Augustine, while Lon remained unlucky and failed to draw a leave again in December. On December 18, however, he wrote home saying that he had successfully bid $1,300 for a furlough that was being auctioned, and as soon as it was approved in a few days, he expected to be on his way. Billy, now called William, had already returned to camp and filled Lon's ears with the beauty of the San Augustine girls that he had seen. Lon was eager to visit the girls even though his old love, Anna Kaufman, had married in November and moved to Washington County.[21]

When Lon finally reached San Augustine at the end of 1863, he was delighted to see his brothers and to find his old school friends, John and Joel Massey, also on leave. Joel had had his foot amputated and was fitted with a cork foot so lifelike that Meck was unable to detect which was which. When their visits ended, John and Lon traveled back east together as far as the camp of the Third Texas Cavalry in Yazoo County, Mississippi. John, captain of Company K, First Texas Regiment, Hood's Brigade, returned to his command at Zollicoffer in eastern Tennessee on April 6, 1864. He wrote Lon a long letter expressing his sorrow in parting again; exactly one month later John was killed during the three-day battle between Lee and Grant in The Wilderness of northern Virginia. Lon did not learn of John's death until August.[22]

Meanwhile, the Union's Red River campaign was underway with a goal of capturing Shreveport and invading northeastern Texas. Ten thousand troops embarked at Vicksburg for the Red River on March 10, 1864, escorted by thirteen ironclads and seven gunboats commanded by Admiral David S. Porter. Four days later the Federals landed at Simsport and captured the partially completed Fort De Russy near the mouth of the Red River. Union troops entered Alexandria on March 18 without

21. A. P. Cartwright to Mother, Aug. 16, 1863, CFP; Mary Cartwright to Leonidas, Nov. 13, 1863 (quotation), ibid.; Leonidas Cartwright to Father, Dec. 18, 1863, ibid.

22. Mary to Lon, Nov. 13, 1863, CFP; W. S. Holman to Anna W. Cartwright, Mar. 27, 1864, ibid.; John H. Massey to Leonidas, Apr. 6, 1864, ibid.; Extract, Special Order no. 8, Headquarters, Second Texas Brigade, Oct. 22, 1864, ibid.; Leonidas Cartwright to Sister Anna, Mar. 22, 1865, ibid.

opposition, while Confederate forces, following orders from Gen. Kirby Smith to pull back cautiously toward Shreveport and avoid confrontations, retreated north to Natchitoches to await reinforcements from Texas. The general had asked Gov. Pendleton Murrah to put "immediately every armed man in Texas into the field." Shirkers were arrested and sent to military service, noncombatant troops returned to active commands, and guard regiments in Texas were shifted to Louisiana, leaving coastal defense to state troops. Low water at the rapids near Alexandria delayed the Union fleet, and federal troops did not reach Natchitoches until April 2, 1864.[23]

Matthew and other San Augustine residents became uneasy with the occupation of Natchitoches, only seventy-five miles away. On April 5 he sent a letter by express to Maj. Richard Waterhouse, whose father had leased Matthew's store, at Mansfield, Louisiana, asking about the strength and placement of the various Confederate units and the chances of federal troops crossing the Sabine River. Waterhouse replied two days later, giving detailed statistics and assuring Matthew that the Confederate army "will make a desperate fight. . . . I should apprehend no danger of any force crossing the Sabine." The Yankees would not risk sending a small cavalry force into Texas, he explained, because "we are too well supplied [sic] with cavalry ourselves & are watching their movements."[24]

Even as Waterhouse's letter sped to San Augustine, the two forces met at Sabine Crossroads near Mansfield (about forty miles south of Shreveport) on April 8. The result was a Confederate victory that ended the Union advance towards Texas. The Federals retreated to Pleasant Hill, where a second battle occurred the next day in which the Confederates suffered heavy loses. The demoralized Southerners pulled back to Mansfield, but fortunately for them, the Yankees continued their withdrawal downriver to Grand Ecore. The Union soldiers were forced to march along the river bottoms because their transports were useless in the low water. Porter's retreating fleet was delayed at

23. Mark Mayo Boatner III, *The Civil War Dictionary* (New York: David McKay Co., 1959), 685–686; Allan C. Ashcraft, *Texas in the Civil War: A Resume History* (Austin: Texas Civil War Centennial Commission, 1962), 23 (quotation).

24. Richard Waterhouse to M. Cartwright, Apr. 7, 1864 (quotations), CFP.

Alexandria until May 13, 1864, when engineers completed wing dams to provide sufficient water to ease the vessels over the shallow rapids. Major's brigade (Meck's old command) and others harassed the Federals along the banks of the Red River until May 26, when all the Yankees finally escaped.[25]

Although they missed the battles at Mansfield and Pleasant Hill, Columbus and Meck (on sick leave since October 1863) heeded the call to defend Texas and joined General Major's cavalry below Natchitoches by April 24. The brothers were among the Confederates who followed the retreating Union boats along the river banks, and Columbus participated in at least one exciting attack before his old kidney ailment sent him to the rear. Meck, on the other hand, saw "very active service" against the gunboats descending the river and wrote home that his unit had not "unsaddled our horses for about ten days." On May 1, 1864, he helped capture the transport *Emma,* loaded with commissary stores and outbound Yankee mail. Meck and others were assigned the job of reading the letters, which provided valuable information: the Union troops thought themselves "badly whiped [sic]" and that their generals believed they were surrounded "on all sides with an overwhelming Force of Rebs." By May 9 the Confederates had captured eight Yankee vessels.[26]

By mid-May Cumby moved to a private residence near the town of Evergreen in Avoyells Parish, where he remained for two weeks. He suffered severe back pains and what he thought was "something like diobetis [sic]" because he had trouble controlling his urine. The doctor, however, told him that his kidneys and bladder were inflamed, probably from the hard riding and stress, and prescribed medicine that helped him for awhile. The family where he was posted had sent their slaves to Nacogdoches, and now that the Union army was in retreat, their son-in-law would carry a letter to Sallie on his way to recover the blacks and return them to the plantation below Alexandria. Sallie, just twenty-three, had her own problems with her two boys, the livestock, and renegade Confederate soldiers passing along the road. One

25. Boatner, *Dictionary of the Civil War,* 686–689.
26. Columbus Cartwright to Sallie, Apr. 27, 1864, CFP; Priv A. P. Cartwright to Father, May 9, 1864 (1st and 2nd quotations), ibid.; Maj. W. P. Saufley to Col. Matthew Cartwright, May 9, 1864 (3rd and 4th quotations), ibid.

had stolen her black horse and others killed the sow and four hogs. "I have had no trouble with the negroes yet—they seem to be trying to do their duty." One slave woman was very ill, and in fact dying. Young Matthew came each evening to spend the night with her, which was a comfort although he was only eight years old. This kind of news only upset Cumby, who returned to duty near Opelousas on May 31. By the end of July 1864, Cumby was home on a furlough he had bought for $380. His health remained bad and his leave was extended until November.[27]

On May 12 Meck ceased duty as a cavalryman and was promoted to courier dispatcher at General Major's headquarters, first at Moreauville, then south in the vicinity of Opelousas, but by June he was back in Alexandria. He considered asking for a furlough when his three-year enlistment ended in early June 1864, but decided that "I have got a very good place now and but little to do, and if I go home I will stand a chance to lose [it]." Meck remained with General Major's headquarters through October, when the general moved into winter quarters in southwestern Arkansas, where food and fodder were more plentiful. Talking among themselves, the troops agreed there was little chance for peace even if former Union general George McClelland, the Democratic candidate, was elected president of the United States in November. "I am fearful that we will have to fight four years longer . . . though if necessary I am willing . . . to achieve our rights and liberties," Meck wrote his parents. Others agreed, and "None are willing to reconstruction of the Union . . . I don't think it can ever be done." The greatest problem in Meck's division was the lack of pay, he wrote, and "a great many are becoming dissatisfied on that account."[28]

East of the Mississippi River, the Third Texas Cavalry had moved to Georgia, where Lon was a member of Gen. Lawrence Sullivan Ross's scouts near Atlanta. "It is an honorable position

27. Columbus Cartwright to Sallie, May 19, 1864 (1st quotation), CFP; Columbus Cartwright to Sallie, May 31, 1864, ibid.; Sallie to Dear Husband, n.d. [probably end of May] (2nd quotation), ibid.; Sallie to Columbus, July 4, 1864, ibid.; Matthew Cartwright to Americus, Aug. 6, 1864, ibid.; Account Book no. 12, p. 27, ibid.

28. A. P. Cartwright to Dear Father, May 20, 1864, CFP; A. P. Cartwright to Dear Parents, May 23, 1864, ibid.; same to same, June 11, 1864 (1st quotation), ibid.; A. P. Cartwright to Col. Matthew Cartwright, Oct. 14, 1864 (2nd–4th quotations), ibid.

though sometimes a very hard one," Lon wrote Meck. He had lost two horses, one killed in a riding accident and the other stolen, leaving him with only a sorrel mare. On August 20, 1864, Ross's brigade tangled with four thousand Yankee cavalrymen at Lovejoy Station on the railroad south of Atlanta. It was "quite a muss," as the Federals tried to drive "the Rebs from Atlanta." Lon and his servant Dick were in the advance, and the Yankee attack scattered "horses, negroes (Wild Dick flew and alighted demoralized in the wilderness)." But the Yankees pulled back "before the deadly fire of the Texas Ranger." The Yankees took many prisoners, including Noel G. Thomas, I. D.'s brother. In spite of the brave stand, the Confederates abandoned Atlanta on September 1, 1864, and the Third Texas Cavalry retreated with Gen. John Bell Hood to Tennessee, where they participated in his ill-fated campaign against Nashville in December. By February 1865, Lon and the Third were back in Mississippi and spent the next three months north of Vicksburg.[29]

Before the end of 1864, Meck's unit moved to Nacogdoches because fodder and grazing were plentiful for the horses. Gen. William Steel had succeeded to Major's command, and Meck was busy "working in new harness . . . in new business that is entirely new to me." Although he did not explain his duties in his letters, he was obviously doing clerical work at headquarters: "I am kept quite busy all of the time. We have had more business in the office than usual." He had access to mail and dispatches coming into the office and told his father that "Hood . . . was in possession of Nashville," which was not true. He added that it was "quite a difference from the news we received last week." Communication across the Mississippi River remained difficult and those in Texas wanted to believe the good news even though Hood was in retreat to Mississippi at that time.[30]

Meck had an opportunity to visit at home just before Christmas 1864. His mother wrote to him about the seasonal festivities, and Meck replied, "I regret very much that I could not be home to participate in the enjoyments." Amanda also inquired if he was

29. Leonidas Cartwright to A. P. Cartwright, Aug. 24, 1864 (quotations), CFP; Leonidas Cartwright to Parents, Feb. 20, 1865, ibid.; Leonidas Cartwright to Anna, Mar. 22, 1865, ibid.

30. A. P. Cartwright to Father, Jan. 16, 1865 (1st, 3rd, and 4th quotations), CFP; A. P. Cartwright to Mother, Jan. 20, 1865 (2nd quotation), ibid.

seeing any young ladies. He replied, "I have not been at anybody's homes . . . though I have received several invitations. . . . As I am not a candidate for matrimony yet awhile I will drop this subject." At this same time, Lon was obsessed with young ladies in Mississippi, where the people "have extended . . . great hospitality in the way of barbecues, parties, etc. . . . I . . . found some very nice young lady acquaintences." One, Miss Mattie Wildy, was a cousin of Mary Garrett, and wanted Lon to forward a letter to her. "Miss Mattie is very intelligent and pretty . . . about twenty years old [Lon was twenty-two], would be pleased to live in Texas," Lon told his sister. Matrimony was definitely on his mind. Seventeen days after writing home, on April 8, 1865, Lon was captured by the federal forces while scouting in the area of Satartia, south of Yazoo City.[31]

Civilian morale in Texas was low in January 1865, and Meck wrote that the people in Nacogdoches were "very despondent." He told his father that everything was "dull about this place. No trading. . . . I bought a hundred dollars new issue at twenty for one," but he heard that the bills sold for ten to one in Austin. When his mother asked how the ladies in Nacogdoches were enduring wartime, Meck assured her that they did not "compare with the ladies of our town . . . in beauty, style . . . , or elegance. . . . The people here all look dejected, not much animation about them. I believe it is worse than San Augustine."[32]

On April 9, 1865, less than three weeks after Lon's last letter from Mississippi, General Lee surrendered to General Grant at Appomattox Courthouse in Virginia, ending the four-year war. Six days later, on April 15, President Lincoln died from gunshot wounds suffered the previous evening, leaving Vice-president Andrew Johnson of Tennessee to cope with the myriad of problems. The news traveled as rapidly as possible to Marshall, where the *Texas Republican* reported on April 14 that Richmond had fallen, and word of Lee's surrender reached the East Texas town on April 28. Since the fall of Vicksburg, Marshall's telegraph office could communicate with Shreveport but no farther east;

31. A. P. Cartwright to Mother, Jan. 20, 1865 (1st and 2nd quotations), CFP; Leonidas Cartwright to Anna, Mar. 22, 1865 (3rd and 4th quotations), ibid.; Jackson and Erwin, "Rebels from the Redlands," 283.

32. A. P. Cartwright to Father, Jan. 16, 1865 (1st and 2nd quotations), CFP; A. P. Cartwright to Mother, Jan. 20, 1865 (3rd quotation), ibid.

however, lines connected Marshall with Houston and Galveston by way of Crockett. Some die-hards west of the Mississippi River considered fighting on, perhaps with foreign support. On May 12 Gen. E. Kirby Smith convened a meeting in Marshall of the governors of Louisiana, Arkansas, Missouri, and Texas. They worked out proposals to end the war without a formal surrender, but that proved impossible when morale in the Trans-Mississippi Department disintegrated. Two weeks later, on May 26, Kirby Smith capitulated at New Orleans; this was followed by another surrender at Galveston on June 2.[33]

Confederate officers in Texas lost control of their troops during April and May. Many went home, taking their arms and horses with them. Disillusioned and discouraged, some soldiers pilfered military stores from Confederate warehouses, and a few turned against citizens. Looting of state property led to an order from the governor on May 25 for sheriffs to protect and store state-owned property for more equitable distribution. But civil order was also breaking down; some sheriffs joined bodies of armed men—former military officers and civilian officials fearful of retribution from the victorious Yankees—passing through Texas towns on their way to Mexico. There, French troops defending Emperor Maximilian from the republican army of President Benito Juárez welcomed Confederates into their cause. In June 1865, Governor Murrah, former Governor Clark, and generals Kirby Smith and John Bankhead Magruder joined the flight to the Rio Grande.[34]

At Marshall the situation worsened in May, and Confederate commanders issued orders "to place strict guards around their respective commands . . . and adopt such other measures" as needed to keep their men in camp to prevent "further molestation of the citizens." But many slipped away, leaving the arsenal and powder mill open for looting. Local residents and absconding soldiers opened bags and kegs until spilled "powder covered the floor." K. M. Van Zandt, the Confederate tax-in-kind collector at

33. Campbell, *Southern Community in Crisis,* 216; Charles H. Dillon, "The Arrival of the Telegraph in Texas," *SHQ,* LXIV (Oct., 1960), 206–207.

34. Charles William Ramsdell, *Reconstruction in Texas* (1910; reprint, Austin: University of Texas Press, 1970), 32–35, 39. This book is still a standard for events and dates, although the author's interpretations are out of date.

Marshall, let it be known that his storehouse was unlocked, and the contents were soon well-distributed.[35]

The end of the war was difficult for Matthew. Like others he did not know what to expect and made a quick trip to Marshall for advice. While there he paid $495 in Confederate money for three dresses for his wife and daughters and also purchased ten yards of domestic for $120. He was home by May 2, but did not record what he learned from Confederate military headquarters. His sons were not yet home except for Columbus, who had not returned to service after his illness the previous year. Inflation was at its peak; Matthew spent $150 for one gallon of whiskey on May 5, a soporific badly needed during these times. A few days later his horse Blacky sickened; Matthew spent $50 to treat him, but Blacky died on May 11 and it cost another $10 to have the carcass removed. Three days later, on May 14, Matthew recorded in his ledger book that "Confederate Currencies Ceased to pass." By May 30, a gallon of rum cost only $2.50 in United States currency, and the dreadful inflation caused by the worthless Confederate paper money was at an end. Matthew had cannily managed to keep a supply of gold, however, and would not suffer as much as those less fortunate.[36]

Meanwhile, the editor of the widely read Marshall *Texas Republican* speculated about what the Union might do: military occupation, confiscate property, disenfranchise the whites, and "elevate" the Negro. The editor hoped instead for a policy of reconciliation to bind the wounds of war and revive the southern economy. He urged his readers to accept federal authority gracefully and hoped that Negro slavery would continue in some form, perhaps with gradual emancipation well in the future. But on June 17, 1865, his hopes were dashed when Lt. Col. Loyd Wheaton, U.S. Army, and his cavalry company arrived from Shreveport followed by the Eighth Illinois Infantry Regiment. Colonel Wheaton informed Marshall residents that military government would replace civil authority for the present, and that slavery had been destroyed by Lincoln's January 1, 1863, Proclamation. Thus, East Texas learned about Union intentions two

---

35. Campbell, *Southern Community in Crisis,* 218–219 (quotations).
36. Account Book no. 12, pp. 30–31, CFP.

days before Gen. Gordon Granger reached Galveston to make the official announcement.[37]

Exactly when Meck was discharged is unclear; probably toward the end of May, when the troops were disbanded. The family heard nothing from Lon, but soon after his capture on April 8 he was exchanged and paroled. Lon was mustered out at Vanton, Mississippi, at the end of May, and each Texas cavalryman was given transportation by boat from Vicksburg to Alexandria for himself and a horse. Lon reached home on June 5.[38] A family story relates that Meck and Lon, coming from different directions, reached the front gate at the same time and that Matthew wept for joy when he saw them. The Cartwrights were luckier than many Texas families, as both sons returned safely.

President Andrew Johnson rejected the demands of the Radical wing of the Republican party that those in the Confederate states be forced to take an oath of past loyalty (which would have denied amnesty to most) as well as future loyalty, as proposed by Lincoln and Johnson. On May 29, 1865, the president issued his Amnesty Proclamation restoring citizenship to those who would pledge future loyalty to the United States; however, those holding high military and civil offices in the Confederate government and those with taxable property valued over $20,000 would have to petition him for individual pardons. The latter group, of course, included Matthew Cartwright.

At the same time, Johnson named Andrew Jackson Hamiliton provisional governor of Texas. A long-time resident of Austin, Hamilton was a Unionist and had fled the state in 1862. Like his counterparts in other Southern states, he had authority to call a convention to amend the state constitution, abolish slavery, and repudiate the state's war debt. By December 1865, all the states except Texas had conformed, and Johnson announced that the Union was restored. Not until April 1866 did Texas grudgingly meet the requirements.[39]

In August 1865 Governor Hamilton began replacing county officials elected under the Confederacy. Lacking sufficient Union-

37. Campbell, *Southern Community in Crisis*, 245, 246 (quotation, citing Marshall *Texas Republican*, May 26, 1865), 247.

38. Jackson and Erwin, "Rebels from the Redlands," 283; Account Book no. 12, p. 31, CFP; Johnson, *Texas and the Texans*, V, 2200.

39. Ramsdell, *Reconstruction*, 55–58.

ists in San Augustine who were willing to serve, he removed the county court but retained the sheriff and county clerk, choosing longtime residents to replace those dismissed. The governor issued a proclamation on August 19 to register voters in each county: the chief justice, the district clerk, and the county clerk would set one day each week to register those who had taken the general amnesty oath and also those who needed to petition for presidential amnesty.[40]

Matthew, the pragmatic businessman, wanted to get his special pardon as soon as possible so that he could resume his activities and protect his property. Unlike some who were reluctant to apply for a presidential pardon with its inference of wrong-doing, Matthew put the past behind him and looked to the future. Some slaveholders hesitated to take the amnesty oath for fear it might jeopardize future claims for compensation for their slaves. Matthew, of course, had lost only fifteen slaves, so his pecuniary loss was small compared with that of William Garrett or W. W. Holman. Many continued to believe that the government would pay them for the loss of their laborers, or perhaps allow compulsory labor for blacks with gradual emancipation. To put these unrealistic expectations to rest and to encourage everyone to become full citizens, Governor Hamilton issued a statement in September 1865 asserting that slavery was dead and could not be restored, and that forced labor laws would only offend the North and delay reconstruction.[41]

Matthew bought a new horse and went to Shreveport in August to see U.S. Army officials about petitioning for his presidential pardon. He took his amnesty oath on August 29 in the Caddo Parish District Court and received a copy to carry with

40. Ibid., 61; Campbell, *Southern Community in Crisis*, 248; San Augustine County Commissioners' Minute Book, 1860–1885: election, Aug. 1, 1864, p. 112; Last meeting of court, May 22, 1865, p. 129; Names of commissioners and county judge (Hamilton appointees) at called session, Oct. 30, 1865 (Chief Justice C. B. Powell; T. S. C. Wade, James Chaffin, I. D. Thomas, Sr., commissioners), p. 130. The Hamilton appointees all lived in San Augustine according to the 1850 U.S. Census. County officers elected in August 1864 are listed on (June) 1865 tax roll: Chief Justice A. G. Price; Inlow Matthews, John G. Berry, and Donald McDonald, commissioners. County Clerk Frances H. Dixon served from 1860 to 1868; Sheriff Wyatt J. Teal was elected August 1864 and served until June 25, 1866.

41. Ibid., 62.

him in order to conduct business. He later recorded it in the San Augustine District Court. While in Shreveport, Matthew sent a telegram, perhaps to President Johnson, asking for the special presidential pardon. This done, he rode west to Jefferson, Quitman, and Athens, then south to Palestine checking on his business before turning toward Nacogdoches and home. He arrived on September 21. On the way Matthew bought new spectacles, violin strings, and a lead pencil, but otherwise recorded only what he ate and drank each day.[42]

Before his trip, a representative of Waddill & Collins, cotton merchants in Jefferson, visited Matthew to arrange to buy the cotton he had stored in their warehouse. He gave Waddill $20 in specie on August 26 to weigh the cotton and arrange the necessary releases attesting that the cotton had not been pledged or sold to the late Confederate government. Everybody who had cotton on hand rushed it to market because of the favorable prices. By the end of September 1865 the factors informed Matthew that he had 150 bales at an average weight of 468 pounds, but he would have to pay $300 to have the bales repaired and compressed for shipment to New Orleans. This last message was sent collect from Jefferson by the U.S. Army telegraph, but must have been delivered to Matthew's agents in Shreveport because as yet the wires did not come through San Augustine.[43]

Soon marriage was on the minds of Matthew's children. The deaths of so many young men had left an abundance of single young women from whom his sons could choose. But neither Meck nor Lon was financially ready to start a family during these uncertain times. Lon's friend John Dean asked the question succinctly in a letter on August 29, 1865. He wondered "how the boys are getting along and which young ladies they want to take from their homes to starve."[44]

Mary Cartwright's beau Jimmie Ingram could support a wife, and he came to Matthew's door to ask for Mary's hand. The wedding was set for December 14 and Mary gave her father a

---

42. Account book no. 12, pp. 31–32, CFP; Amnesty oath before A. H. Lunans, clerk of Tenth Judicial District, Caddo Parish, La., Aug. 29, 1865, in San Augustine District Clerk's Civil Cases, vol. I, Index; Ramsdell, *Reconstruction*, 41–42.

43. Account Book no. 12, p. 32, CFP.

44. John Dean to Leonidas Cartwright, Aug. 29, 1865, CFP.

long list of necessities before he again left for Shreveport in the first week of October. First he bought spices, sugar, pickles, raisins, almonds, tea, and cheese to be shipped home to Amanda and paid in specie, for which he received a $75 discount on his $226 bill. The next day he purchased $150 worth of dress material, hoop skirts, corsets, three boxes of Lily White (the popular cosmetic that hid blemishes), fancy soap, toothbrushes, combs, ribbons, and belts, again receiving a one-third discount for cash. Some items on Mary's list such as the bridal wreath were more difficult to locate, but he returned home on October 14 with almost all she had requested.[45]

Matthew left again two weeks later for northeastern Texas, to collect rents and money owed for land, but with the high cotton prices in New Orleans, he also bought more cotton. From Henderson, he returned home through Shelby County to see his nephews Matthew and Robert Cartwright, who were attending a boarding school. Matthew reached home in mid-November and within a week started for New Orleans to buy goods to stock the store in San Augustine. Like his own father, Matthew wanted to provide economic opportunities for each son, and now seemed an auspicious time to resume store keeping. Although Columbus decided that he preferred to raise livestock, Meck and Lon would run the store with Matthew as their financial partner.[46]

In the Crescent City from November 24 to 29, 1865, Matthew visited various dry goods and hardware merchants selecting menswear, toiletries, stationery, sewing notions, Barlow knives, looking glasses, dress goods and trimming, mens' and womens' hosiery, cloaks, umbrellas, blankets, groceries, liquor, tobacco, brooms, twine, dishes and cups, buckets, and pans. The total amount came to almost $2,000 including packing, drayage, and insurance. Matthew paid the full amount in cash, in gold and United States legal tender notes, the first paper money issued by

45. Mary's list (original in possession of Mary Ingram Browning, granddaughter; copy in CFP); Receipted statements to Matthew Cartwright from Walsh & Boisseau, Oct. 4, 1865, and Jones & Co., Oct. 5, 1865, CFP; Account Book no. 12, pp. 33–34, ibid.

46. Account Book no. 12, pp. 34–35, CFP; handwritten receipts, Nov. 2–4, 1865, from Stephen Chaffin and H. G. Thompson ("Recd of MC $600 for 3 bales, $668 for three bales, left in each man's care; Jas. G. Credille shelter for 10 bales paid by me to MC will deliver by 15th"), ibid.; Leonidas Cartwright to W. H. Morrow, Apr. 8, 1866, ibid.

James Melville Ingram (1840–1900) and Mary C. Cartwright Ingram (1845–1903), ca. 1890. Courtesy Cartwright Family Descendants.

the federal government in 1863. His boxes and barrels were loaded on board the steamboat *Cuba* to be delivered to S. M. Cooley at Grand Ecore. Matthew remained in New Orleans through December 2, buying a trunk, saddle, and bridle for Mary and a new suit with a black satin vest for himself. Amanda always expected presents of jewelry or notions when her husband or sons traveled, and indulgent Matthew bought three silver calling card cases and sheet music to please the ladies in his family.[47]

Mary's wedding took place as scheduled in the Cartwright parlor, and the newlyweds remained in San Augustine through the holidays. Matthew paid $8 for photographs of the happy couple and the family on January 6, and a month later, just before Mary and Jimmie left for Opelousas, Louisiana, he gave his daughter $2,000 as a wedding gift. Money now had to substitute for the traditional family matrimonial gift of land and slaves. Ingram took his bride to his family's Evergreen farm near Opelousas. He and Mary lived there jointly with his sister Molly and her husband, Dr. Hector McDuffie.[48]

Matthew and Amanda's household continued to function much as it had before the war. Old Nancy, now fifty-five years old, and three of her adult children, Emeline, Virtue, and Walker, lived on the place and agreed to work for room, board, and a little spending money. Dick, more independent after his years with Lon in the army, moved elsewhere in San Augustine, but what happened to Jane and her five children is unknown. When word of emancipation first reached San Augustine, some planters told their bondsmen that the decree would not take effect until Christmas, in order to insure that they would have hands to pick cotton in the fall and also in hopes of government recompense. Many blacks readily accepted the delay because the week-long Christmas holiday was always a time of gifts, and freedom seemed the ultimate present. With only house servants, Matthew perhaps let his people know that they were free and allowed them to remain in the servant quarters.[49]

47. Receipted statements from six New Orleans merchants and the steamboat *Cuba,* Nov. 24–29, 1865, CFP.
48. Account Book no. 12, p. 35, CFP; Mary C. Ingram to Anna Cartwright, Feb. 20, 1866, ibid. It is not clear if "Evergreen" was the name of the farm, or if it was near the town of Evergreen, Avoyelles Parish, a plantation community about twenty-five miles from Opelousas and thirty from Alexandria.
49. Matthew Cartwright Bible.

The Cartwrights, unlike many of their neighbors, survived the Civil War without the loss or maiming of a son. The emancipation of their few household slaves was not an economic loss comparable to those suffered by neighboring planters who possessed numerous field hands. During the war Matthew and Amanda carefully guarded their gold and silver reserves by using Confederate paper money for immediate needs while judiciously dispensing coins for scarce items or negotiating favorable discounts.[50] Long business experience gave Matthew an edge over others when buying, selling, or bartering. With normal commerce about to revive, Matthew looked forward to receiving his special pardon and resuming business activities unhampered.

50. Account Book no. 12, pp. 37–41, CFP.

Eleven

Changing Times

~

1866–1870

San Augustine residents optimistically hoped for a quick return to normal relations as a state in the Union while they ignored national political realities. Unlike Marshall, which was immediately occupied by federal troops, San Augustine saw little change in 1865 and 1866 except from emancipation and the replacement of some county officials.

The Republican party hoped to gain a strong following in the South by placing Unionists in office, but in San Augustine few such men were willing to serve. Governor Hamilton named C. B. Powell, a wagon-maker who had lived in San Augustine since 1850, to be chief justice although he had not previously held political office. Henry Lewis, a longtime resident, became sheriff. The men named justices of the peace, barkeep James Chaffin and elderly I. D. Thomas, Sr., had not participated in the war, and the exact nature of their political beliefs is unknown. The county clerk remained in office although he had served in the state guard.[1]

1. San Augustine County Commissioners' Court Minutes, Oct. 30, Nov.

Matthew and other wealthy men had not yet received their special pardons when voters went to the polls on January 8, 1866, to select representatives to attend a convention in Austin to draft a new state constitution and the necessary laws to reenter the Union. Many Texans were apathetic about the election and only 124 San Augustine men cast ballots, compared with the 335 in the 1861 race for governor or even the 228 who participated in a county election in August 1864. They chose lawyer Richard F. Slaughter, Matthew's nephew-in-law, over Kenneth Loggins, 81 to 43.[2] Slaughter had married Anna Holman, the daughter of deceased Sanford and Clementine Cartwright Holman.

The delegates, many of them Confederate veterans like Slaughter, met in Austin in February and March 1866, and after acrimonious arguments, added the Reconstruction measures ordered by Congress for readmittance to the Union as amendments to the 1845 Texas state constitution. They repudiated state debts incurred during the Confederacy as demanded, but instead of declaring the act of secession null and void, they merely said that it was illegal. In this same grudging manner, they did not ratify the Thirteenth Amendment abolishing slavery, on the grounds that it had already been approved by the required number of states then comprising the Union. Instead, they added a phrase to the state constitution abolishing slavery and also allowed blacks to own property and testify in court in cases involving their own race. Voting rights and office-holding for the freedmen, ideas that were incomprehensible to most Texans, were not considered. Convention members set June 25 for the election of state and county officials.[3]

21, 1865; San Augustine residents to A. J. Hamilton, Feb. 20, 1866, Election Returns, San Augustine County, 1866, Secretary of State Records (TSL); A. A. Metzner letter, July 31, 1867, Bureau of Refugees, Freedmen and Abandoned Lands, Record Group 105 (microfilm roll 3; National Archives), from notes provided by Thomas Nall, S. F. Austin University, Nacogdoches (cited hereafter as Nall, Freedmen's Bureau Notes). For Marshall, see Max S. Lale, "Military Occupation of Marshall, Texas, by the Eighth Illinois Volunteer Infantry, U.S.A., 1865," *Military History of Texas and the Southwest*, XIII (1976), 39–47.

2. Election Returns, San Augustine County, 1861, 1864, 1866, Secretary of State Records (TSL).

3. Campbell, *Southern Community in Crisis*, 254–255.

A total of 294 San Augustine men went to the polls on that date. Matthew Cartwright may have been among them on the strength of his amnesty oath, though he still lacked his special pardon. Judge Powell reported that "several capitalists . . . that have not received pardons . . . cast their votes" and were not challenged by the registrars. Some former Confederates who had taken the oath of amnesty "boldly announced that they did not hold that they were bound thereby," which the judge interpreted to mean they still adhered to the "rebel faith." San Augustine, like most of the state, favored conservative James W. Throckmorton of Collin County for governor 286 to 8 over former Gov. Elisha M. Pease, a Unionist. While a member of the legislature, Throckmorton had favored Sam Houston in 1857 and 1859 and voted against secession in 1861. But once Texas seceded, he supported the Confederacy in various capacities, including briga-dier general on the frontier, and was elected president of the 1866 convention.[4]

The Redlanders also elected former county judge Albert G. Price to head the county government and named Thomas William Blount as state representative. Billy Blount was only twenty-six years old, a CSA veteran, and a former classmate of the Cartwrights at Kentucky Military Institute. What Columbus and Meck thought about Billy as a legislator is not recorded. The legislature met from August 6 to November 13, 1866, and enacted a number of conservative measures meant to ensure the *status quo ante bellum*, such as laws regulating the activities of blacks similar to the earlier slave code restricting their movements. All blacks had to work or be arrested as vagrants. These labor laws reflected the wide-spread fear that the freedmen would not work on the plantations without coercion.[5]

Meanwhile, on August 20, President Johnson announced that the insurrection had ended in Texas and restored the state to the Union. The Radical wing of the Republican party, however, believed that the president had acted too quickly and generously in allowing unrepentant rebels to reenter the Union, and it offered

4. Election Returns, San Augustine County, 1866, Secretary of State Records (TSL).

5. Ibid.; Ramsdell, *Reconstruction in Texas*, 118–126.

a number of illustrations. Texas had not approved the Thirteenth and Fourteenth Amendments abolishing slavery and forbidding states to pass laws that abridged the privileges of citizenship or deprived any person of their life, liberty, or property without due process of law. Moreover, Texas was passing restrictive laws. The South was returning only Democrats to power, thereby endangering Republican control of Congress. Like the other Southern states, Texas legislators named former Confederates to the U.S. Senate: Texas Supreme Court Justice Oran M. Roberts, president of the Secession Convention in 1861; and seventy- eight-year-old David G. Burnet, whose son left the U.S. Army to serve the Confederacy. Roberts and Burnet traveled to Washington "to make an appearance for the State rather than with any expectation of being admitted," and thus were annoyed but not surprised when Republican senators denied them seats in December 1866.[6]

Roberts remained in the capital to take care of business for Governor Throckmorton and also to facilitate pardons "of particular individuals in Texas." Securing the pardons remained critical amid rumors that Congress might confiscate the property of wealthy southerners. Matthew Cartwright, William W. Holman, Dr. Lewis V. Greer of San Augustine, and William Ingram of Sabine, Mary Cartwright Ingram's father-in-law, employed Judge Roberts to secure their pending pardons. Roberts wrote Matthew on December 11, 1866, that he had the four pardons in hand and that "we just got through yours in time," it being "about the last signed by the President," who was waiting to see what Congress was going to do. Judge Roberts added that he did not believe Congress would "undertake to confiscate property" because it was more interested in reorganizing southern state governments to reflect Republican goals. "My advice to the people," he wrote, "is to go to work . . . to develop the material interests of the country and to mend their own fortunes." Matthew was in total agreement.[7]

6. Oran M. Roberts, "The Political, Legislative, and Judicial History of Texas for its Fifty Years of Statehood, 1845–1895," in Dudley G. Wooten (ed.), *A Comprehensive History of Texas, 1685 to 1897* (2 vols.; Dallas: William G. Scarff, 1898), II, 155–157, 160 (quotation) (cited hereafter as Wooten [ed.], *Comprehensive History*).

7. Ibid., II, 161 (1st quotation); O. M. Roberts to Matthew Cartwright, Dec. 11, 1866 (2nd–4th quotations), CFP.

Returning home in January 1867, Roberts sent the four pardons to Matthew. Roberts wrote, "As I mentioned to you, I had to get help to rush them through before the repeal of the law . . . . I was told . . . that about two hundred dollars apiece [*sic*] was the customary fee." The judge reminded his client that Cartwright had said "to be liberal as to any terms" in order to secure the documents. Regretfully, Roberts had no "encouraging news as to our political condition" but felt "confident . . . that the property of all that have been pardoned" was safe.[8]

The two-page pardon, dated December 4, 1866, was signed by President Andrew Johnson and Secretary of State William H. Seward. A return was required from each recipient acknowledging that he would take the 1865 amnesty oath, never use slave labor, pay any costs levied against him or his property, relinquish any property or proceeds from it that had been confiscated by the United States, and sign the enclosed acceptance. Matthew replied on February 8, 1867: "Sir: I have the honor to acknowledge the receipt of the President's Warrant of Pardon bearing date 4th December, 1866, and hereby signify my acceptance of the same, with all the conditions therein specified." The secretary of state returned a copy of the pardon to Matthew on February 23, 1867, which he recorded at the county courthouse.[9] Matthew Cartwright's citizenship was fully restored and his property safe.

Meanwhile, freedmen in San Augustine met stiff resistance from whites regarding the new social order. Following reports that whites were mistreating blacks in eastern Texas, an inspector from the Freedmen's Bureau headquartered in Galveston visited the area and found many questionable incidents. In San Augustine in late 1865, for example, he found that some former slaves did not know that they were free. The inspector also heard about beatings for what was termed disrespectful behavior—a freedman not removing a hat in front of a white, not allowing his wife to be whipped, and so forth. More atrocities against blacks took place during 1866, also a poor crop year, which perhaps added to white frustration. These conditions caused the bureau to increase the number of agents in East Texas.[10]

8. O. M. Roberts to Matthew Cartwright, Jan. 19, 1867, CFP
9. Matthew Cartwright's Pardon, Dec. 4, 1866, CFP.
10. Claude Elliott, "The Freedmen's Bureau in Texas," *SHQ*, LVI (July, 1952), 4–6.

ANDREW JOHNSON,

PRESIDENT OF THE UNITED STATES OF AMERICA,

TO ALL TO WHOM THESE PRESENTS SHALL COME, GREETING:

Whereas, Matthew Cartwright, of San Augustine County, Texas, by taking part in the late rebellion against the Government of the United States, has made himself liable to heavy pains and penalties;

And whereas, the circumstances of his case render him a proper object of Executive clemency;

Now, therefore, be it known, that I, ANDREW JOHNSON, President of the United States of America, in consideration of the premises, divers other good and sufficient reasons me thereunto moving, do hereby grant to the said Matthew Cartwright a full pardon and amnesty for all offences by him committed, arising from participation, direct or implied, in the said rebellion, conditioned as follows:

1st. This pardon to be of no effect until the said Matthew Cartwright shall take the oath prescribed in the Proclamation of the President, dated May 29th, 1865.

2d. To be void and of no effect if the said Matthew Cartwright shall hereafter, at any time, acquire any property whatever in slaves, or make use of slave labor.

The pardon from President Andrew Johnson restoring Matthew Cartwright's citizenship, December 4, 1866. Courtesy Eugene C. Barker Texas History Center, University of Texas at Austin.

3d. That the said *Matthew Cartwright* first pay all costs which may have accrued in any proceedings instituted or pending against his person or property, before the date of the acceptance of this warrant.

4th. That the said *Matthew Cartwright* shall not, by virtue of this warrant, claim any property or the proceeds of any property that has been sold by the order, judgment, or decree of a court under the confiscation laws of the United States.

5th. That the said *Matthew Cartwright* shall notify the Secretary of State, in writing, that he has received and accepted the foregoing pardon.

In testimony whereof, I have hereunto signed my name and caused the Seal of the United States to be affixed.

Done at the City of Washington, this Fourth day of December A. D. 1866, and of the Independence of the United States the Ninety first.

Andrew Johnson

By the President:

William H. Seward, *Secretary of State.*

A totally opposite view of the state of things in San Augustine was given by state representative William Blount in a glowing article about the county for the 1867 *Texas Almanac*. Blount described an elysium: "The freedmen of San Augustine are doing better for themselves, and their employers than in any part of the South of which I have any knowledge." Most had hired themselves to former masters in return for one-third of the crop; the employers "furnish everything for farming . . . as well as feed them on good and wholesome food." Some men were paid $10 per month while women received $4. Blount knew of no outrages "being committed upon freedmen or white men; the freedmen have been taught by their former masters what their social status is, and are not desirous of encroaching upon the rights of others." Blount attributed this good conduct to the "absence of Bureaus, Union soldiers, and internal revenue agents" in San Augustine.[11] By inference, confrontations elsewhere were due, in Blount's mind, to governmental meddling.

Congress had created the Bureau of Refugees, Freedmen, and Abandoned Lands in March 1865 to deal with the problems of the freedmen arising in areas then occupied by the U.S. Army. The temporary agency was to serve for the duration of the war plus one year, but in 1866, in response to the restrictive black codes passed by southern legislatures, its powers and life were extended. If necessary, its agents could ask for military support. The absence of refugees and abandoned lands in Texas meant that bureau agents concentrated on seeing that blacks received fair treatment from employers and in the courts, and also tried to establish schools to educate the freedmen and their children.

The bureau began operating in Galveston on September 21, 1865. One of the first orders instructed agents to disabuse blacks of the notion that they would receive a portion of their former masters' land at Christmas and to stress that freedom brought the obligation to work. The freedmen should make written labor contracts with employers detailing duties and pay. While the planters agreed with the obligation to work, they often resisted contracts. Each bureau agent supervised a large area at first, and thus some counties like San Augustine escaped close surveillance.[12]

11. Thomas W. Blount, "County Seat, San Augustine," *The Texas Almanac for 1867* (Galveston: Galveston News, 1867), 153–154.
12. Elliott, "Freedmen's Bureau in Texas," 1–3.

Learning about the need for contracts from the visiting inspector, Matthew made arrangements in January 1866 with Nancy, Emeline, Virtue, and Walker to work in the house and garden. The three women each received $4 per month and board, while Walker earned $10 per month, just as Rep. Blount had reported. Matthew also allowed them to charge clothing and small luxuries such as tobacco at the store against their annual earnings. Emeline did not work for two weeks toward the end of the year, perhaps in observance of the former Christmas holiday, and at the final reckoning, Matthew deducted $4 for board for fourteen days for herself and her two sons. Perhaps this angered the twenty-nine-year-old woman because her name disappeared from the account book, as did those of her brother and sister, Walker and Virt. Matthew replaced them in January 1867 with Amanda Jones and her two children, Albert and Martha, ages sixteen and fourteen, all of whom served through 1868. The mother earned $5 per month and continued working until December 1869. It is not clear if old Nancy stayed; the name "Nancy McNeely" appeared on the same ledger sheet as "Nancy C—," but a heavy line was drawn under the 1866 charges, perhaps meaning that these were two different women. Other free blacks patronizing the Cartwright store included Peter Cartwright, Columbus and Sallie's former slave, and Jordan, the blacksmith purchased by George Teal. Jordan went by the Teal surname in the account book but was Jordan Barnes on the 1867 voter list.[13]

While Matthew treated his black servants well by local standards, others did not, which caused the bureau to send an agent to San Augustine in 1867. Lt. Albert A. Metzner, U.S. Army, Eleventh Volunteer Reserve Corps, arrived in April to serve San Augustine, Shelby, and Sabine counties. A native of Germany, he had already spent one year with the bureau in DeWitt County

13. Written contracts do not exist for 1866, but Account Book no. 12, pp. 37–40, CFP, gives the pay and deductions for Nancy, Emeline, Virtue, and Walker for 1866. Contracts with Amanda Jones and Nancy McNelly for 1867 and signed with "x," were witnessed by the county clerk; contracts with Milly Hamilton and Albert Jones for 1868 are without witness signatures. For Jordan and Peter, see Account Book no. 12, pp. 60–61, ibid. San Augustine Voter Registration list for 1867 (TSL); published in Mrs. McXie Whitton Martin (comp.), *1860 Citizens of San Augustine County, Texas: An Edited Census with 1862–1865–1867 Tax Rolls and 1867 Voters Registration List* (San Augustine: privately printed, 1984), 94.

and was an experienced agent. He kept the required monthly reports detailing the kind of contracts being made, general economic conditions, what kind of schools were available for the blacks, the social and political situation as it related to racial harmony, and the number of troops he had, or needed, to enforce the laws insuring good treatment of freedmen. At first he got along reasonably well, but later his alcoholism caused problems. Metzner had no military guard for the first month and lacked transportation to visit Sabine and Shelby counties. There was no public stage to those areas, he reported, nor could he hire a horse. Blacks told him that the authorities in those counties allowed crimes to go unpunished, and when Metzner finally announced plans to visit, he received death threats. His nine-man infantry guard arrived, and in July 1867 he asked permission to hire four horses for himself and three soldiers in order to make a two-month tour of the neighboring counties.[14]

Around the same time that Metzner arrived in San Augustine, the Radical wing of the Republican party in Congress passed several new acts undoing President Johnson's generous Presidential Reconstruction plan in the southern states. Congress also divided the South into five military districts to supervise Reconstruction; Texas and Louisiana were the Fifth Military District under the command of Gen. Philip Sheridan. The new arrangement, known as Congressional, Radical, or Military Reconstruction, allowed all adult males to vote except those disenfranchised by their role in the Confederacy, by felony convictions, or by having held political office before 1861 (and thereby taking an oath to uphold the U.S. Constitution) and then taking part in the rebellion. Texas and the other states were to hold new constitutional conventions with delegates chosen by manhood suffrage. Registration of eligible voters would begin in July 1867 by a three-man board appointed by the military. Each board member had to take the 1862 "Ironclad Oath" swearing that he had not voluntarily aided the Confederacy. This test oath was not required of voters, only jurors; other officeholders did not have to swear to it until 1869.[15]

14. Albert A. Metzner to Lt. A. T. Kirkman, Assistant Adjutant General, Apr. 26, 1867, roll 7, Nall, Freedmen's Bureau Notes; Metzner reports, May 30, 31, July 16, 1867 (roll 3); Metzner to Kirkman, May 31, July 16, 1867 (roll 7); July 31, 1867 (roll 21), ibid.

15. Campbell, *Southern Community in Crisis,* 272–276, 290.

General Sheridan, under the authority of the third Reconstruction Act, ordered the removal of Governor Throckmorton as an impediment to Reconstruction in July 1867, and appointed former Gov. Elisha Pease in his place. On the advice of Republican supporters, Governor Pease appointed elderly Roddy Anthony county judge in San Augustine but could find no qualified men willing to be county commissioners and face the derision of their neighbors. Public opinion in San Augustine grew increasingly hostile toward the federal government, and within the year one outsider wrote that "rebel sentiment is rampant and intolerance of anything savoring loyalty . . . openly expressed." Only "loyal" men, meaning those who supported the Republican party, including black preacher Plato Thompson, were named to the three-man voter registration board. The board enrolled voters from July through mid-September 1867 for a canvass of residents to determine whether or not a second constitutional convention should take place, and if so, to select delegates.[16]

Registration of eligible voters, black and white, began on July 16 and fifteen men signed up: twelve whites followed by three blacks. District Judge Charlton Payne, Matthew's former lawyer, led the list while Metzner was eighth, having become eligible to vote because of residence in Texas for twelve months and in the county for three. Plato Thompson was the first black to enroll. The first day's list also included at least two young Confederate veterans: Noel G. Roberts, Jr., and James E. Thomas, both of whom served in Company E with Lon and Meck Cartwright. They were accepted on the strength of their 1865 amnesty oaths.[17]

The next day three more freedmen registered, and on the third day, after word had spread that registering was possible without immediate physical retaliation, ten more braved the growing taunts of the white populace. Among them was Dick Holman, Lon Cartwright's loyal servant during the war. Metzner coached the freedmen so that they could give a surname, place of birth, and length of residence in the county and state. While some blacks

16. San Augustine County Court Minutes, 1867–1868, 169; Election Returns, San Augustine County, 1867–1868; William Sinclair report Aug. 18, 1868 (quotation), roll 15, Nall, Freedmen's Bureau Notes.

17. San Augustine County Voter Registration List, 1867, in Martin (comp.), *1860 Citizens of San Augustine County . . .*, 86–101; List of Company E, Sharp Collection (BTHC); Oath of amnesty for Noel G. Roberts [printed form], Nov. 20, 1865, Sharp Scrapbook (BTHC).

accepted the surname of their last owner, many did not and reached back to former owners or even chose a name at random. On Saturday, the traditional day to go to town, fifty-seven blacks and twenty-one whites received certificates. Registration took place at the courthouse, and, according to the court minutes after unseemly public behavior there, the judge asked that the statute against defacing public buildings be enforced. Under the statute men were arrested for urinating in the courthouse and also for hitching animals to the building.[18] Surely the newly enfranchised freedmen would not endanger their position by urinating in the building, which suggests that white protestors were demonstrating their resentment over the registration process.

Lon Cartwright was the first member of the immediate family to register. He signed on July 31 and was the 335th man to enroll. His brothers and father waited until the end of August to add their names. At first many Texans believed they could prevent the calling of the second constitutional convention by not registering or voting, but after careful scrutiny of the statute, they discovered that a majority of those *voting* on election day, not a majority of the county's population, would determine the outcome. Thus, by mid-August, more whites enrolled than blacks each day until the last, which for San Augustine County was September 19. A total of 604 voters had been enrolled, 298 whites and 384 blacks. Walker Cartwright, Matthew's former slave, did not enroll until November 1869, two years later, although he was over twenty-one years old and no longer employed by the Cartwrights. Perhaps Walker and Peter Cartwright, who also delayed registering, were reluctant to flaunt their new power before their current employers.[19]

The canvass for and against holding a convention took place for four days, February 10 to February 14, 1868, at the courthouse instead of the traditional scattered polling places. Opening day troublemakers tried to stop voting by breaking a window, poking a pistol through the hole, and firing in the direction of the judges. Albert Metzner, who had been chosen election judge to replace William Phillips, a Republican candidate for convention delegate, seemed to be the target. Metzner reported that "respect-

18. San Augustine County Court Minutes, July 1867, p. 164.
19. San Augustine County Voter Registration List, 1867, in Martin (comp.), *1860 Citizens of San Augustine County . . .*, 87, 94.

able citizens" saved the day, although he later said that the sheriff had not made an appearance and that Justice of the Peace S. W. Blount, Matthew Cartwright's neighbor, had only pretended to restore order. Instead, Blount shouted "Go ahead, boys, drive those damned Yankees out." Nonetheless, the election continued for the next three days, although neither Plato Thompson nor the clerk, too intimidated by hostile whites, reported for duty.[20]

Predictably, more blacks than whites went to the polls to vote, yielding the following results:

for the convention	*against the convention*
whites 7	whites 137
blacks 248	blacks 4
255	141

Altogether 396 men voted, and 255—over one-half of those voting—favored holding the convention. The Republican candidates to attend the convention, William Phillips and John Morse, received 255 votes each, defeating the "rebel" candidates who received 137 white votes. Neither of the rebel candidates was registered to vote. Phillips had been a merchant in San Augustine since before 1850 and had bought the old Cartwright building on the southwest corner of Main and Harrison. His Unionist sentiments were well known in 1861 when Anna Cartwright wrote to her brother that Phillips had "taken the oath of allegiance [to the Confederacy] at last contrary to everyone's expectation."[21] Perhaps Anna was wrong, or his expedient lapse in loyalty was forgiven.

While the convention struggled to write an acceptable constitution in 1868 amid internal wrangling among Radical and Moderate Republicans, racial tension increased in East Texas. The Republicans organized Loyal Leagues to educate black voters, while the whites retaliated by refusing to hire "radical loyal league negroes," as had been suggested by the Marshall *Texas Republican*. If economic coercion failed, some whites resorted to threats and violence. San Augustine historian George L. Crocket, who was born there in 1860, says that two hundred men joined

20. Election Returns, San Augustine County, [February] 1868; Metzner to J. P. Richardson, Feb. 21, 1868 (quotation), roll 13, Nall, Freedmen's Bureau Notes.

21. Ibid.; U.S. Seventh Census (1850), San Augustine County, Texas; Crocket, *Two Centuries*, 219; Anna Cartwright to A. P. Cartwright, Oct. 10, 1861, CFP.

the Ku Klux Klan under the leadership of I. D. Thomas, Jr. "The Invisible Empire," Crocket had been told, included "not only the young men who had lately returned from the war, but also many well advanced in years." One evening the Knights "don[ned] their spectral armor" and rode in double file from one side of San Augustine to the other before splitting into smaller groups to drag black miscreants out of their homes for "a good flogging" until the victims promised to reform.[22] Whether any of the Cartwrights took part in this 1868 effort is unknown, but peer pressure must have been strong.

One terrifying night early in December 1868, the Cartwrights watched the old university building across the road from their house burn to the ground. According to Crocket, whose details may be intentionally inaccurate, the Methodist East Texas Conference met in San Augustine, and one evening "a lecture was delivered to the negroes." Irate white youths locked the door to their school building to prevent the second scheduled meeting the following night. Although parents sent the boys back to undo their mischief, Crocket writes, the blacks had discovered the insult and around midnight the building was in flames. George Baker, a black whose name does not appear on the 1867 voting list, confessed to the crime and was placed under guard. Dr. I. J. Roberts, formerly surgeon with Company E, let Baker escape during the doctor's turn at guard duty because he feared "serious trouble" with the Union soldiers. Frank B. Sexton, the former CSA congressman, wrote to Oran M. Roberts on December 9 deploring the destruction of the university and mourning the decline of the town.[23]

Although several murders of both blacks and whites occurred in San Augustine County during those uneasy times, other counties experienced even more racial violence. At the close of 1868, Gen. J. J. Reynolds, then commander of the army in Texas, stationed one white infantry company in San Augustine, one at

22. Campbell, *Southern Community in Crisis,* 288 (1st quotation), 289; Crocket, *Two Centuries,* 347 (2nd–4th quotations).
23. Crocket, *Two Centuries,* 348 (quotations); F. B. Sexton to Oran M. Roberts, Dec. 9, 1868, Roberts Collection. Michael Butler replaced Metzner as agent in August 1868 and reported having troops from October through December. Notes concerning organization of the Freedmen's Bureau courtesy of Cecil W. Harper, North Harris County College.

Tyler, another at Palestine, and twelve at Jefferson. The cavalry companies, composed of both white and black troopers that had earlier occupied East Texas, had been sent to the Rio Grande and western frontier to cope with Indian problems. In 1869, however, a small troop of white cavalrymen returned to Nacogdoches while larger numbers were posted at Tyler and Jefferson, clearly demonstrating the need for more mobility in the areas of greater tension. Both cavalry and infantry remained at Jefferson and Tyler until March 1870, when military rule ended and Texas was readmitted to the Union.[24]

Amid this civil unrest and political confusion, Matthew Cartwright endeavored to carry on business. No contracts exist providing details about storekeeping arrangements between father and sons between 1865 and 1870. Only the ledger books and one or two letters provide any information. From the varying handwriting in the ledgers and the dates of purchases made by Meck and Lon, it appears that they took turns minding the store and traveling the countryside collecting debts and contracting for cotton. Matthew reserved the New Orleans buying trips for himself through 1868, after which details become less clear. In March 1869 Matthew gave each son a credit of $2,500 on the ledger book for "interest in merchandise" following their respective marriages. Evidently this was a wedding gift, not a buying-out of their interests. While other San Augustine merchants placed advertisements in the local newspaper, no paid notices for the Cartwright store appeared in extant newspapers, although occasionally the editor might remark that new goods had arrived. Apparently the Cartwrights eschewed paying for space in the newspaper when everybody knew where they were and what kind of stock they carried. In 1869 six merchants advertised, quite a number for a town with only 920 people and an additional 3,276 in the county.[25]

24. Final Report of Metzner, June 19, 1868, roll 21, Nall, Freedmen's Bureau Notes; Report of Inspection tour of eastern Texas made by William Sinclair in July, to Capt. C. S. Robert, AAAG, Aug. 18, 1868, roll 15, ibid.; William L. Richter, *The Army in Texas During Reconstruction, 1865–1870* (College Station: Texas A&M University Press, 1987), 153, 176, 185.

25. Account Book no. 14, 1867–1870, 153, 170 (quotation). For Lon, see pp. 11–14, 117–119, 169–170; for Meck, pp. 15–18, 151–154. Population statistics, *Texas Almanac for 1964–1965*, 120, 125; *Red-Land Beacon* (San Augustine), July 31, 1869.

As senior partner, Matthew continued to ship cotton to his New Orleans factors, Clapp Brothers & Company; prices fluctuated almost daily in 1868 and 1869 but remained between twenty-three and twenty-nine cents per pound for low-to-middling cotton. One uninsured shipment of ten bales on board a steamer caught fire at Baton Rouge, and though damaged, most was salvaged and sold at a discount by Matthew's agents. Apparently Matthew preferred risk to the high cost of insurance. Postwar crops in East Texas suffered from adverse weather and worm infestations, which led Matthew to find other products, such as salt and raw wool, to send to market. East Texas wool, however, was not profitable, and evidence in the Cartwright ledgers suggests Redlanders began eating the sheep that had provided wool for clothing during the war.[26]

Matthew spent most of his time in the little office at home answering letters about buying and leasing portions of his land. Most inquiries came from the blackland prairies north and west of San Augustine, but regular correspondents kept Matthew apprised of activities affecting his interests elsewhere. He had a number of contacts in various counties, including lawyers who helped make sales and poor farmers who watched for timber thieves and squatters. Nephew William S. "Billy" Holman had moved to Bell County where, in addition to his own business, he watched over Matthew's investments. William's sister Anna and her husband, lawyer Richard F. Slaughter, moved to Kaufman County soon after the war, but their relationship with Matthew seemed strained by his handling of some of her inheritance. At this time, Matthew owned tracts of land in fifty-six counties ranging in size from 100 to 4,428 acres and totaling more than 360,000 acres. Thus, it is not surprising to find letters about inaccurate surveys, unpaid taxes, and unregistered and conflicting claims.[27] Matthew no longer could travel long distances to

26. Clapp, Brothers & Co. to M. Cartwright, Mar. 31, Apr. 9, Oct. 7, 1868, CFP; Hill and Company to M. Cartwright, July 27, 1869, ibid.; Clapp, Brothers & Co. to M. Cartwright, Jan. 15, 1868, ibid. For eating of mutton, see Account Book no. 12, 1866, 42, and Account Book no. 14, 1867, 3, ibid.

27. For representative letters to Matthew Cartwright in 1868, see the following in CFP: D. W. Broughton, Jan. 13; John B. Meeks, Jan. 18; D. T. Richardson, Feb. 4; J. R. Cocke, June 2; Nathaniel Robinson, June 28; J. T. Victory, July 30; T. A. Harris, Oct. 21; James H. Starr, Oct. 24; T. E. Rowe, Nov.

visit his remote holdings, but if serious problems arose, Meck and Lon were able to tend to the business.

Matthew also entered into a railroad venture after the war. Along with San Augustinians Stephen W. Blount, Dr. Lewis V. Greer, and John G. Berry, and seven others from eastern Texas, Matthew applied for a charter for the Orange, Jasper, and Henderson Railroad. The charter was granted in October 1866. Twenty-five miles of track had to be completed by January 1870 on the line from the mouth of the Sabine River through Jasper and San Augustine to Rusk County, to be financed by $5,000,000 in stock. Capital being short, no stock had been sold by March 15, 1869, when a Sabine County promoter suggested building an interim tramline and sawmill to generate income as a means to save the charter, but nothing was done. Six years earlier, Matthew had owned eighty-two shares of stock in the Eastern Texas Railroad, the forerunner of the 1866 venture, which had laid some track before the war. But in 1863, Lt. Dick Dowling used the rails to fortify Fort Sabine. While willing to promote better transportation in his own area, Matthew had turned down an earlier opportunity to invest in the Buffalo Bayou, Brazos and Colorado Rail Road Company. Its promoter unsuccessfully argued that the road would increase the value of Cartwright's Oyster Creek land in Fort Bend County.[28] The lack of investment capital in railroads resulted in the isolation of San Augustine during Matthew's lifetime and beyond. Not until 1883 did rails connect Nacogdoches and Houston, and no railroad came closer to San Augustine until the twentieth century.

A second postwar business venture of Matthew's was the search for "petroleum or rock oil" on his one-half league in Jefferson County south of Beaumont, a tract better known as Spindletop. Benjamin Taylor Kavanaugh, a sometime Methodist

---

10; R. Knowlen, Dec. 27; Richard F. Slaughter to Matthew Cartwright, Nov. 26, 1868; also see William S. Holman to Dear Uncle, Oct. 22, 1869, ibid. Inventory and List of all Community Property, 1870, ibid.

28. An Act to incorporate the Orange, Jasper, and Henderson Railroad Company, Oct. 11, 1866, *Special Laws of the State of Texas Passed by the Eleventh Legislature* (Austin: State Gazette Office, 1866), 120–124; J. C. Alney to Matthew Cartwright, Mar. 15, 1869, CFP; DeWitt Clinton Harris to Matthew Cartwright, Sept. 19, 1853, ibid.; N. I. Moore to M. Cartwright, May 15, 1860, ibid.; Webb, Carroll, and Branda (eds.), *Handbook of Texas*, I, 537.

minister, physician, and amateur mineralogist, traversed eastern Texas in 1865 looking for oil seeps and bored two commercially unsuccessful wells in Nacogdoches County. He contracted with Matthew on August 12, 1866, to explore near the spring called Spindletop in Matthew's James W. Bullock league. Kavanaugh had two months in which to make test holes with his "mineraloger," a boring device that could drill down 142 feet. If he found production within two months, the lease would continue for twenty years and Matthew would receive 10 percent of the oil as royalty but would have to furnish the barrels at the well for his portion. The crude equipment did not reach a productive stratum, and in 1868 another speculator wanted to buy "50 or 100 acres . . . [at] the Spindletop," but warned Matthew to "bear in mind that land in this county is almost entirely *worthless.*" Excitement about rock oil, the basis for producing kerosene, continued in the Redlands, and on October 24, 1866, the San Augustine Petroleum Company was incorporated with Greer, Berry, Rufus Price, Charles I. Polk, and Kavanaugh, but not Matthew Cartwright, among the stockholders.[29]

Family matters also demanded Matthew's attention. He still served as administrator for the two sons of his deceased brother Robert, and he brought the boys to San Augustine in 1867 to finish their education. Their sister Amanda and her husband A. D. McCutchan had moved to Upshur County in 1861, and after brief service with the Confederate army, McCutchan was discharged because of poor health. He asked Matthew for help in disposing of the property he had left in San Augustine and also in identifying all of the land Mandy had inherited from her father. Mandy died sometime in the late 1860s, leaving a daughter, Mary, and a son, James D. The son later worked for the Cartwrights and lived in Shelby County in 1888.[30]

29. Lease agreement between B. T. Kavanaugh and M. Cartwright, Aug. 12, 1866, CFP (a copy is displayed at the Institute of Texan Cultures in San Antonio as perhaps the oldest extant lease in the state); S. W. Geiser, "Benjamin Taylor Kavanaugh and the Discovery of East Texas Oil," *Field and Laboratory* (1941), 47–53; G. A. Nations to Matthew Cartwright, June 12, 1868 (quotations), CFP; *Special Laws . . . Passed by the Eleventh Legislature*, 158.

30. Entries in Account Book no. 14, for Matthew and Robert, minors, pp. 103, 126, 162–163, 192–193; William N. Rainey to Matthew Cartwright, Mar. 3, 1868, CFP; Matthew Cartwright, Jr. (Robert's son), to Uncle Matthew, Mar. 10, 1868, ibid.; A. D. McCutchan to Col. M. Cartwright, Dec. 6, 1862, ibid.;

Lon, Anna, and Meck all married within a two-month period between December 1868 and February 1869. After a four-year courtship, Lon wed nineteen-year-old Lucilla "Ludie" Ingram at her home at Sexton in Sabine County on December 17, 1868. She was the youngest sister of Jimmie Ingram, Mary Cartwright's husband. Like Sallie, Columbus's wife, Ludie had attended a "female" college, an educational advantage that was still regarded as unusual at this time. Ludie's father, already a widower, had died eleven months earlier and she inherited one-half of her parents' rural home at Sexton. Lon agreed to move there for one year to superintend the farm in partnership with Dr. Gustavus Hendrick, the husband of Ludie's sister Ann. The arrangement led to a quarrel that was settled in court in December 1869, with Lon forced to buy the property for $8,100 in specie.[31]

In October 1868 Anna finally gave in to Ben Roberts's ardent and patient courtship and set the wedding for January 10, 1869. Anna wrote to Mary just before she actually said yes to Ben, leaving the distant sister anxious for details. Mary replied, "Here you have been telling Ben 'no' (so you say) for the ninety ninth time and are on the point of telling him 'yes' . . . why don't you relieve the poor fellow by telling him positively what you are going to do." No details about the wedding exist, but the twenty-four-year-old bride moved briefly to Ben's farm just beyond the old John Cartwright place. Using money from her father's wedding gift, Anna bought the 1839 Ezekiel Cullen house in December 1869, registering the transaction in her own name, an unusual practice for married women at that time. Built by Augustus Phelps, who had contracted Matthew's house, the classic one-story home with its finished attic was located on Congress Street

same to same, May 14, July 28, 1863, ibid.; J. D. McCutchan to Lon Cartwright, July 26, 1888, ibid. See Marion County Probate Records, W.P.A. file (BTHC), for death of A. D. McCutchan and guardianship of his two children; Editor McCutchan mentions his "blue-eyed little Mary" in San Augustine *Red Land Express,* Mar. 30, 1861.

31. Ingram family genealogy, CFP. Poem by Lon to Ludie, Feb. 8, 1869, mentions four-year courtship. Lon Cartwright to Ludie Ingram at school, Oct. 14, 1867, ibid.; Sidney Bryan to James M. Ingram, Jan. 11, 1869, ibid.; Deed of conveyance, filed May 17, 1870, and again September 2, 1879, Gustavus Hendrick, executor, to Leonidas M. Cartwright, Sabine County Deed Records (typescript photocopy, no vol. or pp.), ibid.

Americus P. "Meck" Cartwright (1840–1873), the second son of Matthew and Amanda, and his wife, Ophelia Margaret Smith (1845–1939), in their 1869 wedding picture. Meck's pose does not entirely conceal his injured eye, which had been closed since an infection in 1855. Courtesy Cartwright Family Descendants.

*Anna W. Cartwright (Mrs. Benjamin T.) Roberts (1844–1903), ca.
1890.* Courtesy Cartwright Family Descendants.

Leonidas Cartwright (1842–1922), ca. 1900.

Lucilla Ingram "Ludie" Cartwright (1850–1908), ca. 1900.
This image and the one on the previous page appear in Frank W.
Johnson and Eugene C. Barker, A History of Texas and Texans
(1914).

only a few blocks from her parents' home. The comfortable home had been occupied previously by a number of prominent San Augustine residents including Matthew's lawyer J. M. Ardrey, Felix G. Lovell, Crabb Griffith, and E. A. Kellogg.[32]

Anna told Mary about Meck's pending marriage plans in the same letter announcing her tentative engagement. "I cannot believe Meck is going to be married until the ceremony has been performed," Mary replied, echoing everyone's surprise. The bride, Margaret Ophelia Smith, was the youngest daughter of Dr. Charles J. Smith. She was born in San Augustine in 1845, but her mother soon died and she was raised by her older siblings; in 1860 she lived in Jefferson with her brother Addison and his wife. Meck may have renewed his casual acquaintance with Ophelia during his May 1866, trip to Jefferson for his father, because Addison Smith kept a store and had also served in the Third Texas Cavalry. No letters document the romance or even Meck's activities between 1866 and his marriage in Jefferson on February 10, 1869, at the home of Ophelia's brother. The couple posed soon afterward for a photograph in which Meck is seated in profile to hide his closed left eye and tall, handsome Ophelia is standing.[33]

On March 22, five and one-half weeks after Meck's wedding, the newlyweds visited Matthew and Amanda, as did Lon and Ludie from their home in Sabine County. A note written by Matthew and slipped into a book said: "Americus & wife, Leonidas & wife here. Cool & Pleasant. Americus Fishing . . . an Eal & Some fish. He's been Sick, now in better Spts. Lon on the Rise now 1/2 after 8 O'clock, Playing violin." On this same day Matthew gave each son the $2,500 credit in the account book. Music was still popular with the Cartwrights; both Lon and

32. Ben T. Roberts to Anna Cartwright, Nov. 30. 1867, Sept. 17, 30, 1868, Eugenia Porter private collection (photocopy deposited in CFP); Anna W. Cartwright to B. T. Roberts, Oct. 15, 1868, ibid.; Mary C. Ingram to Anna W. Cartwright, Jan. 18, 1869 (quotation), copy by Patty C. Tennison from illegible original in CFP; San Augustine Deed Records, A, 95, H, 450, J, 247, 625, 628, and J-2, 9 as abstracted by Martin in 1987.

33. Mary C. Ingram to Anna W. Cartwright, Jan. 18, 1869 (quotation), CFP; U.S. Seventh Census (1850), San Augustine County, Texas; Tombstone in San Augustine Cemetery; U.S. Eighth Census (1860), Marion County, Texas; Account Book no. 12, p. 36, CFP; U.S. Ninth Census (1880), Marion County, Texas; Marion County Marriage Records, A, 163. The record was filed on Febr. 10, although the Jefferson *Home Advocate,* Febr. 13, 1869, gives Feb. 11 as the date of the wedding.

Meck bought violin strings at the store from time to time, as did their Shelby County nephew, Robert Cartwright, Jr. In September 1869, Meck and Ophelia bought eight chairs, a table, and bedroom furnishings and settled into housekeeping in San Augustine.[34]

Matthew and Amanda enjoyed their roles as heads of the family, and Matthew managed to combine business with family visiting occasionally. In March 1867, two years before Anna married, Matthew took her, his niece Mary Garrett, and her stepbrother William Garrett to New Orleans. They stayed at the City Hotel for two weeks while he conducted business and the cousins shopped for sewing machines and clothing. They bought three Wheeler & Wilson machines, each in a mahogany and blackwalnut case, for $110 apiece. The third one was for Mary Cartwright Ingram, whom they planned to visit at Opelousas on their way home. Mary had recently lost her only child, Matthew C. Ingram, and Anna told her mother that Mary "was perfectly overjoyed" when they unexpectedly arrived on March 26. Mary had complained previously that her father had not taken time to visit her when he went to New Orleans. Anna had missed her sister when Mary left home, and upon arriving at Opelousas Anna wrote her mother that "a sister's love is very great . . . no one . . . can fill the place." Amanda well understood that sentiment; her sister, Betty Thomas, had recently left San Augustine for Tennessee after the death of her husband. Amanda was alone in Texas while her three sisters lived near each other in Tennessee. Matthew and the Garretts left the Ingram farm in a few days, but Anna remained for a long visit with Mary. The house at Evergreen, she wrote, was comfortable and her room was almost as large as her room at home. The sisters played duets on Mary's piano just as they had during the war.[35]

That same fall, Matthew and Amanda welcomed Mary home for a long visit while awaiting the birth of her second child. Little

34. Scrap of paper found by James I. Cartwright, Jr., inside book (quotation), CFP; Account Book no. 14, pp. 151, 197, 193, 213, ibid.

35. Account Book no. 12, p. 43, CFP; Memorandum Book for 1867, pp. 1, 24, ibid.; Various receipts, Mar. 11–22, 1867, Account Papers folder, ibid.; Anna to Mother, Apr. 4, 1867 (quotations), ibid.; Mary Ingram to Anna Cartwright, Aug. 5, 1866, ibid.; J. C. Akin to Columbus Cartwright, Feb. 9, 1867, ibid.

William Holman Ingram, born December 23, 1867, became Matthew's favorite grandchild for awhile as the child of his youngest daughter. Columbus and Sallie had three boys by this time and had lost three infants. Not until March could her father escort Mary Ingram home, leaving Jimmie Ingram to wait impatiently to see his new son. Matthew entertained his ten-week-old grandson in the stagecoach to Grand Ecore and also on the steamboat to New Orleans, to the amusement of the other passengers. They waited a week at the City Hotel before Mary could get a boat to Opelousas. Matthew had to remain in New Orleans, and Mary, a much more traditional Victorian lady than her sister, told Anna that she "felt a little timid about starting . . . by myself," but all went well.[36]

When the patriarch returned home at the end of March he became ill and was unable to see visitors or do business for several weeks. But soon he was back making lists, keeping the household accounts totaled in his memorandum book, and answering correspondence. He seems not to have traveled anymore after 1868 but remained active, visiting the store where he bought himself or Amanda a rocking chair. Having settled wedding gifts on his married children, he looked forward to the education of young Matthew, now fourteen years old. By early 1870, four of his five married children had provided heirs for the Cartwright fortune. Columbus and Sallie lived down the road with their four: Robert, almost ten; John Matthew, eight; Clinton, four; and a new "Meck," Americus Holman Cartwright, born on December 20. Meck and Ophelia's first baby was born on November 24, 1869, and they named him Matthew Charles for his two grandfathers. Anna gave birth on January 18, 1870, to Matthew Cartwright Roberts, and Mary, still at the farm in Louisiana, also had another baby boy on December 27 and named him Matthew C. Ingram, with little Willie now two years old. Only Lon and Ludie in Sabine County remained childless and were not expecting one soon.[37]

36. Lon Cartwright to Ludie Ingram, Oct. 14, 1867, CFP; Family genealogy charts, ibid.; J. M. Ingram to Anna Cartwright, Feb. 22, 1868, ibid.; Mary Ingram to Anna, Mar. 26, May 16, 1868 (quotation), ibid.

37. G. J. Hampton to Col. Cartwright, Apr. 14, 1868, CFP; Memorandum book for 1867, pp. 24–30, ibid.; Account Book no. 14, 206, ibid.; Family genealogical chart, ibid.

Matthew's health gradually failed, and in March medicine was charged to his account at the store. Cartwright descendants recall hearing as children that Matthew suffered from a cancer on his leg that they suppose led to his death on Friday, April 1, 1870, at the age of sixty-three. The printer made up the customary funeral notice card:

The friends and acquaintances of
MATTHEW CARTWRIGHT, Sen.
are respectfully invited to attend his funeral tomorrow morning at 10 o'clock, A.M. He will be buried with Masonic honors, at his late residence in the town of San Augustine.
SAN AUGUSTINE, TEXAS, April 2d 1870.[38]

Amanda chose a burial plot several hundred feet east of the house, probably a selection that they had agreed upon. All except the Ingrams would have been able to attend the funeral on Sunday, April 3; George Cartwright and his family and Lon and Ludie had ample time to come from Sabine County. Mary and Jimmie arrived as soon as possible and remained for several weeks. There are no extant accolades for Matthew in the form of an obituary in the San Augustine newspaper, though surely one ran on the Saturday following his burial. The Marshall paper ran a death notice which was reprinted in the Houston *Daily Telegraph* on April 26, 1870. The San Antonio *Daily Express* carried the brief obituary on May 1 and, presumably, so did the Austin paper. All items were identical:

DIED at his home in San Augustine, 1st day of April, Matthew Cartwright, one of the pioneers of Texas, and one of the largest, if not the largest, land holder in the state.[39]

Now the business affairs of the Cartwright family passed to Amanda and her sons. The father had trained his three oldest sons well, and his widow, as the next two decades would prove, understood the business better than anyone suspected.

38. James I. Cartwright, Jr., to Deolece Parmelee, July 2, 1987, Cartwright research files; Funeral Notice, Sharp Scrapbook (BTHC).
39. Mary C. Ingram to mother, May 9, 1870, CFP; Houston *Daily Telegraph*, Apr. 26, 1870; San Antonio *Daily Express*, May 1, 1870, in C. L. Greenwood Index, obituaries (BTHC).

T w e l v e

The Legacies

—

1870–1900

*M*atthew's death left the fifty-three-year-old widow and her teenage son alone in the big house. To ease the transition, Meck, Ophelia, and little Matthew (born in November) moved into the upstairs bedroom. Meck was keeping the store on the courthouse square and worked on the account books in Matthew's old office adjoining the house. When the census enumerator visited the home in July 1870, he found, besides the five Cartwrights, three servants living in the quarters on the north perimeter: a twenty-year-old man and two teenage maids. These appear to have been newcomers and doubtless needed close supervision. The constantly changing household help must have annoyed Amanda and her daughter-in-law. The servant situation was a little better at Columbus and Sallie's residence, where one black family lived on the property and another next door. The men worked on the farm while the women washed and cleaned and a twelve-year-old girl helped Sallie with the two youngest children. At Ben Roberts's farm Anna had only a maid, but probably employed a woman by the day to wash clothes, as did many other households, according to the number of black washerwomen listed on the 1870 census.[1]

The first task for the widow and her children was to compile an inventory of Matthew's estate. Although he died intestate, the patriarch had maintained complete and orderly records in his office concerning his acreage in the various counties, plus his debts and the money owed to him. Within six weeks, Columbus and Meck with young Matthew's help prepared a list showing 298 parcels of land in 56 counties totaling 361,632 acres with a value of $353,304. Also included in the estate were nine town lots in San Augustine, including the store, valued at $800; the homestead at $1,200; two horses at $125 each; thirty head of cattle at $120; and miscellaneous items worth $630. The total valuation of the estate was $356,304, and on May 9, 1870, Amanda signed a document attesting to the accuracy of the inventory before I. D. Thomas, Jr., clerk of the San Augustine district court. This listing, however, failed to take notice of Matthew's debts or the amounts owed to him. A preliminary list showed fourteen unpaid notes made since 1859 that totaled $4,829.70, ranging from $10.00 to $1,120.00, all at 12 percent per annum, plus $3,000.00 due Matthew from his partnership in the store.[2]

Amanda, of course, had a one-half interest in what she and Matthew had accumulated since their marriage, and thus the estate would be divided in half, one-half (176,652 acres) to the widow and the rest to be equally divided among the six children. Their shares would amount to 29,442 acres each if divided by simple arithmetic and without considering differing values or gifts previously given by Matthew. But how to make the portions equally fair posed problems: some land was worth only fifty cents per acre while other tracts might bring between one and three

1. Account Book no. 14, A. P. Cartwright's order for Mrs. Amanda Cartwright for 200 pounds of ham from New Orleans, May 10, 1870, CFP; U.S. Ninth Census (1870), San Augustine County, Texas (see roll 170 for a cook and wash woman).

2. "Inventory and List of all the Community Property Real, Personal & Mixed belonging to the late Matthew Cartwright Deceased . . . ," n.d., 9 pp. ms, CFP; "Inventory of M. Cartwright," 1 p. with Amanda's signature and that of Clerk of District Court, filed May 10, 1870, ibid.; "Inventory and list of all notes and a/c due M. Cartwright Deceased," n.d., ibid. Many documents concerning Matthew's estate are no longer on file in the San Augustine Courthouse.

dollars per acre. The sons made tentative lists and finally Amanda and her six children drew lots, and the final division was made one year later.[3]

William Phillips, the census enumerator for San Augustine County in 1870, visited Amanda on July 6. She or Meck estimated the value of the real estate at $343,281, which agrees reasonably well with the manuscript inventory of Matthew's acreage. The personal property valuation of $75,529, however, was much larger than the amount that appears in extant estate papers or in the San Augustine County tax roll for that year. This statement of real and personal property on the 1870 census totalling $418,810 ultimately placed the Cartwright property as the fourth-largest estate in Texas, following those of Richard King in South Texas and Galveston merchants J. J. Hendley and George Sealy.[4]

In August 1870, most likely at the urging of Amanda, Lon and Ludie returned to San Augustine from the old Ingram farm at Sexton in Sabine County. They moved into Amanda's house and Lon took charge of his father's estate. Meck, increasingly restless and moody, found living even temporarily with his mother difficult, and he and Ophelia gladly returned to their private quarters, where he could concentrate on closing the store accounts. At the time of the patriarch's death, there were $1,500 worth of goods on hand and $3,000 in notes and accounts due, the latter representing the deceased Matthew's one-half interest. Also, Meck and Lon had 18,000 pounds of cotton in storage, purchased by them at fifteen cents per pound ($2,700), that needed to be sent to market. Neither Lon nor Meck wanted to continue storekeeping, particularly since they needed to oversee their inherited property once the estate was settled. On February 1, 1871, the brothers closed Lon's account in the partnership, leaving Meck to settle matters and dispose of the store.[5]

Amanda sent young Matthew to school in Upshur County in

3. Various lists, undated, filed with inventories, CFP; Amanda Cartwright's share, San Augustine County, Deed Records, J-2, 188–191.

4. Ralph A. Wooster, "Wealthy Texans, 1870," *SHQ*, LXXIV (July, 1970), 29–35.

5. Matthew Cartwright to Lon in San Augustine, Aug. 6, 1870, CFP; "Inventory and list of all notes and a/c due M. Cartwright Deceased," n.d., ibid.; Account Book no. 14, pp. 277, 286, ibid.

Amanda Holman Cartwright (1817–1894) in her widow's veil after Matthew's death. Courtesy Cartwright Family Descendants.

the fall of 1870, probably following a plan conceived by his father. Morgan Harbin Looney, a native of Georgia, had opened his academy in Gilmer in 1860, and its excellent reputation kept it crowded even during the war. In 1864 Looney had to turn students away because of a lack of boardinghouses. Judge Oran M. Roberts joined the faculty in 1868 to teach law, agriculture, and bookkeeping while his children attended classes. His presence, of course, added to the school's prestige. Fifteen-year-old Matthew, however, was not impressed with his 140 fellow students. "I find it very easy . . . to take the head of my classes . . . . I never did see such common boys. They can't learn at all," he wrote to Lon. His teachers quickly promoted the bright young man from San Augustine to advanced classes in several subjects. Away from home for the first time, Matthew complained about the beds and food and bragged about his prowess in pistol shooting with his colleagues. As it turned out, Matthew stayed only one term and left the school in December.[6]

With Columbus and Meck in poor health, Amanda chose Lon to handle her business. Amanda had no inclination or need to take charge of the bookkeeping or correspondence, unlike other widows without sons or other male relatives. Instead, she began exhibiting a surprisingly keen business sense and required Lon to produce profits.

Amanda gave Lon a power of attorney to act as her agent in selling land and settling debts, a position he held for the rest of his mother's life. In December 1870, Lon left San Augustine for Gilmer, where Matthew joined him at the end of the school term. Almost thirteen years older than Matthew, Lon began training the younger brother in business practices, thereby continuing a family tradition. The pair remained on the road in Upshur and Wood counties for three weeks, returning home on January 1, 1871, in time for the end of the holiday parties. Amanda demanded meticulous bookkeeping and Lon provided it. The broth-

6. Unidentified clipping about Looney school by D. T. Loyd, vice-president, First National Bank of Gilmer, in Matthew Cartwright [Jr.] scrapbook, CFP; Anna Holman Traylor, daughter of Isaac, to Cousin Anna W. Cartwright, Mar. 13, 1864, ibid. (original in possession of Marilyn Bloemendal); Printed circular, Gilmer School, for Spring, 1868, p. 404, O. M. Roberts Scrapbook (BTHC); Frank B. Sexton to O. M. Roberts, Dec. 9, 1868, O. M. Roberts Collection (BTHC); Matthew Cartwright to Leonidas Cartwright, Oct. 23, 1870, CFP.

ers collected $1,151.83 in gold on this first trip while Lon spent only $109.80 for food, lodging, and a valise and proper clothing for Matthew, plus fees to record various instruments at the courthouses. Amanda allowed Lon to spend two months at home for the birth of Ludie's first baby; Amanda Holman Cartwright, called "Mantie," arrived on March 19, 1872. This infant Amanda was one of three born in 1871: Anna Roberts's "Manda" came in January while Mary Ingram's "Manda" did not appear until November. Eight years later, young Matthew named his first daughter Amanda. In April, Lon and Matthew journeyed to New Orleans to collect money and buy staple groceries and luxuries for their mother. They returned by steamboat to Jefferson and then took the stage to Marshall and rail to Shreveport to take care of estate business in each place. Lon collected over $4,500 in the Crescent City and almost $4,000 in Jefferson for cotton sold for the Cartwrights. Again, expenses were modest compared with profits.[7]

The formal division of Matthew Cartwright's estate was recorded at the courthouse on May 30, 1871. Even before the final partition, two heirs changed their residences in anticipation of the settlement. Jimmie Ingram had sold his Evergreen farm near Opelousas in October 1870 and thought he would like to live in either northern or central Texas on land Mary would inherit. But Mary wanted to live near her mother and sister, so the Ingrams settled on Columbus's 428-acre farm on the eastern edge of San Augustine. The Ingrams went to New Orleans and bought staples and new furniture, including one "Brilliant Stove" that was shipped by steamer to the Sabine River for delivery.[8]

In turn, Columbus moved his wife and four children to the old Ingram family farm at Sexton in northwestern Sabine County.

7. Power of attorney, Dec. 12, 1870, CFP; "Statement of a/c . . . in interest of Estate of M. Cartwright," Dec. 12, 1870–Jan. 2, 1871, April 24–May 13, 1871, Leonidas Cartwright Account Book, pp. 1–3, ibid. (cited hereafter as L. Cartwright Account Book). Columbus and Sallie lost an infant named Amanda. Only Ophelia and Meck had no daughter named Amanda, and only Leonidas failed to name a son Matthew.

8. James M. Ingram to Lon Cartwright, Nov. 15, 1870, CFP; Clapp Brothers of New Orleans invoice, Jan. 24, 1871, ibid.; San Augustine County, Tax Roll, 1872 (1871 has pages missing), lists Ingram on the former Columbus Cartwright farm while the 1871 Sabine County Tax Roll shows Columbus on the old Ingram family farm (microfilm; CL).

This was the same land that Lon had bought at auction in 1869 after the suit with his brother-in-law. Oddly, the old Ingram farm on the John Horton league appeared in Columbus's share of his father's estate in May 1871; one can only guess that Matthew Cartwright had provided the money for Lon's purchase, although the league was not listed on the May 1870 estate inventory. In any event, Cumby and Sallie lived there for over two years until July 5, 1873, when they exchanged the property for their old home in San Augustine while Jimmie and Mary Ingram moved to Sexton.[9]

Meanwhile, Lon and Matthew resumed their travels and in April and May 1872 visited Shelby, Henderson, Smith, and Gregg counties and then went east to Shreveport and eventually New Orleans. All was not work: they attended the theatre in both Shreveport and New Orleans, charging Matthew's tickets against his mother's account. In the Crescent City Lon bought an expensive set of rosewood furniture for his mother and a bedstead for himself, the latter a gift from Amanda. He also paid $225 for a sewing machine for Ludie and filled extensive lists for clothing, yard goods, and other items wanted by his wife and mother, totaling almost $1,000. Utilizing the swiftest and most comfortable means of transportation available, Lon and Matthew left New Orleans by steamboat for Galveston on May 2, and then took a train to Austin. After finishing estate business in the state capital, they boarded a stagecoach to Bastrop and Giddings, and again connected with rail to Houston. After several days of business and pleasure, they started home on horseback. No railroad connected Houston with Nacogdoches or San Augustine.[10]

Amanda sent Matthew back to school at Gilmer in the fall of 1872 even though the respected Mr. Looney had left. Doubtless Matthew found schoolwork tame after nine months traveling

9. Sabine County, Tax Roll, 1871, 1872, 1873, includes the list of properties owned by Columbus in other counties (microfilm; CL); *Gustavus Hendrick, exec. and wife, v. Leonidas Cartwright and wife,* August term, suit no. 1001, San Augustine County, Deed Records, Jan. 4, 1870 (photocopy), CFP; "Inventory Estate of M. Cartwright," May 10, 1870, ibid. In a handwritten contract (in possession of Sandra Kardell Calpakis) between Columbus Cartwright and James M. Ingram to exchange the Horton league in Sabine County for one of Cartwright's leagues in Hill County, Ingram agreed to sell the San Augustine farm for $5,000 in gold and a down payment of animals, tools, and crops on the Horton league.

10. L. Cartwright Account Book, 9–11, CFP.

with his brother. He complained in early October about poor beds, food, and a lack of letters from home, and within a few days he returned to San Augustine but soon enrolled in a school in nearby Shelbyville. In typical teen fashion, he told his mother that he was studying hard, reading the poetry of Sir Walter Scott and John Milton, and attending church. He planned to return home in November at the end of the 1872 term.[11]

Matthew's holiday at home was marred by tragedy. The night after Christmas, Matthew caused his family acute distress when he and forty-year-old Carroll Ballard exchanged pistol shots near the old customs house in San Augustine. A sophisticated seventeen year old and a good shot, Matthew was well acquainted with men who drank too much (including brother Meck, and probably his two deceased uncles) and who settled their quarrels with gunfire. Details of the affray were suppressed by family and friends, but one can imagine that Ballard made insulting remarks about the Cartwrights and Matthew took offense. While Matthew was not injured, he severely wounded Ballard. Friends of the victim tied him on his horse and led him home to his wife, Clementine Texas "Tet" Ingram, the older sister of Mary's husband Jimmie Ingram and of Lon's wife Ludie. Tet was a widow with three children and lived near Sexton in Sabine County when she married Ballard. They settled at Buena Vista in Shelby County, but the relationship was stormy and the couple had quarreled and separated several times. Ballard had a violent temper, and since 1861 he had appeared in court several times on charges of attempted murder. Fortunately for Matthew, the older man did not die, although he remained an invalid for several months.[12]

The sheriff arrested Matthew but Uncle Billy Holman, Ben Roberts, and Lon posted a $100 bond to guarantee his appearance before a grand jury on February 7, 1873. Meantime, rumors indicated that Matthew's life might be in danger from friends of the Ballards, and the family considered sending him to stay with Cumby in Sabine County. Columbus, however, thought Matthew

11. Matthew Cartwright to Mother, Oct. 9, 28, 1872, CFP.
12. McXie Martin to Deolece Parmelee, interview, Sept. 23, 1987; F. Knight Parker to D. P., interview, June 11, 1986; Mary Sharp Smith to D. P., interview, May 6, 1984 (transcribed as narrative in Cartwright research notes); San Augustine County Courthouse Records, 1861 (Special Collections, Steen Library, Stephen F. Austin University).

would be "safer at town then here," although most Sabine County residents had no animosity toward Matthew. Nonetheless, the family decided that Matthew should leave the area until the grand jury hearing.[13]

Early on January 8, with $500 in gold and $100 in paper money provided by Amanda, Lon and Matthew quietly left San Augustine on horseback and rode for two days to the International Railroad at Palestine. There they put their mounts on board and rode the rails to Hearne, where they left the animals on January 11. Reboarding the train, the brothers continued to Austin and then Houston, where they bought some clothing and other items, went to the theatre, and perhaps attended to family business. After a short time they took the train to Brenham and Austin, making collections due to the Cartwrights, and then transferred to another line to travel north to McKinney and Denton before starting leisurely toward Nacogdoches and home. Frugal Lon returned Amanda's $600 advance plus the money that they had collected. By exchanging gold coins at favorable rates for paper currency, Lon always made a profit that covered his expenses.[14]

The grand jury indicted Matthew for assault to kill Ballard and for unlawfully carrying a gun. One week later a jury acquitted him on the first charge but convicted him for carrying the weapon, an irony at a time when many East Texans went around armed. He paid the $25 fine and the sheriff confiscated his pistol. Within a month, the family sent Matthew to Cumberland University in Lebanon, Tennessee, well out of reach of Ballard's friends, who still bore a grudge. On the way, he was to take care of Cartwright business in New Orleans, an indication that he had graduated in his business training.[15]

Matthew was accompanied by George Garrett, the son of William and Lucetta Teal, and John Polley from Sabine County, and the three found a boardinghouse near the college. Matthew entered the university as a sophomore but said he was the young-

13. San Augustine County, District Court Minutes, 1860–1872, H, Cause no. 992; Columbus Cartwright to Lon Cartwright, Jan. 2, 1873 (quotation), CFP.
14. L. Cartwright Account Book, 15–17, CFP.
15. San Augustine County, District Court Minutes, H, 633, 652–653; Amanda Cartwright to Matthew Cartwright, Mar. 28, 1873, CFP.

est student enrolled. Matthew believed that he could graduate within two years and perhaps study law until "I am twenty-one," in August 1876. In June Amanda and Lon successfully petitioned the San Augustine District Court to have Matthew's age disability removed, and two months before he was eighteen, he was declared to be legally competent to handle his own affairs except for voting. Now he could sell some of his land with ease when opportunity occurred, as it did by the end of the year.[16]

In May 1873 Lon, for a change, was ill and so Meck and Columbus made the long trip to Denton County to take care of business. Lon suffered "dispepsia or disordered stomach" but still went "on one or two camp hunts & fishing," which he thought improved his health. He was better by June and he took Columbus's eldest son, Robert "Bobbie" Lane, age thirteen, on a quick trip to Central Texas, continuing the tradition of training young Cartwrights. Lon returned home in time for the birth of his second daughter, Annie, on July 2; the proud but annoyed grandmother wrote that they had "music a plenty" when "Mantie's little sister" helped her cry.[17]

Amanda suffered another tragedy in August 1873, when word arrived that Meck had died while on business at a hotel in Carthage. For some time he had suffered from various ailments, including jaundice, for which he took calomel or blue pills, both containing mercury. His consumption of alcohol contributed to his liver problem, but like others, he used liquor to mitigate pain. In any event, Meck's time ran out on August 11, and the doctor pronounced him dead of black jaundice, a severe form due to blood poisoning. Lon hurried to Carthage to bring the body back home for burial. Anna Roberts, obviously disturbed by the events of the past year, wrote a sisterly lecture to young Matthew warning him against the evils of dissipation: "We all grieve so much over poor Meck's lamentable end . . . sober he could have been such an assistance to his family, and a *great* asset to society." She told Matthew to "*never* let wine or strong drink pass your

16. Matthew Cartwright to Mother, Apr. 1, 19 (quotation), 1873, CFP; Matthew Cartwright to Leonidas Cartwright, Oct. 13, 1873, ibid.; San Augustine County, District Court Minutes, H, 664.

17. Lon Cartwright to Matthew Cartwright, Apr. 24, 1873 (1st and 2nd quotations), CFP; L. Cartwright Account Book, 21, ibid.; Amanda Cartwright to Matthew Cartwright, July 12, 1873 (3rd and 4th quotations), ibid.

Matthew Cartwright (1855–1925), ca. 1874. Probably taken while he was a student at Cumberland University in Lebanon, Tennessee. Courtesy Cartwright Family Descendants.

lips." Lon and Columbus assumed the task of paying Meck's debts and helping Ophelia and her two children, Matthew Charles, not quite three, and Annie T. (called "T" to distinguish her from Lon's Annie), approaching two. Ophelia gave birth to a daughter five months after Meck's death, and the grieving mother named her America Peyroux, to be called "Meck." Like other children born after the death of their fathers, many people believed America had extraordinary powers for healing others.[18]

Matthew was a good scholar and popular at Cumberland University. His mother received postal cards with his grades each month, and he regularly managed 9+ out of a possible 10. He reported that "the young ladies" were lavish in their praise of his good looks, and he became tentatively engaged to one. He joined Sigma Chi fraternity and the debating society and regaled his family with his successes. Doubtless his father would have been proud of his accomplishments. He even sent his mother an invitation to a major debate scheduled for the evening of January 16, 1874, when M. Cartwright of Texas would challenge Joel B. Fort of Tennessee.[19]

Disquieting news reached Matthew that Carroll Ballard had died on December 29, 1873, a year after the shooting, and that Ballard's friends blamed it on the old wound. In fact, Ballard had recovered sufficiently to ride long distances on horseback and apparently died from overexposure to the elements. Sabine County residents told Mary Ingram that during his last feverish days, Ballard had expressed no animosity toward Matthew: the dying man believed that God had arranged the shooting to punish him for past misdeeds and to inspire repentance. Nevertheless, rumors circulated in San Augustine that Matthew was so guilt-ridden in Tennessee that he was drinking heavily. Matthew quickly replied

18. Panola *Watchman,* Aug. 13, 1873, courtesy of Deolece Parmelee; Account Book no. 14, pp. 213, 286 (for medicine in 1869–1870), ibid.; L. Cartwright Account Book, 23, ibid.; Anna Roberts to Matthew Cartwright, Sept. 28, 1873 (quotations), ibid.

19. Matthew Cartwright to Mother, Aug. 10, 1873, CFP; Postal card grading reports, Sept.–Dec. 1873, Jan.–May 1874, ibid.; A. B. Humphreys to Matthew Cartwright, May 19, 1874, ibid.; Matthew Cartwright to Lon Cartwright, Oct. 13, Nov. 19, 1873, ibid.; Printed invitation for "Intermediate Exercises, Amasagassean Literary Society," Jan. 16, 1874, ibid. Family stories told to Deolece Parmelee in 1987 by Anne L. Allen Rutherford and Pauline Gill Sullivan.

that even if Ballard had died of his wound, it would not have interfered with his studies or caused him to become "dissipated" because he did not feel guilty. His actions, he wrote his mother, "were not a transgression of either the laws of God nor . . . of my country." Finally, he would never give his enemies the pleasure of seeing him "follow in the footsteps of poor Meck."[20]

Matthew left Cumberland University in May 1874 for a visit home to decide what he should do. Friends wanted him to tour Europe, an idea that the family did not approve, while others suggested law school in Virginia. At age nineteen, Matthew had no firm plan except that he did not intend to remain in San Augustine. Returning from Tennessee by rail via St. Louis into northeastern Texas, he realized that economic opportunities lay along the rail lines. The International and Great Northern and the Texas and Pacific Railways had built tracks into North and Central Texas, crossing counties in which the Cartwrights owned land. Like his father and grandfather before him, Matthew sensed new economic opportunities and determined to investigate North Texas instead of resuming school. He ended his train trip at Jacksonville in Cherokee County northwest of San Augustine instead of at Marshall, perhaps to avoid going through Shelby and Sabine counties because of the Ballard trouble. Either way, Matthew had an eighty- or ninety-mile journey by stagecoach from the railroad to San Augustine, a fact that strengthened his resolve to leave the stagnating Redlands.[21]

Matthew began his tour of North Texas in August, riding horseback from San Augustine to Longview and then traveling by train to Dallas. He explored land he owned in Johnson County south of Fort Worth, which he found particularly pleasing, and then made stops in Kaufman, Rains, Woods, and Upshur counties before returning home in September. Because of the economic hard times in North Texas, he could not make many collections

20. Mary C. Ingram to Matthew Cartwright, Feb. 27, 1874, CFP; Matthew Cartwright to Mother, Mar. 6, 1874 (quotations), ibid.

21. Leonidas Cartwright to Matthew Cartwright, Feb. 23, 1874, CFP; Matthew Cartwright to Mother, Mar. 6, 1874, ibid.; Matthew Cartwright to Mother, May 4, 1874, ibid.: Webb, Carroll, and Branda (eds.), *The Handbook of Texas*, II, 752: Kaufman County Historical Commission (comp.), *A History of Kaufman County* (2 vols.; Austin: Taylor Publishing Company, 1978, 1979), II, 36.

or trades during his travels. The recession was due to the widening effects of the panic of 1873, which had stemmed from overspeculation in railroad building, heavy industry, and agriculture, compounded by the failure of Jay Cooke's banking firm. Nevertheless, the towns along the railroads east of Dallas were growing. Matthew chose Kaufman County and the new railroad town of Terrell as his new home. Immigration to the blackland prairies was assured by good transportation and the return of conservative government to Texas.[22]

By 1874 the political climate in Texas had changed. Although the Cartwrights seldom wrote each other about politics, Lon rejoiced over recent events that made living in Texas palatable again to former Confederates. Referring to the victory of the Democratic redeemers that ended Republican rule in Austin, Lon praised "a democratic, free government": "Coke and Hubbard her executives, [O. M.] Roberts the head of her judiciary and much of her best talent filling her legislative halls." Having recovered full citizenship with readmission to the Union in 1870, Texas Democrats flocked to the polls in November 1872, voting for Horace Greeley over the Republican incumbent, Ulysses S. Grant, by a majority of 19,000, and also sending Democrats to Washington and to Austin. The new legislature set December 1873 for state elections; the Democrats again triumphed, electing Richard Coke governor over incumbent Republican, E. J. Davis, by 85,549 votes to 42,663. Although the Republicans staged last-minute, armed demonstrations before and after the inauguration ceremonies in January 1874, Governor Coke and the Democrats prevailed.[23] For the Cartwrights and their friends, the political landscape had almost returned to normal.

While his brothers and sisters remained rooted in San Augustine and Sexton, Matthew was ready for adventure. Having missed the excitement of going to war, he did the next best thing: he headed west in 1875 just after Gen. Ranald S. Mackenzie had defeated the Plains Indians. It was a journey he would repeat

22. Matthew Cartwright to Mother, Aug. 29, 1874, CFP; Matthew Cartwright to Lon Cartwright, Sept. 3, 1874, ibid.; Matthew Cartwright to Mother, Sept. 12, 1874, ibid.

23. Leonidas Cartwright to Matthew Cartwright, Feb. 23, 1874 (quotation), CFP; Ramsdell, *Reconstruction in Texas*, 312–317.

twenty-one years later when he took his family by wagon to see the glories of the Palo Duro Canyon. No letters document Matthew's first journey to the Texas Panhandle, but he recalled details for the Terrell *Daily Tribune* in 1923 on the town's fiftieth anniversary.

In April Matthew and six other men from Terrell plus a cook and teamster boarded the train for the Fort Worth terminus of the Texas and Pacific Railroad with two prairie schooners and a saddle horse each. The purpose of the trip was hunting and prospecting for ranch land:

> We laid in a ten-day supply for man and beast, and left in a northwest direction for Fort Griffin [a U.S. army post in Shackleford County] . . . [spent] a few days on the post, and on leaving carried a month's rations. . . . We would depend on grass for our horses and game for our meat. We followed the old McKenzie Trail, leading to Santa Fee [*sic*] . . . until we got within a day's travel of the New Mexico line.

There they turned southeast when they learned that the recently defeated Comanches had massacred Colorado-bound prospectors: "We . . . traveled about 1200 miles . . . had a good time, killed lots of game including buffalo, deer, and antelope."[24]

Having had his adventure, Matthew returned to Terrell at the close of 1875 and opened a grain farm on inherited land on the prairies south of town. A manager would raise grain and tend to cattle and horse raising. In the spring of 1876 Matthew invested in a mare and a Durham bull to start his herds and was building a house on the farm suitable for his mother to visit. His real focus, however, was the land business. To impress customers, he ordered engraved stationery bearing his name, with "Dealer in Real Estate" below it, and a dateline with "Terrell, Texas." Lon was still using plain writing paper, but soon adopted his brother's style for his own land business. Matthew, just past twenty, understood the

24. "Reminiscence by Matthew Cartwright . . . ," clipping from special edition of Terrell *Daily Times* (n.d.), CFP. The 1896 adventure in family letters in CFP: Mary Cartwright to brother Lon D., Apr. 25, 1896; Mary Davenport Cartwright to son Lon D., Apr. 26, 1896; Matthew Cartwright to Leonidas Cartwright, July 27, 1896; Mary Cartwright to Ludie and Mary Cartwright, Aug. 8, 1896.

importance of appearing a modern businessman and was willing to spend money to do so.[25]

The town of Terrell had been created in 1873 when the Texas and Pacific Railroad announced plans for its route between Longview and Dallas. Named for pioneer Robert A. Terrell, who had established his farm there in 1846, it was a typical railroad boomtown. Within its first seven months of life, 150 houses were built, while stores, saloons, and gambling halls proliferated along the railroad tracks and livestock roamed the streets at will. Within three years, however, solid citizens like Matthew Cartwright and former San Augustine resident Gen. John Summerfield Griffith had replaced the transient speculators and the little town grew more respectable and tidy. In 1879 the growing city, approaching a population of 2,000, unsuccessfully tried to have the county seat moved from Kaufman to Terrell, an effort that would be repeated every few years without success.[26]

On July 24, 1876, Matthew journeyed northeast of Terrell to Pittsburg in Camp County to marry twenty-year-old Mary Cynthia Davenport. Orphaned when she was very young, she had often visited her aunt, Mrs. John H. Broocks (Elizabeth Jerome Polk), in San Augustine, but she lived with her maternal uncle, David Polk, in Pittsburg. The young couple settled into a boardinghouse in Terrell, a common arrangement, but it was not suitable for a young expectant mother. Early in 1877, Matthew took Mary to San Augustine to await the birth of her first child amid friends and relatives while he traveled on business. Mary did not stay at the house of sixty-year-old Amanda, where Lon and Ludie and their three children occupied the upstairs bedrooms, but went instead to stay with Anna Roberts, who was expecting her sixth child in July. Ophelia Cartwright and her three little ones were nearby; Ophelia also saw to the comfort of her elderly father, who had a house close by. Cumby and Sallie and their six children lived down the road where they raised horses, cattle, and hunting hounds.[27]

25. Matthew Cartwright to Mother, Nov. 13, Dec. 8, 1875, CFP; Matthew Cartwright letterhead, Mar. 19, 1876, ibid.; Leonidas Cartwright letterhead, Sept. 6, 1877, ibid.
26. *History of Kaufman County*, II, 20–21, 28.
27. Genealogical material in CFP.

Matthew Cartwright (1855–1925) and his wife, Mary Cynthia Davenport (1856–1937), ca. 1882. Courtesy Cartwright Family Descendants.

Matthew returned to San Augustine in time for the birth of Leonidas Davenport on May 9, but had to leave soon after. Mary and "Jake," as his father affectionately called him, remained with Anna and Ben Roberts through the summer because there was no home for them yet in Terrell, and summer travel with a small baby was unwise. Matthew arrived in August to take Mary, the baby, and their recently employed servant back to Terrell; he even managed to persuade Grandmother Amanda to accompany them to Terrell for her first train trip. Unlike her sister, widow Bettie Thomas, who traveled alone to San Augustine from Tennessee that same summer, Amanda seldom left her home. She now weighed over two hundred pounds, but Matthew informed Lon that "Ma seemed to enjoy the trip . . . and stood it much better than she expected." They made a leisurely journey, spending one day in Marshall before taking the train to Terrell. Matthew took rooms at the Terrell House near the railroad station for his family and mother, instead of at a boardinghouse, but they soon decided to eat their meals at a private boardinghouse.[28]

Amanda started home in October without going to see the Dallas Fair as she had planned, and by chance met her sister Bettie in Marshall, also en route to San Augustine. At the end of the year, Matthew bought a four-bedroom home on the edge of town on the road to Rockwall for his little family, and Mary invited her younger sister to live with them and attend school in Terrell. Lizzie Davenport's presence made Matthew's long absences more tolerable for Mary. Matthew was following in his father's footsteps and increasing his land holdings in developing areas, and by 1878 he had $18,000 in taxable property in Kaufman County alone. Besides his farm and ranch, he owned eight town lots in Terrell (some with improvements), livestock, and a horse and buggy. He built brick buildings on his commercial lots, which became known as the Cartwright Block.[29]

While Matthew was on his way to building a fortune, Lon remained in San Augustine to care for his mother and her busi-

28. Leonidas Cartwright to Matthew Cartwright, Feb. 23, 1874, CFP; Matthew Cartwright to L. Cartwright, Sept. 16, 1877 (quotation), ibid.

29. Matthew Cartwright to Mother, Nov. 2, Dec. 29, 1877, CFP; Elizabeth Thomas to Sallie Cartwright, Dec. 6, 1877, ibid.; Mary Davenport Cartwright to Amanda Cartwright, Feb. 10, 1878, ibid.; U.S. Tenth Census (1880), Kaufman County, Texas; Kaufman County, Tax Rolls, 1878–1890 (microfilm; CL).

ness. A good manager himself, Lon became more appreciative of his father's accomplishments when he began reordering and systematizing the voluminous land records in the old office. "The more I see of Pa's work," he wrote to Matthew, "the more I am impressed with his superior ability as a financier."[30]

Lon and Matthew entered into a partnership in 1878 raising cattle on a league, leased from their mother, seventeen miles south of Terrell, and by the following spring, they fenced it (not with barbed wire, which Matthew hated) and improved their herd with good stock. Including their mother's cattle, they had three hundred head, but a scorching summer forced them to move the animals when the water supply dried up. Lon spent a lot of time at the ranch and even missed the birth of his fourth child in San Augustine on April 16, 1879. Ludie was unusually understanding for a new mother and urged him to complete his business before coming home. Following family custom in employing relatives, the brothers hired William T. Cartwright of San Augustine, the son of their father's cousin Hezekiah, as ranch foreman. A few years later, Lon employed William Holman Cartwright, the orphaned son of Clinton Cartwright and Elvira Holman Wheeler, to manage the new ranches Lon opened in Cooke County north of Denton and in Stephens County west of Fort Worth.[31]

San Augustine, bereft of a railroad, remained quiet and stagnant. In 1880, the town had a population of 503 and the county a population of 5,084, while Terrell and Kaufman County were booming with 2,003 and 15,448 residents respectively. Matthew continued to beg his mother to move to Terrell to live with him, but she resisted change. Lon wanted to move to the boomtown, where traveling by train would make overseeing his ranches easier. Hoping to persuade his reluctant mother, he bought a large residential block on Griffith Avenue in Terrell and divided the property with Matthew. Lon and Ludie and their five children were cramped in his mother's house in San Augustine, and when

30. Leonidas Cartwright to Matthew Cartwright, Mar. 9, 1874, CFP.
31. In CFP: Amanda Cartwright to Leonidas Cartwright, Apr. 18, 1879; Matthew Cartwright to Mother, May 18, 1879; Leonidas Cartwright to Mother July 8, 1879; Matthew Cartwright to Lon Cartwright, Sept. 27, 1879; William T. Cartwright to Leonidas Cartwright, July 1, 1880 (W. T.'s son-in-law Jim Williamson succeeded his father on the ranch); William H. Cartwright to Leonidas Cartwright, Sept. 10, Nov. 7, 1883.

Matthew began building his large house in Terrell in 1882 Amanda's intransigence must have irritated them. Moreover, Amanda, not Ludie, remained the lady of the house, although Amanda permitted her long-suffering daughter-in-law to assume more household tasks as Amanda grew older.[32]

Terrell's Griffith Avenue became a showcase of late nine-teenth-century mansions, although the road itself remained a dusty track leading out of town. Matthew's three-story, five-bedroom frame house with its square tower ranked among the most impressive. A center hall, twelve by forty-four feet, sepa-rated four large rooms, each eighteen by twenty feet, on both the first and second floors, all with fireplaces. The attic contained two rooms ventilated by dormer windows. A spiral staircase gave access to the two upper floors, and high ceilings, bay windows, and ample galleries made it a comfortable dwelling even in summer. As in the San Augustine house, Matthew ordered a one-story ell at the rear for a large dining room, twenty-four by eighteen feet, plus an ample kitchen.[33]

The house was finished by November 1883 when Matthew's fifth child, daughter Jerome Broocks, was born; Matthew told Lon that the total cost would probably reach $7,500, but it would "be a superb building." In anticipation of Lon's eventual move to Griffith Avenue, Matthew ordered a deep, bricked well and a twelve-foot windmill constructed on the line between their lots so both would have ample water for the "house, Kitchen, lots, and gardens." He also had "a splendid barn built 30 x 40 frame and Dressed weatherboarding."[34] Reflecting his father's tastes, Matthew of course planted an orchard. The handsome house Matthew built in 1883 still stands, now surrounded by smaller modern homes.

Meanwhile the Ingrams, Robertses, and the families of Lon and Columbus continued the life-style dictated by East Texas custom. The women devoted themselves to home, children, church,

32. Population figures, *Texas Almanac, 1964–1965,* 119, 120, 125; Mat-thew Cartwright to Leonidas Cartwright, Sept. 13, 1890, CFP.

33. Jerome Cartwright Head and Mildred Griffin Miller, "The Matthew Cartwright House, Terrell, Texas," unpublished ms (Texas Historical Commis-sion, Austin).

34. Matthew Cartwright to Leonidas Cartwright, June 28, 1883 (quota-tions), CFP.

Matthew Cartwright (1855–1925) house, 805 Griffith Avenue, Terrell, Texas. The house, which remains in the possession of descendants, was built in 1883. Courtesy Cartwright Family Descendants.

and garden while the men pursued their interests in land speculating, farming, livestock raising, hunting, and fishing. As had their parents, the oldest children went off to college when they finished in the local schools. At first they attended schools east of the Mississippi River, but later they enrolled in the growing number of colleges in Texas. Columbus's son Robert, the eldest of Amanda's grandchildren, was the first of this generation to leave Texas to attend college; in 1879, at age nineteen, he entered Vanderbilt University in Nashville. In 1886, the five female cousins, Columbus's Mary, aged fourteen; Meck's Annie, fifteen; and the three Amandas (Lon's, Anna's, and Mary's), all fifteen, spent a year at the Athenaeum in Columbia, Tennessee. Jimmie Ingram and Lon visited the girls at Christmas and posed for a photograph. The importance the Cartwrights placed on a good education continued as each child reached the proper age. Boys often spent time with uncles to obtain ranching experience or business training before going off to college. Throughout these years of growth within the family and in their business ventures, the

*Matthew Cartwright (1855–1925) and his wife Mary (1856–1937)
with their ten children in Terrell, Christmas 1908. Front row (left to
right): Mary D., Matthew, Mary, eldest son Lon D., youngest son
Bourke; back row (left to right): Jerome, William Holman, Eugenia
"Jean," Matthew, Jr. "Mapps," Estelle, John Reagan, and Amanda
"Mant." Although Lon D., Mant, Jean, Estelle, and Jerome, the five
oldest, were married, their spouses are not pictured.* Courtesy
Cartwright Family Descendants.

Cartwrights remained closely knit and concerned about the next
generation.[35]

During the 1880s, Columbus Cartwright formed a business
partnership with his sons Robert and John Matthew, both of
whom had moved to Mt. Calm in Hill County. C. Cartwright &
Sons, Dealers in Real Estate and Live Stock, raised fine horses on
a ranch five miles north of Mt. Calm. Columbus remained most
of the time in San Augustine, maintaining a race track where he
trained his favorite animals. Beginning in 1885 he bought thor-

35. Material about the education of the children up until the 1940s is
available in the biographical sketches in both volumes of *Four Families*, and
other details are available in numerous family letters. Photograph of the five
girls and the two men, CFP.

oughbreds and was listed in S. D. Bruce's *American Stud Book* and semimonthly magazine, *Turf, Field and Farm*.[36]

Intrigued by Columbus's success with racing stock, Lon soon invested in thoroughbreds, much to Matthew's disgust. The ever-practical younger brother chided his mentor for risking money on exotic horses when mules were the real money-makers. "Mules are a staple article," Matthew wrote, "and will command money; horses can scarcely be bartered for trash." That statement, of course, was not true of his brothers' purebred horses. By the 1890s, Lon's stationery letterhead not only mentioned his land "in all parts of the state," but also announced that he bred thoroughbred saddle and harness horses, registered and grade Jersey cattle, and grade-level Holsteins and Shorthorns. His stock farm was eight miles southwest of Gainesville, and by 1898 it was the responsibility of his eldest son Leonidas, Jr., age twenty-two. The young Leonidas opened another stock ranch at Reed in Cooke County where he and his father raised Durham cattle and Berkshire hogs in addition to fine horses.[37]

The almost idyllic rural pleasures of San Augustine were interrupted at the end of 1887 when Ben Roberts died at age fifty-one. His eldest son Matthew Roberts, only seventeen, withdrew from the University of the South at Sewanee, Tennessee, and returned home to help his mother. As a young girl Anna Cartwright Roberts had displayed more independence of mind than many of her friends and cousins, and even her mother deplored her occasional "contrariness." Instead of relying on male relatives to administer Ben's estate, she applied to the court and was immediately appointed administrator. Although no prenuptial agreement appears at the courthouse, Anna had kept her property separate from Ben's even though local tax assessors followed custom and assessed it as his. She spent the next several months trying to collect numerous large debts owed to Ben, while she sold

36. *Turf, Field and Farm*, 1885–1904, and *The American Stud Book* (Sanders D. Bruce [ed. of *Turf, Field and Farm*], 1889), V, 567 (both in possession of Sandra Kardell Calpakis); *Bruce's American Stud Book* (New York: Sanders D. Bruce, 1894), VI, 233, 374, 446.

37. *Bruce's American Stud Book*, VI, 233, 446; Matthew Cartwright to L. Cartwright, Dec. 16, 1889 (1st quotation), CFP; Leonidas Cartwright letterhead, Jan. 22, 1892 (2nd quotation), ibid.; Leonidas Cartwright letterhead, Feb. 18, 1898, ibid.; Leonidas Cartwright letterhead Sept. 6, 1899, ibid.

Five of John Cartwright's granddaughters at school in Tennessee, with Leonidas Cartwright (second from left) and James Ingram, Christmas 1886. Cartwright and Ingram visited their daughters and nieces, all about the age of fifteen, at the Athenaeum in Columbia, Tennessee. The girls pictured (left to right) are Americus's daughter Annie Tomlinson Cartwright (1871–1960); Columbus's daughter Mary C. Cartwright (1872–1954); Leonidas's daughter Amanda Holman "Mantie" Cartwright (1871–?); Anna Cartwright Roberts's daughter Amanda Holman "Manda" Roberts (1871–1949); and Mary and James Ingram's daughter Amanda Holman "Manda" Ingram (1871–1948). Courtesy Cartwright Family Descendants.

tracts of his land to pay his many creditors. Some of the sales appear to have been for less than their appraised value, suggesting that some opportunists took advantage of Anna's vulnerable financial status.[38]

When Matthew offered to build a house for Anna on Griffith Avenue in Terrell, she agreed to make a fresh start in an area that offered business opportunities for her sons. Matthew often said: "The place to make money is where it is in circulation the most."

38. Amanda Cartwright to Lon Cartwright, July 5, 1879 (quotation), CFP; San Augustine County, Probate Minutes, F, 129–130, 141–142, 147, 159, 174–179, 185, 198–199, 216–219, 274, 312–313, 363; also loose papers, "Estate of Ben Roberts," ibid.

While Anna had resources from her own property, she was not well-off when she and her seven children moved to Terrell in October 1888. Like her mother, Anna had become quite heavy, but that did not prevent her from becoming a businesswoman. Within eighteen months of her move, she and young Matthew Roberts had opened a real estate and loan office with the aid of Matthew, and they soon purchased an insurance agency to augment their income. Before long, brother Matthew turned over his interest to his sister and nephew, and the firm name became M. C. Roberts & Co. Twenty-year-old Matthew C. Roberts, already on his way to becoming a successful entrepreneur like his uncle, soon found reasons to make regular business trips to Dallas in order to see Emily Griffith, the daughter of Gen. John Summerfield Griffith, who had moved there from Terrell. They were married at the end of 1890, but like many of their contemporaries, the newlyweds continued living with their parents for awhile.[39]

To appease his mother, Lon reluctantly relinquished the idea of moving to Terrell, but he was vexed by the inadequacies of her old house. In the summer of 1888, he and Ludie became seriously ill. The nursing care they required demonstrated the need for more downstairs bedrooms. Before Ludie had completely recovered, their eldest daughter Mantie fell ill at Southwestern University in Georgetown and was sent home. She was too weak to wait on herself, which further demonstrated the need for a one-story house. Not long after the invalids recovered, Amanda suffered a stroke at church. Taken home to her downstairs bedroom and partially paralyzed on one side, the seventy-two-year-old matriarch stubbornly struggled to walk, resulting in a sprained ankle. Typically, however, she continued to move about by catching hold

39. Matthew Cartwright to Leonidas Cartwright, Sept. 13, 1890 (quotation), CFP; Matthew Cartwright to L. Cartwright, Sept. 10, 1888, ibid.; Anna Roberts to Lon Cartwright, Oct. 6, 1888, ibid.; Matthew Cartwright to L. Cartwright, Apr. 28, 1890, ibid.; Matthew C. Roberts to Uncle Leonidas Cartwright, May 8, 1890, ibid.; Matthew Cartwright to L. Cartwright, Oct. 15, 1889, ibid.; Anna Roberts to Mother, Dec. 7, 1890, ibid. Matthew Roberts was later mayor of Terrell and in 1919 moved to Dallas, where he was president of the First National Bank. His son Summerfield G. Roberts married Annie Lee Warren, the granddaughter of Meck and Ophelia Cartwright. Summerfield and Annie Lee Roberts used their extensive fortunes to further research in Texas history.

of the furniture even though one hand and foot remained virtually useless.[40]

Lon seized the opportunity to find a better home for Ludie, who was expecting her eighth (and next to last) child in December 1889. He decided to enlarge a modest house that he owned on a small tract on the south side of Main Street several blocks east of his mother's home. Schoolteacher William R. Leonard, a native of Ireland who taught Lon's Mantie and Meck's Matthew and Annie in 1878, had bought the site from Columbus Cartwright the following year. For some reason he sold it to Lon in 1880, and Lon purchased additional acres from Cumby until the tract contained fifty acres. When Lon finished remodelling the house in early 1890, he had fourteen rooms, mostly on one floor, which he furnished with new pieces ordered from Chicago. He did not know for sure that his mother would leave her home to live with him, but she finally agreed. Amanda left the house intact except, perhaps, for her bedroom furniture. The old house remained unoccupied until 1898, when Americus H. Cartwright, Columbus's son, and his wife Minnie Clementine Sublett bought it and its contents. The historic home remains in the hands of Meck and Minnie's descendants.[41]

Meanwhile, Jimmie Ingram prospered on his plantation at Sexton, where he also owned a cotton gin and conducted land business like his Cartwright brothers-in-law. Mary decorated the comfortable house with fashionable furnishings and retained her interest in music and painting, hanging a number of her own works on the walls. Ingram relatives often lived with them, including a spinster who provided company for Mary when

40. Miss E. C. Watts to Ludie Cartwright, Aug. 17, 1888, CFP; Matthew Cartwright to L. Cartwright, Sept. 10, 1888, ibid.; Mantie Cartwright to Mother, Oct. 28, 1888, ibid.; Ludie Cartwright to Leonidas Cartwright, Oct. 3, 1889, ibid.; Matthew Cartwright to L. Cartwright, Oct. 15, 1889, ibid. Details of Amanda's infirmity are from Jane Weed to Deolece Parmelee, June 9, 1986, Cartwright research files.

41. San Augustine County, Deed Records, J-3, 291–293, 487, 664, N, 169–171; San Augustine County, Tax Rolls, 1878–1893; Statement for tuition, W. R. Leonard to L. Cartwright, Oct. 25, 1878, CFP; Statement for tuition to Columbus Cartwright, administrator of A. P. Cartwright estate, June 13, 1878, ibid.; Anna Roberts to L. Cartwright, Dec. [illeg.], 1889, ibid.; A. H. Cartwright family tradition, Sandra Calpakis to Margaret S. Henson, interview, July 18, 1991.

*A family trip to Mineral Wells, Texas, ca. 1898. Anna Roberts is
seated at center, with Americus's widow Ophelia Smith Cartwright
and Ludie and Lon Cartwright to her left. To her right are Ophelia's
eldest daughter Annie, with husband Robert Lee Warren; Ophelia's
son Matthew Charles and his wife Blanche Griffith are standing. The
reclining three-year-old cousins are Annie Lee Warren, the future
Mrs. Summerfield G. Roberts, on the left and Pauline Allen, the
daughter of America and Walter P. Allen of Terrell, on the right.*
Courtesy Cartwright Family Descendants.

Jimmie traveled on business. Lon and Ludie and their children
made frequent visits to enjoy the rural pleasures of hunting and
fishing. In 1888 Jimmie became the state senator for District 2,
composed of Sabine, Shelby, San Augustine, and Rusk counties.
Mary accompanied her husband to Austin for the first session
from January to April 1889, staying briefly at the new Driskill
Hotel before settling into one of the numerous boardinghouses
near the capitol. She discovered, however, that few wives accompanied their legislative husbands to Austin. Gov. Lawrence Sullivan
Ross, who had been Jimmie's commanding officer during the
Atlanta campaign, was starting his second term, and meeting him
was perhaps an inducement for Mary to visit Austin. Doubtless
she enjoyed touring the new capitol that had been finished in time

for Ross's first term. She did not go Austin again when Jimmie was reelected for a second term in 1891.[42]

Ophelia Cartwright, Meck's widow, was the next family member to leave San Augustine. Her elderly father, Dr. Charles Smith, died in December 1886, which allowed Ophelia to join her two oldest children, Matthew Charles, almost nineteen, and Annie, seventeen, in Georgetown, where they were enrolled at Southwestern University. Teenage Meck accompanied her mother and entered the Georgetown high school. Ophelia said that she could not bear being separated from her children for long periods. The four returned to San Augustine the following summer when she asked her Terrell brother-in-law Matthew for advice:

> Matthew is very anxious to attend a business college either at Waco or Dallas. . . . We have catalogues . . . and I see that they transact real business . . . which must be very improving . . . the girls can go there too, and I suppose I will have to go with them, as I could not keep house without them.

Within weeks, Ophelia and her family were in Waco, and when Matthew Charles completed his course in January 1890, he went to Terrell to work and live with his Uncle Matthew. Ophelia and the girls remained in Waco until their school term ended in June 1890, when they joined the Cartwright clan in Terrell, boarding briefly with Anna Roberts. Matthew, the administrator of Meck's estate, offered to buy a nearby house for Ophelia. She readily accepted, and by the end of the year she and her children were settled in Terrell.[43]

42. A. H. Cartwright family tradition, Sandra Calpakis to Deolece Parmelee, June 11, 1986 (cited in Deolece Parmelee, "Family and Land: The Cartwrights of East Texas," ms [1986], 661 n. 45 [copy in possession of author]); J. M. Ingram to L. Cartwright, July 23, 1881, CFP; Ludie Cartwright to Leonidas Cartwright, Apr. 30, 1882, ibid.; *Members of the Texas Legislature, 1846–1962,* 133, 140; Austin *Daily Statesman,* Jan. 8, 20, 1889; *City Directory, Austin Texas, 1889–1890.*

43. Mantie Cartwright (Lon's daughter) to Mother, Oct. 28, 1888, CFP; Ophelia Cartwright to Matthew Cartwright, Aug. 11, 1889 (quotation), ibid.; Ophelia Cartwright to Amanda Cartwright, Mar. 19, 1890, ibid.; Matthew C. Cartwright to Leonidas Cartwright, May 8, 1890, ibid.; Matthew Cartwright to L. Cartwright, July 21, September 13, 1890, ibid.

Only Lon and Cumby remained in San Augustine with their mother. Amanda gradually declined although she was in reasonably good health four months before her death, which occurred at Lon's home on June 26, 1894, at age seventy-seven. The family gathered for her funeral and, as she had wished after almost a quarter of a century of widowhood, she was buried next to Matthew in the little private graveyard east of her old house. Lon composed suitable facts about her life on a sheet of paper entitled "In Memoriam" for the use of the minister. Besides providing her birthdate, parents' names, date of arrival in San Augustine, and marriage date, and noting the loss of one of her six children, Lon added, "She was one of the Kindest of Mothers and devoted wife, a faithful Christian, charitable to all in need and beloved by all who knew her." She had joined the Methodist Church in 1858, and, he added, she had been a faithful and consistent member. These remarks were embellished by her minister and printed in the local paper as her obituary. Two weeks later, Lon, who once wrote poetry for Ludie, wrote six stanzas praising motherhood.[44]

The heirs knew that, in addition to bank accounts in several cities, their mother had always hoarded cash, but when they unlocked the safe from which she occasionally doled out funds, they found $60,900. An even greater surprise awaited them in her personal secret safe, unknown to all except Lon, who had never had access to it. When Jimmie Ingram opened the strong box, it contained $19,250 in gold coins and $9,710 in other currency. This secret hoard of $28,960 brought the grand total of cash on hand to $88,960. Amanda's habitual thrift during her married life culminated in this treasure trove, accumulated in large part since the death of her husband. Matthew had set an example for her by always keeping gold and silver on hand, especially during the Civil War.[45]

---

44. "In Memoriam," n.d. (quotation), and "Mother," July 15, 1894, Lon's handwriting, CFP; Obituary signed D. A. McRae, clipping, n.d., Sharp Scrapbook.

45. "Statement of Distribution of Cash Funds . . . Est. of Mrs. A. Cartwright;" CFP; Statement of cash found, signed by J. M. Ingram, n.d., on sheet of Leonidas Cartwright's letterhead, ibid.; Joiner Cartwright, *Early Morning Coffee With Father* ([n.p.]: privately published, [n.d.]), 2.

A little shaken by the discovery of so much cash, Lon, Cumby, Matthew, and Jimmie packed up the money, quietly left town in a buckboard—presumably well-armed—and headed for the nearest railroad. Jimmie and Matthew boarded the train with the treasure and arrived safely in Terrell. They spent the night on pallets on the living-room floor around the heavy pile of money, along with Matthew's seventeen-year-old son Lon D. The next morning, still nervous, they took the train to Dallas, where they deposited $73,500 in the American National Bank and the remaining $15,460 in the Exchange National Bank. Bank officers often recalled in later years the day the Cartwrights made the large deposits. Why Matthew took the money to Dallas instead of placing it in the First National Bank of Terrell, of which he had been president since 1891, is unclear.[46]

During the months following Amanda's death, the heirs inventoried her jewelry, cash, and land and endeavored to distribute them equitably. Once the jewelry was appraised, representatives of the five branches of the family (Lon abstained) drew lots for the different pieces, and a monetary value was given to make up any differences in value. The cash was easily divided into six equal shares of about $9,400. Dividing the land again posed problems, and portions had to be adjusted depending on the value of the tracts. For example, Columbus received 39,000 acres while Matthew's total was only 22,000 acres.[47]

Almost immediately, Lon and Ludie made plans to move to Terrell, where their eldest daughter Mantie and her husband lived. They began building a house on Griffith Avenue on the lot they owned alongside Matthew's house. By mid-January 1895, the elegant Queen Anne structure with its wraparound verandas was underway, and in April they moved in. During its construction, Matthew wrote, "Mary says she gets mad every time she comes up from town, because your house is much prettier than hers." Matthew used the opportunity to make improvements to

46. Cartwright, *Early Morning Coffee,* 2; "Statement of Distribution of Cash," CFP; First National Bank of Terrell letterhead, Sept. 24, 1891, through 1903. Matthew remained president for twenty years.

47. "List of lands drawn by Columbus . . . 20th August 1894," in collection of Anna V. Cartwright; List no. 3, "List of Lands Drawn by Matthew Cartwright from Estate Aug 29 18[??]" [recent pen-and-ink copy, no source given], CFP; Statement of Deposits of Mrs. A. Cartwright in various Banks, ibid.

Columbus Cartwright (1837–1901) and his hounds at his home in San Augustine, 1890s. Courtesy Cartwright Family Descendants.

his own house by adding the columns, balustered porches, circular portico, and Italianate trim on the dormer windows and tower that gave the house its distinctive character. Three years later, Mary and Jimmie Ingram built a large, comfortable house in Terrell, completing the family circle except for Columbus.[48]

Columbus remained in San Augustine by choice, although at one time he thought about moving to Waco, where his eldest sons lived. Once the Cartwright overachiever, Cumby had learned over the years that his kidney ailment could only be controlled by

48. Lon Cartwright to Ludie, Sept. 10, 1894, CFP; Matthew Cartwright to Leonidas Cartwright, Jan. 17, 1895 (quotation), ibid. Picture of the Ingram house in CFP carries that date.

quiet living; raising racehorses and other livestock suited his life-
style. Moreover, Sallie had not been well since the mid-1880s,
when she had suffered severe bouts of intermittent fever; she died
at age fifty-three in 1895, seven months after Amanda. Columbus
was also tied to San Augustine by his devotion late in life to the
Methodist Church. Among his gifts to the church were a com-
munion service and an entire adjoining block with the understanding that it would provide an area for hitching the members'
horses. Earlier, he had been annoyed to find that somebody had
untied his horse from a nearby tree and allowed it to roam.[49]

How Columbus responded in 1896 when Matthew proposed
moving their parents' remains to Terrell is unknown. The idea
seemed sensible because the old Matthew Cartwright house stood
vacant and would perhaps be sold to strangers. If the remains
might have to be moved to the new city cemetery in San Augustine, why not move them to Terrell instead? Matthew made the
arrangements in September 1896, and the pair was reinterred in
Terrell with a suitable marker. At the same time, Anna and
Ophelia moved the remains of Ben Roberts and Meck Cartwright
to the Terrell cemetery. Columbus must have felt that he had been
abandoned except by those of his children who remained in San
Augustine.[50]

About this same time, Lon received a request from L. E.
Daniell, who was preparing the recently deceased John Henry
Brown's *Indian Wars and Pioneers of Texas* for publication in
1896. Daniell asked Lon to write an article about Matthew and
Amanda Cartwright and to send portraits of each. The article
recounts the family's history beginning with their arrival in San
Augustine in 1825, mentions the three sons' Confederate service,
and offers a paragraph about each of the six children of Matthew
and Amanda.[51]

49. Sallie Cartwright to Husband, Nov. 2, 1882, Anna V. Cartwright
collection; Obituary, clipping, Sharp Scrapbook; Deed to Board of Trustees,
Feb. 15, 1897, CFP; Columbus Cartwright to Rev. J. B. Turrentine, ibid.
50. Matthew Cartwright to L. Cartwright, Sept. 19, 1896, CFP.
51. L. E. Daniell to Matthew Cartwright, Sept. 12, 1896, CFP; Matthew
Cartwright to Leonidas Cartwright, Sept. 19, 1896, ibid.; Brown, *Indian Wars*,
632–633; John H. Jenkins, *Basic Texas Books: An Annotated Bibliography of
Selected Works for a Research Library* (Austin: Texas State Historical Association, 1983), 57–59.

Columbus became increasingly ill in 1901. In November his four children living in San Augustine, sons John Matthew and Americus H. and daughters Mary (Mrs. James J. Bewley) and Ella (Mrs. William G. Sharp), called the other two to come to their father's deathbed. All of Columbus's heirs were present when he died on December 12, 1901; they buried him next to Sallie in the San Augustine City Cemetery the next day.[52]

Lon and Matthew were left to carry on the Cartwright name and legacies, along with the male heirs of their deceased brothers. Matthew continued land speculating in the 1890s along with banking and ranching. He owned the Fleur de Mustard Ranch in Stonewall County where he raised both cattle and horses, while still operating the two ranches in Kaufman County. Oak Land, only seven miles southwest of Terrell on Brushy Creek, had cattle and horses, while the mule farm was at Cotton Wood Ranch fifteen miles southeast of town. He also advertised that he was a dealer in baled hay.[53]

While Matthew and Amanda's sons abandoned retailing and the commission business to concentrate on land trading and ranching, many of the grandchildren became lawyers and businessmen in banking, real estate, and insurance. Just before the turn of the century, the Cartwright heirs ventured into the search for petroleum on land they had inherited near Corsicana and Beaumont. Exploration at Corsicana began in the early 1890s and the Cartwrights expected to collect royalties when oil began flowing in 1894. Negligence in recording deeds in subdivided tracts, however, forced the family to take opportunistic trespassers to court. The heirs won the case, and a substantial monetary award, in 1903.[54]

When the Lucas gusher blew in on Spindletop Hill near Beaumont on January 10, 1900, Anna Cartwright Roberts's twenty-three-year-old son Claude was already on the spot. He and two associates had established a real estate and insurance

52. Columbus Cartwright to Matthew Cartwright, Jan. 16, 1901, CFP; Robert L. Cartwright to Leonidas Cartwright, Nov. 29, 1901, ibid.; Obituary and funeral notice, Sharp Scrapbook.

53. Matthew Cartwright letterheads, Apr. 8, 1889, through Mar. 26, 1891, for the hay, but later letterheads mention only the two Kaufman County ranches.

54. R. L. Cartwright to Matthew Cartwright, Mar. 7, 1903, CFP.

office in Beaumont several years earlier and were developing a ten-acre residential tract, Oakwood, on the southwest edge of town. The heirs of Matthew and Amanda owned portions of the David Brown league south of town, where the Oakwood Addition was located, and also part of the contiguous J. W. Bullock league, the site of the big gusher. Matthew, now forty-five years old, and his nephews planned a stock company in April 1900 and the Cartwright Oil & Development Company, Producers of Fuel Oil, received a charter from the state a year later. A letterhead boasted capital stock of $500,000 (each share valued at $100) with Matthew Cartwright of Terrell as president and nephews and friends as the other officers.[55]

Besieged by offers to buy or lease the properties, the directors decided to sink their own well on a 2½-acre tract at Spindletop in May 1901, and by January 1902 they were shipping oil by rail to Louisiana. A glutted market, however, dropped the price from an earlier high of seventy-five cents per barrel to only fifteen cents in March. The following year more disasters ensued. An inept drilling crew caused delays when pipe collapsed at the bottom of the hole and the well had to be abandoned. A fire on the crowded Spindletop dome in April 1903 destroyed many wells, including the Cartwright rig. The company lost $3,000 worth of machinery and tools and had to store or lease to others its ten railway tank cars, some salvaged machinery, and the 37,500-barrel steel storage tank.[56]

A new well was started in August 1903 on a different tract five hundred feet southwest of the hill, but a gas blowout caved in the well. Moving the rig eight feet to one side, the driller struck caprock at 1,076 feet and within days the well was producing modestly. By 1903, however, Matthew had lost interest in what seemed an unprofitable enterprise, and turned the presidency over to his eldest nephew Robert L. Cartwright of Waco, only five

55. C. C. Roberts to Matthew Cartwright, Jan. 28, 1900, CFP; M. C. Roberts to Matthew Cartwright, Apr. 1, 1900, ibid.; R. L. Warren to Matthew Cartwright, Apr. 11, 1901, ibid.

56. Matthew Cartwright to R. L. Cartwright, May 11, 1901, CFP; Leonidas Cartwright, Jr., to Matthew Cartwright, Mar. 10, 1902, ibid.; R. L. Cartwright to Matthew Cartwright, Mar. 7, July 30, 1903, ibid.; Cartwright Oil & Development Co. Annual Report, Jan. 13, 1903–Jan. 15, 1904, ibid.

years younger than himself. Although the annual report of January 15, 1904, listed net resources of $188,140 including lots in the Oakwood Addition, several local oilfield tracts, and the oil equipment, the directors, with capital stock of $343,800 outstanding, decided to liquidate the Cartwright Oil & Development Co. on September 16, 1905.[57]

Matthew, the youngest of the San Augustine Cartwrights, outlived his siblings and all but two of their spouses. James Ingram enjoyed his new house only briefly before he died in 1900; Columbus, of course, died in San Augustine the following year. The two Cartwright sisters passed away in 1903: Anna Roberts in May and Mary Ingram six months later. Frail Ludie, in poor health for years, succumbed in 1908, while Lon survived until 1922. Matthew died on November 11, 1925, at the age of seventy, while his wife Mary lived until 1937. Ophelia's three married children built houses next door to each other on Griffith Avenue, and Ophelia lived with her daughter Meck and Meck's banker husband, Walter P. Allen, until her death in 1939.[58]

In the 1790s John Cartwright, the pioneer Texas immigrant, had moved as a boy with his father from North Carolina to the Tennessee frontier, where both transformed themselves from relatively modest farmers to diversified agrarian entrepreneurs. John brought a cotton gin, blacksmith tools, mill equipment, and retail goods to East Texas and also invested in Texas land, thereby establishing the foundation of a sizeable estate; the associated country store was critical to his success when money was in short supply. John's sons and grandsons further expanded the family's land holdings and, unlike their more timid neighbors, were always willing to explore new entrepreneurial opportunities when times and technologies changed.

Throughout the nineteenth century, the Cartwrights had contributed to the establishment and growth of San Augustine by their commercial and entrepreneurial skills. By the turn of the century, however, all but one branch of the family had abandoned the piney Redlands. John's grandson Matthew, the youngest son

57. Cartwright Oil & Development Co. Annual Report, CFP; Printed notice of liquidation, Sept. 16, 1905, ibid.

58. Genealogical material in CFP; Deolece Parmelee, narratives of the six children of Matthew and Amanda, "The Land and the Cartwrights," (manuscript, 1987), in possession of author.

of Matthew and Amanda, was the first to leave San Augustine to start anew in Terrell. Other family members followed, except for Matthew's oldest brother Columbus and his children, most of whom remained in San Augustine. By the 1890s the grandsons and sons-in-law of Matthew and Amanda were scattered over Texas looking for new enterprises.

The Cartwright traditions of hard work, education, civic duty, striving for success, and the judicious use of accumulated wealth were deeply ingrained in family members. Fathers and uncles trained sons and nephews, and peripheral members of the extended family were also offered opportunities in family enterprises. Although the women received little business training, several demonstrated an acute understanding of their husbands' activities, and when necessary assumed considerable responsibility. With such a human network and diversified economic activities, the Cartwrights survived the hard times and political turmoil of the nineteenth century better than many other families. They carefully guarded accumulated wealth, giving the lie to the old saying "shirtsleeves to shirtsleeves in three generations." When ventures like the Cartwright Oil & Development Company failed to produce sufficient income, the Cartwrights sensibly cut their losses and fell back on banking, real estate, and ranching. Family ties and pride in their San Augustine and Terrell roots still unite Cartwright descendants today.

Appendix

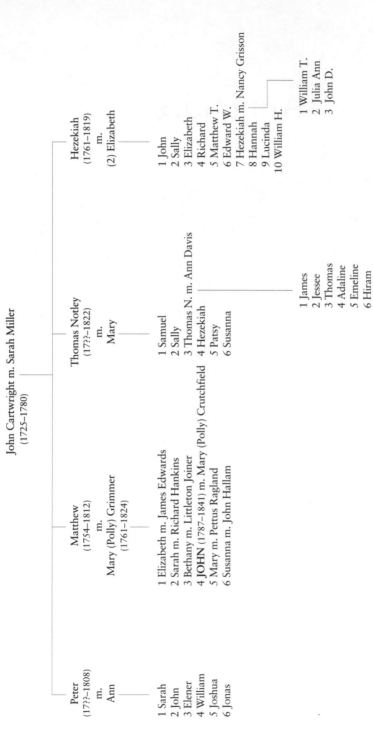

John Cartwright m. Sarah Miller
(1725–1780)

Peter
(172?–1808)
m.
Ann

1 Sarah
2 John
3 Elener
4 William
5 Joshua
6 Jonas

Matthew
(1754–1812)
m.
Mary (Polly) Grimmer
(1761–1824)

1 Elizabeth m. James Edwards
2 Sarah m. Richard Hankins
3 Bethany m. Littleton Joiner
4 **JOHN** (1787–1841) m. Mary (Polly) Crutchfield
5 Mary m. Pettus Ragland
6 Susanna m. John Hallam

Thomas Notley
(17??–1822)
m.
Mary

1 Samuel
2 Sally
3 Thomas N. m. Ann Davis
4 Hezekiah
5 Patsy
6 Susanna

1 James
2 Jessee
3 Thomas
4 Adaline
5 Emeline
6 Hiram

Hezekiah
(1761–1819)
m.
(2) Elizabeth

1 John
2 Sally
3 Elizabeth
4 Richard
5 Matthew T.
6 Edward W.
7 Hezekiah m. Nancy Grisson
8 Hannah
9 Lucinda
10 William H.

1 William T.
2 Julia Ann
3 John D.

Chart I: Forefathers of John Cartwright of San Augustine

First generation children of John Cartwright (with spouses):

- Matthew (1807–1870) m. Amanda Holman (1817–1894)
- Robert Grimmer (1809–1853) m. Mary Lanier (1819–1852)
- Dicey Hoskins (1811–1820)
- George W. (1812–1881) m. Ann Oliver (1830–1880)
- Mary (Polly) (1814–1846) m. William Garrett (1808?–1884)
- Clementine (1819–1847) m. Sanford Holman (1816–1843)
- Martha E. (1822–1822)
- J. Clinton (1823–1848) m. Elvira Holman (1825–1854)
- Richard Hankins (1828–1856) m. Ann Berry

Robert Grimmer's children:
1 Amanda m. A. D. McCutchan (1843–1860s) (1837?–1871)
2 Matthew (1847–1921) — 1 Mary, 2 James D.
3 Robert George (1849–1933)

George W.'s children:
1 Sanford H. (1844–1887)
2 Mary

Clementine / Sanford Holman's children:
1 Clementine m. B. F. Price (1836–1864)
2 Mary m. H. W. Sublett (1837–1883)

J. Clinton's children:
1 Anna m. Richard F. Slaughter (1839–1923)
2 William S. (1847–?)

Richard Hankins's children:
1 William Holman (1845–?)
(daughter) (alive 1890)

Columbus (1837–1901) m. Sallie Lane (1841–1895)
1 Matthew C. (1859–1860)
2 Robert Lane (1860–1943)
3 John Matthew (1862–1920)
4 Amanda (1864–1864)
5 Annie H. (1865–1865)
6 Clinton C. (1866–1906)

Americus Peyroux (1840–1873) m. Cphelia Smith (1845–1939)
1 Matthew Charles (1869–1960)
2 Annie T. (1871–1960)
3 America P. (1874–1959)

Leonidas (1842–1922) m. Ludie Ingram (1850–1908)
1 Amanda H. (1871–1957)
2 Annie E. (1872–1947)
3 Leonidas II (1876–1944)
4 James Ingram (1879–1960)
5 Columbus William (1882–1957)
6 Ludie (1885–1570)
7 Mary Lillian (1887–1584)
8 Grover Cleveland (1889–1562)
9 Velma (1892–1575)

Anna W. (1844–1903) m. Ben T. Roberts (1837–1887)
1 Matthew C. (1870–1931)
2 Amanda H. (1871–1949)
3 Annie W. (1872–?)
4 Ben Shadrach (1874–1966)
5 Felix M. (1875–1900)
6 Claude C. (1877–1924)
7 Mary C. (1878–1936)

Mary C. (1845–1903) m. James M. Ingram (1840–1900)
1 Matthew C. (1866–1867)
2 William Holman (1867–1923)
3 Matthew (1869–1870)
4 Amanda Holman (1871–1948)
5 James M., Jr. (1872–1949)
6 Leonidas (1877–1965)
7 Sidney (1881–1882)

Matthew (1855–1925) m. Mary Davenport (1856–1937)
1 Leonidas Davenport (1877–1963)
2 Amanda H. "Mant" (1879–1977)
3 Eugenia Polk (1880–1937)
4 Estelle (1882–1972)
5 Jerome Broocks (female) (1883–1976)
6 Mary D. (1885–1964)
7 John Reagan (1887–1917)
8 William Holman (1889–1980)
9 Matthew, Jr. (1892–1962)
10 Bourke (1894–1965)

Chart II: John Cartwright's Children and Grandchildren

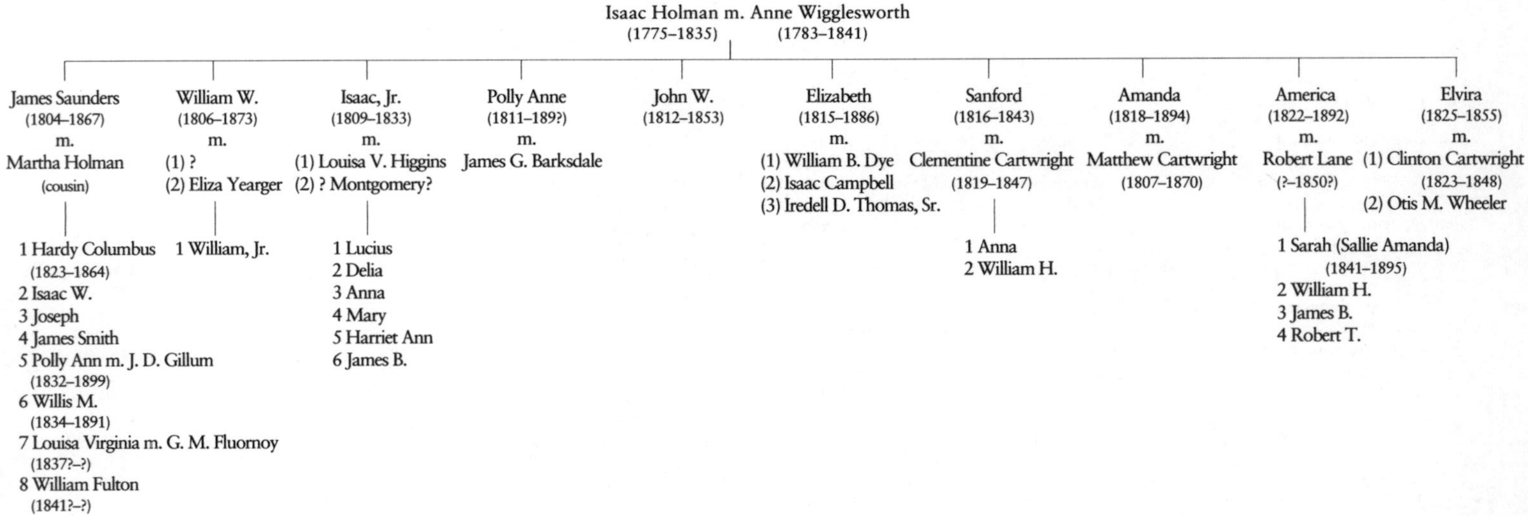

Isaac Holman m. Anne Wigglesworth
(1775–1835) (1783–1841)

| James Saunders (1804–1867) | William W. (1806–1873) | Isaac, Jr. (1809–1833) | Polly Anne (1811–1899) | John W. (1812–1853) | Elizabeth (1815–1886) | Sanford (1816–1843) | Amanda (1818–1894) | America (1822–1892) | Elvira (1825–1855) |

m.
Martha Holman
(cousin)

William W.
m.
(1) ?
(2) Eliza Yearger

Isaac, Jr.
m.
(1) Louisa V. Higgins
(2) ? Montgomery?

Polly Anne
m.
James G. Barksdale

Elizabeth
m.
(1) William B. Dye
(2) Isaac Campbell
(3) Iredell D. Thomas, Sr.

Sanford
m.
Clementine Cartwright
(1819–1847)

Amanda
m.
Matthew Cartwright
(1807–1870)

America
m.
Robert Lane
(?–1850?)

Elvira
m.
(1) Clinton Cartwright
(1823–1848)
(2) Otis M. Wheeler

1 Hardy Columbus
(1823–1864)
2 Isaac W.
3 Joseph
4 James Smith
5 Polly Ann m. J. D. Gillum
(1832–1899)
6 Willis M.
(1834–1891)
7 Louisa Virginia m. G. M. Fluornoy
(1837–?)
8 William Fulton
(1841?–?)

1 William, Jr.

1 Lucius
2 Delia
3 Anna
4 Mary
5 Harriet Ann
6 James B.

1 Anna
2 William H.

1 Sarah (Sallie Amanda)
(1841–1895)
2 William H.
3 James B.
4 Robert T.

Chart III: Isaac Holman's Descendants

Index